U.S. Landscape Ordinances

U.S. Landscape Ordinances

An Annotated Reference Handbook

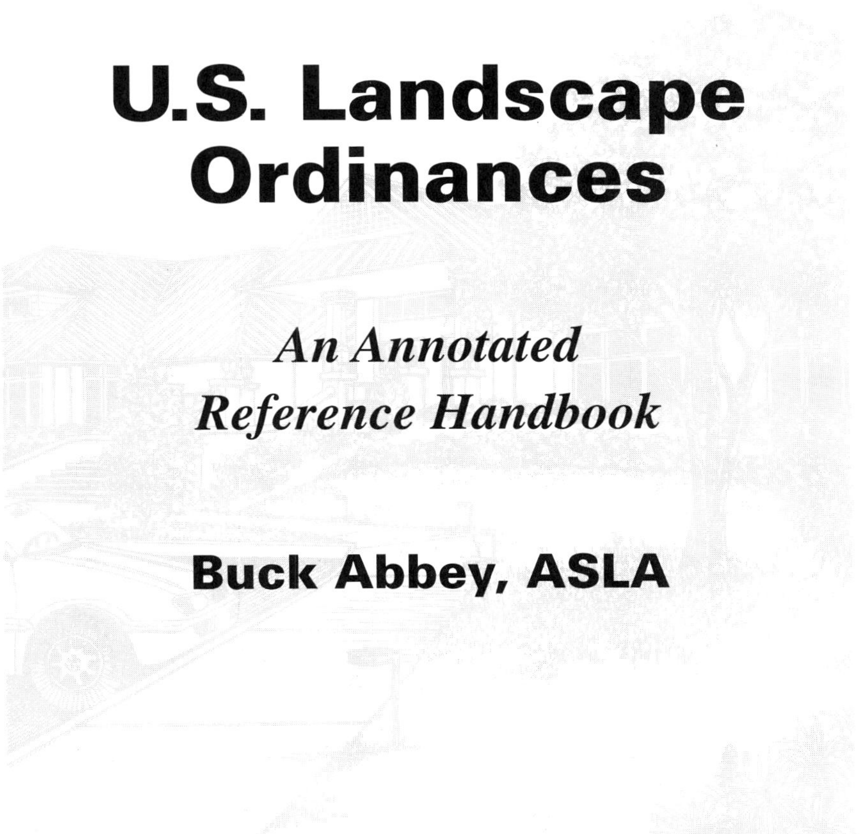

Buck Abbey, ASLA

John Wiley & Sons, Inc.

New York • Chichester • Weinheim • Brisbane • Singapore • Toronto

Dedicated to the memory of David Lee Abbey, as well as to Violet, Anne, Kris, Gail, Steve and LSU alumni worldwide.

This book is printed on acid-free paper. ♾

Published simultaneously in Canada.

Library of Congress Cataloging-in-Publication Data:

Abbey, D. Gail
U.S. landscape ordinances : an annotated reference handbook / Buck Abbey.
p. cm.
Includes bibliographical references and index.
ISBN 0-471-29276-1 (cloth : alk. paper)
1. City planning and redevelopment law—United States—States.
2. Landscape protection—Law and legislation—United States—States.
I. Title.
KF5692.Z95A23 1998
346.7304′5—dc21 98-24358

Printed in the United States of America

10 9 8 7 6 5 4 3 2 1

CONTENTS

Special Note on Content

Each day communities across the nation enact landscape ordinances or make revisions to existing ordinances.

Should your community be annotated in this study, the author would appreciate hearing about any changes in your community ordinance since the date of this publication. Should your community not be included in the study, you may send the author a complete copy of your community ordinance for future inclusion. Be sure to include the exact ordinance citation, as well as any supplemental data or graphics that your city normally provides to readers.

The "green law database" maintained by the author will store this information and keep the data updated so that in future editions of this book your community can be mentioned and the knowledge shared with others wishing to know about it. In addition, some of the data will be presented periodically on the LSU "Green Law Web Page" (http://www.design.lsu.edu/greenlaws) so that the information can be broadly shared.

Laws, codes and statutes change from time to time as they are amended, merged, deleted, challenged or revised. Readers are cautioned to consult the original documents housed in the various planning agencies of each community cited within this document prior to preparing landscape plans. The addresses in the Directory (Appendix B) have been included for your use to facilitate this activity.

PREFACE

Green Law Research

This work has been undertaken over the last ten years while I was teaching at Louisiana State University. It has been prepared to assemble knowledge about community landscape ordinances and their impact on the design and planning professions that work with this type of legislation. Directly, as well as indirectly, these ordinances impact the design professions in America today. To some extent, the general distribution of design professionals in America is shaped by these laws. Where such laws are in effect, the design professions are influenced by them. Moreover, where the laws are in effect, there are more design professionals who practice their craft.

It has always been my thought that in a country of laws, laws must leave some imprint on the landscape in which we all live, work and play. Do laws shape the landscape? This study makes a case for the argument that they do. Part of the reason for this study, then, was to determine the impact of law on the way communities are designed, redesigned and built. There is a growing relationship between landscape ordinances and the way modern cities are designed. Laws are now supporting design, and designers are assisting with the establishment of laws. Many of such green laws are being written by design professionals.

A university professor would be interested in this subject for two other reasons.

It is my hope that by undertaking a research project such as this, the professor may help to expand the understanding of these public laws in the minds of the practicing planners, landscape architects, architects and engineers who are largely responsible for the way communities look. The general public too may be influenced by this work in the way it reacts to new construction and natural landscape destruction. Second, too few academic people have chosen to investigate the landscape ordinance and its impact on our environment and the urban design of our cities, towns and villages. The very nature of urban areas across the country is being shaped by the language of these laws, which are popping up across the country as some of the newest planning tools available for directing growth and preserving trees and native landscape character.

By encouraging this type of research, I hope to get other professors and writers interested in the subject so that the range of scholarship will increase as a result of the leadership of this book. Today, little has been written on this subject.

Undertaking a project such as this was not possible without the support of my colleagues in the School of Landscape Architecture at LSU. Their encouragement has been most helpful.

Assistance was given by many people from across the country as well. I wish especially to thank many LSU graduates who are working in the field, making a living as landscape architects, planners, arborists and community leaders. Some of them work with landscape ordinances each working day of the year. Many LSU graduates who practice throughout the United States have sent ordinances back to the "ole war school" for analysis, critique and use in this study. Their information has been incorporated into this book. They are thanked for their kind remembrances of by-gone days.

Landscape architects, planners, foresters and others trained at the other fine schools around the nation have also contributed to this study. They are appreciated for helping us acquire this information and for their kind letters of support. Many of these people have indicated in their letters that they or their firms have been directly involved with the research and implementation of ordinances on a local level in many communities. Many others tell us that they comply with design guidelines and landscape ordinance standards during the course of each workday. They find it encouraging that universities now have an interest in this subject.

Special recognition must go to individuals and firms who have been involved with the creation of landscape ordinances and who have assisted with this project: Bob Smith, ASLA; Keith Villere, ASLA; Rhett Roy, ASLA; and Foster Conant & Associates. The work of Gary O. Robinette on the subject of local landscape ordinances is of special importance. All merit mention for helping to get this project started.

The firm of Abbey Associates, Incorporated, Landscape Architects-Planners, of Baton Rouge and New Orleans, Louisiana, has contributed much time and energy to this project. Many of the drawings in this book were prepared on their computer system.

My former student and good friend Kay Orlando Ourso has contributed greatly to the look of this book. Kay is a landscape architect and accomplished artist who did her first pen-and-ink landscape architectural perspective in my sophomore class almost twenty years ago. She is the only student ever to take my drawing class twice—she liked it so well. She earned A's both times! She is a terrific artist, as her pen and ink drawings included here show.

Many other landscape architects, planners, foresters, lawyers, horticulturists and administrators have been helpful by sending information and sharing experiences. Particularly noted are those offices and agencies listed in Appendix B, "Directory to Landscape Ordinances," in this book.

Few research projects are accomplished without money and project assistance.

I give thanks to Walter Imahara of the Louisiana Association of Nurserymen for getting this project off the ground many years ago with a grant and a question: "Why don't you read these new California ordinances that were sent to me and see if something like this would be useful in Louisiana?" With that charge, and with a grant from the Louisiana Association of Nurserymen, we have learned a lot about the subject over the last ten years. Without additional financial support during the same time period, the background research leading to this document would not have been possible. Research support to allow the project to continue was received from the Dow Chemical Company, the Louisiana Department of Agriculture and Forestry, the Louisiana Chapter of the American Society of Landscape Architects and graduate assistant research stipends from the Graduate School of Louisiana State University.

Projects like this do not happen without special people. Debra Smith Henderson, the best administrative assistant anyone would want, was most helpful with all of the administrative aspects of this project. Jennifer Gubert, "Jen Jen," was the best word processor and computer operator to have when times were busy with classes, grades, papers and reports. Leonard Martin served ably as proofreader.

Special recognition is given to the angelic Dr. Robert "Doc" Reich, who is my hero, friend and "down South father."

Finally, universities are about students. Without the assistance of student researchers, acting as data entry personnel, assistants or gofers, I would have given up the research that formed the basis of this project long ago. Their enthusiasm, support, inquisitiveness and humor turned very routine, and sometimes very trying, legal inquiry into a puzzle of exceptional fun.

Several of the students turned their part-time jobs into a landscape ordinance thesis. Specifically, Tim Leguaite and Sissy Foster have added to the body of knowledge concerning landscape ordinances. Their carefully thought-out thesis work is cited in this document. Other student assistants are noted for their attention to detail and writing, especially Mary Blakeney and Jeff Edwards. Both are exceptional researchers and will do well in the future. Michael Seymour, Les Southards and Jeanie Lin were always there with helpful criticism and a smiling willingness to help out when times were really busy.

The twins, Becca and Debbie Deubler, were a constant inspiration during the course of this project. They often added to the confusion during the early days of this project, when I would get them mixed up with each other. They have been most helpful and supportive since.

D. G. Buck Abbey, ASLA
Orange Beach, Alabama

Kay O. Ourso

CHAPTER 1

Introduction: Landscape Ordinances

He has refused his assent to laws,
the most wholesome and necessary for the public good.
He has forbidden his Governors to pass Laws of immediate and pressing importance
unless suspended in their operation till his assent should be obtained,
and when so suspended, he has utterly neglected to attend them.

Declaration of Independence 1776

Any community wishing to establish a landscape ordinance is committed to improving that community through long-term environmental care and improvement. A landscape ordinance is a tool that can help.

A landscape ordinance in a community certifies that the community thinks that it is important to protect, preserve and promote nature in the city and to keep nature as a cleansing agent and tool of environmental quality. A healthy environment is an indication of a healthy community. Healthy communities have landscape ordinances. Keeping nature in the city is a means of protecting the public health, safety and welfare of the citizens of that community, and that is one of the prime measures for enacting this type of legislation (see Abbey, 1988, in the Selected Bibliography).

Many important benefits can be cited as to the good work that nature does for cities. We know, for instance, what trees, shrubs, ground covers and associated natural features do within the urban context. Trees provide a host of benefits—from cooling shade to air filtering. Books have been written about the carbon intake-oxygen release-energy cycle mechanisms of trees and other plant materials.

We know further about the importance of clean air, pure water and friable soils and what they do to make cities livable. Scientists have even studied the special environmental role of urban wildlife in the design of cities. The function of landscape ordinances is to ensure that nature is an important part of the city (see Figure 1.1).

Landscape ordinances provide for the preservation of natural features such as wetlands, erodible slopes, special native habitats and specimen trees. In some communities, the total context of their ordinances is the protection of the public water supply, whereas in other communities it is the tree canopy that is important to preserve. Some landscape ordinances provide for the rebuilding of nature following the common construction activities sure to happen in places where people settle. Subdivisions, commercial developments and industrial activities take their toll on nature. This type of ordinance places nature back in the city following construction activities. Other landscape ordinances have been enacted simply to make city living more pleasant and to provide for the subtle psychological needs of city dwellers. Examples of each type of ordinance can be found in this study.

1. Street (yard) landscaping and planting
    a. Front
    b. Side
    c. Rear
    d. Corner
2. Open space planting
3. Land use buffers
4. Parking lot screening and interior plantings
5. Irrigation of planting
6. Protection of landscaped areas
7. Views—blocking traffic, screening with plants
8. Maintenance of plantings
9. Sight triangles
10. Garbage and utility service screening
11. Size of plant materials, approved species
12. Lighting
13. Median strips, street edges, public rights-of-way
14. Grading and drainage
15. Tree preservation and tree protection
16. Habitat protection and native plant preservation

FIGURE 1.1. Technical issues addressed by landscape ordinances, Louisiana State University.

Nature's Odyssey in the City

Landscape ordinances are among the nation's newest planning tools. They do not have a long history, having been developed only in recent decades. Community landscape ordinances have been created to supplement zoning or subdivision laws, both of which are well-known and long-used planning tools. In some communities, landscape ordinances are used to regulate and control growth and are seen as major growth management tools.

During the 1930s, the 1970s and now in the 1990s the pendulum of public interest has turned toward landscaping, tree planting and environmental preservation on a national scale. Why is this so? Why is the replanting of our towns and cities becoming important to the citizens of this nation?

During the 1930s many public tree programs were undertaken for erosion control and cropland preservation, which was very important in that day and age. Later, during the 1970s, following the first Earth Day, the environment became a critical topic, especially among college-age kids and their parents, the "beat generation." The 1970s saw the introduction of new types of urban legislation to protect the environment, rebuild the city and slow the rapid growth that was doing much to destroy the countryside. During the 1990s the fruits of these programs are being reaped, with landscape ordinances sprouting up throughout the nation as a means to control growth and preserve nature in the city.

Communities no longer allow developers to build construction projects without considering nature. Many communities have enacted at least one of three typical kinds of landscape ordinances.

A city may have a *comprehensive landscape ordinance*, sometimes called a land alteration ordinance. Landscape ordinances of this type have been enacted to prevent complete site clearing and habitat destruction. These are very sophisticated, highly regulatory ordinances that regulate not only landscaping but land alteration, tree protection, tree removal, storm water management, erosion control, groundwater recharge and land clearing. This type of ordinance is the most modern and is still somewhat rare. When found, it is often in a community with fragile natural resources or where the public wishes to severely control land development. Often this type of ordinance is heavily lobbied and supported by citizens groups and mainstream environmental societies. Developers find this type of ordinance highly restrictive, but not impossible to work with.

Typically, these ordinances will not allow grade changes or changes to natural drainage that destroy native habitats including vegetation and wildlife. In some instances they may require off-site mitigation of any damage during alteration. This type of landscape ordinance is highly restrictive, and compliance often costs a great deal of money. Prior to any site clearing, design and planning documents must be prepared in order to obtain a clearing permit.

These ordinances usually have interesting names, such as Wetland Preservation Ordinance, Shoreline Development Ordinance or Erosion and Drainage

Mitigation Ordinance. Often, the rare and fragile resource is identified in the name of the ordinance, such as in Beach Dunes Impact Ordinance.

Postconstruction landscape ordinances, commonly called simply *landscape ordinances,* are increasingly common in America's larger cities, towns and villages and are fast becoming the most common of all green laws. These ordinances require planting of building sites following construction. The most usual function of such ordinances is that they reserve site open spaces and require planting of these spaces with ornamental trees, shrubs, ground cover, grasses, annuals or perennials.

A postconstruction landscape ordinance may be a single-issue ordinance, such as an ordinance that simply requires the planting of parking lots, or a multiissue ordinance that regulates design, installation of planting and maintenance of the landscape following construction.

The type of landscape ordinance most commonly cited in this book typically requires planting of parking lots, buffering incompatible land uses and separating construction from streets with street yard plantings, berms and decorative features. This type of ordinance often requires planting of open spaces, creation of parking lot screens and planting of sign monument zones. Restrictions on plantings at the street sight triangle zone or the access-way sight triangle zone are found in most ordinances. Site service areas such as loading zones, trash receptacles, storage areas and the like are often screened from off-site viewpoints by this type of ordinance.

In addition to land preservation and planting, other aspects of site development are often included in this type of ordinance, such as design requirements for fences and walls and the design of earth berms and drainage features. Many ordinances set standards for irrigation and maintenance, and a few have regulations for the design of landscaping in fire-prone or hurricane-susceptible regions or in places where snow loads are a problem.

Some communities actually include design requirements for vehicular use areas (parking lots) in their landscape ordinances. Still others codify soil erosion design standards within their community ordinances. The complete paving of any site from lot line to lot line is prevented by this type of ordinance. This is one of the most common features seen as a result of a community green law of this type. No longer can sites be completely paved. No longer can storm water freely run off-site to cause flooding problems downstream! Landscape designs and irrigation plans are required to be submitted at the same time construction plans are reviewed by the city. Design occurs prior to issuance of a building permit.

Figure 1.2 illustrates the typical geography and terminology of a postconstruction landscape plan. Not all communities require that all of the site zones illustrated in this drawing be treated following construction of a typical commercial development. When you read the annotations later in this book, you will be able to see which of the site zones are required to be included in each city. A public agency, such as a planning commission, a city landscape architect, a building official or a city forester reviews the plans, inspects installation, issues necessary

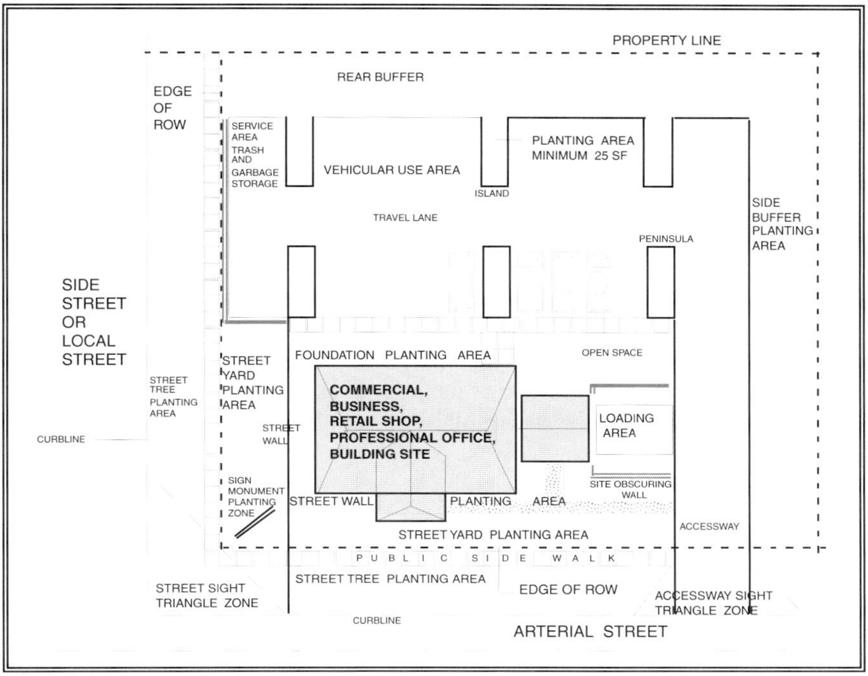

FIGURE 1.2. General landscape ordinance site terminology, Louisiana State University.

permits and receives appeals for waivers. Some communities leave the administration of these ordinances up to the Department of Public Works or the city engineer. Wherever the administration takes place, the person in charge should have the proper training and sensitivity to nature in the city.

In short, an ordinance that attempts to put nature back into a city after existing natural features have been removed is a postconstruction landscape ordinance. Not surprisingly, this type of ordinance is commonly drafted, administered and complied with by the landscape architecture profession. Where landscape architects are in greater concentrations, such as in Florida, California and Texas, we find more landscape ordinances enacted into law. Is there a relationship here?

Tree ordinances are a third type of landscape ordinance. These are the oldest of the landscape ordinances because of their single-issue nature that has made them popular throughout the county. Most communities at one time or another have established tree boards or public commissions to look after public trees. These groups undertake responsibility for maintenance of public trees or the planting of trees along streets, in parks and on other public lands. In some instances the focus is on preserving tree canopy or specimen or historic trees. Since the 1930s this type of ordinance has been promoted by public agencies, forestry associations and urban forestry groups.

A tree ordinance attempts to put nature back into the city in the form of tree plantings, usually street tree plantings and plantings for parks, public buildings and public memorial sites. Some of the newer ordinances are attempting to protect wildlife, retain soil structure and prevent destruction of wetland habitats.

Not surprisingly, this type of ordinance is commonly drafted, administered and complied with by the landscape architecture profession or the profession of urban forester or arborist. Where people and trees are in greater concentrations, as in Minnesota, Georgia and Massachusetts, we find more tree ordinances enacted into law. Is there a relationship here?

All of these types of ordinances enable the professions of landscape architecture, horticulture and urban forestry, and the various green professions have grown explosively as a result. Recent research shows evidence of this trend.

History of Landscape Ordinances

Few ideas of mankind are more significant than the concept of written law. Western civilization is based on written law. For centuries laws have been written to regulate the relations between human beings. Laws were handed down orally until the Babylonian king Hammurabi developed his famous code in 1750 B.C. This code, inscribed on a stone column, consisted of 3,600 lines of cuneiform text. Within the Hammurabi code can be seen the first language that prescribed the proper way to build.

Many builders, even today, operate under the general direction and intent of this seminal law of building construction. The code has been handed down, modified and changed over the centuries, but still relates to the way modern cities are built.

To some extent, Hammurabi's code is the basis of landscape ordinances, which did not appear in the historical record as we understand them today until some 5,450 years later.

The earliest of all recorded landscape ordinances is the Pennsylvania Shade Tree Law which dates from the eighteenth century. This early community ordinance mandates that landscaping is to take place in the village for the public good and health benefits. This law can be considered a descendant of the Hammurabi code in that it regulates the behavior of human beings living in association with each other. Keep in mind that the purpose of the king's code was to benefit the public good while excluding the arbitrary administration of justice.

This law can also be cited as the first American landscape ordinance because it cites specific design standards, landscape plant species and the benefits to be derived by the proper installation and maintenance of nursery stock.

The law states that

> *every owner or inhabitant of any and every house in Philadelphia, Newcastle and Chester shall plant one or more trees, viz., pines, unbearing mulberries, water poplars, lime or other shady and wholesome trees before the door of his, her or their house and houses, not exceeding eight feet from the front of the house, and preserve the same to the end that the said town may be well shaded from the violence of the sun in the heat of summer and thereby be rendered more healthy.*

This law contains some of the same features found in modern landscape ordinances.

For instance, the early law sets forth the context and reasons for the law and explains how it applies in the various villages of the Pennsylvania community. The shade tree law is also typical of a landscape ordinance in that it consists of both design components that must be considered and technical standards that specify types of materials, sizes and how they are to be used. Notice that specific dimensions and plant material species are cited.

The history of landscape ordinance legislation closely parallels the history of zoning laws in this country, and some of their roots may be traced to early case law decisions (see Harr, 1971, in the Selected Bibliography). One of the first critical turning points in the history of this type of legislation occurred in 1886 with a seminal land use law decision handed down by a California court. In *City of San Francisco v. Yick Wo and Hang Kie* the decision certified the right of a city to impose restrictions on land use and property development. The court indicated that the city did have an interest in keeping certain land uses separate and in controlling where things are to be built. In this case, Chinese laundries constituted the unwanted land use; these were thought to be fire hazards, unwanted in most middle-class neighborhoods of the day.

Soon thereafter, other actions on the other side of the country led to the nation's first comprehensive zoning ordinance. In 1913, New York set a landmark in the evolution of land use controls that would eventually lead to the establishment of zoning ordinances throughout the land. Much later, landscape ordinances would grow out of zoning ordinances.

For many years the battle over city-applied restrictions on the use of private land was fought out in courts of law. It was not any easy struggle. Often cited as the original case law settling the issue of zoning is the *Euclid v. Ambler Realty* decision of 1926. In this decision the Supreme Court of the United States stated that "every community had the right to determine its own character and the nature of development within," thereby settling the controversy between cities and private landowners for once and all. This decision of the Court has never been challenged since.

But still the specifics of requiring developers to set aside specific amounts of private property for planting with trees, shrubs and ground covers remained untested. Following *Euclid v. Ambler*, many cities set development standards for land use, size, building setback, bulk, height and safety codes that developers and builders would have to meet in order to stay in compliance with the law (see Laguaite, 1985, in the Selected Bibliography). Standards for setting aside land for planting trees, shrubs and ground covers, the main purpose of a landscape ordinance, were never tested until they were challenged in Los Angeles.

In 1949, in *Ayres v. City of Los Angeles*, a trial court upheld the city council and planning commission, which imposed planting requirements in a subdivision of the Westchester District of the city at the intersection of Arizona Avenue and Sepulveda Boulevard. A condition was imposed by the planning commission that required a ten (10)-foot strip along the rear of lots to be restricted to the planting of trees and shrubs. The purpose of this planting requirement was to confine traffic and circulation to and from the lots and to screen lot owners from traffic noises, fumes and views of fast moving traffic on Sepulveda Boulevard. Plant materials and set-aside space were seen as useful tools. This was thought reasonable by both the planning commission and the city council as a way to provide safety islands for residents crossing the street in this new subdivision. The imposition of the condition was reasonably related to the protection of the public health, safety and general welfare.

This decision of the trial court is the first example of a modern landscape ordinance that was tested based on safety and public health and the police power of zoning. By the 1940s zoning was acknowledged as a common practice across the land, but it did not settle the issue of aesthetics, which is an important aspect of landscape ordinances as we know them today. The legal question of aesthetics and its relationship to zoning and setting aside private lands for planting, an important part of the landscape ordinances of today, would be tested later in the mid-1950s.

A decision in 1954 did address the issue of aesthetics and a city's ability to require plantings as a means of beautification. In *Berman v. Parker*, which eventually made its way to the United States Supreme Court, Judge Douglas, writing for the majority, shed clear light on the subject of community aesthetics. The court said,

> *The concept of the public welfare is broad and inclusive. The values it represents are spiritual as well as physical, aesthetic as well as monetary. It is within the power of the legislature to determine that the community should be beautiful as well as healthy, spacious as well as clean, well balanced as well as carefully patrolled.*

This decision, as depicted in Figure 1.3, can be pointed out as the most likely instance in which the idea that plantings of trees, shrubs, and ground covers can be used to make cities beautiful, healthy, spacious and clean. All of these factors mentioned by the judge are important characteristics of the ordinances cited in this study.

Modern landscape ordinances can be tied to the date of the *Aryes* decision. What we have today are the results of all of these early court decisions and certain state enabling laws set in place sometime after Earth Day 1970.

***Euclid v. Ambler Reality,* 1926**
Judge Sutherland, U.S. Supreme Court
With the increase and concentration of population, problems have developed which require additional restrictions in respect to the use and occupation of private lands in communities. . . . Every community has the right to determine its own character and the nature of development within.

***Berman v. Parker,* 1954**
Justice Douglas, U.S. Supreme Court
The concept of the public welfare is broad and inclusive. The values it represents are spiritual as well as physical, aesthetic as well as monetary. It is within the power of the legislature to determine that the community should be beautiful as well as healthy, spacious as well as clean, well balanced as well as carefully patrolled.

***Ayres v. City Council of Los Angeles,* 1949**
Justice Shenk
Subdivision of the Westchester District in the City of Los Angeles at the intersection of Arizona Avenue and Sepulveda Blvd. A condition was imposed by the planning commission and approved by City Council and upheld by the trial court required a ten-foot strip along the rear of lots to be restricted to the planting of trees and shrubbery . . . the purpose being to confine ingress and egress to and from the lots; and to screen the lot owners from traffic noises, fumes and views of fast moving traffic on the boulevard; and to provide safety islands for residents crossing the boulevard. The imposition of the condition was reasonably related to the protection of the public health, safety and general welfare, so said the court.

FIGURE 1.3. Early landmark case law decisions (after Haar 1971, Laguaite 1985).

This study contains ordinances that were written in the 1970s, 1980s and 1990s. There is no law herein that dates to the 1960s, although many of the ordinances are direct descendants of earlier provisions of zoning codes or city tree ordinances developed in the 1930s to combat the Dutch elm disease or the American chestnut blight then sweeping the nation.

Many of the ordinances in this study were written in the mid-1970s and revised in the 1980s and again amended in the 1990s. Some of the earlier language from the 1970s can been seen in the later ordinances.

The very early ordinances (1970s) took a more regulatory tone and seem to be aimed at eliminating bad practices in the landscaping industry. They required such things as the grassing of construction sites, mowing vacant lots or protecting vegetation on public properties such as along streets and in public parks.

In the 1980s the emphasis shifted toward encouraging better design. Ordinances were developed primarily to provide for better design of parking lots and buffer yards between zoning districts. These ordinances required uniform plantings based on plant size and spacing requirements and encouraged a mix of plant materials. It was during this time that clauses such as the Alternative Compliance provision were inserted to encourage innovative landscape design practices and more sophisticated administration and enforcement.

The language of the 1990s landscape ordinances are trending toward habitat preservation, land alteration restrictions, tree protection and Xeriscape® or water-efficient landscape design principles. Provisions directed toward the preservation of natural resources have been written and inserted into landscape ordinances in many communities. Additional emphasis has been placed on design by requiring licensing and by establishing community appearance boards.

Another trend seen in many of the ordinances of the 1990s is the inclusion of standards for those who are qualified to prepare landscape designs, irrigation plans, grading plans, tree surveys and tree preservation plans. Many states are now requiring that such plans and specifications for landscape improvements be developed by registered, licensed landscape architects or, in some instances, by other licensed professionals in providing horticulture or forestry services.

Louisiana State University Landscape Ordinance Index 10

The Louisiana State University (LSU) Landscape Ordinance Index 10 is a list of what the author considers the best ordinances of their type contained within this book (see Figure 1.4). Readers should turn to the annotations to get a full description of each cited entry in this index. Should any researcher care to review a

Fairfax County, Virginia—Tree preservation
San Diego, California—Well defined and written
Hillsborough County, Florida—Land alteration requirements
Denham Springs, Louisiana—Community involvement
Raleigh, North Carolina—Very thorough, well documented
Southlake, Texas—Well organized
Carlsbad, California—Exceptional user manual
South Holland Village, Illinois—Emphasis on design
Medina, Washington—Organized permit process
Dublin, Ohio—emphasis on selected plant material

FIGURE 1.4. LSU Landscape Ordinance Index 10, Louisiana State University.

minimum number of ordinances in order to see the range of possibility, the LSU Index should be consulted first. From time to time, as new information becomes available and ordinances are revised, this list will change to reflect the changing nature of American landscape ordinances.

Objectives of This Study

No one has reviewed landscape ordinances in a scholarly or organized manner. There is no standard text on the subject. In fact, only two titles exist on the subject, and these titles are limited in scope and narrow in content. Any search of the Internet, for instance, will reveal no great body of scholars working on this subject that is so fundamental to the practice of landscape architects across the nation.

This is the first attempt to bring academic rigor to this subject on a national scale. The object of this research project, which began ten (10) years ago, is to survey the nation, define the nature of landscape ordinances, standardize the vocabulary, define various technical requirements and compare and contrast ordinances from different environmental regions. Once this data becomes easily available, other ordinances will spring up, based on the knowledge it provides.

Methodology

A direct mail survey was conducted in two parts. The first part sought out ordinances from the general membership of the American Society of Landscape Architects (ASLA) by direct letter and by placing requests in chapter newsletters and professional publications. This method uncovered approximately one hundred forty (140) ordinances. Second, a mailing list of landscape architects working in public agencies was assembled through a direct mail request to each of one hundred sixty-five (165) cities that employ landscape architects, ostensibly to manage these ordinances. This approach had a response rate of forty-six (46) percent (seventy-six ordinances), well above that which would be considered average for a survey of this type.

All cities were asked to submit one current copy of its community landscape ordinance along with any supporting materials used to administer the law.

Following receipt of the materials, each ordinance was analyzed along three main lines of inquiry: the contextual basis of the law, technical requirement adopted locally and administrative procedures followed to implement the program. Each ordinance was annotated and entered into a data base by data entry people under the direct supervision of the landscape architect. The data base consisted of two hundred sixteen (216) cities, towns, villages or municipal jurisdictions from forty (40) of the fifty (50) states. Additional information, such as model community ordinances, a directory to landscape ordinances, standard landscape ordinance definitions and a select bibliography, was included for reference. The information data base will be updated as needed, and new ordinances will be entered as they are uncovered.

Results and Findings

The data that has been assembled can be used by any researcher who cares to peruse a variety of landscape ordinances in one sitting. By reading the annotations one may ascertain the nature of individual community landscape ordinances and how they differ from place to place. It is expected that this information, being the first of its kind, will act as the standard reference for any community, agency or firm wishing to draft or update an ordinance.

The long-term results of this research will add to the beauty and environmental quality of the nation, at the same time helping to expand citizen interest in public trees, landscape, open space and the work of the various landscape industries, including landscape architects, horticulturists, arborists and urban foresters.

How to Read the Annotations in This Book

This work was undertaken to furnish the reader with critical explanatory notes concerning a wide range of landscape ordinances found in a nationwide survey.

The annotations are shortened versions, or snapshots, of each ordinance in the "green law data base" housed at the School of Landscape Architecture at LSU. They should not be considered as correct legal text, in that each annotation attempts to capture the spirit and uniqueness of each community ordinance rather than its exact text. The annotation format is appropriate for describing laws that may change from time to time. Ordinance language changes as a result of legal modifications, challenges and finding better ways to do things prescribed by law. The exact language of a law may change, but the annotation should remain essentially correct for a great number of years.

With each annotation we have identified the city, the state and the name or ordinance number of the law to facilitate locating the law by writing directly to the city planning agency involved. Several landscape ordinances listed are devoid of proper titles, in which case a standard generic title has been substituted. For example, the substitute title for an ordinance without a title in Sacramento, California, would read "Landscape Ordinance of Sacramento." Refer to the "Directory of Landscape Ordinances" in Appendix B for the mailing address, telephone number or fax number of our contact representative.

With each annotation we have concentrated on writing about three things. We have been interested in the *context* or purpose of the ordinance. Why was this ordinance enacted in this community? is the question we tried to answer. Whenever a unique reason was uncovered, we tried to point it out. Second, we took great interest in the *technical language*, including design components or standards of all ordinances, because this part of a landscape ordinance is what most people have to comply with in order to get the permits for construction. In many instances we noted different terminology for the same thing. This led us to put together the "Standard Landscape Ordinance Definition" section (Glossary) of this book, with the hope that we could help clarify the language differentials across the country. When unusual technical requirements were noted, we cited them in the annotations. Third, we made an effort to mention in the annotation how the *administrative components* of the ordinance work. We paid special attention to those ordinances that require sealed drawings and review by a licensed landscape architect working for the permitting agency.

Finally, any unique feature noted in the ordinance was generally cited, along with any special remark that the annotator thought would be helpful to the reader. The following outline was used to guide the annotations of the documents on file in the author's data base.

I. *Identification.* State, City or County, Title or Short Name of Law, Public Act Number, Date

II. *Purpose.* Context of the ordinance

III. *Components.* Subsections of the ordinance, design components or standards

IV. *Requirements.* Technical or administrative requirements

V. *Unique Features.* Anything particular to this community

VI. *Reviewer's Comments.* Personal thoughts by the reviewer on issues of importance

The following sample was used as a guide in writing the annotation for each original landscape ordinance document. The topic, as seen in the outline, is in boldface type, and the sample statement or explanation is written in plain type.

---

1. Designated state

Michigan

2. Designated city, town or village

City of Leslie

3. Jurisdictional authority, name of ordinance and date of enactment

[Authorizing document, Chapter, Article, effective date.]

City of Leslie.

Landscaping, Section 155.125, Zoning Code, February 16, 990

[The designation *n.d.* means that no date of enactment could be determined from the data reviewed. Where the proper name of the ordinance could not be determined from the literature, the term *City of ______ Landscape Ordinance* serves as a title.]

4. Annotation of ordinance

Like many of the landscape ordinances from the Great Lakes region, this ordinance combines postconstruction landscaping ordinance requirements with a tree preservation ordinance and screening and buffering requirements. The intent of the ordinance is to establish standards for the installation and maintenance of landscaping and landscaped open green space within the city. By doing so, the City of Leslie hopes to promote environmental quality, preserve and encourage open space and protect the natural beauty of the city while preventing the unnecessary destruction of trees, wildlife habitat and other natural resources.

5. Ordinance application

This ordinance applies to all development within the city and shall go into effect at such time that a development permit is issued that alters the previous use of any given area of land. All zoning classifications fall under this ordinance, and each classification has slightly different landscaping requirements. Single-family residential zones need not comply with the vehicular use area and buffer area requirements of this ordinance.

6. Enforcement

Enforcement is centered on withholding the Certificate of Occupancy until all landscape requirements are met. The Code Enforcement Officer under the Director of Planning and Growth Management is responsible for overseeing compliance with this ordinance.

Landscape plans illustrating compliance with the ordinance must be submitted for review by the Director of Zoning's office. Quality is ensured by requiring that anyone providing landscape services for hire, especially those who provide inspection, installation, maintenance, design, pruning and removal, be properly licensed. Plans must be prepared, signed and sealed by a Florida-registered landscape architect and must show specific technical information in order for the plan reviewers to ascertain whether the design components of the ordinance are being addressed in the design.

Technical standards or performance standards are given for plant materials, installation, maintenance, irrigation, tree protection and tree preservation.

An unusual example of these standards pertains to the size of installed trees. The tree height chart shown in Table 1.1 has been developed to ensure that fifty (50) percent of all required trees on a plot be related to the height of the main structure.

7. Descriptive or analytical table of technical data

Table 1.1 is a typical descriptive table giving factual information about the design standards or technical requirements of the referenced city.

This table illustrates in graphic format the relationship of plant material height to the height of an existing structure. In this community, the size of

TABLE 1.1. Tree Height Chart, Leslie, Michigan

Height of Structure	*Shade and Ornamental Tree Height and Spread*	*Palm Height/ Clear Trunk Measurement*
To 15 feet	12 feet; 6 feet	14 feet; 4 feet
15 to 25 feet	14 feet; 7 feet	18 feet; 8 feet
26 feet or more	16 feet; 8 feet	22 feet; 14 feet

a plant to be installed must be in relationship to the scale of an existing building. Large buildings require large trees; smaller buildings may be planted with smaller trees.

8. Typical design components addressed within the ordinance

Specific components that must be addressed in the design include street trees, open space planting requirements by zoning district, buffer requirements, vehicular use areas, waterway frontage, screening, sight distances at intersections and exterior lighting. These standards are based on linear measure in the case of street trees, unit measure in the case of landscape parking islands, square foot measure in the case of plot size. Plant materials are based on height, spread, caliper, container size and grade. Topsoil and mulch are based on depth, and berms are based on height and slope. Irrigation is based on percentage of coverage.

9. Typical technical standards

Widths of buffers and perimeters are generally ten (10) feet, and vehicular use areas must reserve fifteen (15) percent of the area for landscaping. Five (5) feet of landscape area shall separate vehicular use areas from single-story buildings. An additional five (5) feet must be added for each additional story up to a maximum landscape width of twenty-five (25) feet. Outdoor storage areas must be screened on seventy-five (75) percent of the perimeter, and trash receptacles must be enclosed with a six (6)-foot masonry wall and an opaque access gate.

Plant materials used in conformance with the provisions of this ordinance shall conform to standards promulgated by the American Association of Nurseryman in "American Standards for Nursery Stock" (ANSI Z60.1-1980) as well as standards set forth by the Horticulture Commission. All plant materials are to be free of disease and pests and in vigorous health. Class B trees shall be of a species having an average mature crown of greater than twenty-five (25) feet but less than forty (40) feet and having trunks that can be maintained with more than six (6) feet of clear trunk. A grouping of three (3) palms shall be equivalent to one (1) Class B tree.

Tree requirements shall be a minimum of five (5) Class B trees for each eight thousand (8,000) square feet of lot area, excluding building and parking footprints. For lots over eight thousand (8,000) square feet, add one additional Class B tree for each fifteen hundred (1,500) square feet.

Shrub requirements shall include one three (3)-gallon shrub for each linear foot of building frontage, excluding entries and openings, planted eighteen (18) inches on center or fraction thereof. All shrubs are to be twenty-four (24) inches in height at time of planting.

This ordinance has special language creating what might be called a "police surveillance view zone." This open view zone is to occur above the top of thirty-six (36)-inch hedges and below the bottom limbs of trees, which cannot be lower than six (6) feet. Landscape architects who prepare the plans must specify the proper plant materials, and property owners must maintain a clear view into property abutting a public right of way. This will enable police officers on patrol to see into the site.

10. Descriptive graphics

This descriptive graphic, Figure 1.5, has been prepared to illustrate compliance with specific ordinance requirements concerning the amount of

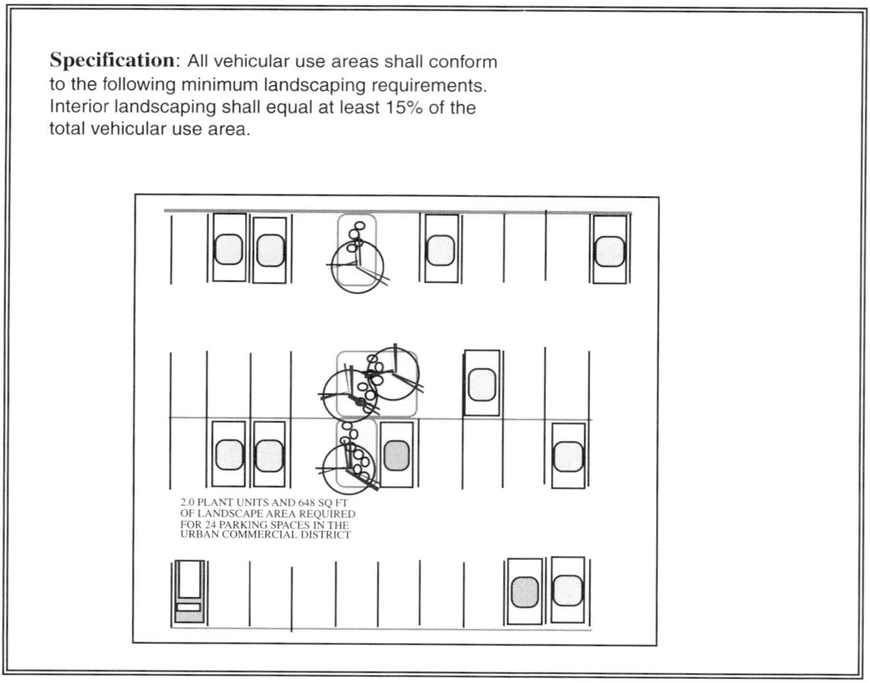

FIGURE 1.5. Sample descriptive graphic.

open space required within designed parking lots. The requirement described in Figure 1.4 is referenced to the City of Leslie, Michigan.

Each graphic within this book describes written ordinance language in a drawing showing the technical requirements or design standards applied to a facsimile site. Each drawing includes a written specification statement as well as notes concerning technical requirements or design standards derived from the meaning of the ordinance being examined. Notes and labels directly from the original text of the ordinance are used to further the communication of relevant site design facts. The intent of the graphic is to portray the law in a geospatial manner.

Throughout the book, descriptive graphics have been prepared to graphically portray the spatial and visual relationships depicted in the landscape ordinance language. Simple graphic conventions, as seen in Figure A.11 in Appendix A, are used to show trees shrubs, ground covers, walls, fences, and other landscape elements.

11. Annotator's comments and unique features

This ordinance is very specific and covers all of the normal concerns of a contemporary landscape ordinance. Reading the ordinance is somewhat difficult because of the way requirements seem to run together. Reorganization into a structure that clearly differentiates the code between the contextual, technical and administrative requirements would be helpful. The city does make available a landscape manual that provides graphic and illustrative interpretation of the code requirement herein. This is a must-read type of ordinance.

Tennis Club
Golf Course
Club House
Marina
Kay O. Oursa

CHAPTER 2

Annotated Landscape Ordinances

Alabama

Daphne

Daphne, Landscaping Regulations, within the city ordinance, n.d.

The landscaping regulations for this beach town address parking lots and development. Parking areas are to be compatible with the "beach resort character of the community." Mature shade trees are required at intervals of five (5) parking spaces, and no more than twelve (12) spaces in a row are allowable without a parking island. Each island must be sixteen (16) square feet. At least ten (10) percent of the total interior area for off-street parking must be suitably landscaped. Some industrial zones are exempt from the requirements.

The landscaping ordinance for new development stresses the use of native vegetation. Landscaping plans submitted for review must identify the native species. In addition, existing trees are to be conserved and integrated into the landscape design plan. Figure 2.1 illustrates the design standards to be used for the design of vehicular use areas in this community.

Fairhope

Fairhope, Ordinance No. 829, amending Ordinance No. 557, "The Zoning Ordinance of the City of Fairhope, Alabama," February 1989.

This landscaping ordinance opens with a series of definitions for terms such as *drip line* and *visual screen*. The ordinance requires that a landscaping plan be submitted to a zoning officer for any new construction or redevelopment. The regulations address landscaping adjacent to public rights-of-way, interior landscaping for parking areas, curbing, screening of storm water detention areas and maintenance of landscaping.

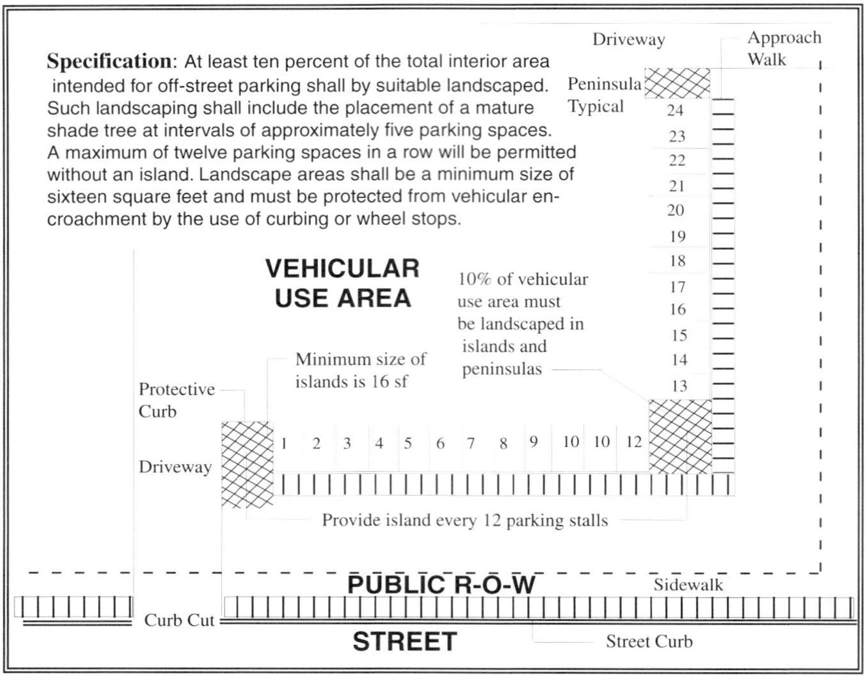

FIGURE 2.1. Vehicular use area design standards, Daphne, Alabama.

Fairhope requires interior landscape areas of grass, trees or shrubs for all parking areas of fifty (50) or more spaces. Large parking lots, such as for shopping centers, must have a continuous landscape strip at least six (6) feet in width at every fourth parking row, and no more than eighteen (18) continuous parking spaces without an intervening planting area at least six (6) feet wide. Owners of existing parking areas are requested to conform fully to the provisions unless conformity results in the loss of established parking spaces.

Huntsville

Article 71, Off-Street Parking and Vehicular Use Area (PVA) Landscaping Requirements, "The Zoning Ordinance of the City of Huntsville, Alabama," February 1989.

This is a very common "first-generation limited-issue" type of landscape ordinance, found in many cities across the United States. This landscape ordinance pertains to parking lots and parking structures only, making it a limited-issue ordinance. Often, this type of first-generation ordinance is improved upon by the addition of other design components or further technical or administrative requirements. In the case of

Huntsville, it has tried to make improvements to its ordinance but has found the political climate not conducive to change.

The essential purpose of this ordinance is to improve the visual appearance of parking and vehicular use areas (PVAs) while preserving trees and other landscape elements so as to protect streams and water courses from excessive runoff. These requirements apply to all PVAs with twenty (20) or more parking spaces containing six thousand (6,000) square feet or more.

Landscaping is to be added to the perimeters for all PVAs covered by this requirement. For PVAs of forty (40) or more spaces, or twelve thousand (12,000) square feet or larger, landscaping is to be added to interiors as well as perimeters. Specifications are given for both of these types of plantings.

Perimeters must be a minimum of five (5) feet in depth. A formula is given for determining interior landscaping requirements. The interior landscape area is determined as:

$$\text{Min. interior landscape area} = \frac{\text{Total PVA (square feet)} \times [1.826 + (0.00435 \times \text{total number of parking spaces planned})]}{100}$$

The interior landscape area need not exceed a maximum of four (4) percent of the PVA.

The only other design component mentioned in this ordinance is a visibility triangle, defined in a companion ordinance.

Credit is given for preserving existing landscape materials. Standards are set forth for plant materials, proper installation, maintenance and submission of the landscape plan and parking lot design. No certification or licensing requirements are mentioned in this ordinance. The ordinance is enforced by the Building Inspector and by withholding the Certificate of Occupancy. Bonds, letters of credit and certified checks may be posted in the name of the city to allow up to six (6) months to comply with landscaping requirements.

This ordinance gives basic parking lot planting design standards. Curiously, it falls short of giving complete parking design requirements for circulation, parking arrangement, travel barriers, enclosure, lighting, signage, safety or other parking lot design considerations. The city should upgrade the ordinance.

Mobile

City of Mobile, Zoning Ordinance of the City of Mobile, Starting with Section IV, Part E, Effective June 1, 1967, with amendments through April 7, 1992.

The purpose of this ordinance is to protect and enhance the ecological and aesthetic environments of the City of Mobile. Further, it is the intent of this ordinance to improve the appearance, quality and quantity of landscaped areas throughout the city, with emphasis on vehicular use areas. The objectives of this ordinance are conservation, reforestation, protection of the environment, flexibility, attractiveness, and tree preservation. The City of Mobile does require a landscape architect or other professional to prepare the landscape plan.

The percentage of land required to be set aside for landscaping varies from year to year. Presently, the percentage is twelve (12) percent. Each area of the site must contain one Heritage Tree for every thirty (30) square feet. If the Urban Forester determines this number to be inappropriate for the site involved, the Urban Forester has the authority to waive any number of trees required; however, those required trees not included in the site must be donated to the Mobile Tree Commission to be planted as public trees.

Parking lot requirements include one (1) tree for every twenty (20) parking spaces. These trees must be placed within the parking area in order to break up the expanse of the lot. Emphasis is given to queuing lanes in order to control drive-through business vehicle circulation.

Signs that contain copy, symbols or other references to products or services are under strict regulations. Signs must be structurally and electrically sound and must not obstruct the view of traffic. Signs must be built in compliance with the Standard Building Code, the city's Electrical Code, or any other applicable code. Permits proving compliance with these codes must be obtained before signs are installed. In addition to permit fees (lighting costs extra), signs also require an inventory fee and a reinspection fee. Signs that are to be located in the historical district must obtain a Certificate of Appropriateness from the Architectural Review Board. There are specific sign requirements for different land uses and zoning uses.

Tree preservation, as indicated by the formation of a Tree Commission, is given major emphasis in this ordinance. Any removal or relocation of a Heritage Live Oak Tree requires a permit granted by the Land Use/Code Administrative Department. The requirements for the issuance of a permit, tree protection during construction, exemptions, removal of public trees, tree removal companies, abuse or mutilation, enforcement of the ordinance, interference with the Urban Forester, tree trails, tree planting and preservation trust fund, appeals, and civic penalties are listed and explained.

Planned Unit Developments (PUDs) are also given major attention. The objectives for PUDs include creative design, flexibility, efficient land use, protection of the environment, open space, and public service.

Alaska

Anchorage

Anchorage Municipal Code, Supplementary District Regulations, Article No. 21.45.125, "Landscaping," 1985.

Few cold-weather communities have landscape ordinances. This cold-weather community has its own "Hardiness Zone Map," which designates lowest average winter temperatures. They range from minus 20 degrees Fahrenheit in Zone 4 to minus 50 degrees Fahrenheit in Zone 1!

Although not very comprehensive as contemporary landscape ordinances go, this ordinance is of interest because of its city's climate. Long, cold winters, almost totally dark days, short growing seasons, increased stress on plant materials and the long periods of time needed for plants to establish themselves or grow make this a unique environment for landscape ordinances.

Landscape materials are an important component of Anchorage's civic infrastructure. In this community the retention of natural vegetation is the most important type of landscaping. Landscape design components consist of parking lots and structures landscaping, screening of roadways, landscaping of public facilities and landscaping in special zoning districts. Specifically, the code addresses visual enhancement landscaping, buffer landscaping, screening and arterial landscaping. Specific standards and design guidelines are minimal. Figure 2.2 illustrates visual enhancement design standards to be used in this community.

Additional standards are given for preparation of landscaping plans, new streets and highways and existing streets and highways. Reference is made to a Master Tree and Shrub List. No standards are given for plant material, installation, maintenance or irrigation. However, irrigation is important. Most outsiders do not realize that Anchorage is a cold "dry desert," receiving only fourteen (14) inches of rain a year. Minimal definitions are given, and there are no licensing requirements.

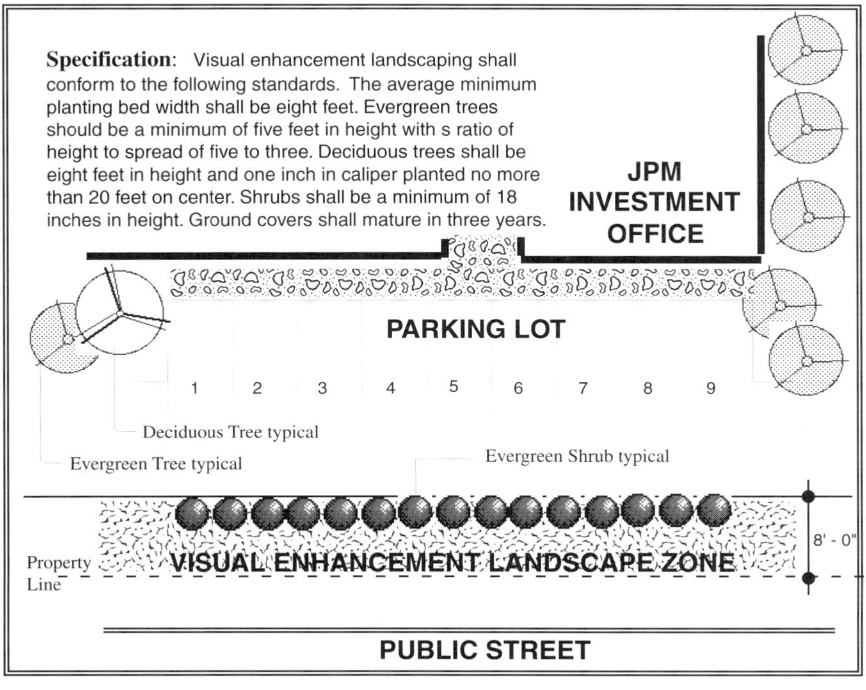

FIGURE 2.2. Visual enhancement landscaping area requirement, Anchorage, Alaska.

TABLE 2.1. Public Review of Landscape Plans, Anchorage, Alaska

Selected Review Criteria	*Reasons for Concern*
Site Visit by Staff	Essential to understand nature of site
Drainage and Topography	How does design respond to each?
Existing Vegetation	Can existing plants be retained?
Significant Features and Wetlands	Are they being impacted by the design?
Adjacent Property	Does design respond to neighborhood?
Are Minimum Landscaping Requirements Being Met?	Must conform to Title 21 AMC
Plants, Planting and Irrigation	Will plants be successful where used?
Vehicular, Parking Lot, Pedestrian and Bike Circulation	Does landscaping respond to these?
Solar Access and Snow Removal and Storage	Effects of sun, shade and snow on landscaping

Administrative practices and contextual concerns are not clear in the documents reviewed for this study. The municipality does have a "Landscape Handbook" that it furnishes to staff and consultants, which helps explain these issues. The purpose of the handbook is to assist in the creative preparation of landscape plans and public review thereof by city staff landscape architects. The section in the handbook titled "How to Review a Landscape Plan" can be very helpful to those who draw the landscape plans for public review. From this section, consultants can learn by what factors the design is being reviewed and approved or rejected.

Table 2.1 illustrates some of the concerns of officials who are charged with the review of the plans.

One of the nice things about this ordinance is the emphasis on streetscape design. The street and roadway landscape design guidelines are very well done. It is curious that in this community ordinance there are not more technical requirements associated with cold weather, wind, snow, low light conditions, frozen soil profiles, safety and wintertime plant material protection.

Arizona

Glendale

Glendale, Ordinance No. 1507 New Series, "Landscape Ordinance of the City of Glendale," August 25, 1987.

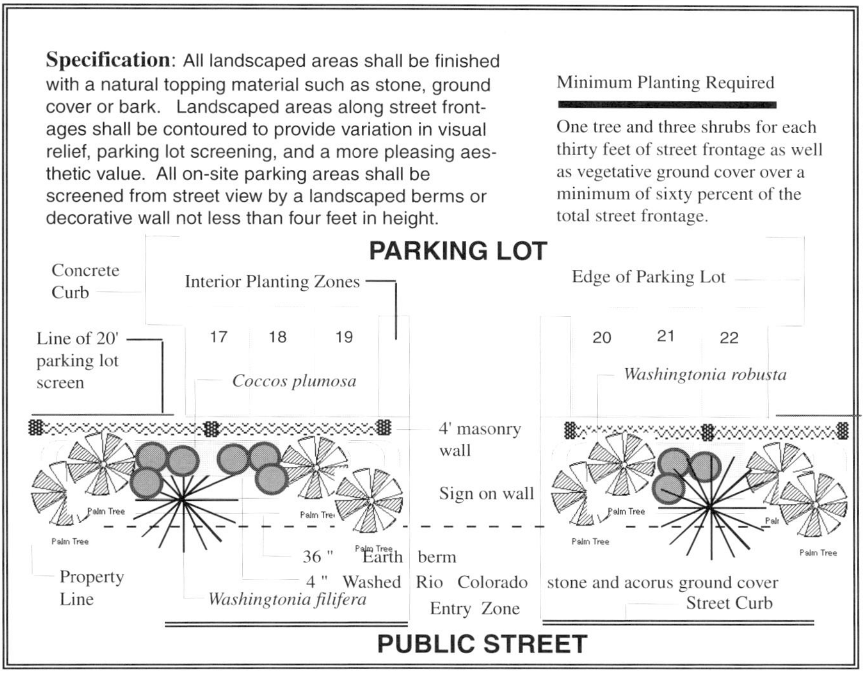

FIGURE 2.3. Parking lot screening and earth cover, Glendale, Arizona.

This ordinance provides standards and requirements for the installation of landscaping and screening walls within the city. All new and expanded development is covered by the regulations. Attractive and logical development, enhancement of property values, attractive appearance, buffers between incompatible land uses and water conservation by using indigenous plants are cited as purposes for the ordinance. Agricultural uses and single-family and two-family residences are exempt from the rules. Preliminary and final landscape plans must be submitted and approved by the director of the Community Development Group.

The Glendale ordinance pays particular attention to street views, setting minimum standards for the planting of trees and shrubs and the construction of contours and berms along street frontages. Figure 2.3 illustrates parking lot screening standards use in this community. In general, one (1) tree and three (3) shrubs are required for each thirty (30) feet of street frontage, and vegetative ground cover must occupy a minimum of sixty (60) percent of the total street frontage landscape area. Parking areas must contain at least one landscaped planter of two hundred (200) square feet for every ten (10) parking spaces provided on the site.

The ordinance also stresses irrigation standards, requiring an automatic irrigation system that promotes water conservation for all landscaped areas.

Mesa

Mesa, Zoning Ordinance, Chapter 14—"Design Guidelines," Chapter 15—"Landscaping and Screening Regulations," Chapter 16—"On-Site Parking and Loading Regulations," December 16, 1991.

The purpose of the Design Guidelines is to provide design criteria for site layout, building elevations, landscaping plan and parking arrangements. The purpose of the Landscaping and Screening Regulations is to provide standards for the installation of landscaping and screening devices in order to control dust, glare, views, noise and erosion. The purpose of the On-Site Parking and Loading Regulations is to provide standards for parking and loading facilities to accommodate the various land uses. These restrictions apply to all buildings and uses of land except single residences and agricultural buildings.

The site plan requirements for the Design Guidelines were written with high priority given to the impact on surrounding property owners and project users. Setbacks, security, walls, areas requiring screening, open space, privacy, lighting, solar exposure, noise impact, pedestrian circulation, and topography are subjects to be emphasized in preparing the site plan. The building elevation requirements stress relating the elevations to the character of the area and enhancing the surrounding vicinity. Exterior materials, relief/rhythm, detailing, height/roof line, signage, landscaping and parking are the features for which standards are given.

One unusual aspect to this ordinance is that a sample of the exterior materials must be provided for the Design Review Board's approval.

The "Landscaping and Screening Regulations" section is divided into landscaping regulations and screening regulations. The landscaping regulations are divided further into general provisions, landscaping design plan, standards for landscape design and development, and maintenance. The general provisions cover landscaped areas, including trees, ground cover, irrigation systems and perimeter landscaping. The landscaping design plan includes a list of all information to be included in the landscaping design plan. The standards for landscape design and development include landscaping for developments adjacent to street rights-of-way, property lines, interior parking area landscaping, multiple-residence open space areas, foundation landscaping and maintenance. The screening regulations are further divided into general provisions and screening design standards. The screening design standards include a list and chart of the types of areas that must be screened, the materials that must be used to screen, and the size requirements of the screens.

The "On-Site Parking and Loading Regulations" section lists general requirements, illustrates required parking stall dimensions and charts the requirements for different zoning districts.

The City of Mesa landscape requirements are quite reasonable. The requirements are presented in a nice, compact booklet, as opposed to the requirements of many cities, which are given in small chapters and must be gathered from larger ordinances. However, the city has organized a complex administrative system including a Superintendent of Building Inspections, a Zoning Administrator, a Board of Adjustments, a Planning and Zoning Board, a City Council, a Design Review Board and a Redevelopment Advisory Board. Despite this complex structure, no landscape architect is required to prepare the landscape plans. New developments must submit plans, fees, and all other applicable information to the Building Inspection Division for approval and granting of a Certificate of Occupancy.

Scottsdale

Scottsdale, Article VII, Section 7.500-7.508, "General Provisions," 1985.

These regulations are intended to establish procedures that ensure the preservation of indigenous plant materials. The Development Review Board has the authority on issues concerning tree removal. Submittals are required to be sent to the Development Review Board for its approval concerning proposed grading around all specified plant materials. Appeals may be granted.

Tempe

Ordinance No. 808, Section 5, "Landscaping, Walls, Screening Devices and Lighting," July 29, 1989, and related ordinance Resolution 90.40, July 12, 1990.

This ordinance provides standards for landscaping, walls, screens and lighting, as well as street tree and landscape guidelines for arterial streets. Used together, this community believes that these landscape features will help ensure privacy, promote logical land development and enhance property values.

The purposes of the standards set by this ordinance for landscaping, walls, screening devices and lighting are to aid in promoting logical land development, enhance property values and create a more attractive community. The City of Tempe encourages the use of low-water plant materials "in such a way that a lush appearance is presented." The ordinance discourages the use of plant material that is high in pollen production and suggests that frost-tender plants be used for accent locations and not primary focal points. All new buildings and any additions to existing buildings fall under the regulations. Site plans and landscape plans must be submitted for building approval. Figure 2.4 shows the tree planting standard used in this city.

An interesting aspect of the Tempe ordinance is a requirement for developers of commercial or office projects with more than fifty thousand (50,000) square feet to provide for public art. "The contribution shall equal or exceed 25 cents per square foot of gross floor area," the ordinance states. The art must be in the form of artwork that is viewable from public spaces, or a cash contribution to the Tempe Municipal Arts Fund. The design and location of the artwork will be reviewed by the Tempe Municipal Arts Commission prior to installation.

Detail drawings, plans and sections are used in the ordinance to illustrate the regulations. A list of designated street trees for the arterial streets is included. For instance, Elliot Road, Wartner Road and Ray Road require the Chilean mesquite.

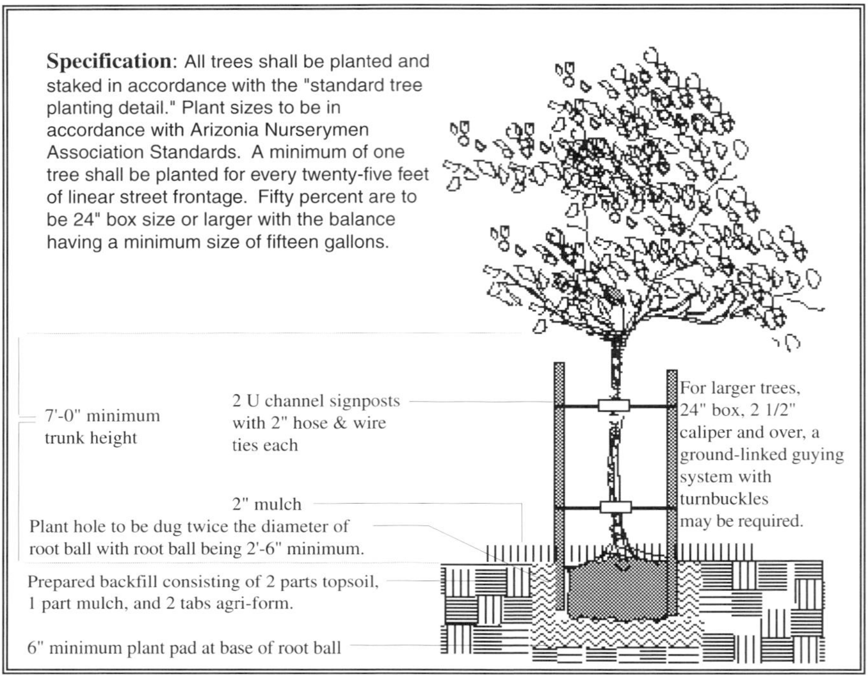

FIGURE 2.4. Standard tree detail, Tempe, Arizona.

Arkansas

Fayetteville

Code of Ordinances, Zoning Code § 160.117, "Off-Street Parking Lot Design" n.d. Related Ordinance No. 3699, "Tree Protection and Preservation," April 20, 1993.

Fayetteville's landscape ordinance consists of language in two distinct ordinances, one prescribing parking lot and buffer plantings and the other tree preservation. They are considered as one for purposes of this discussion.

The parking lot design ordinance requires interior plantings for parking areas of more than ten (10) spaces and perimeter plantings for parking areas of more than five (5) spaces. Special perimeter requirements apply to areas between parking and property lines and/or street frontages.

Buffers of vegetation, fences or walls are required between specified zoning districts. The planting standards are minimal.

Planting requirements for parking lot interiors, perimeters and buffers are based on specified units, area and linear footage measure.

The Tree Protection and Preservation ordinance regulates the planting, maintenance and removal of trees on public grounds and in new subdivisions and large commercial developments. It provides protection for "rare" and "landmark" trees and sets standards for removal of hazardous trees.

This ordinance creates the position of Landscape Administrator and the Tree and Landscape Advisory Committee of citizens and establishes licensure for commercial tree pruning services. The powers, duties and responsibilities of each are defined.

Tree preservation plans must be submitted for large-scale commercial developments when submitting site plans or preliminary plats for review or when applying for a building permit or grading permit for land parcels over one acre. No land disturbance, site clearing or grubbing may take place without approval of the tree preservation plan. Tree preservation standards are illustrated in Figure 2.5.

This ordinance sets a percentage minimum canopy requirement for sites that have had trees removed for construction. For example, residential sites require twenty-five (25) percent canopy, office and professional zoning districts twenty (20) percent and light industrial fifteen (15) percent coverage.

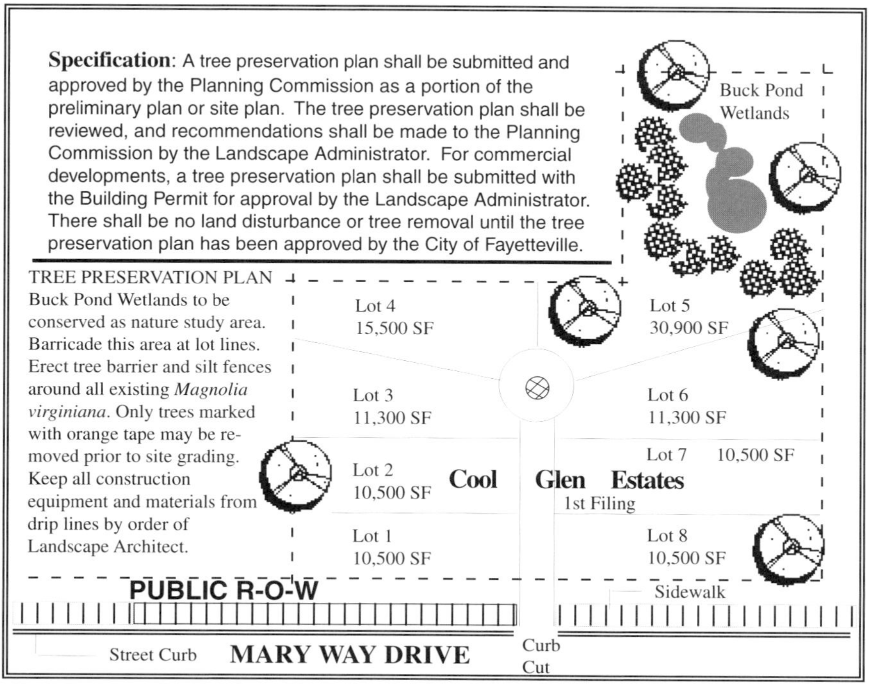

FIGURE 2.5. Tree Preservation Plan, Fayetteville, Arkansas.

The ordinance makes reference to the "City of Fayetteville Landscape Manual." This is a document providing detailed instructions for preparing tree preservation plans, as well as standards and specifications for tree protection, planting, maintenance and design.

Hot Springs

Draft 4, Hot Springs "Landscape Guidelines," September 14, 1995.

The purpose of this ordinance is manyfold. It attempts to promote tourism, economic growth and well-being and to increase property value, protect natural resources and promote responsible land use. This ordinance applies to all new development and renovations of more than five thousand (5,000) square feet within the city limits of Hot Springs. These requirements become applicable at the time of applying for a building permit or a Certificate of Occupancy. This document contains several exemptions, the most important of which is that for a single family with only one building on the property.

In order to be in accordance with this document, the property owner must submit two (2) copies of a landscape plan, which must get approval before the permits will be issued. The requirements for this plan are quite strict, up to the point of including slope percentage arrows, centerlines of water drainage and telling how existing vegetation is to be protected.

This ordinance uses a point system, as can be seen in Table 2.2, which gives points for each landscape element. Points are granted to a proposed plan based on individual plants preserved or installed, with the number of points for each plant specimen determined by the size and landscape value of various types and species of plant material. Total points required are determined by size of site and use. This system, used to provide for the screening of parking and service areas and to require the use of more plant materials, gives the most points for the preservation of native plants. The ordinance stresses the importance of native plants yet allows the property owner many options in the development of the property. The ordinance indicates that this system is intended to be flexible in order to allow the character of the site and of the owner to be expressed, thus creating a more beautiful and unique city.

The ordinance is administered by the City Planning Department and the Office of Code Compliance. A Landscape Development Permit is issued upon submission of a Landscape Development Plan. Upon installation of all landscaping, a Certificate of Occupancy will be issued. Temporary Certificates of Occupancy will be granted prior to installation of landscaping if a bond, letter of credit or certificate of deposit in the amount equal to the uncompleted contract amount, or five (5) dollars per square foot of uninstalled landscaping, is posted in a manner acceptable to the city.

This document also addresses the enforcement of the ordinance. It is to be enforced by the Office of Code Compliance, and if the property owner does not eventually execute the required work, he or she can be forced to pay the city to bring the property into compliance.

TABLE 2.2. Point Schedule, Hot Springs, Arkansas

Landscape Elements	*Number of Points*
TREES	
Existing native trees, 8″ caliper or more	100 points
Existing native trees, 2–8″ caliper	50 points
Introduced trees of 2″ caliper or greater	25 points (40 points for certain native species)
Introduced trees of 1–2″ caliper	20 points (30 points for certain native species)
Introduced trees less than 1″ caliper	8 points (12 points for certain native species)
SHRUBS	
Existing native shrubs, 3 foot minimum height	20 points
Introduced shrubs of 15 gallons or larger	15 points (20 points if native to Arkansas)
Introduced shrubs of 10 gallons	10 points (15 points if native to Arkansas)
Introduced shrubs of 5 gallons	5 points (8 points if native to Arkansas)
Introduced shrubs of other sizes	1 point per gallon (1.5 points if native to Arkansas)
GROUND COVER	
Existing native ground covers, herbs, grasses	5 points per 50 square feet preserved
Introduced ground covers, herbs, lawn	5 points per 100 square feet preserved
BUILT SCREENS	
Earthen berms	2 points per linear foot
Wooden or brick fences or walls	0.50 points per linear foot
Metal fences	0.10 points per linear foot

Removal of any existing site vegetation of more than twelve (12) inches caliper before issuance of a permit, or failure to complete installation or removal at any time of living landscape elements or failure to maintain plantings, will constitute a violation.

Overall, this ordinance is well written, in part because it is based on a point system that works for any site under development. Landscape design requirements are clearly stated. The flexibility of this ordinance as a result of the point system used is probably its most unique feature.

Little Rock

Little Rock, Ordinance No. 13,617 "Landscape Ordinance of the City of Little Rock, Arkansas," 1977.

This ordinance addresses the issue of parking in the urban environment to decrease the visual impact of areas devoted to parking, the storage of automobiles and the like. Minimum requirements and standards for the planting and landscaping of such parking areas are established. Species of trees, shrubs, grasses, ground covers and so forth to be used in vehicular use areas and public rights-of-way are shown. Landscape requirements for vehicular use areas include peripheral coverage requirements, street coverage requirements, and interior coverage requirements (inside the vehicular use area). Landscape plans fulfilling presentation requirements are to be submitted to the Community Service Department in order to receive a permit. Existing plant material is to be preserved. Landscape plans are subject to review and approval. Penalties and rights of appeal are included according to the provisions of the ordinance.

Little Rock, Ordinance No. 13,617, "Landscape Ordinance Illustrative Guide," 1980.

This booklet offers examples of requirements and design solutions for parking areas: plant materials presentation requirements, pavement requirements, parking design, peripheral landscape requirements, street coverage, landscape requirements, plantings in the right-of-way, interior landscaping, design standards, visibility requirements, uncontrolled intersections, controlled intersections, grade adjustment factors, medians, streetlights and growth characteristics of plantings in the right-of-way.

Little Rock, Ordinance No. 13,617 "Zoning Code" No. 225-XX, Chapters 15 and 25,1984; No. 330-XX, Chapter 30, n.d.

This community has a very detailed parking lot ordinance. It requires heavy screening on the sides of any parking lot that abuts a residential area and screening of the parking lot from the street view. This ordinance addresses parking lots more thoroughly than most ordinances do. The drawback is that it addresses only parking lots and nothing else.

Little Rock. "Landscaping and Tree Protection," Chapter 15, Code of Ordinances, n.d.

The Little Rock ordinance presents a combination of site development objectives, which include establishing the City Beautiful Commission, providing for landscaping of parking lots and related areas, tree preservation and buffers between land uses.

The City Beautiful Commission consists of nine (9) members whose duty is to meet monthly to undertake activities to ensure a high level of visual aesthetics.

Among other duties, the City Beautiful Commission hears requests for variances to the provisions of the landscape ordinance. A one hundred (100) dollar variance fee is filed with the Commission.

Trees of more than six (6) inches caliper or twenty (20) feet tall located on public rights-of-way or on other city-owned land may not be removed unless they are diseased, injured or within the area of a proposed structure. This does not apply to the maintenance of utility lines or to the development of subdivision streets, curbs, gutters, storm sewers and utilities. A list of special shade and flowering trees most desired in the city is included in the list of trees to be preserved.

Trees that are removed must be replaced with trees meeting the specifications of the landscape ordinance.

The landscape ordinance applies to site development and vehicular use areas of higher density than two-family sites. Sites not in conformance must eventually comply under certain conditions, such as in rehabilitation or expansion of an existing structure beyond ten (10) percent of existing floor space.

A Landscape Permit must be obtained by submitting a landscape plan to city officials. The landscape plan must present a range of specific information to show compliance with the terms of the ordinance. Upon approval, a Certificate of Occupancy is granted.

Several technical requirements are listed in this ordinance. The design must respond to specific plant species, plant material standards, screening requirements, perimeter planting, interior parking lot planting, building facade landscaping, land use buffers and hillside cuts and slopes.

Hillside treatment is based on percentage of slope. Sod and grass may be planted on slopes of less than thirty (30) percent. On slopes of more than thirty (30) percent but less than forty (40) percent, vegetation must be planted with netting. On slopes of more than forty (40) percent, riprap must be used with soil-separating fabric. Trees must be planted twenty (20) feet on center on benches used on hillside cuts and fills.

Storm water detention basins, hillside buffers and utility easements count toward satisfying landscape area requirements. Specific language is given concerning planting in public rights-of-way.

Specific design criteria are given for buffers between various land uses and streets. Buffers are required for all multifamily, commercial, office and industrial land uses. The size of the buffer is based on a percentage of average width or depth. Screening with a six (6)-foot fence or other device is required for parking lots, drives, sanitation areas, static commercial displays of merchandise, loading docks, heating or air conditioning equipment, dumpsters and trash containment areas.

This ordinance is a little disjointed in that it seems to have been developed segmentally. Certain contemporary site development standards go unmentioned or are briefly discussed. Reorganization of the ordinance for clarity and completeness is recommended.

California

Alameda and Contra Costa Counties

East Bay Municipal Utility District, Model Ordinance, n.d.

The East Bay Municipal Utility District (EBMUD) is a water utility serving one and two-tenths (1.2) million people in Alameda and Contra Costa counties in the San Francisco Bay Area. As part of its water conservation efforts, EBMUD has developed a model ordinance for water-efficient landscapes. Jurisdictions within its service area are encouraged to adopt the ordinance. The California state landscape ordinance (AB325) required local jurisdictions to adopt their own landscape ordinances before January 1993 or fall under the regulations of the state's model ordinance.

The stated purpose of the model ordinance is to manage and use water efficiently. It promotes functional landscapes with plants best suited for the climate, encourages soil conditioning, as shown in Figure 2.6, and urges cities to take a leadership role in water conservation efforts. The ordinance indicates that outdoor

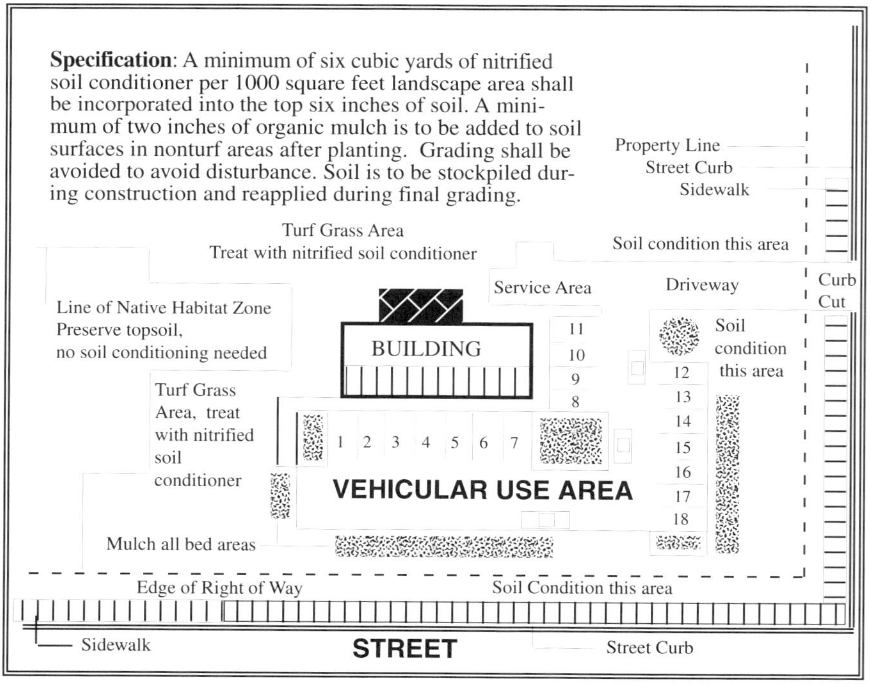

FIGURE 2.6. Soil conditioning specifications, East Bay Municipal Utility District, California.

landscaping consumes approximately twenty-five (25) percent of the water used in the EBMUD.

The model ordinance requires landscape plans for all new construction. At least ninety (90) percent of the plants selected should be well suited to the climate and require minimal water. The ten (10) percent of plants of a non-drought-tolerant variety should be grouped together for easy irrigation. Turf areas are not to exceed twenty-five (25) percent of irrigated areas (except for golf courses, parks, cemeteries and school recreation areas). Turf must have a water requirement less than or equal to that of tall fescue.

The model ordinance sets restrictions for irrigation and sprinkler systems and establishes additional requirements for new construction other than single-family residences. A monthly irrigation schedule for each valve is requested from the designer.

Beverly Hills

Beverly Hills, "Landscape Ordinance of Beverly Hills," 1986.

The intent of this ordinance is to control the construction and maintenance of walls, fences and hedges so as to provide for individual security and privacy by restricting the movement and view of the general public in those areas of a lot where privacy and security are most needed, yet preserving the open garden quality and unobstructed vistas of the front yard.

Carlsbad

Carlsbad, "Landscape Manual: City of Carlsbad, Policies and Requirements," November 13, 1990.

The city's programs, policies and regulations relating to landscaping come in an attractive illustrated notebook. The intent of the regulations is to produce character and a visual image for Carlsbad and to create "an enduring impression of the community." The policies are described as minimum standards, and development projects are encouraged to exceed standards whenever possible.

The regulations concerning plantings are noteworthy. The city has included a "plant palette list" for specific zones within the community, such as "lush landscape," "refined landscape," "naturalizing landscape" and "native landscape." The ordinance goes one step further, to assign an arterial streetscape theme for the city. For example, Alga Road is considered the "Coastal Foothills," requiring plants like the Canary Island pine (*Pinus canariensis*) and the eucalyptus (*cladocalyx*). Other street themes include "Lagoon Vistas and Wetlands," "Agricultural History/Valley Vistas," "Oak Grove Woodland" and "Scenic Sea Coast Drive."

The ordinance also recognizes Xeriscape, outlining the low maintenance and low water usage concept with seven principles. Water conservation policies and requirements for the naturally semiarid region are included in the "Policies and Regulations" chapter. Housing projects featuring "model homes" are required to

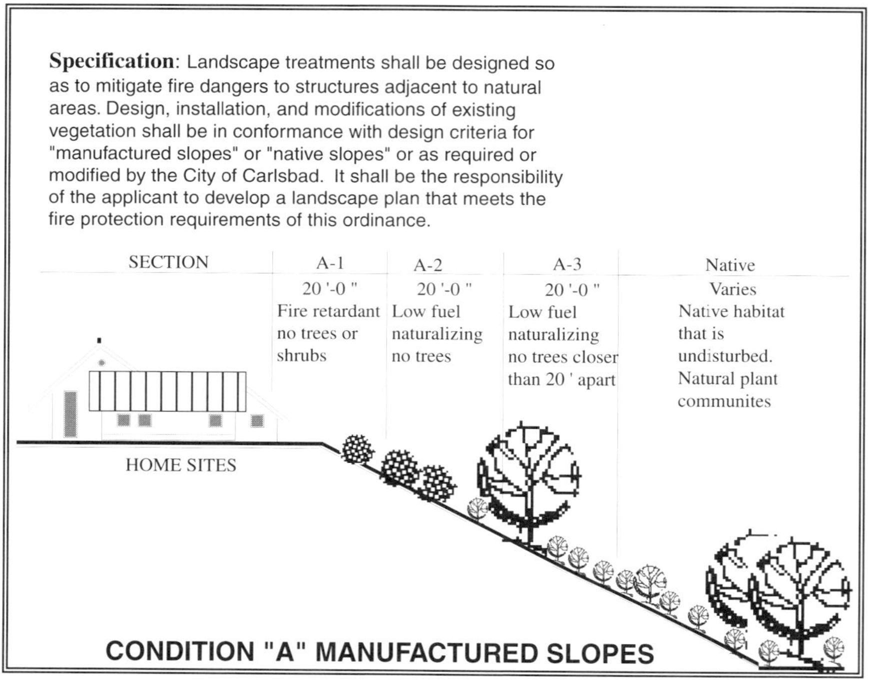

FIGURE 2.7. Fire protection design standard, Carlsbad, California.

designate at least one model as the "Water Conservation Landscape Model" or the "Xeriscape Model." Signs are necessary to educate prospective buyers on water-conserving elements and plant materials used in the design.

Generally, Carlsbad requires one (1) tree for every forty (40) feet of street frontage. The regulations also address slope revegetation, erosion control and fire protection. Figure 2.7 illustrates one of the standards for the design of fire-resistant slopes. The notebook's appendix includes a list of restricted "high fuel species," such as California sagebrush (*Artemisia californica*) and junipers (*Juniperus* species). The appendix also features a handy checklist for those working their way through the landscape permit process.

Claremont

Claremont, Resolution No. 87-192, "Rural Claremont Architectural and Landscape Standards," 1987.

The City of Claremont wishes to retain a "sense of place" by preserving some of the rural and agricultural features of the area and by requiring developments to reflect individuality of design while being visually integrated with the environment in which they are placed. Architectural designs should not overwhelm the site, but rather should be in proportion to the site. In addition, structures and property improvements should consider the following: orientation and siting for mountain views from the site and adjacent properties, solar orientation, minimal paving and outdoor lighting and a landscape design that blends with the natural environment.

Culver City

Culver City, Ordinance No. CS-670, Amending Section 37-2 of the Culver City Municipal Code, Repealing Section 37-88.G of the Municipal Code, and Substituting Section 37-91 of the Municipal Code, September 14, 1970.

The purpose of this ordinance is to establish parking area construction and maintenance requirements in order to preserve public health, safety and general welfare.

Two copies of plans for parking area improvements are to be submitted to the Building Department. Building and electrical permits are to be applied for at the same time. No certified planner or landscape architect is required to prepare the plans.

Specifications for asphalt concrete or portland cement are given on thicknesses, drainage, seal coats, priming coat and soil sterilization. The ordinance explains how the surface is to be prepared, constructed, illuminated and landscaped.

The landscaping requirements for the parking areas include shrubs, ornamental fences or trees of certain heights to separate different land uses. Parking lots shall have a one hundred (100)-square foot area, with one (1) tree and shrubs at its base planter area provided for every fifty (50) parking spaces. All landscaping shall be irrigated and maintained.

This ordinance could easily be mistaken for a parking area specification.

Davis

Davis City Code, Ordinance #920, Section 29-160, "50% Shading of Parking Lots," n.d., and Davis Zoning Ordinance, Section 29-179.5.1, "Water Conservation Standards for New Construction," n.d., and Davis Zoning Ordinance, Section 29-180, " Landscaping and Screening Commercial Zoning Districts," n.d.

Davis is an ecologically aware city that promotes the use of bicycles and discourages automobile travel where possible. Its landscape ordinance is scattered throughout the city code rather than compactly stated in a freestanding document. The various landscape clauses cover water conservation, shading of parking lots and landscaping and screening of commercial districts.

The most interesting part of this ordinance is the parking lot screening language. The city requires that at least fifty (50) percent of each parking lot be screened fifteen (15) years after the building permit is acquired. At the time the building permit is sought, a landscape plan must be submitted that shows the extent of the shade produced by the specified trees. Suggestions as to which trees perform

TABLE 2.3. Water Conservation Standards, Davis, California

Standard	*Expected Results*
Turf grass not to be planted on slopes >15%	Too much runoff on steep slopes
Sprinklers on slopes > 15% to use 0.5 inches per hour or less	Reduces runoff
No turf grass in medians	Reduces waste
No turf grass between curb and sidewalk	Reduces overspray and waste
Sprinkler application rates to be uniform	Cuts down on waste and inefficiency
Valve circuits to be uniform and separated by similar design units	Makes system more uniform
Only head-to-head coverage allowed on valve circuits	More uniform application of water
Use check valve at low point of system	Prevents off-site drainage
Separate trees and shrubs from turf grass in system design	Keeps application rates similar
Mulch soil surfaces two (2) inches deep	Reduces evaporation
Controllers to have multiple programming modes	Less water applied more often
Conduct periodic water audits	Monitors system performance
MUST COMPLY WITH AT LEAST THREE ADDITIONAL STANDARDS	
Conduct soil test	Understanding of capillary action
25% of landscape area to be planted with cool season grass	Reduces water needs
35% of landscape area to be planted with warm season grass	Reduces water needs
Use alternative water where possible	Preserves potable water
Create flat areas at toe of slopes	Slows runoff, allow percolation
Stockpile and preserve topsoil	Utilizes water more efficiently
25% of landscape area not to be sprinkled	Encourages native plants
90% of plants to be well suited to native habitat	Encourages non-use of exotics
Water audit to be conducted by certified water auditor	Capable system analysis
Sprinkler valve circuits inspected per system requirements	Maintains system consistency
Valve circuits to have catch can device test	Monitors exact rate of flow

well are listed in the ordinance. The ordinance also describes how to calculate the shade/pavement ratio. Credit is given for shade produced by nearby structures.

Surprisingly, the ordinance does not tell on which day of the year or hour of the day the calculation is to be made.

Because trees, vines and other landscaping can cool the city and reduce energy use while promoting bicycling, the city requires that ten (10) percent of each commercial site be landscaped. Screening is required adjacent to R (residential) districts.

Few technical standards or design components are mentioned in this ordinance. However, there is more detail in the water conservation measures. Davis promotes efficient use of water in all private and public construction in all zoning districts by encouraging proper landscape design, installation and maintenance practices. The landscape design and construction standards shown in Table 2.3 are given and must be met by all new construction.

The ordinance is more concerned with water and energy and does not place as much emphasis on horticulture or landscape architecture as many contemporary ordinances.

Fontana

Fontana, "Landscape Ordinance of Fontana," n.d.

This pamphlet contains five items: guidelines, standards, general requirements, specific requirements and landscape maintenance districts and their specifications. Topics include park and recreational fees, landscape/irrigation plan reviews, minimum boundary landscape, parkway landscape, inspections for irrigation construction and landscape plans, specific plan requirements for industrial and commercial multifamily residential development and parking areas, operation costs and cost assessment formulas for landscape maintenance districts.

Glendale

Glendale, Section 30-1211, "Glendale Municipal Code—Open Space and Landscaping," n.d.

This code requires that at least twenty (20) percent of the total lot area shall be permanently landscaped open space. Permanent landscaping is to consist of landscaped areas at the ground level, in planters or in potted containers. Decorative design elements such as fountains, sculptures, planters, rocks or other similar elements may be permitted where they are integral parts of a landscape plan composed primarily of live plant materials. Pedestrian walks and vehicular access ways will be permitted in such landscaped areas but may not be counted as landscape open space. Permanent and automatic irrigation facilities are to be provided in all permanent landscaped areas except for potted containers and the like.

Glendale, "Glendale Municipal Code—New Condominium Landscaping Criteria Summary," n.d.

Some of the requirements of this ordinance are listed by their type briefly as the following: landscape setback areas with maintenance methods provided, decorative design elements requirements, permanent and automatic irrigation facilities, plant material conformity to the American Standard for Nursery Stock, minimum street tree size for planting and irrigation drawings and stringent irrigation requirements.

Goleta

Goleta, "Goleta Water District Guide to Landscape Plans," 1988.

This ordinance emphasizes the use of drought tolerant landscape designs that utilize low-water Mediterranean climate plants. Processing procedures for landscape plans are discussed. Irrigation plan requirements and advice on the use of low-water plant materials are provided. In addition, the Goleta Water District includes a checklist for the landscape/irrigation plan review and examples of both landscape and irrigation plan drawings.

Hayward

Hayward Municipal Code, Zoning Ordinance, Ord. No 71-038, "Preservation of Trees," June 22, 1971.
Related ordinance, Hayward Municipal Code, Zoning Ordinance, Ord. No 95-10, "Street Trees," February 21, 1995.

These two related ordinances comprise a single-issue landscape ordinance directed toward landscaping on public streets and in public places, protecting public vegetation and preserving trees on private lands.

The ordinance creates the position of Landscape Maintenance Manager, creates an Official Street Tree List and requires permits from the city for any planting or pruning on public land. The Landscape Maintenance Manager is charged with the care of all public vegetation, with powers that extend to nuisance plants on private property.

Street tree planting specifications and a standard street tree planting detail are included within the law.

The tree preservation ordinance is directed toward reducing the wholesale destruction of trees, which would decimate the scenic beauty of the San Francisco Bay area, at the same time exposing properties to topsoil erosion, mud slides and increased flood hazard.

No tree may be removed without a permit or approval of the city landscape architect. To receive a permit, a developer must make application in writing to the city and show why trees have to be removed and which trees will remain. Trees may be removed only according to stated criteria, which are reproduced in Table 2.4.

TABLE 2.4. Tree Removal Criteria, Hayward, California

Condition of tree in respect to disease, danger of falling, or proximity to utilities
Interference of tree with neighboring property owner's view
Proximity to proposed structures
Necessity to remove tree to allow substantial enjoyment of individual property rights
Topography and the effect of tree removal on erosion, soil retention and increased flow of surface water
Number of trees in the neighborhood and effect of removal on property values
Good forestry practices, how many trees the site will support
Landmark importance of tree and the effect of its retention on use of property

This community values existing trees but has not developed language to encourage replacement of trees nor landscaping of private lands as a method of retaining native tree cover.

Irvine

Code of Ordinances, Division G, "Sustainability in Landscaping," n.d.

Landscape ordinances vary across the nation in response to climate, geography, local conditions and the needs of public policy. A typical landscape ordinance consists of language stating contextual concerns, administrative procedures and technical requirements. These are generally stated in the law's purpose, design components and technical standards or specifications. Most often a landscape ordinance is focused on regulating the construction industry or landscape practices or encouraging good design.

This ordinance is one of the most interesting and perhaps unique in this study. The Irvine ordinance is focused on "sustainability." It is the only landscape ordinance in this study, and possibly the only one in the nation, based on resource conservation.

The ordinance sets forth actions and standards that collectively work to conserve, recycle and reuse resources invested in landscapes, and that work to optimize benefits and reduce environmental impacts. It is the goal of this ordinance to ensure that environmental benefits and impacts be given the same consideration as aesthetic and functional goals and that landscape design will result in increased benefits, decreased impacts and reduced consumption of resources.

Sustainability, utilizing some of the policies indicated in Table 2.5, involves coordination of landscape planning, design and management within the urban environment. A sustainable landscape is one that provides positive levels of carbon

TABLE 2.5. Sustainability Policies, Irvine, California

Policy	*Benefit/Impact Reduction*
Conserve, recycle and reuse resources.	Increases benefits and reduces impacts
Increase efficiency of energy use.	Reduces energy consumption
Use reclaimed water.	Reduces water consumption
Optimum levels of biomass storage.	Removes carbon dioxide from air
Optimum levels of oxygen production.	Increases quality of air
Design landscapes with plant associations.	Similar habitat reduces outside energy needs
Design for optimum microclimatic effects.	Reduces heating and cooling energy consumption
Reduce use of turf grass.	Reduces or eliminates lawn equipment use
Use recycled materials for mulch.	Utilizes organic soil management practices
Conserve significant biotic resources.	Unhindered nature provides positive results
Balance aesthetics, function and sustainability.	Advantage: positive effects over negative impacts
Promote sustainability education.	Increases benefits, reduces impacts community-wide
Reduce or eliminate use of garden chemicals.	Reduces environmental problems caused by fertilizer, pesticides and herbicides

storage and oxygen productivity after all demands for energy, water, soil improvement and maintenance activities have been accounted for. The listed policies have been identified as adding to sustainability.

A landscape permit is required, and all conceptual landscape plans must be approved.

No specific design components or technical requirements are given in this ordinance; rather, the ordinance requires that a "Sustainable Landscaping Guideline Manual" be written to formulate such rules, procedures and interpretations as may be necessary to carry out the objectives of this law.

The *Sustainable Landscaping Guideline Manual* created as part of this ordinance states purpose and goals, sets forth related state law, lists review procedures and defines landscape areas and design guidelines. In addition, the manual is complemented with a glossary and a recommended Plant Association List showing appropriate groupings, water needs, species and habit.

Design guidelines center on (a) Landscape Productivity, (b) Plant Associations, (c) Energy Conservation, (d) Water Conservation, (e) Microclimate Improvement and (f) Soil Management. To measure compliance, performance guidelines are listed rather than technical standards and measurable methods of determining environmental benefits or impact reduction.

This is an interesting ordinance indeed. It should be lauded for its basis in science rather than art, but encouraged to seek, determine and set specific scientific standards to measure the effects of compliance. Other cities could benefit from looking into this ordinance.

Long Beach

Long Beach, Section 18-21.12.210, "Usable Open Space," 1986.

Included in this code are open space requirements for common and private (i.e., patio and balcony) use in R-3 and R-4 zones. Within the landscape requirements, trees of at least twenty-four (24)-inch box size are required in any new construction for each one hundred twenty-five (125) square feet of required yard in R-3 and R-4 districts. A tree of the same size is required for each twenty-five (25) linear feet of street frontage. Tree species must be approved by the Street Division of the Department of Public Works. Alternative requirements regarding street tree codes are provided. Landscape plan, irrigation and planter drainage and inspection are standard. Requirements for truck loading, screening and drive-through facilities are presented. For parking lots, one (1) tree is to be provided for each five (5) parking spaces. These trees may be clustered, but a minimum of one (1) cluster for each one hundred (100) feet of a row or double row of parking spaces must be provided. Parking structures have to meet requirements too (i.e., one (1) tree per twenty-five (25) feet of the perimeter of the structure).

Long Beach, Section 27-21.12.520, "Landscaping Requirements," 1986.

Los Angeles

Los Angeles Municipal Code, Section 12.40, "Landscape—General Requirements," May 12, 1996, Ord. No. 170978.

Los Angeles has one of the most unique ordinances in this study. This ordinance exceeds those of other large American cities and, without doubt, will be looked at for years to come as a model for other towns and cities. The purpose of the ordinance is, in part, to help solve some real urban environmental problems. Notably, this ordinance has been crafted to aid in stabilizing ecological balance by assisting air purification, storm water runoff, groundwater recharge and water cleansing and mitigation of the urban heat island effect. Glare reduction and reducing yard waste are secondary purposes. All reasons are based in science, rather than art, for this community landscape ordinance.

The ordinance contains five major goals that must be met by design, as described in the following paragraphs and shown in Table 2.6.

TABLE 2.6. Design Goals, Los Angeles, California

Purpose	*Requirement*	*Method*
Water Management	Conserve city water	Highly controlled irrigation
Conservation of Energy	Reduce urban temperatures	Tree planting to shade walls
Heat and Glare Reduction	Reduce heat buildup on paving	Parking lot planting
Air Quality Enhancement	Generation of oxygen	Vegetation to produce oxygen filter
Soil and Watershed Conservation	Conserve soil, reduce erosion	Plant all manufactured slopes
Source Reduction of Waste	Recycle all organic yard waste	Compost on-site

The Department of Building and Safety will not issue any building, grading, or use of land permit for any project unless the Department of City Planning determines that the proposed landscaping will meet the design goals.

To meet these goals, permit applicants must demonstrate in their design of the project site how specified landscape ordinance guidelines are being met. A point system has been prepared by the City Planning Commission to measure this compliance. A design manual (user's guide) has been written to explain how the points are calculated. Points are based on landscape features, landscaping techniques utilized in the design and water management strategy.

Standards are included in the guidelines for irrigation, air quality enhancement, planting techniques, slope planting and shading of walls and structures.

Submittal requirements for landscape plans and application fees are set in this ordinance.

This ordinance, based on science rather than art, will help to make Los Angeles a very beautiful city.

Los Angeles, Xeriscape Ordinance No. 163,532, "Water Conservation Requirements," n.d.

The City of Los Angeles requires reduced water consumption in the landscape through a variety of techniques (Xeriscape). The ordinance does not regulate plant size, type or quantities. It affects all new multifamily, commercial and industrial projects. Landscape and irrigation drawings must conform to a performance point system contained in the ordinance. Those qualified to prepare plans and drawings are California-licensed landscape architects, architects, landscape contractors or irrigation designers. A plan check fee of twenty-five (25) dollars is standard. Included in the ordinance are three plan drawings explaining irrigation requirements.

Rancho Mirage, Los Angeles, Chapter 17.20.010, "Landscaping Standards," 1988.

Rancho Mirage, a quality resort community, plans to protect and enhance its desert surrounding, to reduce heat and glare brought on by development and to minimize the impact of physical and visual pollution. The following standards are introduced to help maintain these objectives: tree and shrub installation requirements, parkway treatment standards, special landscape design requirements of corner lots in planned unit developments and landscape maintenance.

Mariposa County

Town Zoning Ordinance, § 17.336.060, "Development Guidelines for Design Review Overlay District," October 1992.

Mariposa has established a design review overlay zone for its community. As part of this ordinance, architectural design standards, site development standards, landscape standards and signage standards are established.

Site development standards have been adopted to allow projects to conform to existing topography and preserve prominent and unique natural features such as rock formations, water courses and vegetation. Properties abutting Mariposa Creek are to take advantage of it as an open space amenity and make use of it as a flood control feature and recreational asset. Landscape standards call for landscaping parking lot interiors, parking lot screens, refuse area screening and perimeter plantings.

Maintenance, irrigation and plant materials are mentioned. Specific plant material quantities are left up to the designer, with the exception of shade trees for parking areas. These quantities are based on providing a specified amount of shade coverage. The town maintains an approved tree list.

It is interesting to see that the landscape requirements are contained within the same legislation that controls the design of buildings, signage, historic structures and site development. Together, these features control the image that is projected by any community.

Napa

Napa Municipal Code, Chapter 15, "Water Efficient Landscaping," December 1992.

In this community, landscape plans are reviewed by the city for landscape design and efficient use of water prior to the issuing of any building permit or grading permit.

To seek approval, a "Landscape Documentation Package" consisting of drawings, calculations, schedules and details pertaining to landscape design, grading design, soil analysis and irrigation design must be submitted to the Planning Department for architectural review. In addition, a prepared irrigation schedule showing efficient use of water and a regular maintenance schedule showing regular inspection and repair of equipment must be included with this package. A standard form, titled "Water Conservation Concept Statement," must be filled out and signed by the person making application for a building permit.

This package must be prepared by a landscape architect, architect or other landscape professional.

One of the major conditions of this permit is to determine the maximum water allowance for each site. A project's maximum water allowance is calculated using the following formula.

$$\begin{array}{c}\text{Maximum water allowance}\\ \text{(in gallons per year)}\end{array} = \begin{array}{c}22^{*} \times \text{landscaped area}\\ \text{(in square feet)}\end{array}$$

Upon completion of the installation of the landscape work, an irrigation audit must be performed by a certified irrigation auditor and a certificate of compliance must be signed by the owner, contractor and landscape architect and filed with the Planning Commission prior to release of the owner's surety bonds held by the city.

Few design standards for either landscape design or irrigation design are itemized in this ordinance. Some reference is made to vehicular use area design, storage areas and landscape maintenance.

The community realizes that to meet the performance requirements of this ordinance, one must have technical training in landscape architecture or many years of experience in the installation of plant material and irrigation systems in its locality.

National City

National City, "Guidelines for On-Site Landscaping," revised June 1992.

National City's ordinance is part of a program to improve the beauty of the city through landscaping. This document is intended to serve as a guideline for property owners in landscaping their properties efficiently and aesthetically.

The ordinance outlines landscape and irrigation plan requirements, design considerations, water conservation, planting, maintenance and alternative water sources. The design considerations include shading, mulching, plant lists, plant selection, water features, lighting, parkways, preservation of existing trees and shrubs and hydrozoning. A landscape architect's or horticulturist's determination and recommendation is required only when an existing tree is being relocated or altered. Water conservation is of extreme importance in this ordinance.

Hardscape is an interesting term found in this ordinance. It refers to landscape elements other than trees, shrubs and ground covers, and includes decks, paved areas and walkways, but not parking areas. *Hydrozone* is another interesting term. Hydrozones are portions of the landscaping containing plants with

---

*22 equals Referenced Evapotranspiration × ET Adjustment Factor × Units Conversion Factor. This factor is calculated by the city and is subject to change based on rainfall and water supply.

similar water needs that are served by one irrigation valve, or a set of valves with the same schedule.

An interesting aspect of this ordinance is the prohibition of lawn turf used for purely aesthetic reasons. The ordinance states that because lawn turf requires so much water and maintenance, it is to be used only in functional areas, such as picnic areas. There are many other restrictions on the use of turf. The use of water features such as fountains and pools is also discouraged.

This is an informal ordinance with few quantifying requirements. The ordinance allows for quality design with explained standards, not simply number requirements. Every possible way to save water is mentioned in this ordinance.

Oakland

Addition to Ordinance No. 9366 C.M.S., "Article 6: Trees," 1976.

This article outlines requirements to regulate the removal of trees, protect trees during building construction and promote appreciation and understanding of trees.

The article protects any tree measuring nine (9) inches DBH (diameter at breast height), except eucalyptus on any undeveloped property, or *Quercus agrifolia* (coast live oak) measuring four (4) inches DBH on any property. The value of a tree to the neighborhood is greater than its potential inconvenience to the owner.

The application process is outlined. The Office of Public Works receives applications for tree removal permits. The Office of Parks and Recreation reviews applications, including a site inspection in two (2) to seven (7) days upon receipt of an application. The Department of City Planning receives recommendations from the Office of Parks and Recreation for any revision of site plans or structural design in efforts to preserve one or more trees. Also addressed are emergency situations, the appeals process, public agency exemptions, enforcement penalties and liabilities.

Ontario

"Landscape and Irrigation Drawings for Residential, Commercial and Industrial Developments," 1986.

The City of Ontario supports water conservation through its stringent requirements regarding drought-tolerant plant materials and water-efficient irrigation systems (Xeriscape).Landscape and irrigation drawings must conform to its extensive list of standards. Other topics listed include solid waste standards, drought tolerant and security plant materials, (ground cover, turf grass, vines, shrubs and trees), slope preparation and maintenance district requirements.

Palm Springs

Palm Springs, "Guidelines for the Design and Installation of Irrigation Systems Which Do Not Deposit Water on Streets, Sidewalks, or Bike Paths," n.d.

These illustrative guidelines for irrigation show types of sprinklers commonly used (i.e., rotor, pop-up, drip, bubblers, etc.) and generally give advice about factors to consider in designing an irrigation system, such as plant water requirements, overspray, irrigation on slopes, narrow spaces, wind, system checks and water pressure standards.

Palo Alto

Palo Alto, "El Camino Real Design Guidelines," 1988.

These guidelines attempt to subdue the intense visual competition caused by automobiles and advertising on commercial streets and instead develop a satisfying visual experience of the city. Topics covered in the guidelines include developing a visual landscape theme, buffers, lighting, site plans, parking lots, architectural review board procedures, off-street parking regulations paving and drainage.

Palo Alto, Chapter 18.83, "Off-Street Parking and Loading Regulations," April 1984.

The purpose of this ordinance is to develop off-street parking, loading areas and bicycle facilities in order to alleviate traffic congestion.

Palo Alto has an Architectural Review Board, which has prepared a document outlining design guidelines for El Camino Real, a major street that runs through the city. The design guidelines set forth street themes, landscaping and paving requirements, suggestions for site plan development and design recommendations for building facades, buffers, parking lots and lighting. Also listed in these guidelines are the Architectural Review Board procedures and administrative policy.

Pasadena

Pasadena, "Xeriscape Policy for City-Owned Facilities," 1989.

In an effort to use water efficiently, the City of Pasadena has designed a mandatory policy for new landscapes built on city-owned facilities. This policy would help reduce water consumption, limit landscapes for a project, and preserve the aesthetic qualities of Pasadena. Listed in this publication are strict turf grass requirements. Turf grass can be used only where it is functionally required in the landscape, that is, in playing fields, golf courses or entertainment areas. Soil tests are mandatory. Low-volume irrigation systems (emitting less than seventy-five hundredths (.75) of an inch of water per hour) are critically important in Pasadena. Furthermore, it stresses the importance of water evaporation reduction through use of mulches and the application of soil polymers that retain moisture.

Pasadena, Chapter 17.64, Section 17.64.290, "Landscaping in the RM Districts," 1986.

This ordinance places restrictions on yard planting areas. For example, forty (40) percent of the lot area not devoted to lot coverage, paved driveways and parking areas is to be maintained in planting. More specific attention is given to the landscaping requirements governing yards and their placement on the lot (i.e., front, side, and rear).

Rancho Mirage

Rancho Mirage, Chapter 17.20, "Landscaping Standards," n.d.

Rancho Mirage is aware of its unique desert setting and has adopted a landscape ordinance to help it distinguish itself as a prestigious quality resort community. The city hopes to do this, in part, by reducing heat and glare generated by development. In addition, to assist in achieving this goal it may require that the landscape plans submitted as part of the compliance process be prepared by a registered landscape architect. The city believes this may ensure that the landscape design will be in harmony with the surrounding desert environment. To further this goal, it requires the use of desert plants.

Fully dimensioned, comprehensive landscape plans are submitted. These plans are to include plant materials, hardscape, water elements and irrigation. Design requirements are very limited in this ordinance. There are standards for plant material sizes, parkway treatment for specific streets, earth mounding, walls, fencing and corner lots. The corner lot requirement is somewhat unusual. Rancho Mirage requires that on corner lots fronting arterial streets, thirty-six-hundred (3,600) square feet be set aside for landscaping. The requirement falls to sixteen-hundred (1,600) square feet for lots fronting collector streets.

Performance standards are included for irrigation systems, installation and maintenance of landscaping. To ensure perpetual maintenance, a covenant must be filed with the Riverside County Recorder. A three (3)-year landscape maintenance agreement, as well as a letter of credit, must be executed between the property owner and the city.

Redlands

Redlands, Los Angeles, "Landscape Plan Evaluation Submittal Requirements," 1988.

General and specific requirements are given for preliminary and detailed landscape plans, which include irrigation and planting plans.

Riverside

Riverside, "Design Review Guidelines," 1987.

The City of Riverside established these guidelines to ensure a high standard of design quality for new developments in commercial, office, high density residential and industrial areas. These guidelines, divided into five (5) sections, are merely recommendations and do not represent actual codes.

The building design section covers maintenance of the architectural character of an area, and the rehabilitation of older buildings.

Site design includes blending architecture and site, planting design and cluster design. There is a large section on signage, including sign relationships to building architecture and site, sign coordination, simplicity, monument signs, use of color and illumination.

The landscape design section discusses the use of plants as buffers and for softening architectural elements, street trees and plant protection devices such as tree stakes and/or guy wires. The irrigation requirements cover subjects such as overlapping sprinkler coverage, controllers, valves and backflow prevention devices.

Furthermore, each section contains fabulous sketches to help clarify the recommendations.

Roseville

Roseville Municipal Code, "Water Efficient Landscape Requirements," February 17, 1993, Res. No. 93-55.

The purpose of this ordinance is to define the standards and procedures for the design of residential and commercial landscapes in order to utilize appropriate plant materials and conserve the scarce public water supply. In addition, this ordinance regulates landscape installation and landscape management. The ordinance applies to all parcels of land within the city. All land uses must follow the guidelines.

Five sets of landscape planting plans, irrigation plans and a soil test must be submitted to the city for the purpose of plan review to determine whether the design is responsive to water conservation and use of drought resistant plants. A Certificate of Compliance, a facsimile of which is shown in Figure 2.7, must be endorsed by a landscape architect to certify that the design has been prepared in accordance with the provisions of the water efficient landscape requirement contained within this ordinance. Following installation, a Certificate of Completion must be endorsed by both the landscape architect and the landscape contractor installing the job.

Definitions are included along with design standards that have been established in the ordinance for preparation of planting plans, irrigation plans and irrigation schedules. Selection criteria for turf grass are an important part of this law. The ordinance contains irrigation design standards, a chart of infiltration rates (Table 2.7) and an exhaustive list of commonly used plants. Water requirements are listed for each plant.

Three classes of plants, based on water use, are established in this ordinance. They include low-use, medium-use and high-water-use plants, as shown in Table 2.8. These plants are to be designed in similar hydrozones. Not included in this ordinance are design components for such site features as parking lots, buffers and screens.

In preparing the landscape design, calculations are required to determine water use requirements. The maximum amount of water that can be used in any one (1) year is limited to thirty (30) inches of artificially applied water. The total

TABLE 2.7. Water Infiltration Rates Based on USDA Information, Roseville, California

	Percent of Slope				
	0–4%	*4–8%*	*8–12%*	*12–16%*	*Over 16%*
Soil Texture, Type	*Infiltration Rates (inches/hour)*				
Coarse Sand	1.25	1.00	.75	.50	.31
Medium Sand	1.06	.85	.64	.42	.27
Fine Sand	.94	.75	.56	.38	.24
Loamy Sand	.88	.70	.53	.35	.22
Sandy Loam	.75	.60	.45	.30	.19
Fine Sandy Loam	.63	.50	.38	.25	.16
Very Fine Sandy Loam	.59	.47	.35	.24	.15
Loam	.54	.43	.33	.22	.14
Silt Loam	.50	.40	.30	.20	.13
Silt	.44	.35	.26	.18	.11
Sandy Clay	.31	.25	.19	.12	.08
Clay Loam	.25	.20	.15	.10	.06
Silty Clay	.19	.15	.11	.08	.05
Clay	.13	.10	.08	.05	.03

TABLE 2.8. Plant Values, Roseville, California

Planting Types	*Planting Value*	*Representative Species*
Low Water Use	0.40	*Cedrus deodara, Elaeagnus angustifolia, Cotoneaster dammeri*
Medium Water Use	1.00	*Magnolia grandiflora, Feijoa sellowiana, Dietes bicolor*
High Water Use*	1.60	*Picea abies, Acer palmatum, Ilex cornuta, Rosa californica*

*This includes lawn turf.

planting area is to be designed with a balanced composition of plant materials with varying water needs. To check a landscape design for compliance with this water budget limit, multiply the planting value of the various landscape zones by their total planting areas in square feet. The sum of these factors must not exceed the total planting area unless the irrigation plan can demonstrate that applied water use does not exceed the thirty (30)-inch limit.

Sample Calculation

Assume a landscape design consisting of twenty-six hundred (2,600) square feet of planting area. The design consists of six hundred (600) square feet of *Cotoneaster dammeri* and six hundred (600) square feet of *Cedrus deodara* in Zone 1, one hundred fifty (150) square feet of *Dietes bicolor* and two hundred fifty (250) square feet of *Hedera helix* in Zone 2 and one thousand (1,000) square feet of *Rosa californica* in Zone 3.

Water Use	*Plant Type*	*Square Feet*	*Planting Value (Total square feet × use = value)*	
Low Use, Zone 1	*Cotoneaster*	600	1,200 square feet × 0.04 =	480
	Cedrus	600		
Medium Use, Zone 2	*Dietes*	150	400 square feet × 1.0 =	400
	Hedera	250		
High Use, Zone 3	Turf grass	500	1,000 square feet × 1.6 =	1,600
	Rosa	500		
			Sum of planting values	2,480
			Maximum value allowed	2,600

Analysis: Design is acceptable; 2,480 < 2,600.

Special criteria and standards in this ordinance apply to model homes and developer-installed single-family residential landscapes.

Sacramento

Sacramento, Ordinance No. 2550, "Landscape Ordinance of Sacramento," 1983.
Sacramento, Chapter 25, Article 1-9, "Commercial Land Use Zones General Purposes," 1984.

Regulations of this code are related to commercial land use zones in Sacramento County. Topics covered in this chapter include providing sufficient space for retail development, retail development intensity regulations, promoting the most desirable use of land and direction of building development and protection of each zone's character. Also attached are tables entitled "Permitted Uses Within the Buildable Area of Commercial Lots" and "Permitted Uses in Yards and Open Spaces of Commercial Lots." These tables show relationships between use, facilities and zoning. Districts may include business and professional office, shopping center, limited commercial, general commercial, auto commercial, highway travel commercial, commercial recreation and industrial office park zones.

Sacramento, Chapter 15, Article 5, Section 315-40,44, "Commercial and Business and Professional Use Development Standards in Commercial Land Use Zones," 1984.

This article includes more specific restrictions for the regulations given in the tables presented in Chapter 25, Article 8, mentioned previously. Topics discussed in further detail are lot frontage (width and depth), front, side and rear yard regulations, building height restrictions, landscape planter restrictions and regulations for perimeter fencing along interior boundary lines of specific zones.

Sacramento, Ordinance Amending Sections 3-d-4, 6-d-5 and 6-d-19 of the Comprehensive Zoning Ordinance of the City of Sacramento, Ordinance No. 2550, "Parking Lot Tree Shading," 1983.

This ordinance requires a shade plan with fifty (50) percent shading over parking areas within fifteen (15) years. Parking areas must also be screened from view of city streets by a planter area with a minimum width of four (4) feet. The ordinance calls for tree lawns (planters) with a minimum width of ten (10) feet in H-C zones and requires an irrigation system in all planters. The city has also developed a list of trees acceptable for planting as shade trees in parking areas to comply with regulations.

Sacramento, Ordinance No. 4096, Fourth Series, "Off-Street Parking and Vehicle Trip Reduction Regulations," 1983.

This ordinance greatly details the requirements of off-street parking and trip reduction regulations. The off-street parking section is concerned with spaces required for specific land uses (i.e., residential, church, hospital, offices, motel, etc.). Minimum parking dimensions include parking angles, stall width, stall depth, maneuvering width, bicycle parking and the like. This is a complete compilation of parking regulations; because of the vast subject material given, only the highlights are mentioned here.

Trip reduction regulations are concerned with reducing the number of employee vehicles in the workplace by providing bus pool/shuttle bus programs, van pool programs, ride sharing, light rail, and similar programs.

Sacramento, Chapter 30, Article 1-6, Section 330-01-3330-133, "Off-Street Parking General Provisions," n.d.

The zoning code of Sacramento County includes passages that cover landscaped areas and planters within parking areas. It is weaker than the comprehensive Little Rock ordinance in that it does not address adjacent areas and its requirements are less stringent. The City of Sacramento does have a parking lot Tree Shading Ordinance. This ordinance details the types of vegetation to be used and requires a landscape plan to be submitted, but does not state who is qualified to prepare the plan for submission.

San Bernardino

San Bernardino, "Landscape Design Guidelines," Development Code 1991.

The City of San Bernardino is greatly concerned about the quality of life in its community. It realizes that the quality of life in a city is linked to the physical design of all segments of city life. It acknowledges in this ordinance that it is important to enhance the aesthetic appearance of the city by providing standards relating to quality, quantity and functional aspects of landscaping.

San Bernardino believes that appropriate screening and buffering increases compatibility between commercial, residential and industrial land uses. Through screening, the impacts of all forms of physical and visual pollution can be reduced while preserving the integrity of neighborhoods and enhancing pedestrian and vehicular traffic safety. Various types of screens are defined in this ordinance, as shown in Table 2.9. The requirements for screens are based on opacity, or the ability of a screen to block views.

San Bernardino's ordinance is different from most, based more upon performance standards rather than strict compliance with technical standards. In fact, the title of the ordinance, "Landscape Design Guidelines," is evidence that the ordinance is directed to landscape architects rather than developers or property owners. The city couches all of its requirements in language it believes will lead to better design results. For instance, it provides specific planting design concepts,

TABLE 2.9. Suggested Screening Methods, San Bernardino, California

OPAQUE SCREENS (screens opaque from the ground to six feet in height)
Small shrubs planted thirty inches on center
Six foot high evergreen screening shrubs planted four feet on center
Small trees planted thirty feet on center
Large trees planted forty feet on center
Six foot tall masonry wall
Tall evergreen trees stagger planted with branches touching ground
SEMIOPAQUE SCREENS (screens that are opaque from the ground to three feet in height, intermittent visual obstructions to a height of at least twenty feet)
Small shrubs planted thirty inches on center
Three foot high wall
Small trees planted 20–30′ on center on top of berm
Three foot high berm with ground cover
Large trees planted forty feet on center
Three foot high evergreen shrub hedge planted three feet on center
BROKEN SCREENS (consist of intermittent visual obstructions from the ground to a height of at least twenty feet)
Small trees planted thirty feet on center with an open fence
Large trees planted forty feet on center
Assorted shrubbery

as illustrated in Table 2.10, various screening options, required plant material sizes, and a specified landscape design review process that will result in a high standard of design performance.

Landscape designs must be in harmony with the surrounding environment and must emphasize drought-tolerant landscaping. In addition, landscape design should include structures such as arbors, trellises, berms and walls when appropriate. Landscaping should incorporate a tiered (layered) planting structure, which includes ground covers, shrubs and trees. Specific planting design concepts are given.

All zoning districts and all development projects fall under this ordinance. Landscaping is required in residential districts. An early stage concept plan is submitted to provide the review authority with a clear understanding of the landscape program for each site. This is followed by a detailed comprehensive landscaping plan that consists of landscaping, hardscape, waterscape, irrigation and any other information deemed necessary by the city.

The design review, building permit, Certificate of Occupancy and maintenance agreement are approved by either Parks and Recreation, Planning and Building Services, or Public Works and the city attorney.

Specific design requirements in this ordinance are minimal. They do include screening, buffer plantings, street tree plantings, setback and parkway areas. Standards are listed for plant material size and spacing, installation and maintenance. Tree removal is discouraged. Permits are required if more than five (5) trees are removed in a thirty-six (36)-month period. For each tree removed in a subdivision, a new tree is to be planted.

TABLE 2.10. Suggested Planting Design Concepts, San Bernardino, California

1. Specimen trees used in informal grouping and rows at major focal points.
2. Extensive use of flowering vines, both on walls and arbors.
3. Pots, vases, walls or raised planters.
4. The use of planting to create shadow and patterns against walls.
5. Trees to create canopy and shade, especially in parking areas.
6. The use of flowering trees in informal groups to provide color.
7. Informal massing of colorful plantings,
8. Use of distinctive plants as focal points.
9. Berms, plantings, and low walls to screen parking areas from view of public rights-of-way while allowing filter views of larger buildings beyond.

TABLE 2.11. Required Plant Material Mix, San Bernardino, California

TREES
Twenty (20) percent in 24-inch box
Fifty (50) percent in 15-gallon container
Fifteen (15) percent mature specimen trees in 36-inch box
Fifteen (15) percent mature specimen trees in 48-inch box
SHRUBS
Eighty (80) percent in 5-gallon containers
Twenty (20) percent in 1-gallon containers
GROUND COVER
One hundred (100) percent coverage in 1 year

This ordinance specifies a distinct mix of plant material sizes to be incorporated into the landscape design, as depicted in Table 2.11.

San Diego

San Diego, Ordinance No. 16650, "User's Guide to the City of San Diego's Landscape Regulations," 1986.

The purpose of this ordinance is to improve the appearance, quality and quantity of landscaped areas that are visible from public roadways and adjacent developments. The citywide landscape ordinance requires landscape improvements in three (3) distinct areas of development: street yards, vehicular use areas and remaining yards.

Of particular interest in this code is the point system for minimum plant material requirements, based on the quantities and sizes of trees and shrubs planted in required landscape areas and in the public right-of-way. A point value is determined for trees and shrubs based on their container size. Points are also given for existing trees located in the required landscape plan. To satisfy minimum landscape requirements, one must achieve a certain minimum number of points per square foot of required landscaped area.

Excellent computer drawings appear throughout this ordinance, which help to explain principles of the code. Figure 2.8 is typical of the descriptive graphics used in this ordinance. Example drawings of typical commercial, industrial and residential projects are provided.

Other topics included in the ordinance are: landscaping and irrigation standards for slopes and improvements in the public right-of-way, submittal requirements (i.e., planting plan, irrigation plan, grading plan and site plan), application procedures and installation verification.

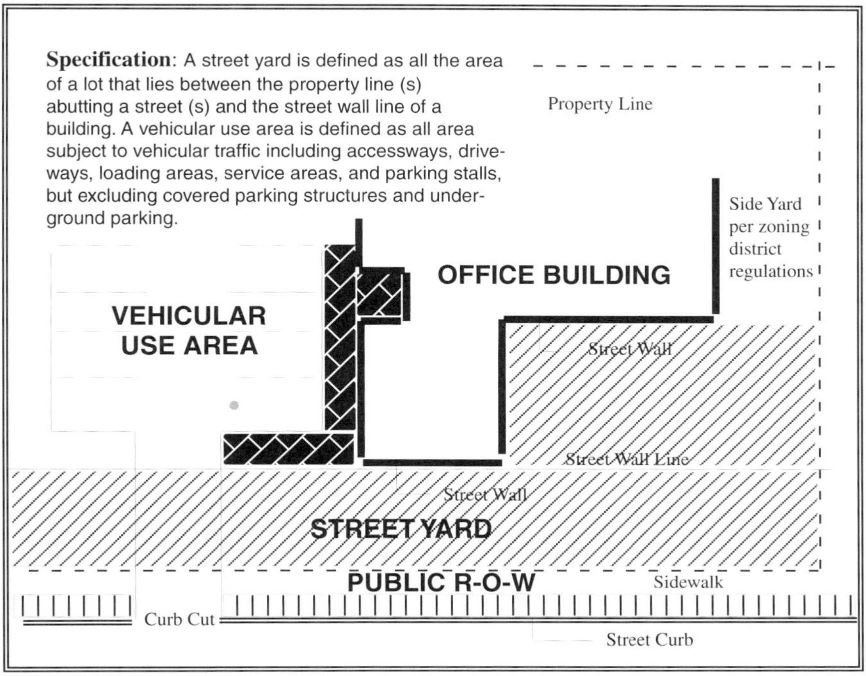

FIGURE 2.8. Street yard definition, San Diego, California.

Santa Clara County

"Landscape Design Guide for Highways and Expressways," March 1971.

This is a design document very similar to a design manual that was put together some years ago by the landscape architecture firm of Eckbo, Dean, Austin and Williams to assist Santa Clara County in preparing public policy concerning landscaping of community streets. The document is included in this study as an example of a public design study typical of those that can be undertaken by any community desiring to develop a design-based landscape ordinance.

This type of study often precedes enactment of an ordinance and is a superb way of determining community needs and defining site design issues that should be addressed in an ordinance format. The document sets forth philosophical background, principles of landscape design and plant selection criteria, rather than detailed technical standards. The document is accompanied by a *Landscape Design Plant Encyclopedia* and standard design details and specifications.

The document presents design in an easy-to-read format with many photographs, sketches and drawings to explain important concepts.

Santa Monica

Santa Monica, "Guidelines to Select Native Plants for Various Aesthetic and Ecological Considerations as Well as Garden Situations," 1988.
Santa Monica, "City of Santa Monica Architectural Review Board, Landscape Requirements," 1986.

Standard landscape and irrigation plans are required to be reviewed by Santa Monica's Architectural Review Board. The city encourages the following percentage of landscaping per site: industrial—ten (10) percent, commercial—fifteen (15) percent, institutions—fourteen (14) percent, office—fifteen (15) percent, multiple residential—twenty-five (25) percent. Other topics presented are size and type of planting, location, maintenance, fencing, hedges and buffer landscaping, along with an example drawing of a planting plan and a plant materials list.

Santa Monica, Section 9127C–Section 9127J.1, "Santa Monica Municipal Code," n.d.

This ordinance focuses primarily on yard regulations, projections into yards (i.e., fences, canopies, hedges, landscape architectural features, guard railings), property boundary walls in H or industrial districts, screening standards and, more specifically, vehicle parking and storage areas.

Simi Valley

Simi Valley, "Landscape Ordinance of Simi Valley," 1988.

The City of Simi Valley ordinance contains an assorted array of landscape requirements information. Landscape submittal requirements are mandatory for standard planting plans and irrigation plans and for unconventional landscape district plans and landscape annexation maps. A sample copy of a landscape annexation map is provided, showing a proper legend, vicinity map, title block and North arrow. Planting and staking specifications are presented for parkway tree planting. General requirements for retaining walls are shown. This ordinance contains an official list of trees for public places. Plant size ranges from small trees (for narrow parkways, narrow areas, cul de sacs, planting in three (3) to four (4)-foot parkways and four (4)-foot tree wells) to large trees (for six (6)-foot and larger parkways, open areas, parks, greenbelts, etc.). More information on approved tree species can be located in the City of Simi Valley Ordinance No. 204 (Parkway Trees) (Section 9103-1 and Section 1903-5).

South San Francisco

South San Francisco, "A Guide for the Preparation of Planting and Irrigation Plans in the City of South San Francisco," n.d.

This is a prepared packet of a few documents needed to prepare landscape and irrigation plans. The various sections include Design Standards and Submission

Requirements, Requirements for the Design of City-Maintained Landscaped Areas, Zoning Ordinance Requirements and Street Trees. Accompanying the packet is Standard Planting and Irrigation Details, which illustrates and describes many planting and irrigation methods. The Design Standards and Submission Requirements section provides general requirements for site planning, parking areas, plant selection, street trees, irrigation design and maintenance. It then describes the submission process. This section is informal and serves as a summary of the requirements to be implemented. The Requirements for the Design of City-Maintained Landscaped Areas section is simply a list of the items the city must be able to locate in order to provide maintenance. It includes a list of trees that are invasive and should not be used. There are also a list of recommended irrigation fixture parts and a list of names of professionals and companies that are certified for general public testing of irrigation systems.

Any project larger than eleven thousand (11,000) square feet requires the execution of a comprehensive maintenance contract between the owner and a licensed landscape contractor, to extend a minimum of eighteen (18) months after the completion of the project.

The Zoning Ordinance Requirements section is the meat of this packet; it is the landscape ordinance. The purpose of the ordinance is to provide standards for landscaping, buffering, and screening. The ordinance gives general regulations for each component and for maintenance. It outlines the maximum screening heights for different uses. General requirements for residential, commercial and industrial land uses are then given. Landscaping and screening requirements for parking and storage areas are listed last. Illustrations of the general requirements for residential, commercial and industrial districts are included to facilitate the understanding of the requirements.

Parking illumination in residential districts must be nonflashing and directed away from abutting lots. Open storage, open parking and loading areas must be screened from abutting lots by a six (6)-foot high screen. Open parking and loading areas located on front or side street yards must have a three (3)-foot high screen. One (1) tree for every six (6) commercial parking spaces must be provided.

The Street Trees section contains the City Official Street Tree List, the Proposed Plant List for the *South Airport Boulevard Improvements Master Plan*, Soil Sampling Procedures and a few illustrations detailing tree staking, planting and a root barrier planter detail.

State of California

California, "Model Water Efficient Landscape Ordinance," Assembly Bill 325, June 15, 1992.

The purpose of this ordinance is to address statewide water usage in California. The ordinance applies to all cities and towns in California that do not have their own landscape ordinance addressing water efficiency. It applies to all new and rehabilitated landscaping for public agency projects, private development projects that require a permit and developer-installed landscaping in single-family and multifamily projects. It does not apply to home owner-provided landscaping at single- and multifamily projects, cemeteries, registered historical sites, ecological restoration projects that do not require a permanent irrigation system, mined-land reclamation projects that do not require a permanent irrigation system or any project with less than twenty-five hundred (2,500) square feet of landscaped area.

The ordinance requires a *Landscape Documentation Package*, which is the submittal package required in order to receive any permits necessary for occupancy. The ordinance gives a thorough explanation of what is required for each item in the package. The items include a water conservation concept statement, maximum applied water allowance calculation, estimated applied water use calculation, estimated amount of water expected from effective precipitation calculation, estimated total water use calculation, landscape design plan, irrigation design plan, irrigation schedules, landscape irrigation audit schedule, grading design plan, soil analysis and certificate of substantial completion.

Hydrozone design areas, shown in Figure 2.9, must be identified in the submittal package.

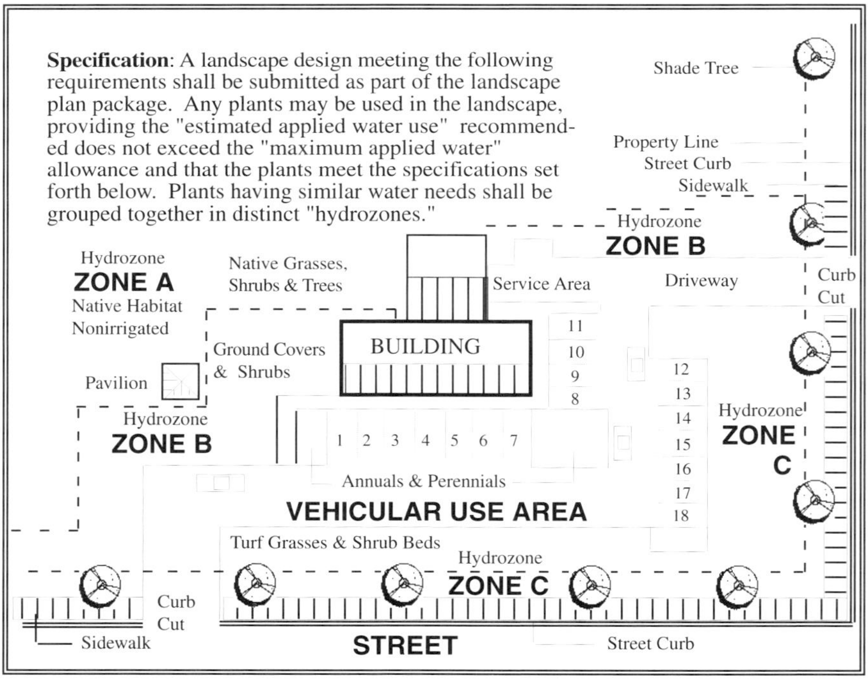

FIGURE 2.9. Hydrozone design areas, State of California.

A copy of the *Landscape Documentation Package* is to be submitted to the city or county, the property owner or site manager and the local retail water purveyor. No landscape architect or other professional is required to prepare the plans, but a landscape architect, contractor, certified irrigation designer or other licensed or certified professional in a related field is required to conduct a final field observation and sign the irrigation audit, certifying that work has been installed in accordance with the contract documents.

California, "Model Tree Ordinance," California Department of Forestry and Fire Protection, April 1991.

This model ordinance is contained within a recent publication prepared for the California Department of Forestry and Fire Protection. *Guidelines for Developing and Evaluating Tree Ordinances*, prepared by Plant Science Consulting & Research for the State of California, presents a model outline that can be used by anyone wishing to draft a local tree ordinance. Fifteen (15) "basic provisions" of a well-drafted ordinance are provided, along with twenty-two (22) additional "optional provisions" that the research firm recommends ordinance crafters to consider.

Any community can produce a draft ordinance by combining the necessary basic provisions with locally appropriate goal-oriented optional provisions. Sample language culled from one hundred sixty eight (168) city and county California ordinances is provided in the document for each of the basic provisions as well as the optional provisions.

The authors also present a logical sequence for planning, drafting and evaluating an ordinance and provide many extra pieces of helpful information.

One of the interesting things in the study is the authors' attempt at classification of tree ordinance types. They correctly define the two (2) common types of tree ordinances found in America, "street tree ordinances" and "tree protection ordinances." A third type is classified as "view ordinances," that is, tree ordinances designed to help resolve conflicts between property owners who have trees that block views or sunlight.

Thousand Oaks

Thousand Oaks, "Guidelines for Landscaping Planting and Irrigation Plans," 1988.

Under the general requirements of this ordinance, plans are to be prepared by a California-registered landscape architect (or other qualified designer, subject to approval of the planning director) and are to be submitted to the planning department for review prior to the release of a building permit. The submittal package must include five blueline copies of the planting and irrigation plans, details and specifications, one copy each of the approved site plan (with vicinity map), grading plan, architectural elevation plans and city resolution of project approval; a filing fee of fifty (50) dollars necessary for the landscape review is to be attached.

All drawings submitted, especially planting and irrigation plans, should follow standards set forth in this code. A sample submittal form complete with a checklist is provided.

Ventura County

Ventura County, "Ventura County Guide to Landscape Plans," 1988.

This guide's intent is to offer the applicant as much freedom as possible in designing a landscape project while meeting the minimum landscape standards of the county.

Overall, this complete guide explains the steps in the process of landscape plan approval, requirements for submittal of landscape plans, minimum landscape standards, the proper use of landscaping and a list of preferred native and exotic plant materials.

Figure 2.10 illustrates one of the planting standards defined in this ordinance.

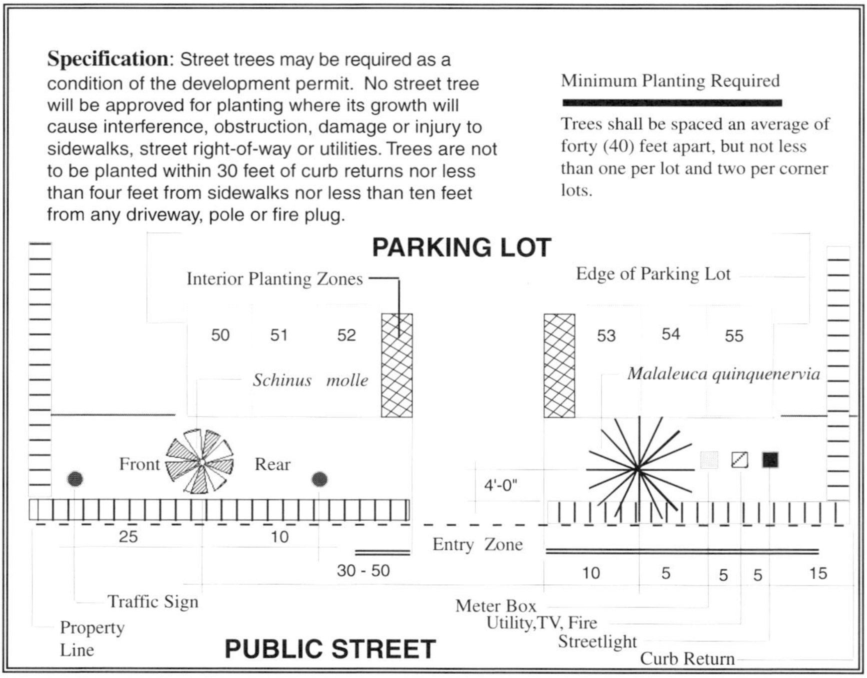

FIGURE 2.10. Street tree planting location standards, Ventura County, California.

Colorado

Aspen

Aspen Municipal Code, Chapter 21.20, "Trees and Landscaping on Public Right-of-Way," 1975.

This ordinance regulates all trees, shrubs, foliage and other landscaping in sidewalk areas or other public rights-of-way. The City Engineer and Director of Parks must approve all locations and types of plant materials planted. Planting for all new construction must be coordinated with the adopted street landscaping plan.

Several specifications for landscaping sidewalk areas are given in the ordinance. In addition, property owners may not pave planting areas or remove or damage existing trees and are required to maintain all plantings in the sidewalk area of the adjacent rights-of-way. A three (3)-year maintenance period is required for all new plantings, and a financial assurance in the amount equal to one hundred twenty (120) percent must be tendered to the city to guarantee replacement. The Director of Parks encourages the efficiency of water use on all public rights-of-way and has included standards for efficient irrigation techniques and systems to be used in sidewalk areas. These standards are shown in Table 2.12.

This ordinance is a limited component landscape ordinance. It applies to a very narrow spectrum of landscape design concerns. The administrative aspects of this ordinance are not spelled out and are unclear.

TABLE 2.12. Water-Efficient Irrigation Standards for Sidewalk Landscape Zones, Aspen, Colorado

Technique	*Expected Results*
Limit functional area of water use.	Reduces volume used
Hours of irrigation prohibited from 11:00 A.M.–3:00 P.M.	Reduces peak demand loads
Employ nonpotable water, reuse water.	Preserves potable water supply
Analyze and improve soil zones.	Reduces frequency of use
Use mulch on all planting zones.	Preserves topsoil moisture
Use lower water demand plants.	Reduces volume and demand
Eliminate weeds and excess vegetation mass.	Reduces demand, limits use
Use proper maintenance techniques.	Reduces waste
Use evapotranspiration data.	Calculates needed supply more accurately
Use native turf where practical.	Reduces demand

Aspen Municipal Code, Chapter XI, as amended, "Tree Removal and Basic Value," July 24, 1995.

This is a related ordinance recently enacted in the City of Aspen. It repeals Section 13-76 of the Aspen Municipal Code and amends Section 6-206(C) to require tree removal permits for specified trees of certain sizes and related items. Trees cannot be damaged, relocated, altered or subjected to environmental changes. Dead trees and trees in emergency situations may be removed with notice to the Director of Parks.

In order to relocate trees, an application must be submitted to the Director of Parks, along with a site plan that shows the following information:

A. Location of proposed driveways and other planned structures
B. Location of all trees of four (4) inches or more, identified by trunk diameter and species
C. Designation of all diseased trees and any trees endangering any roadway, structure or utility service line
D. Any trees to be removed, retained or relocated and areas that will remain undisturbed
E. Any proposed grade changes that will impact trees.

It is the responsibility of the Director of Parks to determine the value of the trees to be removed, based on the following criteria:

A. Do the trees minimize flood or snowslide, or do they protect watersheds?
B. Do the trees to be removed prevent excessive water runoff?
C. Do the trees prevent wind erosion?
D. What is the condition of the trees in respect to disease, breakup and interference with utility lines?
E. Number of trees in the neighborhood and their contribution to natural beauty and effect on property values in the area.
F. The impact of denial on the reasonable economic use and enjoyment of the property.
G. The effects of good forestry practices on the land.
H. The adequacy of the methods proposed to relocate any trees.

Based on a review of these facts, the Director of Parks may grant or deny a permit.

Where trees must be removed to adequately develop the land, the Director of Parks may require that any trees removed be replaced with trees of comparable value. Comparable value is to mean trees of equal aggregate value or cash in lieu of comparable value.

The valuation of trees under this ordinance is calculated as follows. The basic value is thirty-six (36) dollars per square inch of the cross-sectional area of the tree at the point where the diameter of the tree is measured. In calculating the basic value of the removal of a twenty-four (24)-inch tree, the following equation is to be used.

$$\text{Basic value} = \$36.00 \times 3.13 \times (D/2) \text{ squared}$$

Given, D = diameter of tree, 24 inches; therefore, $\$36.00 \times 3.13 \times (24/2)$ squared, or $\$36.00 \times 3.13 \times 144 = \$16{,}225.92$.

This ordinance is a basic tree protection ordinance. It is not clear as to the derivation of the formula used to determine basic value. The preceding sample calculation results in a monetary amount that seems rather high.

Aurora

"Council Policy on Preservation of Existing Trees," 1987.

This ordinance requires that site plans make all efforts to accommodate existing trees. All relocation plans should be executed by a professional forester or nurseryman to ensure the health of the trees. A plan for mitigation (equivalent replacement of lost vegetation) should be outlined.

Breckenridge

Zoning Code, Article 22, "Landscaping," n.d.

This community is perhaps at the highest elevation of any community in this study. In fact, one of the reasons for implementing a landscape ordinance is to retain the sense of a mountain environment and mitigate the adverse effects of climate, aspect and elevation. In addition, in this area it is important to abate erosion, stabilize steep slopes and preserve air and water quality.

Breckenridge uses a performance-based zoning ordinance to administer the needs of its high-altitude alpine climate. For that reason, many of the requirements are suggestive rather than very detailed and regulatory. Under this system, some of the landscaping requirements are "absolute" and some are "relative."

Landscape design is required for vehicular use area interiors, screening, buffering residential districts and street edges. The ordinance contains few technical standards or design guidelines. These have been included in a supplemental document, "The Town of Breckenridge Landscaping Guide," prepared by the Community Development Department.

Standards are given in the ordinance for maintenance, plant material quality and size.

Little emphasis is placed on design in this community. Tree protection standards for specimen trees, significant tree stands and tree clusters are encouraged (relative landscaping) but not made mandatory in Breckenridge.

Colorado Springs

Colorado Springs, City Code, Chapter 14.1, "Zoning," Article 8, "Parking"; Chapter 14.1, "Zoning," Article 10, "Landscape Requirements"; Chapter 18, "Parks and Recreation," Article 4, "Trees and Shrubs," Part 1, "Planting and General Requirements," 1988; and "Landscape Policy Manual," City of Colorado Springs Planning Department.

Like many cities, Colorado Springs' landscape ordinances are included in various places throughout the City Code. Like only a few cities, Colorado Springs has gathered the pertinent ordinances into a landscape policy manual, with illustrations and examples to clarify the regulations.

Concerning parking, the regulations generally require three (3)-foot screening, by berms or shrubs, around open parking areas, and one (1) shade tree for every fifteen (15) parking stalls. Trees must be in islands or fingers to qualify. Recommended trees and shrubs are included in Appendix A of the policy manual.

The city's ordinances address landscaped setbacks, buffers, internal landscaping, percentage of ground cover in living materials, irrigation, assurances for installation and completion, administrative relief, nonconforming uses, development plans, street trees and plantings under power lines. The policy manual includes a couple of interesting examples of requests for waivers from the stated policies. The Planning Department's approval or denial is also included for the examples.

Under the policy manual's Part 13, "Miscellaneous Policies and Explanations," Colorado Springs prohibits the planting of elms because of the trees' negative qualities, such as "disease proneness, weak branches, suckering and uncontrollable spread of seeds."

Colorado Springs Parks and Recreation Department Parks Division, "Significant Tree Program, Policies and Procedures," n.d.

The purpose of this program is to recognize and preserve trees in the community and to continue the heritage begun by General William Jackson Palmer, the city's founder, who initiated street tree planting programs in the late 1800s. The Significant Tree Program applies to trees on public and private properties, with the "significant" designation encouraged. However, on private land, the property owner must approve of the designation.

Significant trees must be associated with the city's history or the lives of significant people, have a strong sentimental value to a neighborhood, be on the State or National Big Tree Register or be of botanical, aesthetic or ecological significance. The trees should be of sound quality and have a life expectancy of more than ten (10) years.

Anyone may nominate a tree for designation. The Forestry Staff reviews nominations, with the Parks Manager and Director of Parks and Recreation making the final determinations. If designated, the tree is placed on the Significant Tree Roster, which is maintained by the City Forester. Heavy pruning or removal of Significant Trees goes through a public review process, with public notices and public meetings.

City of Colorado Springs Park and Recreation Department, Forestry and Natural Resource Division, "Forestry Rules and Regulations," n.d.

This document outlines rules and regulations concerning tree service work and general forestry practices, as contained in the City Code. The regulations address planting and maintenance of trees in public rights-of-way, maintenance of tree and plant growth on private property, standards for tree pruning, safety standards for tree pruning and removal, registration of persons involved in the pesticide business, excavation and trenching near public trees and hearing procedures and penalties for noncompliance.

Colorado Springs, "Urban Forest Management Plan," n.d.

This is not an ordinance, but a guide for the city's administration of tree programs. It includes information on the current condition of Colorado Springs' trees, current maintenance and planting of the city's trees, the future of the tree population in the community and budgeting for community tree programs.

Denver

Denver, Zoning I-0, I-1, I-2 "Districts," n.d.

This zoning ordinance has a few landscape ordinances including the subjects of landscaping for setbacks, application of the landscaping requirements for existing uses, use and maintenance of off-street parking space, and the requirements for submitting landscape plans.

Denver, "Denver Parks and Recreation Median Design Guidelines," June 10, 1991.

This is a small packet of guidelines prepared in order to visually connect the parkways and boulevards with the city parks. The guidelines must be followed by landscape architects and other professionals. They briefly explain and illustrate the requirements for medians and parkways, including soil preparation, planting area widths, plant materials, curbs and gutters, splash guards, irrigation, signage and sight triangles.

Denver, "Denver Streetscape Design Manual," June 31, 1992.

This is another packet of guidelines for the City of Denver; however, these guidelines are for the entire city. Subjects include street trees, shrubs and ground covers, lighting, paving, furnishings, buildings, signs, parking, maintenance and irrigation.

The section on street trees includes tree location; size; selection; species recommended, not recommended, and not allowed; and special uses. The shrubs and ground cover section includes recommended shrubs and ground covers, recommended turf grass, and ground covers not recommended and not allowed. The subjects in the lighting section include pedestrian lighting, spacing and location, style and materials, street lighting and special-effect lighting. Paving includes sidewalks, amenity zones, curb ramp and curb cut guidelines, crosswalk pavements, entry walks, step-out strips and paving not recommended. The section on furnishings includes neighborhood entry monuments, commercial district gateway markers, walls and screens, seating, tree grates, fencing and railing, trash receptacles, bollards, planting pots and planters, newspaper racks, bicycle racks, kiosks, fountains, mailboxes, parking meters, utility boxes, meters and manholes, bus stops and public art. Commercial building guidelines include character, scale, continuity, interest and comfort. Sign guidelines include business signs, placement and regulatory signs. Parking includes structures, lots, landscaping, plant materials, screening, lighting, walkways, irrigation and maintenance. The section on maintenance and irrigation includes trees, shrubs, sod, irrigation systems, lighting, furnishings and sidewalks. The approval process for landscape plans includes the streetscape completion process, revocable permits, maintenance districts and business improvement districts.

Denver, "Rules and Regulations for the Landscaping of Parking Areas," May 10, 1989.

The intent of this ordinance is to improve the appearance of off-street parking areas, to protect the appearance and value of the surrounding properties and neighborhoods, to protect the users of parking areas and to improve environmental conditions. These objectives are to be achieved by providing for the installation and maintenance of landscaping and lighting for screening, aesthetic qualities and security. Parking areas excluded from these requirements include parking garages, structures and areas containing fewer than fifteen (15) parking spaces.

Areas for which the ordinance provides requirements include street frontage landscaped planting strips, perimeter boundary landscaping or screening, internal parking area landscaping and special requirements for B-5, B-7 and B-8 zones. The ordinance provides quality standards for plant materials, fences, planter boxes, walls, heights, visual screens, walkways, irrigation, maintenance and lighting. The submittal process and exceptions are also detailed. The requirements are explained and illustrated.

Fort Collins

Zoning, Annexation and Development of Land, Subsection D, Sec. 29-491 "Off-Street Parking and Vehicular Uses," n.d., and Related Administrative Documents, n.d.

Written landscape design components, standards and requirements in this community are scattered among ordinances, administrative guidelines, technical schedules and memoranda. They include such items as landscape plans for commercial uses, an off-street parking and vehicular use ordinance, City of Fort Collins Landscape Guide, graphic details, native plant, street tree and park tree lists.

The written material composing the landscape ordinance in this community is very disorganized. Any consultant wishing more detail is advised to contact the Park Planning and Development Division of the City of Fort Collins.

Lakewood

Lakewood, Article 15: Site Development Standards, "Site Development Ordinance," n.d.

It is the intent of this ordinance that the qualitative standards serve as a guide in the review of site plans; no one development is expected to meet all the qualitative guidelines set forth. The purpose of the ordinance is to ensure quality design or, at least, to improve weak design. The ordinance is enforced through the approval for a building permit. Most residential, commercial and industrial zoning districts are subject to this ordinance.

The two major emphases in this ordinance are the application process and the parking requirements. The ordinance is focused mainly on commercial and industrial applications in this regard. Landscaping standards are few; they are listed by landscaping materials such as deciduous trees, ornamental and flowering trees, evergreen trees, shrubs, and rock and stone. A recommended plant list is provided. All new parking lot structural sections must be designed by a professional engineer. No landscape architect or other professional is required to develop the landscape plans.

This ordinance is unique in that its requirements are extremely few and simple (except for parking lots). As stated in the intent, no one development is expected to meet all these requirements—this aspect is extremely unusual.

The intended purpose of this ordinance and the simple requirements given allow a developer to design without the pressures experienced by a designer with a more limiting ordinance.

Pueblo

Zoning Ordinance, Section 17-4-7, "Landscape Performance Standard," July 10, 1995.

Landscape performance standards have been adopted to enhance neighborhood character and property value. Pueblo's ordinance applies to most zoning districts.

Design components of this ordinance include landscape setback areas, parking lots, parking lot screens, buffers, outdoor storage areas and landscaped storage areas. For each of these components, specific plant materials, quantities, spacing and other criteria apply. These standards are outlined in Table 2.13.

Other standards apply to plant material, maintenance and installation. Use of native plant material is encouraged, and certain species are prohibited.

TABLE 2.13. Design Standards, Pueblo, Colorado

Technical Standard	*Requirement*
Setback Areas	1 tree, 5 shrubs, 25 SF ground cover
Setback Area Coverage	50%, or plants to be evergreen or ornamental
Parking Area Landscape Percent	5% of paved area, 75 SF islands with curbs
Island Plantings	1 tree, 3 shrubs, or 1 shade tree and 25 SF of ground cover
Parking Lot Screening	1 tree 30 feet on center
Parking Lot Screening Options	1 shrub 3 feet on center, 3 feet tall at maturity
Parking Lot Screening Options	Berm with 25 SF of ground cover
Parking Lot Screening Options	Opaque structure minimum height of 3 feet
Sight Triangle	No planting over 2 feet tall
Buffer Between Residential Uses	10 feet wide, 1 tree 20 feet on center, 6-foot fence
Trash Storage	Screened from public view, fence, wall, 5′ evergreen planting
Landscape Open Space	70% living landscape material
Landscape Open Space	1 tree, 5 shrubs, and 25 SF of ground cover for every 500 SF
% Plant Material Cover	70% of landscape area
Shrub Spacing	5 gallon 5′ OC, 2 gallon 3′ OC
Perennial Plantings	18 inches OC
Water Features	May count up to 50% of minimum landscape requirements
Nonliving Landscape Materials	No more than 30% of required landscape area
Irrigation Requirement	Permanent system installed

Landscape plans must be submitted in applying for a building permit. No Certificate of Occupancy will be granted until landscaping is installed. The Director of the Department of Zoning may contract with a licensed landscape contractor to bring a property into compliance if the owner fails to install the required landscaping.

This is a good example of an ordinance that specifies standards in such detail that the ordinance becomes a "cookbook" solution. Ordinances of this type do not stress design, but rather place emphasis on meeting certain designated numbers, quantities or formulas.

Thornton

Thornton, Chapter 58, "City of Thornton Development Code," Article VII, Landscape Regulations, and Article VIII, Design Regulations, August 10, 1992.

The purpose of this ordinance is to improve livability, increase customer draw, increase property values, improve compatibility between adjacent land uses, screen undesirable views, contribute to the image and appeal of the community, protect the vision of motorists and preserve existing trees and the wildlife they support. The ordinance is enforced through approval or denial of occupancy certificates. No landscape architect or other professional agency is required to develop the landscape plans.

Preservation and maintenance of trees and shrubs is emphasized.

For single-family, duplex, nonresidential and multifamily properties and single-family attached and manufactured home park common areas, all portions of these properties that are not occupied by streets, roads, driveways, sidewalks, parking areas, other vehicle use areas or city-approved trails or paths are to be landscaped, and no property shall allocate less than twenty (20) percent of the total property for landscaping. At least seventy-five (75) percent of the landscaped area is to have ground cover plant materials. The front yard must contain a landscaped area at least twenty (20) feet in depth. The side and rear yards are to contain a landscaped area at least fifteen (15) feet in depth. Parking areas of one hundred (100) or more spaces shall must allocate ten (10) percent of the total hard surface area to landscaped islands. Within parks, detention areas and drainage channels, one (1) tree or ten (10) shrubs are to be added for every four thousand (4,000) square feet and must blend in with their adjacent uses. The development projects adjacent to city rights-of-way, medians and I-25 will be responsible for the landscaping of these areas. Parkways are to contain one (1) tree and five (5) shrubs for each fifty (50) feet of street frontage. Medians are to contain one (1) tree for each fifty (50) feet of street frontage and twenty (20) shrubs for each four hundred (400) square feet. Requirements for I-25 adjacencies are included in a Landscape Master Plan, and developers of this area are to pay the city an amount calculated on square footage of ownership.

Requirements within landscaped areas include one (1) tree or ten (10) shrubs for every six hundred (600) square feet of area to be landscaped. Landscaped parking islands are to be at least one hundred (100) square feet in area and contain four (4) shrubs and one (1) tree. All landscaped areas must be served by a functioning automatic irrigation system. Landscaping materials required by these provisions are to be distributed throughout the areas to be landscaped. Elm trees are prohibited within the city. Boxer elms, or trees of the *Salix* and *Populus* genera are prohibited within twenty-five (25) feet of any street or public right-of-way. Substitutions for reductions in the amount of landscape materials used are specified.

If a temporary Certificate of Occupancy is issued because the landscaping was not completed under specified conditions, the city is to be given an irrevocable letter of credit, certified check or performance bond payable to the city equaling one and one-half (1½) times the cost of all incomplete landscaping and including a one (1)-year guaranty cost as determined by a landscape architect, commercial landscape nursery or commercial landscape contractor and deemed reasonable by the Department. If the installation is not completed within six (6) months after the issuance of the temporary certificate of occupancy, the security will be used by the city to complete the installation.

Connecticut

Wilton

Zoning Ordinance, Article No. 29-8-C, "Landscaping, Screening and Buffer Areas," March 15, 1993.

This landscape ordinance applies to all properties that require site plan review. This is a very basic landscape ordinance that has only three (3) design components. These include landscaped buffers between conflicting land uses, screening of objectionable views from adjacent properties and vehicular use areas.

The ordinance indicates that existing trees and all trees over eight (8) inches in caliper should be saved. However, there is probably insufficient language to enforce it, and there is an appeal clause.

Technical standards for compliance in terms of size, area or width are equal to or perhaps a little better than those of many other communities. For instance, this community requires that all shade trees be three (3) inches in caliper, evergreen trees be seven (7) feet in height, flowering trees be two (2) inches in caliper and that ten (10) percent of parking areas be set aside for landscaping. The latter calculates to twenty (20) square feet of planting for each parking space.

One interesting requirement not often seen in ordinances restricts paving to within six (6) feet of any structure except at points of entry, building terraces or driveways. Another unique requirement not seen often is a provision restricting the use of stone mulch ground cover to no more than ten (10) percent of any planting areas. This is perhaps an appropriate clause for a state with excess fieldstone highly desirable for landscaping.

This is a limited landscape ordinance with reasonably good, but limited, technical standards.

Florida

Altamonte Springs

Land Development Code, Article VIII, "Landscaping and Tree Protection," in effect September 24, 1993.

This ordinance was enacted to provide minimum landscaping, tree maintenance and tree protection in order to protect and preserve the appearance, character and value of properties within the city. The ordinance has four divisions and numerous sections that describe many standards and requirements, as shown in Table 2.14.

This table gives a snapshot view of the entire ordinance. One can easily see the design components and the types of standards included in the law. To understand the many technical requirements, such as dimensions, spacing, sizes, quantities and calculations, one must carefully read the entire ordinance with pencil in hand. It is beyond the needs of this discussion to itemize all of these details, many of which are generally common to most of the ordinances in this study. For instance, by now

TABLE 2.14. Outline of the Landscape Ordinance, Altamonte Springs, Florida

Division	*Issue (Section)*	*Typical Standard*
I. General Provisions	Definitions	Defines language used in the ordinance
	Plan Requirements	Standards and licensing for drawing preparation
	Permit Application	Procedure for seeking approvals
II. Landscaping	Plant Materials	Plant species, sizes and quality standards
	Installation	Plant care, installation and maintenance
	Natural Vegetation	Preservation of native habitat and trees
	Design Requirements	Perimeters, buffers, VUAs, tree shading, sight triangle, hardscape, topiary
	Administrative Permits	Tree bank, enforcement, waiver, permit and fees, tree removal permit and conditions
III. Tree Protection	Tree Replacement	Standards and sizes
	Emergencies	Emergency removal rules
	Protection	Protection during construction, barriers, inspections
	Planting and Replacement	Prohibited species
IV. Enforcement	Methods	Civil action, payment to tree bank
	Replacement	Criteria for replacing plant loss, lack of shade
	Technical Information	Recommended species and use, shade value

the reader knows that the average spacing of large trees across the country is forty (40) to sixty (60) feet on center.

A noteworthy feature of this ordinance is the method of calculating shade point requirements. An example will illustrate how this is done.

In this community, it is the objective of the ordinance to achieve a fifteen (15) percent shade coverage within surface parking areas within a five (5)-year or ten (10)-year time frame. If this goal is not met, the city assumes that improper maintenance (perhaps none) is taking place and the property owner can be fined, can be subject to replacement rules or may have to make a contribution to the tree bank.

The key to making sure that this does not happen is to properly design parking area plantings and calculate shade point requirements. To do this you will need:

1. Information about the shading ability of the trees on the site
2. A table listing the trees to be retained on site, with their shade values
3. A table listing the required plantings, with species, number of trees, shade value per species and the total square feet for all of the shade values
4. A shading plan to demonstrate that the retained and new trees will meet or exceed the shading requirements.

Calculating Shade Point Requirements for Altamonte Springs, Florida

1. Determine required shade coverage by multiplying square footage of parking area by 15%.
2. Measure average crown spread of all trees to remain on site. For each tree measured, use the following formula, where R equals radius: $R \times R \times 3.14 \times 125\%$. (Note that by using the factor 125%, a 25% bonus is being given for preserving existing trees.)
3. The shade provided by existing trees is subtracted from the shade requirements of the property. The required planting total needed will remain. This remaining amount is determined by totaling the "shade points" in a prepared table of "shade values" for each type of tree selected for the site.

The following sample calculation, using the Table of Shade Values prepared by horticulturists, will demonstrate the calculation by example.

Table of Shade Values at Five and Ten Years

Genus, Species	*Common Name*	*Height at 5 Years (ft)*	*Height at 10 Years (ft)*	*Shade (sq ft)*
Cornus florida	Dogwood	7	14	155
Acer rubrum	Red Maple	6	12	115
Lagerstroemia indica	Crape Myrtle	7	14	155
Taxodium distichum	Red Cypress	10	20	315
Quercus michauxii	Cow Oak	10	20	315

Example

(1) Determine Shade Coverage Requirement

Parking area	20,000.00 sq ft
Multiply by 15%	× .015
Shade coverage required for parking area	3,000.00 sq ft

(2) Existing Trees to Remain

Species	Crown Spread	Shade Value Points
Cow Oak	25′	491 × 1.25 = 614 sq ft
Dogwood	10′	79 × 1.25 = 99 sq ft
		Credit 713 sq ft

(3) Required Plantings (3000.00 − 713.00 = 2,287.00 sq ft.)

Species	Number	Value per Tree	Shade Value Points
Red Cypress	3	315	945 sq ft
Crape Myrtle	5	155	775 sq ft
Red Maple	5	115	575 sq ft
Required plantings total			2295 sq ft

Therefore:

Existing Tree Credits	713 sq ft
Required Plantings	2295 sq ft
Shade Value Total	3008 sq ft

Result: Exceeds requirement by 8 points, or (3,008 − 3,000 = 8)

This ordinance is well thought out, nicely organized and easy to read and understand. The requirements are fairly general, not very complicated and not as restrictive as some of the other ordinances in this study. One suggestion from the annotator might be to provide some standard graphic details to illustrate the technical requirements mentioned earlier as being too numerous to remember at first reading.

Boca Raton

Boca Raton, Chapter 21A, "Tree Preservation," April 11, 1972, Ord. No. 1651.

The purpose of this chapter is to establish rules and regulations governing the protection of trees and vegetative cover within the limits of the City of Boca Raton. In effect, this ordinance encourages the proliferation of trees and vegetation in recognition of their meaningful contribution to a healthful, aesthetically pleasing and safer community. Trees absorb carbon dioxide, produce oxygen, filter dust, reduce wind and noise, prevent soil erosion, protect against beach erosion, improve surface drainage, enhance wildlife habitat, beautify and enhance improved and vacant lands and generally promote the health, safety and well-being of the community.

Among the topics detailed in this code are tree removal, relocation or replacement permit fee, tree protection, hazardous trees exempt from written requirement, tree removal exceptions owing to emergencies (hurricane, tropical storm, tornado, flood), exemptions to nurseries, tree and vegetation removal criteria for landscape betterment plans, disposal of diseased trees, designation of specimen and historic trees, natural vegetative cover on beach dunes and preservation of mangrove areas.

Boca Raton, Ordinance No. 2926, Section 302.2.1, "General Landscaping Criteria," 1981.

This code emphasizes landscaping as a means of achieving beauty in the community. Landscaping not only includes trees and planting, but paving, fountains, benches, fences, exterior lighting fixtures and any other item of exterior furniture. Features in the landscape are to be both functional and aesthetic and must complement the whole. Existing natural landscape character must be preserved whenever possible.

Requirements are given in the code regarding tree species use, screening, turf grass establishment, landscape installation and landscape maintenance. Selected technical standards applying to parking lot design are presented in Table 2.15.

The rest of the code consists of criteria for parking lots and vehicular use areas. Fifteen (15) percent minimum of the gross parking area is to be devoted to living landscaping, which includes grass, ground cover, plants, shrubs and trees. Other subtopics of this criteria section include lighting and screening planter islands. In Boca Raton, parking lots are considered a transitional space between buildings and roads, building groups and other parking areas. The atmosphere within the parking lot and vehicular use area is to be parklike rather than harsh.

TABLE 2.15. Design Standards, Boca Raton, Florida

Technical Standard	*Requirement*
Parking lot landscaping	15% of gross area
Landscape screen area	four (4) inch-wide minimum
Parking lot screen	minimum 36 inches tall, plants spaced 30 inches on center
Perimeter landscape area plant spacing	one tree, 40 feet on center
Parking lot planter islands	spaced every ten parking spaces and at ends of rows
Planting island minimum size	5 feet wide by ¾ length of parking stall
Interior planting requirement	1 tree for each 125 square feet of parking area
Tree species selection	50% from a selected list
Palms	minimum 12 feet tall

Boca Raton, Ordinance No. 2110, Section 2-132.1 "Community Appearance Board," 1975. Amended with Boca Raton, Ordinance No. 2926, Section 302.2.2, "Criteria for Parking Lots and Vehicular Use Areas," 1981.

This landscape ordinance is unique in that it is unusually comprehensive in its interpretation of the landscape. It is concerned with many factors that affect community appearance other than just landscaping. The ordinance creates a citywide Community Appearance Board, charged with the task of making Boca Raton a more beautiful city in which to live. It does this with a heightened understanding of design, good taste and those elements that contribute to the image of Boca Raton as a place of beauty, spaciousness, harmony, fitness, broad vistas and high quality.

The Community Appearance Board recognizes the fact that beautiful communities can be created only through a quest for beauty by community leaders, architects, planners, Realtors and the general building industry, supported by an appreciation of the visual world by the people of the city. The task of the Community Appearance Board is to identify and preserve various elements of urban beauty and require that new building projects enhance the existing environment.

The Board conducts its business in a similar fashion to that of subdivision review committees. Most people have come to expect certain design oversight when building in developments with restrictions. In this city, this Board performs the function of reviewing certain information about building projects submitted by permit applicants above and beyond that which is normally required by the various building and planning departments of the city. It checks to see that all projects are in compliance with the Community Design Plan and meet certain standards of taste and aesthetics.

The general requirements of this code are minimum aesthetic standards required of all site development, structures, buildings, signage, exterior space, parking and landscaping. They ensure that all building projects show proper design concepts, express honest design construction and be appropriate to surroundings within the corporate limits of Boca Raton, Florida. Special conditions apply to designated areas, business districts and thoroughfares in the city.

Landscape criteria are particularly identified in this ordinance. Some of the main technical requirements are cited earlier in the discussion of Ordinance No. 2926. Various aesthetic standards are clearly defined and further explained in the code.

Other cities in the United States would be well served by community appearance boards that take on the issues of aesthetics and design, something that most planning agencies, permit offices and elected officials are hesitant to do.

Brevard County

Brevard County, "Comprehensive Landscape Ordinance," n.d.

This ordinance addresses issues such as (a) land clearing, (b) tree protection, preservation and replacement, with specific instructions regarding mangrove trees and (c) landscaping requirements. Subheadings include information on procedures and requirements for applications concerning land clearing permits and landscaping plans; minimum landscape requirements for off-street parking required adjacent to vehicular rights-of-way and to other properties; enforcement; penalties and appeals.

Broward County

Broward County, "A Compendium of Municipal Landscape Codes in Broward County, Florida," 1986.

The Florida Chapter of ASLA (Broward Section), along with several firms in the Broward area, has compiled this handy directory of communities within Broward County that support and uphold landscape ordinances. The directory includes twenty-nine (29) communities having landscape ordinances. Among the items included in the compendium are city name, contact name, address, telephone, reviewing agency, enforcing agency, current date of the landscape code, cost of the code, application fee, whether or not the code requires a separate building permit for landscape installation and whether or not processing includes a public hearing and/or board reviews or staff review only. Code information between each municipality is compared in matrix form.

Collier County

Land Development Code. Zoning, Division 2.4, Section 2.4.1, "Landscaping and Buffering," n.d.

Known as the Collier County Landscaping Code, this ordinance in part was enacted to establish uniform standards of installation and maintenance of landscaping. In addition, it recognizes that it is important to this community to promote water conservation by encouraging the use of native and drought-tolerant vegetation.

In this community, landscape plans for satisfaction of this article must be prepared and sealed by registered landscape architects. Single-family, two-family and mobile home sites are not required to have the drawing sealed. The landscape plan, consisting of specific site and design information, as shown in Table 2.16, is submitted to the Development Services Director at the preliminary subdivision phase, final site development phase or building permit phase. The required design information must address the standards described in the following paragraphs.

Standards are contained in this ordinance for plant materials, installation and maintenance.

Plant material standards are further subdivided into quality, place of origin (native or exotic), type, prohibited species, credit for plant preservation and plant materials preservation. Detailed specifications for trees, shrubs, hedges and ground covers are given. They include such particulars as spacing, heights, spreads and composition percentages, which control the percentages of particular plants on a project.

TABLE 2.16. Landscape Plan Prepared by a Licensed Landscape Architect, Collier County, Florida

Drawing Contents	*Reasons for Illustration*
Property Lines and Easements	Determine site ownership and control
Access Points	Ascertain safety upon entry and exit
Utilities	Comply with public utility law, safety
Parking	Determine parking lot planting requirements
Vehicular Use Area	Determine planting zones, auto movement
Buildings	Ascertain pedestrian circulation, shadow zone
Vegetation Communities	Review existing site ecology
Vegetation Protection Devices	Methods of preserving native vegetation
Planting Areas	Calculate required sizes of planting areas
Code Required Landscaping	Must be identified on plans
Plant Material Schedule, Quantity, Species, Size	Judgment of suitability for site and planting purpose
Drought-Tolerant Ratings	Determine water and irrigation needs
Native Plant Status	Evaluate changes to site character
Dimensions	To determine quantities, sizes, and areas
Calculations	To ensure compliance with the code

The ordinance emphasizes the use of native southern Florida species. A Xeriscape Plant Guide and other Florida botanical studies and manuals are cited as references. Design standards are also included for such site features as landscape berm design, storm water management systems and irrigation water distribution systems.

Specific standards are given for the design and operation of automatic sprinkler irrigation for all cultivated landscaping. Standards are in accord with Florida Irrigation Society Standards and Specifications. Irrigation plans must be prepared and submitted by a registered landscape architect or irrigation designer as part of the review process. These plans must include, as a minimum, the information shown in Table 2.17.

The main part of the ordinance is devoted to the various design components that must by dealt with by the designer. They include vehicular use areas, shopping

TABLE 2.17. Irrigation Plan Prepared by a Licensed Landscape Architect, Collier County, Florida

Drawing Contents	*Reasons for Illustration*
Existing Vegetation to Remain	Determine native plant zones and water needs
Buildings	Determine routing, electric sources
Other Site Improvements	Determine routing and water zones
Parking Spaces, Aisles, Driveways	Figure spray areas
Mains, Valves, Pump Locations	Examine system components and connections
Pipe Sizes	Ascertain water flow quantities
Specifications	Manufacturers' quality and standards
Controller	Examine water schedule
Backflow Preventer	Protection of public water supply
Rain Sensing Device	Reduce quantity of water needed
Sprinkler Zone Plan	Water needs of various plants, water distribution

center courtyard green space, screening and landscape buffering of adjacent land uses. The latter includes four (4) types of buffers, and their specific use is dictated in a table of buffer yard requirements. Of these components, the shopping center courtyard green space is the most notable. In this community, when someone builds a facility with more than forty thousand (40,000) square feet, he or she is required by the landscape ordinance to set aside seven (7) percent of the size of the vehicular use area as "green space." This space is set aside for pedestrian use within front yards or courtyards of the shopping areas. Within these spaces decorative plantings and site features such as fountains, sculpture, site lighting and gazebos may be designed to make the spaces environmentally sound, scenic and pedestrian friendly. Specific standards help to make this happen. For instance, in these areas a minimum of one (1) foot of park bench is required for one thousand (1,000) square feet of retail space, and one (1) tree for each two hundred fifty (250) square feet of green space is helpful. Building perimeters must set aside ten (10) square feet per one thousand (1,000) square feet of gross floor space for plantings.

Collier County is located in the southwest section of the Florida peninsula, just north of the tropics. Naples, Florida, is one of the main towns in this area. This landscape ordinance is thought by some to be one of the better ordinances in the State of Florida. The ordinance is very well thought out and fairly comprehensive in scope. Perhaps some additional language in regard to storm water management, erosion control and hurricane resistance might be included.

Cooper City

Cooper City. Minimum Landscape Requirement Ordinance, Ord. No. 83-3-5, SS2 (11A-1), 3-22-83.

Cooper City is concerned with aesthetics, water conservation, preservation of native plants and efficiency in land development. Consequently, it adopted this ordinance in order to encourage innovative approaches to design that would promote environmental quality in the community.

Landscape requirements that are part of this code include perimeters, vehicular use areas, buffer zones, storage areas and "street swales." Street swales, often called street yards in other communities, lie between the sidewalk and the street. In this area, Cooper City requires one (1) fourteen (14)-foot tree for each forty (40) linear feet in most zoning districts and one (1) ten (10) foot tree in residential districts.

This ordinance applies to both commercial and residential areas, with specific treatment mentioned for certain types of land uses such as gas station districts, electrical substations and construction facilities.

Standards and technical data are included in this ordinance for the design of berms, trash enclosures, plant materials and plant species mix. Certain plants that have a tendency to become nuisances or are nonnative or artificial are prohibited.

A separate ordinance has been enacted by the community as a tree preservation ordinance.

Landscaping plans showing specific information for all building or paving must be submitted to the Planning and Zoning Board, Building Department and the Community Appearance Board for all projects other than single or duplex family projects. Plans for multifamily and commercial projects must be prepared and sealed by a registered landscape architect. Landscape contractors may prepare plans for single-family residences.

A development permit or occupancy permit can be withheld and penalties can be assessed for noncompliance with the terms of the ordinance. The chief building official or code enforcement officer oversees development under this code.

It is of interest that this community has seen fit to determine the character of the community tree canopy. It has included in the code the types of street trees (swale trees) that are acceptable for planting; seven (7) species are listed. There is also a provision for "tree species mix" for on-site plantings to ensure that the community has vegetative diversity.

Coral Gables

Coral Gables Municipal Code, Section 2-67, "Landscaping," n.d.

This city has minimal landscape requirements contained within the city zoning ordinance. Provisions contained within the ordinance define landscaping and set certain standards for land set aside for open space for single-family, commercial and special use buildings. No specific technical standards are given.

Coral Springs

Coral Springs. Minimum Landscape Requirement, Article IX, City Code, 1972.

The City of Coral Springs has prepared a landscape manual that contains the landscape ordinance as well as city's list of recommended plants, planting details, National Arborist Association Standards for pruning, guying, fertilizing, lightning protection and pesticide applications. Additional information prepared by the National Arbor Day Foundation is included. The manual has been prepared by the planning department for use by the general public for interpretation of the landscape ordinance.

This ordinance follows the general ordinance format often found in the communities of south Florida. The ordinance puts forth definitions, specifies technical design components and sets forth standards for plant materials, installation, maintenance and irrigation.

Maintenance standards include insect and disease control, mulching, turf edge trimming, pruning, root system management, control of nuisance species and watering.

Landscape requirements are tailored for various zoning districts. Most districts include general site planting, perimeter planting, parking lot interiors and street trees. Screening, storm water retention and landscape buffers are not included in this ordinance.

Provisions are included with the ordinance for providing credits for preserved trees, preventing tree abuse and designating specimen or historic trees. Thirty (30) percent of all trees and forty (40) percent of all shrubs are to be water conserving native plants.

Administrative procedures begin with landscape plan approval, include waivers and end with permits, denial or penalty.

Dade County

Code of Metropolitan Dade County, Chapter 18A, " Dade County Landscape Ordinance," Ordinance 95-222, December 5, 1995.

The largest city in Dade County, Florida, is Miami. This ordinance was recently enacted to apply to all of the incorporated and unincorporated areas of Dade County. The ordinance consists of minimum standards that will be enforced by either the county government or one of several municipal governments in the county. Municipalities may enact more stringent regulations if necessary. The regulations apply to all private and public development when a permit is required, except for single-family, duplex family and agricultural sites. Existing development must comply with street tree requirements and parking lot buffers under certain circumstances.

Several purposes of the ordinance are mentioned. They include, among others, promoting Xeriscape principles, defining the hierarchy of roadways, preserving existing forest communities, reducing energy consumption and improving environmental quality. Mention is made of buffering the effects of hurricane storms. Fifty-one (51) definitions are given, covering the subject matter of this forty-eight (48)-page ordinance.

The ordinance requires the submission, review and approval by the Department of Planning, Development and Regulation of landscape plans, irrigation plans and tree surveys.

The tree survey referenced in the ordinance must be prepared according to the following standards, as shown in Table 2.18.

All plans, except for one-family and two-family developments, must be prepared by and bear the seal of a landscape architect licensed to practice in the State of Florida, as required by Chapter 481, Florida Statutes. All plans are to be accompanied by calculations, tabulations and statistical information and quantities. They are reviewed according to design criteria listed in Section 18-A-7 of the ordinance.

A tree removal permit or natural forest community vegetation permit is required prior to the removal of trees.

This ordinance sets minimum design standards for lawn areas, irrigation, plant materials, buffers and parking lot interiors. A typical standard for this ordinance is described in terms of performance, sizes, quantities, spacing and formula, as follows:

> *Shrubs shall be a minimum of eighteen (18) inches in height when measured immediately after planting. Hedges, where required, shall be planted at a maximum spacing of thirty (30) inches on center, and maintained so as to form a continuous, unbroken and solid visual screen with a maximum of one year after time of planting. Shrubs shall be provided at a ratio of seven (7) per required tree. Thirty (30) percent shall be native species.*

TABLE 2.18. Standards for Preparation of the Tree Survey, Dade County, Florida

Drawn at the same scale as the site plan.
All existing trees four (4) inches in DBH or larger.
Identify all trees to be removed, relocated or preserved.
List scientific and common name of all trees.
Determine DBH of each tree or sum of all trunks on multiple-trunk trees.
Map all specimen trees on site.
Estimate height, canopy cover, and physical condition of trees.
Delineate boundaries of native plant communities.
Delineate boundaries of natural forest communities as required by Department of Environmental Resources Management (DERM).

CERTIFICATE OF COMPLIANCE

The signature below of a licensed landscape architect, registered in the State of Florida pursuant to Chapter 481, Florida Statutes, certifies that the project constructed on Lot 12, Parcel 17, Tract 46, of the Tiger Valley Business Park has been implemented by the contractor / owner according to plans prepared by the landscape architect.

This certifies that the work has been installled in compliance with the requirements of the Code of Metropolitan Dade County, Chapter 18A, " Dade County Landscape Ordinance."

Certified this date________October 20, 1996________________________________

D.E. Deubler, ASLA Landscape Architect ___ LA 0009999______LC C 05555_____

FIGURE 2.11. Facsimile of a Certificate of Compliance, Dade County, Florida.

Other standards are listed for plant material quality and prohibited or controlled species.

A landscape manual providing illustrative interpretation of the standards is available from the Department of Planning, Development and Regulation.

A Certificate of Compliance, as shown in Figure 2.11, is issued to the county by the designing landscape architect, certifying that landscape installation and irrigation are complete and installed as designed. Upon completion of the landscape installation, the county issues a final Certificate of Use and Occupancy or a Certificate of Completion to the owner.

The Committee of Landscape Adjustment has been formed to receive applications for adjustment of landscaping requirements. It has the authority to approve, modify or deny requested adjustments or variances.

It is interesting that one of the stated purposes of this landscape ordinance is to promote the use of trees to protect and buffer the effects of high winds on structures. Few landscape ordinances encourage the use of hurricane resistant landscaping as a protective measure. The ordinance points out the need but does not go very far in specifying criteria, standards or regulations in how to meet this need. Perhaps this is an issue to be considered by all areas that are susceptible to hurricane impact.

Dania

Dania. Vegetation, Chapter 26, Dania, Florida, Code, April 12, 1994.

The Dania landscape ordinance is a tree preservation and landscaping ordinance. It is designed to reduce tree loss, at the same time replacing lost trees and adding new landscaping following development activities. This ordinance is not a land alteration ordinance but goes a long way to preserve native vegetation. The stated purpose of the Dania ordinance is to enhance the natural environment and beauty of the city by providing landscaped green spaces in relationship to paved areas and structures. The city also wishes to promote Xeriscape principles in the maintenance of landscapes as a means of reducing water consumption.

This ordinance contains both design components and standards.

Standards are included for plant materials, plant installation, irrigation and landscape maintenance. These are both technical and performance standards. For instance, "Shade trees shall be a minimum height of fourteen (14) feet, with a minimum diameter at breast height of two (2) inches and a minimum of four and one-half (4½) of clear trunk immediately after installation" is a good example of a technical standard found in this ordinance. "The owner of land shall be responsible for the maintenance so as to present a healthy, vigorous and neat appearance free from refuse, debris and weeds" is a typical performance standard for maintenance.

Plant installation standards give specifications for the proper planting, staking and pruning of vegetation. Plant standards pertain to trees, shrubs, hedges, vines, ground covers and turf grass. There is also a list of restricted plant species based on brittle wood, invasive root systems and exotic nuisance plants. Maintenance standards describe how the landscaping is to be cared for after planting, and irrigation standards set forth parameters for area coverage, water zones, system control, water quality and times when watering is permitted.

Design components contained within this ordinance require that technical drawings and specifications be prepared to demonstrate how the developer of the property will comply with the provisions of the ordinance. Both a landscape plan and an irrigation plan must be submitted for approval prior to receiving a permit. The irrigation plan is submitted to the building department, and the landscape plan, along with a site plan, is given to the planning and zoning board for review and approval.

The landscape plan and preliminary irrigation plan must be prepared by a registered landscape architect. The landscape plan must show all trees to remain, to be relocated and to be removed, as well as all proposed plantings, site lighting, retention ponds, parking, driveways, walkways and site improvements. The plan must be accompanied by details, specifications and a table of data showing such technical information as gross and net area, required quantities, square footage of vehicular use area and other information that may be required to give a complete understanding of the proposed plan.

The landscape plans must show design solutions for the following site areas: vehicular use areas, landscaping adjacent to public rights-of-way, landscaping adjacent to abutting properties and interior landscaping for all vehicular use areas. Landscaping for nonvehicular open space must meet the following standards, as presented in Table 2.19.

Turf, ground cover, shrubs, trees and other landscape materials shall be installed to cover all open spaces, excluding buildings and paving.

TABLE 2.19. Nonvehicular Open Space Standards, Dania, Florida

Percentage of Site Nonvehicular Open Space	*Trees and Shrubs*
Less than 30	1 tree and 10 shrubs/2,000 square feet
30 to 39	1 tree and 8 shrubs/2,500 square feet
40 to 49	1 tree and 6 shrubs/3,000 square feet
50 or more	1 tree and 6 shrubs/3,500 square feet

Other design components include landscape buffers between various land uses.

In this community trees are as essential as clean air and pure water. A person cannot remove any tree nor clear land without first obtaining a permit. Tree abuse is prohibited. Historical trees cannot be removed without a variance from the commission. There are certain exceptions to this rule, which include nuisance trees, agricultural or nursery operations, public works and damaged trees in emergency situations such as hurricanes.

Trees can be removed or relocated under certain circumstances. All cut and removed trees must be replaced. A determination of the number of trees to be replaced shall be performed by the developer. This determination is based on the area of impact and the category of replacement trees. The rule is that the canopy replacement at tree maturity shall at least equal the canopy removed.

When allowed by a tree removal license, any trees that are removed and not relocated are to be replaced by the developer's paying a tree replacement fee into the Dania Tree Preservation Trust Fund, which is defined in the ordinance. The cost of replacement is based on current trade prices multiplied by a factor of two and seven-tenths (2.7). Specimen trees and natural forest communities, such as high hammock, natural forests and beach and dune communities, have special tree preservation standards.

Any violation of this code results in fines, which are placed in the city's Beautification Trust Fund.

This is one of the most complete and detailed landscape ordinances reviewed in this study. It is easy to see that a community like Dania, Florida, highly values the landscape and has enacted legislation to see that overwhelming growth does not destroy the environment or character of the place. This ordinance might be a model for others that wish to ensure that vegetation, wildlife, clean air, pure water and beauty are part of the fabric of the community.

Davie

Davie Code, Section 12-100, "Site Landscaping, "June 19, 1996, Ord. No. 96-27. Ord. No. 91-13, "Tree Preservation," February 6, 1991.

The town of Davie has both a landscape ordinance and a tree preservation act. Together they comprise the city's comprehensive landscape ordinance. The purpose of the two ordinances, considered together, is to provide minimum landscaping standards to reduce land use conflict and establish regulations governing the protection of trees while promoting the proliferation of trees and other vegetation in the town of Davie.

Standards are cited in the ordinance for plant materials, Xeriscaping, plant material installation, tree preservation and tree protection during construction. Tree removal, relocation, replacement and maintenance are also mentioned.

Design components for landscaping lots and sites are discussed on a zoning district basis rather than a townwide basis. Townwide standards are most common in the ordinances in this study.

As an example of district standards, we might look at one land use. For instance, in the single-family or two-family district there are technical requirements for site tree planting, street tree planting, shrub and ground cover planting and implementation of landscape buffers adjacent to streets. Technical requirements vary for zero-lot-line developments, multifamily, commercial and industrial districts.

Special standards apply to parking lots in all districts. Interior landscape area requirements are specified as are the sizes of islands and amount of plant material to be planted. Townwide standards also apply to outdoor equipment screening, sight triangles and trees under power lines.

Plant material quantities are based on square footage and linear measure.

Permits required for removal, relocation and replacement of trees are obtained from the Development Services Department. This department also reviews and approves all proposed landscape plans and irrigation plans, which must be prepared and sealed by a licensed landscape architect. Plans must be prepared according to stated specifications, some of which are shown in Figure 2.12.

Upon completion of a project, a Certificate of Occupancy is granted to the owner as evidence that all landscape requirements have been met.

The city has published a categorical landscape materials inventory that lists plants by size and use. In addition, the ordinance makes reference to tree care standards promulgated by the National Arborists Association.

The ordinance in this community has some innovative ideas that might be considered by any community wishing to draft an ordinance based on land use districts.

Daytona Beach

Land Development Code, Section 2, "Landscaping," n.d.

Daytona Beach is one of the most famous beaches in the world. People visit Daytona Beach to partake of its scenic and cultural resources. This city strives to keep the "Florida image" so important in the tourism industry. Thus, it has enacted its landscape ordinance to provide for sound ecological site design that preserves native vegetation and the character of the city.

This ordinance applies to all new development and any renovations, under certain conditions, exceeding five thousand (5,000) dollars in cost.

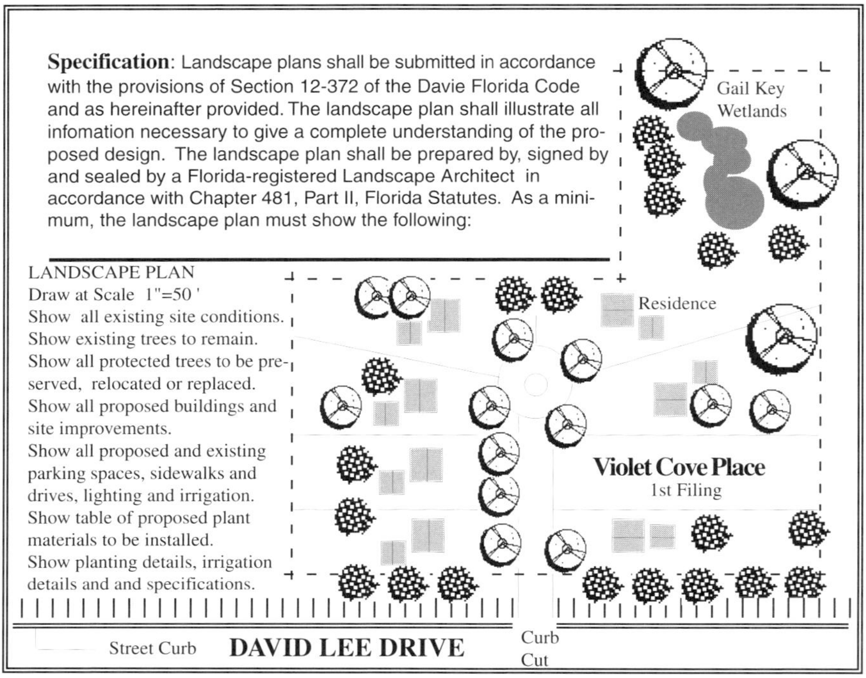

FIGURE 2.12. Landscape plan preparation specifications, Davie, Florida.

Design components of this ordinance include property perimeters, building perimeters and vehicular use areas.

Standards include requirements for plant selection, planting design, landscape materials, irrigation and maintenance. The planting design standards in this community, as shown in Table 2.20, are very specific and easy to understand by a reader with minimal training in landscape architecture.

One of the most distinctive aspects of this ordinance is its emphasis on providing planting design standards to guide the creation of the design. Most communities cite far fewer design requirements. To follow these design standards, many calculations must be made and submitted to the Planning Board at the time of application for a building permit.

Land Development Code, Section 3, "Trees and Native Vegetation," n.d.

A closely related ordinance is the tree preservation ordinance. This ordinance was enacted to further the work of the landscape ordinance by controlling the removal of trees and native vegetation. The community believes that it is in the public interest to protect the value of land, improve water quality, modify climate, promote soil stabilization and oxygen exchange and minimize air pollution.

TABLE 2.20. Planting Design Standards, Daytona Beach, Florida

Planting Design Standard	*Requirement*
Building perimeters	5 to 10 foot depth
Property perimeters	Minimum depth 5 feet
ROW perimeter	15% hardscape, 25% flowering plants
Plant arrangement	Grouped with similar water requirement and aesthetic appeal
Planting areas	At least three species, one of which must be a tree
Parking-to-tree distance	75 linear feet maximum
Tree ratio	One each 200 sf of landscape area, one each 2500 sf of site
Tree composition	75% shade trees, 50% of shade trees to be evergreen
Ornamental and palm trees	25% of required tree count
Building perimeter trees	Placed on corners and each 50 lf on center
Shrub ratio	25% of landscape area to be shrubs, ground covers, vines
Plant spacing	80% coverage of landscape area, 100% in two years
Accent plantings	Spaced 40 lf on center in property perimeter areas
Internal parking area	10% of paved area, minimum size 80 sf, 3 foot-transition radius
Tree size (shade ornamental)	2½ inch caliper, 10 feet tall or 1½ inch caliper, 8 feet tall
Palm size	6 feet of clear trunk at time of planting
Shrubs	12 inches general, 24 inches VUA screens, 36 inches property screens
Ground covers and vines	12 inches at maturity, spaced 18 inches on center at planting

A permit is required to remove, relocate, cut down or damage any tree or any native vegetation protected as part of required landscaping, buffers or preservation areas. Landscape plans and vegetation plans must be submitted for review under some circumstances. These plans must show the location, type, density and timbering history of each site.

Timbering of pine on land zoned for agricultural use is allowed. On lands not so zoned, a fifty (50)-foot buffer must be maintained on arterial and collector streets and a twenty-five (25)-foot buffer along other streets and property perimeters. All hardwoods are to be preserved.

TABLE 2.21. Tree Preservation Standards, Daytona Beach, Florida

Specimen Trees per Acre	*Existing to Be Preserved*
Less than 3 per acre	80%
3.0–5.0 per acre	65%
5.1–8.0 per acre	50%
8.1 or more per acre	4 per acre

Certain exotic trees are not protected and can be removed without permits.

This ordinance provides tree coverage and tree preservation requirements as shown in Table 2.21.

Fifteen (15) percent of the square footage of each development is to be designated for the preservation of existing trees. A minimum of one (1) tree must be preserved for every two thousand five hundred (2,500) square feet of site area. Where an insufficient number of trees exist, two and one-half ($2\frac{1}{2}$)-inch replacement trees must be planted. Specimen trees, those over twelve (12) inches DBH, must be preserved according to the guidelines shown in Table 2.21.

The ordinance provides protection and maintenance standards, as well as restoration requirements if trees are removed or damaged without a permit. Restoration is based on one (1) restoration tree for each six (6) inches DBH of removed tree or eight (8) trees per acre in the case of prematurely cleared land in which all evidence has been removed.

To ensure fairness to developers, reasonable and understandable review criteria are provided along with a modest procedure for modification and appeal.

Where it is impractical to comply with tree coverage requirements, the developer may apply for a waiver of alteration and deposit a fee of three hundred (300) dollars (two thousand four hundred (2,400) dollars/acre) in the city Tree Reserve account. This account uses the money for the purchase and installation of trees and irrigation on public lands.

Deerfield Beach

Deerfield Beach, Florida, Ordinance No. 1988/57, Section 5931, 1988.

The existing tree canopy of Deerfield Beach has been reduced to fifteen (15) percent, and the use of indigenous plants and trees is therefore highly encouraged for ecological and aesthetic reasons. Xeriscape design is recommended for maintenance and conservation considerations.

The ordinance requires variety in plant choices. For example, if a space requires one hundred fifty-one (151) to two hundred (200) shrubs as outlined elsewhere in the document, there is a minimum of four (4) different species. Furthermore, at least ten (10) percent of required trees must be flowering, and twenty (20) percent of required trees must be palm species. Native species must comprise at least twenty-five

(25) percent of the total provided trees. Three (3) years from the effective date of the ordinance, the requirement for natives increased to forty (40) percent.

Also addressed briefly are installation and irrigation standards.

Deerfield Beach, Land Development Code, Section 98-80, Landscape Requirements, 1984.

Landscaping is recognized in Deerfield Beach as a necessary ingredient of the urban environment. Minimum landscape standards are set forth for the design, installation and maintenance of landscaping.

Included in the ordinance are specifications for landscape perimeter requirements, off-street parking area requirements and plant material type and size requirements. Xeriscaping, to reduce water consumption, is required by this ordinance. Special landscape requirements are included for various zoning classifications. Certain streets used as thoroughfares are set aside as "arbor streets." Shade trees over and above the minimum requirements apply here.

Other sections of the ordinance describe screening, irrigation and maintenance.

Planting standards are based on square footage, linear measure and units.

Permits are required from the city forester to remove any native trees. However, exotic trees and nuisance trees may be removed. Credit is given toward landscape requirements for preserving existing native trees.

A landscape plan and tree survey prepared, signed and sealed by a registered landscape architect must be submitted to the city forester for approval. All landscaping must be installed according to accepted good planting procedures as prescribed by the American Society of Landscape Architects. A Certificate of Installation must be prepared by the same qualified firm or landscape architect who prepared the approved and installed plan. This postconstruction certification statement represents the designer's understanding of compliance with the plans, specifications and requirements of the landscape ordinance. The landscape architect, by signing this certificate, certifies that the landscape contractor has complied with provisions of the ordinance.

Enforcement is ensured by withholding the Certificate of Occupancy or Occupation License of the land user. Penalty provisions apply for violations of this code.

Ordinance Section 98-81 is a closely related landscape ordinance. This section deals with tree preservation. Requirements are given for removal, relocation and replacement of trees. Tree abuse, remedial actions and tree protection methods are outlined. A host of special arboricultural definitions are given to make it easier to understand the technical language included in this complementary ordinance.

Delray Beach

Delray Beach, "Landscape Design Standards," Sections 4.6.16E, and related "Landscape Regulations," Sections 4./6.16, Zoning Ordinance, September 13, 1971.

The purpose of Delray Beach's ordinance is to promote the general welfare of its citizens by providing minimum standards for the installation and maintenance of landscaping. This ordinance not only applies to the setbacks, yard areas and parking lots of new developments, but attempts to address existing ones as well. It addresses compliance and relief, site design requirements, landscape design standards, irrigation requirements, prohibited and controlled species, minimum landscape requirements and minimum maintenance requirements.

Landscape design standards are set forth in this ordinance. They include criteria for reducing water usage, development of soil structure and moisture retention, selection of proper turf, ground cover, shrubs, palms and trees. Special emphasis is placed on appropriate planning and design to include consideration of size, shape, soil and topography of individual sites.

A plan must be submitted before a building permit will be issued. Planting standards are based on square footage and linear footage. This ordinance recognizes the need for water conservation in Florida by dedicating a fair portion of the requirements to Xeriscape principles and water conservation requirements. Furthermore, the ordinance promotes the use of native plants and "phases in" the requirement of their use. Eventually, fifty (50) percent of trees and twenty-five (25) percent of all other plants will be required to be native. A unique feature of this ordinance is that it prohibits certain species of plants within the City of Delray Beach. One can surmise that in the climate of south Florida these invasive plants can become an environmental problem, and this ordinance is the community's way of addressing this issue.

Required maintenance consists of mowing, edging, weeding, shrub pruning, fertilization and inspection and repair of irrigation systems.

Overall, this ordinance is proactive in its approach. It applies to single-family homes as well as duplexes, apartments and commercial sites. However, the document is easy to read and establishes clear principles for landscape design within Delray Beach.

Fort Lauderdale

Broward County, City of Fort Lauderdale, Ordinance No. C-90, Section 47-58, "Landscaping and Tree Preservation," 1989.

This ordinance emphasizes landscape requirements for vehicular use areas and tree preservation. Sections within the ordinance include definitions, landscape plan submittal requirements, installation, irrigation, maintenance, landscape requirements for vehicular use areas (VUAs), landscape requirements for zoned districts, specific requirements for signs, townhouse developments, parking structures, churches, fences and walls (buffer yards are mentioned) and tree preservation, with subtopics such as tree removal, tree services and arborists registration, tree protection, tree abuse and tree cutting, removal of trees and dead trees constituting a public nuisance and street tree planting.

Gainesville

Gainesville Code, Article VIII, "Environmental Management," June 10, 1992, amended.

In this community landscaping is seen as being an essential part of environmental quality. Gainesville's landscape ordinance is contained within a comprehensive law that addresses many aspects of city environment that include, among other elements, landscape regulations, tree management policy and storm water management.

This ordinance contains forty two (42) points of justification for its existence, perhaps the most of any ordinance examined in this study. Justification is based on many environmental reasons, land use reasons and quality of life issues.

All property within the city including expansion, except for certain exempt areas, is subject to these regulations. At least twenty (20) percent of the area devoted to development on each site must be reserved for landscaping. All zoning districts, including new subdivisions, must comply with these regulations.

This ordinance addresses several issues of design, including vehicular use areas, landscape buffers and site reforestation. Site reforestation requires that each development have a minimum number of trees planted. For sites of less than five (5) acres this would be one (1) tree for each twenty-eight hundred fifty (2,850) square feet; for larger properties this becomes one (1) tree for each thirty-eight hundred (3,800) square feet. There are additional design components that include subdivision tree canopy requirements, subdivision street trees and special plantings for selected "gateway streets." Subdivision tree canopy requirements specify that no more than thirty (30) percent of the existing tree canopy may be removed. Developers of subdivisions must also plant street trees.

Tree removal permits are required for all trees of more than eight (8) inches DBH. Special commercial forestry permits are available for trees associated with forestry management, tree harvesting and other similar purposes. No clearing or grubbing of a site may begin until the site has received development plan approval and or a building permit. Credit is allowed for all preserved trees, as shown in Table 2.22.

TABLE 2.22. Tree Credits for Preserving Trees, Gainesville, Florida

Existing Crown Spread		*Diameter of Tree at DBH*	*Number of Credits*
90 feet or greater	or	36 inches or greater	7
60–89 feet	or	30–35 inches	6
50–59 feet	or	26–29 inches	5
40–49 feet	or	20–25 inches	4
30–39 feet	or	13–19 inches	3
20–29 feet	or	8–12 inches	2
10–19 feet	or	2–7 inches	1

Performance, administrative and technical standards are included in this law. These include plan submission requirements, design standards, tree protection and relocation standards. Standards for plant materials, replacement stock, installation and maintenance are included as well. Gainesville has established an official tree list and has defined "Champion Trees" and "Heritage Trees." Invasive, nonnative plant species are prohibited.

Hallandale

Broward County, City of Hallandale, Article IX. Section 1-7, "Landscaping Requirements," 1979. Broward County, City of Hallandale, Chapter 32, Article 2, 8, "General Site Design Standards," 1989.

This is a very large and complete ordinance (forty-one (41) pages) containing standard requirements for tree planting, right-of-way (r-o-w) planting, parking areas, nonvehicular use areas and irrigation. Standards are given for a certain desired species mix and for tree credits, as shown in Figure 2.13. A minimum of open space is required to be planted on all sites and in all zoning districts, including residential.

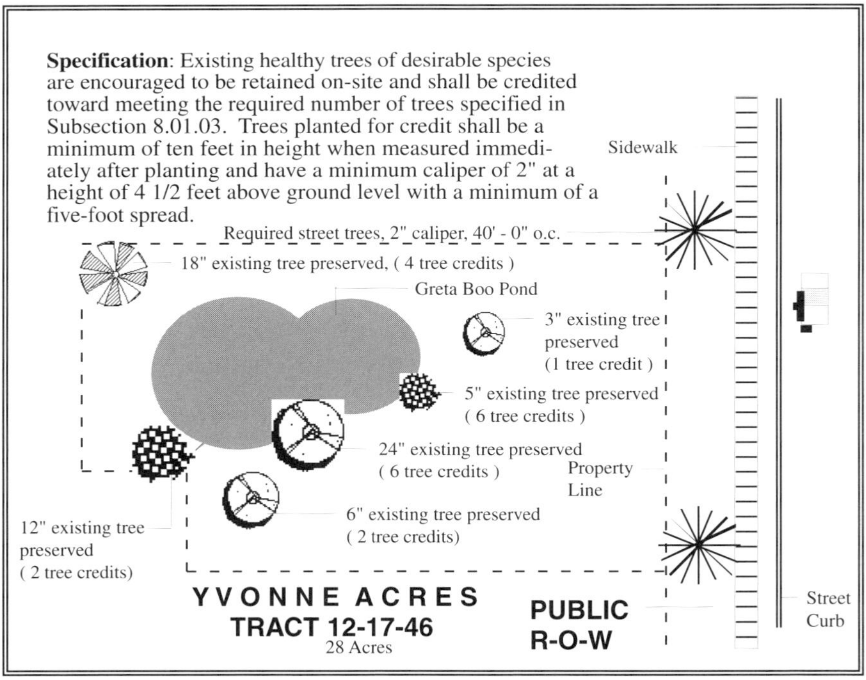

FIGURE 2.13. Tree credits, Hallendale, Florida.

This ordinance is complemented with sketches and tables that help to clarify the code requirements. The City Manager in this community is responsible for its enforcement and administration.

Hillsborough County

Hillsborough County, Ordinance No. 92-05, "Hillsborough County Land Development Code," March 4, 1992.

The Hillsborough County Land Development Code contains seven separate articles. Article 1 includes the provisions of general applicability, Article 2 deals with zoning, Article 3 explains development requirements, Article 6 describes the administrative and decision-making bodies and Article 7 contains definitions. The articles of interest for this annotation include Article 3—Division 3.5, Land Alteration Regulations, and Division 3.6, Landscaping Regulations; and Article 7—Division 7.1, Rules of Construction, and Division 7.3, Definitions.

Division 3.5 of the Hillsborough County Land Development Code, "Land Alteration Regulations."

The purpose of the land alteration regulations is to set forth regulations regarding land alteration, the protection of trees and other vegetation and the protection of environmentally sensitive areas, in order to maintain the quality of life in Hillsborough County and protect the health, safety, welfare and general well-being of the citizens. Land alteration is any activity that removes vegetation from or changes the topography of the land by grubbing, tree removal, clearing, grading filling or excavating, except for activities undertaken to maintain existing grounds. Any development intending to alter the land in any way must first acquire a Land Alteration Permit from the County Administrator. Land alterations that do not require a Land Alteration Permit include activities such as agricultural businesses, maintenance procedures and small alterations. This ordinance is enforced through the issuing, and possible revoking, of building permits, Certificates of Occupancy, development orders, development permits or development approval.

Article 3.5 discusses the review procedures for land alterations. The factors considered in evaluating an application for a land alteration permit, the criteria for granting the permit and the submission requirements are listed. An in situ field permeability test of any area to be excavated and dewatered must be performed by a civil engineer registered in the State of Florida. The land alteration standards and guidelines include illustrations and topics such as protection of soil and water resources, protection of surface water flow, protection and replacement of trees, protection of environmentally sensitive areas and uplands providing significant and essential wildlife habitat, protection of natural plant community vegetation outside conservation and preservation areas and an environmental restoration fund. Appendix B of Division 3.5 discusses "prescribed ecological burns," requiring authorization from the local fire department to burn and at least one (1) certified burn manager present on-site.

There are many unusual aspects of this ordinance—too many individual interesting elements to mention. For instance, the ordinance contains unique topics and has a unique organization. Division 3.5 involves "land alterations," which is an unusual term for development. Preservation is of major importance in this division. This ordinance also contains Appendixes A, B, and C, which summarize research studies such as "Significant Wildlife Habitat Minimum Width/Size Criteria," "Habitat Management Guidelines" and "Guidelines for Listed Species." Each Division of this ordinance is outlined as a separate ordinance.

DBH, the diameter of a tree at breast height is referred to repeatedly. "Wildlife corridors" are defined as contiguous stands of significant wildlife habitat that facilitate the natural migratory patterns and other habitat requirements of wildlife. Agencies or organizations referred to frequently include the County Administrator, County Commissioners, Zoning Administrator, County Code Enforcement Board, Environmental Protection Commission, Florida Game and Freshwater Fish Commission, U.S. Fish and Wildlife Service, Florida Department of Agriculture and Consumer Services Division of Forestry, Environmental Restoration Fund and Geographical Information Systems. Hillsborough County has many plans for the future of the county, such as the *Future of Hillsborough Comprehensive Plan* and the county's *Future Land Use Plan Map.* Reports documenting the necessary information for these future master plans include *Significant Wildlife Habitat in Hillsborough County, Natural Plant Communities, the Florida Game and Freshwater Fish Commission Natural Systems* and *Land Use Cover Inventory Map.*

Division 3.6 of the Hillsborough Land Development Code, "Landscaping Regulations."

The purpose of this division is to set forth the regulations regarding the installation and maintenance of landscaping in order to conserve energy and water, promote safety and quality, protect property values and create compatible boundaries for differing land uses. The purpose of parking area landscaping is to provide shading throughout the entire lot. It is unlawful for any development to commence within Hillsborough County without first having obtained a Landscaping Permit from the County Administrator. A site inspection must be performed and approved after installation of a development before a Certificate of Occupancy is issued.

Division 3.6 deals with the specific landscaping requirements. It recommends using Xeriscape and native species. It lists the minimum number of species required for the number of required trees and explains credit given for preserving existing trees. Maintenance involves an irrigation system for all landscaping. The number of required trees is based on the type of development and the area. For example, single- and two-family residential lots of less than ten thousand eight hundred ninety (10,890) square feet require only two (2) trees; lots greater than ten thousand eight hundred ninety (10,890) but less than twenty-one thousand seven hundred eighty (21,780) square feet require four (4) trees; lots greater than twenty-one thousand seven hundred eighty (21,780) but less than forty-three thousand five hundred sixty (43,560) square feet require six (6) trees; lots greater than forty-three thousand five hundred sixty (43,560) square feet require eight (8) trees. Multi-family residential lots less than twelve (12) units per acre require eight (8) trees per gross acre; lots greater than twelve (12) units per acre require six (6) trees per gross acre. Commercial and industrial land uses require four (4) trees per gross acre. Parking area requirements are also included in this section. Illustrations are provided to further the understanding of the requirements set forth in this section. The illustration subjects include stormwater detention basins; perimeter buffers adjacent to road rights-of-way; perimeter buffers adjacent to parking area driveways; and parking area terminal islands, internal islands and divider medians.

A very interesting and unique aspect of this ordinance is the statement that when native plants are used, the irrigation system requirement can be waived.

Hollywood

Hollywood. "Vehicular Use Area and Landscaping Regulations." Article 9, Zoning and Land Development Regulations. Ord. 0-94-26, June 7, 1994.

The landscape ordinance was set up to assist in meeting the goals and objectives of the *Hollywood Comprehensive Plan.* The ordinance seeks to preserve natural areas, add native plants to the community through landscaping and enhance wildlife habitat. It applies to all projects coming under development or rehabilitation requiring site plan approval.

Landscaping will be installed in perimeter landscaped setbacks and in terminal islands in parking lots. Parking lot interior planting space is based on a percentage of area. Vehicular use areas with a width of more than fifty (50) feet are to have twenty-five (25) percent of its area set aside for landscaping. Lots of less than fifty (50) feet are to have fifteen (15) percent set aside

This ordinance has what might be called a "natives ratio" or native plant requirement. Hollywood requires that by June 1, 1997, each site must have sixty (60) percent native trees and forty (40) percent native shrubs.

Performance standards are given for water conservation, irrigation and plant material installation. Landscaping shall be designed using the principles of Xeriscaping promulgated by the South Florida Water Management District.

A related ordinance, "Trees," Chapter 106 of the Land Development Code, requires that one (1) public street tree must be planted for each fifty (50)-foot section or portion thereof of the street frontage designated in every building permit application. The trees used in the design must be those from an approved list as provided by the city. Table 2.23 summarizes this list in tabular format.

Trees are of such value in Hollywood that they may not be removed except by permit. Permits are given to remove trees under certain circumstances such as disease, storm damage or their reputation as a public nuisance. Casuarina trees, better known as Australian pine, have such a bad reputation that they cannot even be planted in the city.

Replacement trees are to be of a type and species from an approved list and of equivalent value to the tree that is being removed.

TABLE 2.23. Approved Street Trees, City of Hollywood, Florida

Bottlebrush (*Callistremon citrinus*)	Queen's Crape Myrtle (*Lagerstroemia speciosa*)
Geiger Tree (*Cordia sebestena*)	Golden Shower Tree (*Cassia fistula*)
Gumbo-limbo (*Bursera simaruba*)	Dahoon Holly (*Ilex cassine*)
Red Maple (*Acer rubrum*)	Laurel Oak (*Quercus laurifolia*)
Paradise Tree (*Simarouba glauca*)	Pigeon Plum (*Coccoloba diversifolia*)
Slash Pine (*Pinus elliottii* var *densa*)	Satinleaf (*Chrysophyllum oliviforme*)
Wild Tamarind (*Lysilima bahamensis*)	Yellow Tebeuia (*Tabebuia argentea*)
Pink Trumpet Tree (*Tabebuia pallida*)	Jerusalem Thorn (*Parkinsonia aculeata*)
Southern Red Cedar (*Juniperus siliciola*)	Silver Buttonwood (*Conocarpus erectus*)
Carrotwood (*Cupaniopsis anacardioides*)	Royal Poinciana (*Delonex regia*)
Bald Cypress (*Taxodium distichum*)	Jacaranda (*Jacaranda auctifolia*)
Pongam (*Pongamia pinnata*)	Red Mulberry (*Morus rubra*)
African Tulip Tree (*Spathodea campanulata*)	Yellow Poinciana (*Peltophorum pterocarpum*)
Beauty Leaf (*Calopphyllum antillanum*)	Cabbage Palm (*Sabal palmetto*)
Royal Palm (*Roystonia elata*)	Coconut Palm (*Cocos nucifera*)
Queen Palm (*Arecastrum romanzoffianum*)	Live Oak (*Quercus Virginiana*)
Mahogany (*Swietenia mahogani*)	Sea Grape (*Coccoloba uvifere*)

Interestingly enough, preservation of any tree may be considered as the basis for the granting of variance from the literal application of zoning or subdivision regulations.

Homestead

Homestead Code, Chapter 39, Article II, "Landscaping," 1990.

This is one of the earlier landscape ordinances, having been written in the mid-1970s, revised in the 1980s and again amended in 1990.

Some of the earlier language is still in this ordinance, and it can be compared with the more recent language. This ordinance illustrates how the very early ordinances (1970s) took a more regulatory tone and seem to be aimed at eliminating bad practices in the landscape industry.

In the 1980s the emphasis seems to have shifted toward encouraging better design. You begin to see flexibility clauses, such as the Alternative Compliance provision, inserted to encourage innovative landscape design practices. It may be of interest to note here that none of the language of the 1990s has found its way into this ordinance. The language of the 1990s landscape ordinances is trending toward habitat preservation, land alteration restrictions, tree protection, Xeriscape principles and additional emphasis on design.

The City Council of Homestead finds that the peculiar characteristics and the quality of the city justify regulations to perpetuate its aesthetic appeal. Prior to any issuance of a Certificate of Use and Occupancy each site must be seeded or sodded with a minimum of one (1) tree planted on each lot. There are requirements for landscaping adjacent to public rights-of-way, perimeter landscape zones, wall plantings and parking area interior plantings.

Plantings for all of these design components are based on linear foot measure, areas or specified unit quantities. This ordinance has a required species mix clause that regulates and prevents monoculture in species selection. The larger number of trees planted requires more species diversification, as shown in Table 2.24.

Standards are given for hedges, plant materials, installation, maintenance, ground treatment, prohibited plant materials and plan approval procedures. There are no standards of quality for those who prepare the designs, however.

Saving existing vegetation is encouraged but not mandatory. Credit may be given for plant materials existing in the areas where new plant materials must be added.

Everyone will remember Homestead as a victim of Hurricane Andrew in 1992. This city was made famous as pictures were flashed around the country, showing a scene of devastation to both landscape and buildings. It is interesting that in this code there is no mention of hurricane-resistant requirements for plant materials or other landscape material usage. It is well known that some plant materials hold up better in high winds (up to one hundred twenty (120) mph) and that many plants, if properly maintained, will do better than others. Certain types of plants should be added to the prohibited list as a result of their lack of performance in hurricane winds.

TABLE 2.24. Required Species Mix, Homestead, Florida

Required Number of Trees	*Minimum Number of Species*
1–10	1
11–20	2
21–30	3
31–40	4
41+	5

Indian River County

Indian River County Code, Chapter 926, "Landscape and Buffer Regulations," Ord. No. 90-16, September 11, 1990.

The Board of County Commissioners of Indian River County finds that landscape regulations are justified to perpetuate the appeal of the natural environment of the county while preserving property values.

This ordinance has been designed to improve the appearance of setback and yard areas, including off-street parking areas and nonvehicular open spaces, and to promote the use of efficient low-volume irrigation systems as a method of conserving water supply. The ordinance applies to all land in the unincorporated parts of the county that is subject to Site Plan Review regulations.

No construction may take place until a landscape plan has been approved by the planning and zoning commission. A Certificate of Occupancy will not be granted until all conditions of the landscape ordinance are met.

This ordinance consists of general requirements, such as landscape plan preparation standards and standards for landscape materials, irrigation, installation and maintenance. Specific design requirements apply to perimeter buffers, vehicular use areas and nonvehicular use areas. Special requirements apply to upland habitat protection, tree preservation and tree protection. These requirements are referenced to other chapters in the land development code and are not summarized here.

In addition to specific design and planting requirements stated in the text, this ordinance has a point system that must be satisfied. A minimum of thirty (30) points must be achieved from the list of options presented in Table 2.25.

Credits are granted for tree preservation. Four (4) types of buffers, varying in width and density, are defined and illustrated in graphic diagrams. No quality assurance standards, enforcement or administrative provisions are cited in this code.

This ordinance is well organized and easy to understand. It falls into the category of comprehensive landscape ordinances if considered together with other chapters of the Code, such as Chapter 914, Site Plan Regulations, Chapter 929, Upland Habitat Protection and Chapter 927, Tree Protection.

Jacksonville

Municipal City Code, Chapter 656, Land Use, Part 12, "Landscape and Tree Protection Regulations," 1991.

The ordinance for Jacksonville, Florida, combines tree protection provisions (Subpart A) and landscaping (Subpart B) requirements. It has recently been updated to include Xeriscape principles. The ordinance applies to both public and private lands, except for single-family subdivisions. There are cited twelve (12) reasons for this public policy, which range from environmental concerns to psychological

TABLE 2.25. Landscape Point System, Indian River County, Florida

Landscape Element	*Points Earned*
IRRIGATION SYSTEM POINTS	
Use of moisture-sensing controller	5
Low, medium and high water use zones indicated on plan	5
SHRUB POINTS	
Twenty-five to fifty percent of total rated very drought-tolerant	5
Fifty-one to one hundred percent of total rated very drought-tolerant	10
TREE POINTS	
Twenty-five to fifty percent of total rated very drought-tolerant	5
Fifty-one to one hundred percent of total rated very drought-tolerant	10
EXTRA PLANT MATERIALS	
Twenty percent more than required	5
Forty percent more than required	10
DESIGN OPTIONS	
Sod/grass area less than sixty percent of landscape area	5
One hundred percent of landscape area is preserved or reestablished Florida native vegetation	30
75 to 99 percent of landscape area is preserved or reestablished Florida native vegetation*	15

* No more than fifty percent of site may be grassed or sodded

effects to the enhancement of land value. Protection of native habitat, water supply and environmental quality are noteably important in this community.

Design components include a fifteen (15)-foot conservation easement, ten (10) percent of site as open space or one hundred fifty (150) square feet of open space per dwelling unit for multiple-family developments. In addition, other design components apply here, including vehicular use areas, perimeter landscaping, buffer yards and sight triangles.

The conservation easement sets aside land on all new residential development for the protection of native vegetation. Some of the standards for tree preservation are shown in Figure 2.14.

Standards are given for tree protection during development, plant materials, maintenance, irrigation, landscape plan preparation and landscape design. The details of these standards comprise the bulk of the ordinance and should be

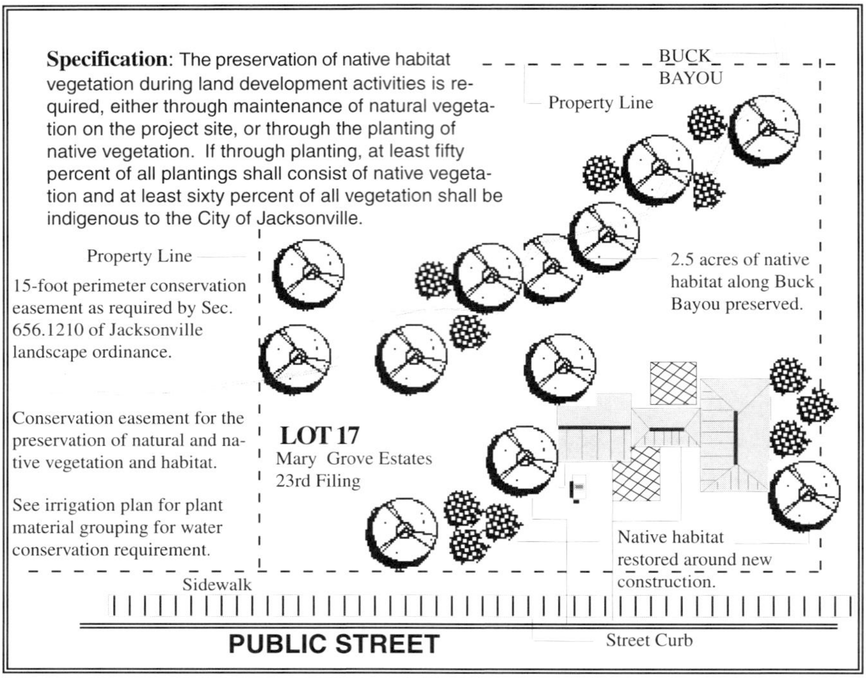

FIGURE 2.14. Native vegetation protection and planting requirements, Jacksonville, Florida.

consulted prior to the creation of any development plans in this community. The landscape design standards illustrated in Table 2.26 and Table 2.27 are examples of the design standards found in this community landscape ordinance.

Prior to the issuance of any building permit, a landscape plan considering these design standards must be submitted to the city. The landscape plan must be prepared by and bear the seal of a licensed registered landscape architect. Under some circumstances, a Tree Replanting Plan and a Site Clearing—Tree Removal Site Plan must be submitted for review and approval.

Trees or native habitat cannot be removed, damaged, or relocated without receiving a permit from the city. No land may be cleared, grubbed or bought under development until this permit is approved. Tree credits against new plantings are given for preserving existing trees. Protected trees that are removed must be replaced on the basis of one-third (⅓) caliper inch per caliper inch removed, except in the instance of live oaks (*Quercus virginiana*). In this instance, the ratio is one to one.

Money collected from permit fees, penalties and contributions are placed in a "tree trust fund" that pays for new plantings on public lands. One of the larger yearly contributors to the Tree Protection and Related Expenses Trust Fund is the city. As a result of street construction and lack of available planting space

TABLE 2.26. Landscape Design Standards, Jacksonville, Florida

Standard	*Expected Result*
Preserve existing plant communities.	Protects plants, animals and water supply.
Reestablish native plant communities.	Maintains character and environmental quality.
Use plant material appropriate for site conditions.	Encourages use of Florida native plants.
Group plant materials with similar irrigation requirements.	Preserves water supply.
Use pervious paving materials.	Promotes ground water recharge, reduces runoff and erosion.

TABLE 2.27. Selected Standards, Jacksonville, Florida

Standard	*Technical Requirement*
Private protected tree	6 inches within 20 feet of street, 8 inches within 10 feet of property line or 12 feet elsewhere on site
Minimum tree planting requirement	One tree per 5,000 square feet of lot area, higher square footage in commercial or industrial
Landscaping area in VUA	10 percent of vehicular use area set aside for landscaping
VUA tree planting requirement	One tree per every 4,000 square feet, 50 percent shall be shade trees
Street frontage planting strip	10 square feet for each linear foot
Street frontage tree planting	One tree for each 50 linear feet, with opaque landscape screen
VUA buffer requirement	5-foot strip between abutting property lines
VUA buffer planting requirement	Planted with trees, shrubs and ground cover, one tree for each 50 linear foot
Buffer strip between land uses	10 feet wide entire length, with visual screen of wood, plants, masonry
Native plant requirements	Fifty percent of landscaping

following utility installation, surplus caliper inches are converted to installation price per inch, and this money is placed in the trust.

An interesting feature of this ordinance is the clause giving the city council the power to designate scenic and historic corridors and regulate development therein. Specific requirements are not mentioned other than to say that the council has the power to impose conditions, procedures and standards. The purpose of this clause is to protect streets with special historic, architectural, archaeological, aesthetic or cultural interest.

Jupiter

"Landscape Ordinance of the Town of Jupiter," 1977.

Jupiter's ordinance intends to improve the appearance of setback and yard areas including off-street parking, open lots and service areas. A minimum strip of five (5) feet between abutting rights-of-way and off-street vehicular use areas shall be landscaped. Landscaped strips include one (1) tree for each forty (40) linear feet, as well as a continuous hedge at a minimum of four (4) feet in height (minimum of twenty-four (24) inches at time of planting). Some of the requirements for interior parking areas are shown in Figure 2.15.

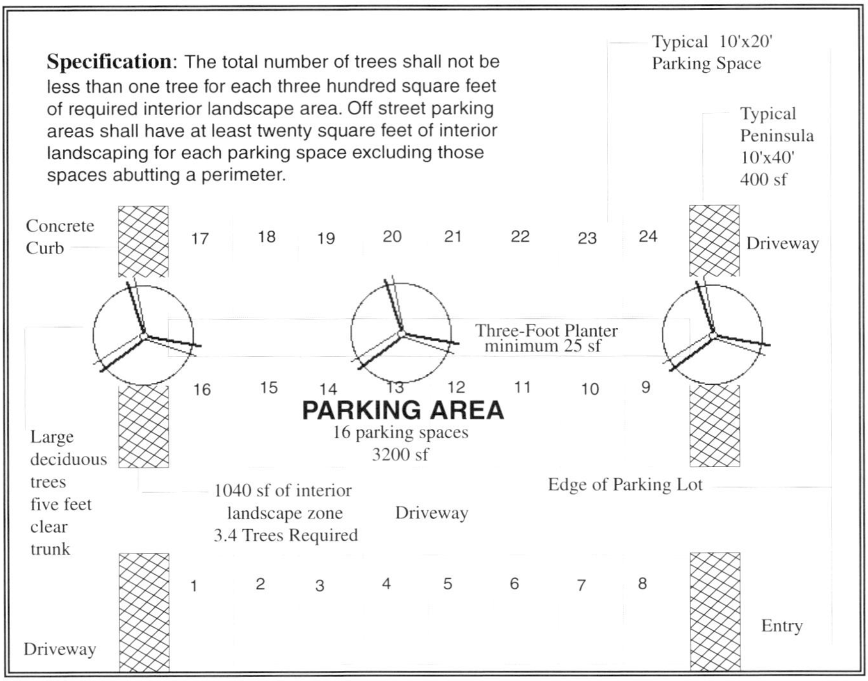

FIGURE 2.15. Landscape requirements, interior parking areas, Jupiter, Florida.

Lake Mary

Code of Ordinances, Chapter 157, "Landscaping and Arbor Regulations," November 27, 1985, amended December 21,1995.

Lake Mary encourages the proliferation, preservation and protection of trees and finds that landscaping enhances property values and aids in addressing a number of environmental concerns. One concern in this city is water recharge. It requires that no more than sixty-five (65) percent of any site be covered with impervious materials.

The design components of this ordinance include buffers, parking lot plantings, screening, and buffers to separate property and street rights-of-way.

This community has defined eight (8) different buffer types. Four (4) of the buffers (Types A, B, C, D) apply to land use buffering and four (4) (Types a, b, c, d) apply to street buffering. They vary according to width, required materials, amount of plants needed, ground coverage materials and types of screen. The buffers vary in width from ten (10) feet to sixty (60) feet. Plant materials for these buffers are based on linear foot measure.

Minimal reference is made in Figure 2.16 to storm water detention design, but few design requirements or technical standards are mentioned in this ordinance.

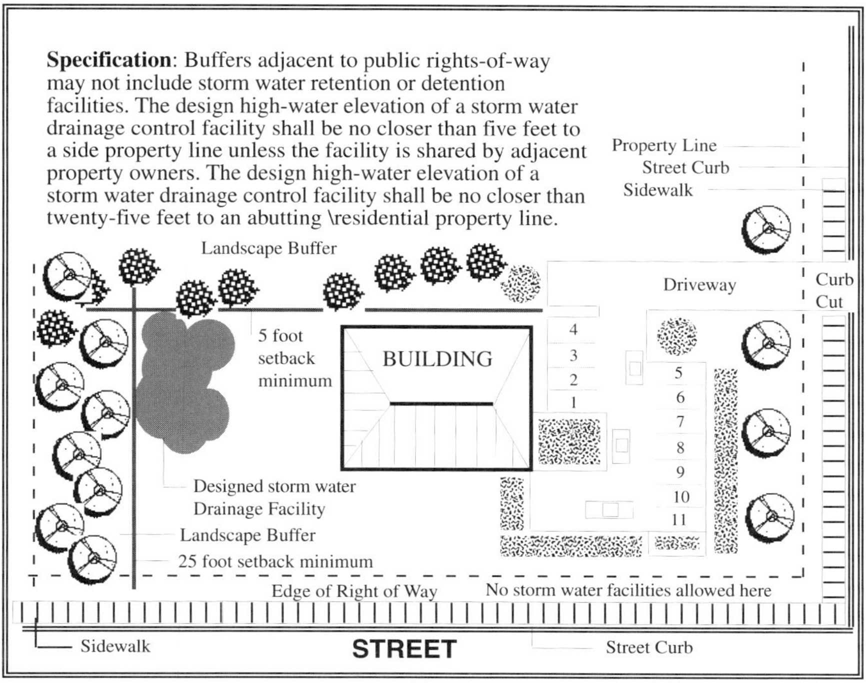

FIGURE 2.16. Storm water detention or retention facility siting standards, Lake Mary, Florida.

Standards are given for drawing preparation, maintenance, plant materials, tree removal and tree protection during construction. Irrigation plans must be submitted, but no standards have been adopted in this community other than requiring that the irrigation plans for all zoning districts other than single-family be prepared by a registered licensed landscape architect. Specifications are given for tree protection fencing and tree protection signs.

Ten (10) percent of any site's native vegetation must be preserved, and forty (40) percent of all new plantings and all replacement tree plantings must be Xeriscape species or highly drought-tolerant species. Permits, called "Arbor Permits," are required for tree removal and pruning, and tree protection signs, as shown in Figure 2.17, must be posted on sites to be cleared. Fines are assessed for removing trees without a permit based on the size of the tree removed. Table 2.28 shows the schedule of fines and mitigation fees that may be charged to non-permitted tree removers.

Owners of single-family and duplex developments may prune without permits, but utility companies must give written notice when extending a line on

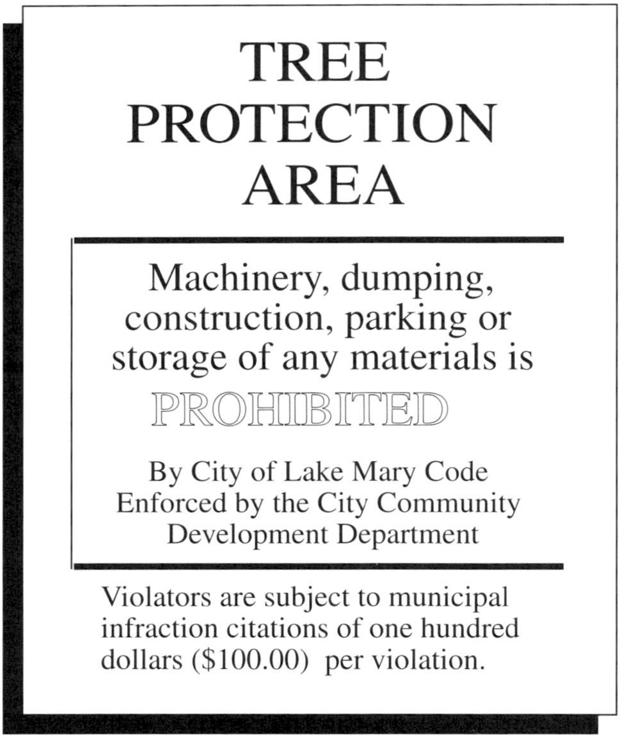

FIGURE 2.17. Facsimile of tree protection area sign, Lake Mary, Florida.

TABLE 2.28. Schedule of Tree Removal Fines, Lake Mary, Florida

Size of Tree Removed	*Initial Fine*	*Mitigation Fine*
Six inches to twelve inches	$100.00	$ 600.00
Twelve inches to twenty-four inches	$100.00	$ 900.00
Greater than twenty-four inches	$100.00	$1,200.00

unimproved properties. Violations for tree removal result in fines based on the schedule shown in Table 2.28.

The mitigation fine can be applied to replacement plantings as determined by using the "replacement ratio" and criteria contained within the ordinance. All money is deposited in the Lake Mary City Tree Planting Fund.

This ordinance covers postconstruction landscaping, tree protection and some aspects of land alteration. It is quite general and not very specific.

Lauderdale

Broward County, City of Lauderdale, Ordinance No. 89-208, Section 1-20 1/2-45, "City of Lauderdale Landscape Ordinance," 1990.

This ordinance emphasizes tree preservation and protection. Application procedures and required fees are covered. Plant material requirements are discussed, as are plant installation, maintenance and tree abuse. Other topics include landscaping public rights-of-way, perimeter landscaping relating to abutting properties and adjacent buildings, buffering of storage areas, mechanical equipment and vehicular parking.

Lee County

Lee County Land Development Code, Division 6, "Open Space, Buffering and Landscaping," January 28, 1983.

The land development code of this county consists of numerous divisions, sections and clauses that pertain to site planning, construction and landscape design. For instance, cross-referenced to the primary landscape ordinance is law that pertains to environment and natural resources, tree protection and zoning in environmentally sensitive areas. All should be consulted to get a clear picture of the extent of landscape requirements in this community near Fort Meyers, Florida.

Design components in this ordinance include buffers, screens, vehicular use areas, street landscape strips and storm water ponds.

This ordinance is intended to create open space and breaks in the urban landscape and to provide replacements for natural vegetation removed during development. Designating open spaces within all developments, within certain zoning districts, is a major concern of this ordinance. The open space standards presented in Table 2.29a apply to residential, commercial, public, industrial and multiple use developments in this community.

Other design standards, as shown in Table 2.29b and discussed in the following paragraphs, apply to other design situations.

Fifty (50) percent of open space must be designed to preserve existing indigenous native vegetation. Minimum dimensions (one hundred eighty (180) square feet) of what can be considered open space apply.

Buffers are defined by linear measure and number of trees per one hundred (100) linear feet. Various zoning districts have different requirements, but they vary in width from fifteen (15) to thirty (30) feet in depth. Fences, berms and walls

TABLE 2.29a. Open Space Standards, Lee County, Florida

Type of Development	*Open Space Percentage*
Single-family detached, two-family	None
Other residential	35% to 40%
Commercial	20% to 30%
Public, quasi-public	20% to 30%
Industrial	10% to 20%
Multiple-use development	Must comply with above as appropriate

TABLE 2.29b. Open Space Standards, Lee County, Florida

Design Criteria and Standards	*Reasoning and Site Engineering Concerns*
Mimic natural systems	Efficiency of design, blending qualities
Shoreline configuration	Increased length and diversity of littoral zone
Slope to water	Steeper than 6 to 1, not more than 4 to 1
Berm shoreline to swales and sinks	Pretreat water in low areas prior to discharge
Vegetation	One herbaceous plant per linear foot
Cluster plantings at water edge	Natural spacing of vegetation
Inlets and outfalls	Cluster plantings for erosion control
Minimum of four plant species	Add diversity in ecology and appearance
Planting techniques allowed	Lining out, mulching or sodding

are used in some buffers. Special buffers apply landward of mean high water elevation and natural waterways. Buffers may be used for passive recreation.

Landscaping must be installed in ten (10)-foot wide streetside landscape strips and throughout the site, based on a tree to square foot ratio. For instance, in a multiple-family development one (1) tree is required per three thousand (3,000) square feet and one (1) shrub every eight and one-third (8⅓) feet.

Parking lots must be landscaped with street buffers and internal planting areas. Parking spaces must be within one hundred (100) feet of a shade tree and there is to be designed one (1) tree planting for each two hundred fifty (250) feet. The landscaped area must be a minimum of ten (10) percent of the parking area. Provisions are included for the planting of islands and divider medians.

Requirements are given for plant installation, irrigation and maintenance of open space and plantings. Landscaping must be irrigated according to Xeriscape principles, and plant materials must meet State of Florida standards. Specified invasive exotic plants are prohibited.

Seventy-five (75) percent of the trees in buffers and landscaping and fifty (50) percent of shrubs must be natives. Credits are given for preserving existing trees and palms that are labeled as protected. Streets must be redesigned to preserve trees larger than twenty four (24) inches (DBH).

An alternative compliance clause (landscape betterment plan) is provided in this ordinance, allowing deviation from minimum requirements for certain stated reasons, particularly for water conservation and better design.

One of the most interesting features of this ordinance is the "archaeological clause" that requires that all identified archaeological sites showing evidence of past human activity be incorporated into the site as open space. Such sites can be disturbed, destroyed or mitigated by certificate of the historic preservation board. Similar clauses are found in few other landscape ordinances.

This ordinance is very comprehensive.

Leon County

Leon County, Florida, Code of Laws, Chapter 7, Art. 1½, "Drainage," 1975.

This ordinance from the Tallahassee area is interesting for several reasons. It links drainage and vegetation together in two separate sections of the Code of Laws for Leon County, Florida. The ordinance recognizes that in low coastal areas, vegetation and storm water management are interrelated, a basic principle of nature.

Chapter 7, Article 1½ and Article 3, provide regulations for storm water management, erosion control, sedimentation abatement and land clearing. In addition, floodplain management, or building within areas delineated on one of several federal government floodplain maps (FHBM—flood hazard boundary map, FIRM—flood insurance rating map, FBFM—flood boundary floodway map), is mentioned in the code.

Permits are required prior to making any changes in land use, land use intensity, or topographic elevation changes. The basic principle of this code is that surface water runoff from the site should be equal to or less than the rate of flow of surface water runoff that would occur following a twenty-five (25)-year frequency storm. In addition, the ordinance recognizes the beneficial functioning of wetlands as areas for the natural storage and filtration of surface water runoff. Vegetation in these areas is protected by design standards and by direct reference to Chapter 12 of the Code of Laws.

Leon County, Florida, Code of Laws, Chapter 12, Art. II, "Landscaping and Tree Protection," 1982.

Landscaping and tree protection are important to the citizens of Leon County. Standards and requirements are given in Chapter 12 of the Code for the preservation of existing vegetation, replacement of removed vegetation, and reforestation of the "county canopy," the latter to stabilize the ecological balance of the community.

Landscape development standards are given, requiring a minimum of fifteen (15) percent of a multifamily, commercial, or public lands and ten (10) percent of industrial land use to be devoted to landscape development. Landscape areas included in the Code include off-street parking and vehicular use areas, perimeter areas and uncomplementary land use buffers. Requirements are given in the law by a ratio formula of units (plants) to area or units to linear footage. Credits to this formula are given for tree preservation. Reforestation of the county canopy is set at one (1) tree for each one tenth (0.1) of an acre of development, for example.

Plant material standards published by the Florida Department of Agriculture and described in *Grades and Standards for Nursery Plants, Part I, 1963, and Part II*, are to be followed. Landscape plans are required prior to receiving a landscape permit, building permit, or Certificate of Occupancy. There are fees for the permits, and variances are allowed. Maintenance, enforcement and penalties are also covered in the Code.

Lighthouse Point

Broward County, City of Lighthouse Point, Article VIII. Section 20-120, 128, "Commercial Landscaping," 1987.

The City of Lighthouse Point has several objectives it wants to accomplish with this landscape ordinance. The first objective is to improve the appearance of certain setback and other property areas, including off-street parking and service areas, for business-zoned properties located in the city. The second objective is to protect and preserve the appearance, character and value of the business-zoned properties in the city. Objective three is to preserve and improve the canopy of the community in order to protect air and water quality.

Among the components mentioned in the ordinance are landscape installation, maintenance, and inspections; plant material standards with approved list of trees and shrubs; plans and their approval (survey, landscape irrigation, changes, etc.); landscape specifications; minimum acceptable standards; perimeter and interior landscaping; parking space requirement; enforcement; and special exceptions.

Lighthouse Point. Commercial Landscaping. Article VIII, City Land Development Code, January 23, 1990.

The objective of this ordinance is to preserve the tree canopy of the community and improve the appearance of business-zoned properties. The ordinance requires installation and maintenance of landscaping for screening, ecological and aesthetics purposes only in B zoning districts.

To accomplish this objective, all developers of property must submit plans to the city building department for review and approval by the planning and zoning board. Accompanying these plans shall be a site survey, a landscape plan and irrigation plans.

Certain landscape specifications (design requirements) are set forth. They include a two (2)-foot perimeter landscape area and a ten (10) percent net interior lot planting requirement. The latter includes planter islands in parking lots. A recommended list of shade trees, flowering trees, palms and shrubs is included in the code.

Properties being renovated within two (2) years of the effective date of the ordinance, for which renovation costs equal twenty (20) percent of assessed valuation, must be brought into compliance with this code.

This ordinance is enforced by the code enforcement board of the City of Lighthouse Point.

This ordinance is minimal in scope and complexity. Performance standards, rather than detailed requirements, are used to convey the intent of the city.

Maitland

Maitland City Code, Chapter 8, "Landscaping," 1971.

This ordinance was enacted under the home rule power of the city for the purpose of regulating landscaping standards for off-street parking and other vehicular use areas.

All off-street parking and other vehicular use areas that require landscaping must meet general landscaping requirements for areas adjacent to public rights-of-way, areas adjacent to surrounding properties, internal parking areas and intersections of access ways (sight triangles).

Planting requirements are based on percentage of area or linear measure. Planting standards are minimal.

Other standards include plant materials, installation and maintenance.

This ordinance applies only to vehicular use areas and is very general and somewhat dated in comparison with other ordinances in the same general region of the country.

Margate

Margate. Landscaping. Chapter 12½, Margate City Code, n.d.

This south Florida city sees its landscape ordinance as a means of maintaining its character as a tropical resort. They also see it as a means of organizing land use and circulation and preserving indigenous vegetation. By achieving these objectives, the city believes it will be able to maintain residential property values and revitalize commercial areas.

The ordinance applies to all zoning categories and will apply to existing permitted uses if and when any building or parking area is expanded, extended or enlarged. When there is a change in occupancy group, as described in the South Florida building code, the land use must be brought into compliance.

This ordinance combines tree preservation with postconstruction landscaping.

Prior to the issuance of any building or paving permit, a landscaping plan prepared by a Florida-registered landscape architect shall be submitted to the city. This rule applies to all building projects other than single- or two-family dwellings. The plan shall include specific information; it must show all proposed structures, vehicular use areas, driveways, surface water areas, fire lanes, zones and hydrants. In addition, the landscape plan shall show location, size, grade and specifications of all landscaping materials, including common and botanical names, planting instructions, soil and fertilizer instructions, mulch specifications, elevations, protective curb details, existing trees and descriptions of any existing conditions that affect the landscaping of the site. Permits are also required for irrigation systems, tree removal and planting of trees in swales.

No person may cut down, destroy, remove, relocate or damage any tree in the city without first obtaining a permit from the city. Damaged trees under emergency conditions are exempted, as are nurseries, botanical gardens and commercial groves. The cost of the permit for each tree is ten (10) dollars. The penalty for noncompliance is an injunction or restraining order issued in any court.

The design components of the ordinance include driveways, abutments to rights-of-way, land use buffers and visual clearance zones at intersections. The landscape design must also address perimeters, waterway frontage, parking areas, planting in swales and storage screening.

Standards are given for plant materials and minimum yard landscaping by zoning category. Performance specifications are given for irrigation, installation and maintenance. Reference codes are cited and made part of the landscape ordinance. These include Grades and Standards for Nursery Plants, Tree Protection Manual for Builders and Developers, and Standards for Pruning Shade Trees.

Planting standards are based on units and linear and square foot measures. For example, in parking areas there are to be at least ten (10) square feet of interior planting space for each parking space and one (1) tree per one hundred fifty (150) square feet or fraction thereof of interior planting area. Along perimeters of abutting property there must be one (1) shade tree for each seventy-five (75) linear feet.

Tree abuse, including hatracking, using climbing stakes, nails, or hooks, and pruning that is not in accord with National Arborist Association Standards are prohibited. Preservation of existing native vegetation is highly encouraged. Thirty (30) percent of all new trees and forty (40) percent of all new shrubs must be native plants.

TABLE 2.30. Recommended Trees, City of Margate, Florida

Common Name	*Botanic Name*	*Tree Type and Use*
Mahogany	*Swietenia mahogani*	Large Shade Tree
Red Maple	*Acer rubrum*	Medium-Size Tree
Live Oak	*Quercus Virginiana*	Large Shade Tree
Laurel Oak	*Quercus laurifolia*	Large Shade Tree
Sea Grape	*Coccoloba uvifere*	Medium-Size Tree
Gumbo-limbo	*Bursera simaruba*	Large Shade Tree
Satinleaf	*Chrysophyllum oliviforme*	Medium-Size Tree
Cherry Laurel	*Prunus caroliniana*	Medium Evergreen Tree
Geiger Tree	*Cordia sebestena*	Medium-Size Flowering
Pigeon Plum	*Coccoloba diversifolia*	Medium-Size Flowering
Silver Buttonwood	*Conocarpus erectus* var *sericeus*	Large Shade Tree
Slash Pine	*Pinus elliottii* var *densa*	Tall Evergreen
Bald Cypress	*Taxodium distichum*	Wetland Deciduous Tree
Royal Palm	*Roystonia elata*	Tall Palm Tree

For any tree being removed the following rules apply. The city requires that the tree be relocated on-site or some public land or be reserved for future use on public land. Replacement trees must be a minimum of three (3) inches in diameter (DBH) and ten (10) feet tall. More than one (1) tree may by used to make a replacement. The aggregate sum of their diameters is to be equal to or greater than the diameter of the tree being removed. Replacement trees must be limited to a list of recommended species, as documented in Table 2.30.

Conflicts, appeals and adjustments to the landscape ordinance are handled by the Beautification Committee, consisting of three (3) members of the Planning and Zoning Board.

Miami

Miami, "Tree and Landscaping Regulations for the City of Miami," 1988.
Miami, "Sections 1 and 2 of Chapter of the City Code, Environmental Preservation, "Off-Street Parking Guides and Standards," and" Landscaping Guides and Standards," respectively, 1983.

Among the topics discussed under "Off-Street Parking Guides and Standards," are landscape material; periphery and interior landscaped areas; deck areas, plazas and roof areas; special exception off-street parking facilities; and maintenance. Interesting to note, within the section entitled "Periphery Landscaped Areas," solid and continuous masonry walls, in certain instances, whose surfaces are stucco, painted, tiled or textured in such a way as to provide a decorative effect if approved, may be used in lieu of the landscape area. Minimum planting well dimensions and minimum shade tree requirements, per area to be landscaped within parking areas, are mentioned under "Deck Areas, Plazas and Roof Areas."

Topics similar to those mentioned earlier are covered in Section 2, with more attention given to plant selection requirements and general landscaping requirements per area.

North Lauderdale

North Lauderdale. Vegetation, Chapter 102, Section 102-01,
Ord. No. 91-11-1800, November 14, 1991.

North Lauderdale seeks to maintain the quality of its environment through the preservation of existing trees and native vegetation while eliminating nonnative nuisance vegetation. It is believed that the quality of the environment will be maintained if landscaping is utilized to create open space, conserve energy and improve the aesthetic quality of the city. This ordinance provides regulations, technical standards and administrative procedures to regulate the design, installation and maintenance of landscaping. General definitions have been included for clarification.

All new development and all existing development, under certain circumstances, must comply with the provisions of this ordinance. Existing properties are not permitted to increase the degree of nonconformity. For example, any expansion of floor space more than fifty (50) percent will trigger the requirement that a property be brought into compliance. This ordinance has specific landscape requirements for each type of zoning district.

General performance standards are given in this ordinance for installation, irrigation and maintenance. Specific size and quality standards for plant materials as put forth by the state Department of Agriculture are to be followed.

This community has a list of approved trees, shrubs and palms, which must be used to satisfy the requirements of this ordinance. There is a separate list for street trees, hedges and native plants. Thirty (30) percent of the trees used in the design and on the site are to be native plants. Credit is given for the retention of existing site vegetation.

Prior to the issuance of a building permit, a landscape plan prepared by a registered landscape architect must be submitted to the development review committee. For RS-5 and duplex zoning districts, the plans need not be sealed by a landscape architect. Irrigation plans designed, signed and sealed by a qualified professional must also be submitted.

Planting standards are provided for each zoning category. In each instance the general site planting requirements are based on linear footage of frontage or square footage of plot, or both. In addition, special planting requirements based on linear measure, square foot measure or percentage of area are added for perimeter landscaping, landscaping adjacent to street rights-of-way, parking area interiors, other vehicle use areas and swale areas. Swale areas lie between the edge of the right-of-way and the curb back and may be planted with approved street trees.

Waivers may be granted by the governing body, subject to a petition in writing by the developer stating the extent and duration of the waiver and what part of the ordinance cannot be designed in compliance.

A landscape manual can be procured from the community development department, which provides illustrative interpretation of design components of the ordinance.

North Miami

North Miami Municipal Code, Appendix A-Zoning, Section 29-8 (h), "Landscape Regulations," n.d.

This act is known as the "comprehensive landscape ordinance," whose purpose is to ensure that all forms of vegetation are planted and preserved with the development, or redevelopment, of structures, drives and parking areas within the city of North Miami. In addition, it is the purpose of this legislation to promote ecological harmony, encourage energy conservation, reduce air pollution, recharge water supply and highlight the positive qualities of the natural environment of the city. The best ecological concepts, environmental objectives and site planning principles are to be utilized to this end.

The community development and planning staff are charged with reviewing landscape plans, certifying compliance with stated landscape design standards and enforcement. The ordinance includes standards for certain yard areas used as buffers and screens, as well as off-street parking, interior parking lot planting and other vehicular use areas. Commercial parking areas, self-serve or valet, are specifically mentioned in this ordinance, as are standards for ensuring solar access and energy conservation.

Standards are given for installation of landscaping, maintenance and plant material quality. Credit is given for preserving existing plant material, although no particular technical standards of tree preservation are cited.

A related section of the ordinance, Section 29-26.1 (C), requires screening of recreational vehicles in residential districts. A special list of trees and shrubs suitable for this type of screening is given.

North Miami Beach

Zoning Ordinance, Article XI, "Landscaping," March 17, 1992.

The purpose of this ordinance is to preserve and maintain viable vegetation within the City of North Miami Beach and to provide for landscaped open space while regulating the installation and maintenance of landscaping.

The ordinance applies to all land uses (including residential) and substantial additions and alterations as allowed by the Director of Community Development. If more than fifty (50) percent of existing landscaping is in need of replacement, then all landscaping must be brought into compliance. Administrative waiver is allowed when, during expansions or additions, it is found to be a hardship to bring the site to compliance with current code requirements.

Landscape plans, designed with the use of Xeriscape principles, and tree surveys must be submitted in order to receive a building permit. Standards are given in the ordinance for preparation of landscape plans, and all such documents are to be prepared, signed and sealed by a registered landscape architect. Following installation, the site must be inspected and a signed Certificate of Compliance must be submitted to the city in order to receive a Certificate of Occupancy.

Specification standards for type, size and quality are given for plant materials, including trees, palms, shrubs, vines, ground covers and lawn grasses. A list of approved plants is available from the city. Certain species are prohibited.

Other standards are mentioned for planting soil, mulch, irrigation and installation methods. One hundred (100) percent of all landscape areas must be irrigated. To ensure water conservation, the use of nonpotable water, rain gauges, pores and flexible drip irrigation pipe is encouraged. Pop up sprinkler heads must be arranged in zones for areas of similar water need.

No tree of more than three (3) inches caliper, other than prohibited species, may be removed without a Tree Removal Permit, and "hatracking" or severe pruning is restricted. Applicable portions of the Dade County Tree Protection Ordinance, ("see Dade County") #89—8 are incorporated by reference. A "landscaping bank clause" is part of this ordinance, allowing equivalent replacement value payment to the City Landscaping Account for trees that must be removed.

Design components in this ordinance include perimeter landscaping, interior landscaping of vehicular use areas (terminal islands, interior islands, divider medians), nonvehicular use areas (open space), vision clearance zones, landscaped or pervious areas, trash storage and retention areas. Planting requirements are based on area, linear or unit measure. In residential zones the schedule of plantings shown in Table 2.31 applies.

A landscape application and review fee, based on lot size, are collected from each building permit applicant.

This is a well written, well organized, easy to understand landscape ordinance applying to all zoning districts, typical of those being written in the 1990s.

TABLE 2.31. Minimum Landscaping Requirements, Residential Districts, North Miami Beach, Florida

Zoning District	*Trees*	*Shrubs*
MH-1	2 Trees	15 Shrubs
RS-5	2 Trees	15 Shrubs
RS-4	3 Trees	20 Shrubs
RS-3	3 Trees	20 Shrubs
RS-2	4 Trees	30 Shrubs
RS-1	6 Trees	50 Shrubs
RD	2 Trees	15 Shrubs

It contains a distinct list of design components, technical standards, minimal administrative standards, alternative compliance provisions, licensing requirements, landscape plan preparation standards and a landscape bank clause.

The Community Development Department in North Miami Beach is proud of this ordinance and believes that it has a "dramatic effect" on the appearance of the city.

Oakland Park

Oakland Park. Landscaping and Fences. Article VIII, Section 24-105, Land Development Code, n.d.

In this community, landscaping is required to improve the appearance of setback and yard areas, including parking lots. This is a minimal ordinance applying to selected land uses.

Planting standards are based on the size of the lot. Twenty (20) percent of any residential, business or industrial district is to be left pervious and landscaped. For instance, in R-1 and R-2 districts the lot tree planting schedule outlined in Table 2.32 applies.

It is required that the trees be of staggered heights. In the event that the required number of trees cannot be installed, the developer is to deposit five hundred (500) dollars per tree in the City Beautification Fund to purchase plant material on public land.

Landscaping is also required for perimeters, with one (1) tree for every forty (40) linear feet. Erosion control buffers five (5) feet in width are required along water courses. Walls and fences are required in certain circumstances.

Plans are subject to approval by the Code Enforcement Department prior to the issuance of any building permit.

TABLE 2.32. Tree Planting Schedule, Oakland Park, Florida

Lot Size in Square Feet	*Number of Trees*
Less than 6,000	2
6,000 to 7,499	3
7,500 to 9,999	4
10,000 and over	5

Orange County

Orange County Code, Chapter 24, "Landscaping," December 15, 1992, Ord. 92-42.

Orange County adopted a comprehensive policy plan several years ago, which mandated changes in several sections of the zoning code in respect to landscaping, buffering, open space, irrigation and stormwater management. Specific

TABLE 2.33. Technical Standards, Orange County, Florida

Design Component	*Technical Standard*
Vehicular Use Areas	Street edge landscaping strip 7 foot depth One shade tree each 40 linear feet Continuous hedge 36 inches high after 18 months 24-inch vehicular overhang zone Opaque and planted 6-foot screens adjacent to residential
Interior Vehicular Use Area	5% of area to be landscaped Minimum planting zone 25 square feet One shade tree for each 100 square feet of interior Islands required every 20 spaces 7-foot center medians planted one shade tree each 60 linear feet
Parking Garages	Designed as building perimeters seen below
Intersection Visibility	Unobstructed views between 24 and 72 inches Landscaped with grass or ground covers 30-foot minimum length at intersections 10-foot minimum length at access way at street edge
Building Perimeters	50% of length of building facing street Minimum depth, 5 feet Landscaped to 30-inch height One tree for each 200 square feet
Service Area Screening	Screened with vegetation, walls or fences Service area screen 10′ wide, 50% opaque Waste storage screen, 6-foot high masonry wall Open storage screened 6-foot wall, 10-foot wide planted strip
Buffer Yards	Type A, 8′ tall, 50′ wide, screens industrial uses Type B, 6′ tall, 25′ wide, screens commercial uses Type C, 6′ tall, 15′ wide, screens commercial, light industrial Type D, 6′ tall, 10′ wide, screens professional offices Type E, 5′ tall, 25–50′ wide, screens mobile home parks Type F, see Chapter 34, Orange County Code One shade tree for each 40 linear feet Incentive width reduction, 20% for better design

goals of this ordinance are to conserve water supply and enhance the visual and aesthetic appeal of the county, while preserving natural terrain, vegetation and property values. This ordinance applies to all properties for which site plan review is required and for all land uses other than single-family and duplex family sites. Certain specified conditions exempt some land uses from this ordinance.

The ordinance contains design components, as well as technical standards for landscaping, water efficient design and design of open spaces. Many of these are indicated in Table 2.33. There are minimal standards for plant materials, maintenance, and installation. There are no standards for tree protection or tree preservation. Some mention is made of on-site storm water management, but it seems that most of these requirements are actually contained within a complementary ordinance (Chapter 34, Article VII).

Tree surveys are required for larger planned developments, according to Section 15-301(b) of the code.

Water efficient design standards include deep mulching and grouping of plant materials with similar water needs. The ordinance also requires the designer to use native plants, freeze-tolerant plants and drought-resistant plants. All plants are to be Florida No. 1 Grade. Turf grass, a high-water-use plant, should be restricted to only those areas receiving pedestrian circulation or recreational use or being used for erosion control in swales and on slopes. Rain sensors and rain gauge equipment are required.

Certain irrigation incentives are established to encourage preservation of native habitat and plantings. Otherwise, one hundred (100) percent of all landscaped areas must be irrigated by a permanent underground central irrigation system.

The ordinance is enforced by requiring submittal and approval of landscape and irrigation plans prepared by "qualified professionals," which include registered landscape architects. Sites are inspected after installation of landscaping, and Certificates of Occupancy are issued following receipt of a signed Certificate of Compliance. Penalties can be assessed, as can be seen in Figure 2.18.

One of the interesting features of this ordinance is the special landscape ordinance in regard to the "overlay zone" that has been created in this community. Special conditions and requirements apply to Activity Centers/Tourist Commercial Developments. This overlay zone is discussed in the following paragraphs concerning the related landscape ordinance.

Related Ordinance. Orange County Code, Chapter 24, § 24-10, "Activity Center/Tourist Commercial Development," December 15, 1992, Ord. 92-42.

Enhanced standards apply to all properties designated as Activity Centers. Design components include streetscape buffers, perimeter landscaping, parking lot screening and property buffer planting. Conventional storm water retention facilities are to be treated as site amenities or screened. Parking lot interiors and building perimeters are to be treated in an enhanced manner as well.

The descriptive table of technical data, Table 2.34, gives an idea of the skillfully enhanced technical standards developed to meet the requirements of the ordinance in this district.

Penalties For Violation

Orange County, Florida

(g) Penalties. Failure to have viable landscaping consistent with the approved landscape plan shall constitute a violation subject to penalties and shall be prosecuted and punished in accordance with Orange County Code, Sec. 1-9. The Board of County Commissioners may bring suit in the Circuit Court to restrain, enjoin or otherwise prevent violation of and / or enforce compliance with this Chapter.

Orange County Code,
Chapter 24,§ 23-3.(g)
"Landscaping"
December 15, 1992,

Ord. No. 92-42.

FIGURE 2.18. Penalty clause, Orange County, Florida.

TABLE 2.34. Overlay Zoning Technical Standards, Orange County, Florida

Design Component	*Technical Standard*
Streetscape Buffers	One shade tree each 40 LF of road frontage Tree height to be 16′ tall, 3½″ caliper
Perimeter Landscaping	One shade tree each 50 LF
Vehicular Use Areas	Continuous hedge 30″ high, 48″ high at maturity, 80% opacity
Interior Vehicular Use Area	10% of total paved area to be landscaped 100 SF minimum size landscape area One shade tree for each 75 SF of landscape area 50% of all landscape areas shall be planted with shrubs Islands required every 15 spaces 7′ center medians planted one shade tree each 50 LF

TABLE 2.34. (*Continued*)

Design Component	*Technical Standard*
Building Perimeters	50% of length of building facing street or parking areas Landscape area shall encircle building Minimum depth, 5′ Landscaped to 30″ height One tree for each 100 SF 50% planted with shrubs
Perimeter Landscaping	Along r-o-w, one tree each 50 LF Along side and rear lot lines, one tree each 75 LF 50% of all trees located within 15′ of property line Credit given for existing trees that are retained Design is flexible, but no tree planting exceeding 150 LF All paved areas and storm water retention areas to be screened Berms 2′ to 5′ high, supplemented with landscaping to 36″ Berms not to exceed 75′ in length Berms between parking and abutting properties

Orlando

"Landscaping and Vegetation Protection," Section 60.200-60.234, September 1991.

This ordinance stresses goals, objectives and policies found in the conservation and urban design elements of the city's Growth Management Plan. The requirements attempt to maintain a balance between environmental and conservation concerns and the need for development and integration of nature into existing and future development. The ordinance provides for the conservation of soils, native vegetative communities and urban woodlands; protects trees during development and sets standards for buffering and screening. The code also sets standards for planting lake edges and for vegetative screening of above-ground utilities.

An interesting aspect of the Orlando ordinance is its acknowledgment and promotion of Xeriscape, which is described as a set of landscape design and maintenance principles that promote good horticultural practice and the economic and efficient use of water. The term *Xeriscape* is the registered trademark of the National Xeriscape Council, and means water conservation through the use of drought-tolerant landscaping or appropriate plant materials that do not require special attention and require little supplemental water to survive. But the ordinance points out that Xeriscape designs "do not resemble desert landscapes, but reflect the lush traditional appearance of Florida gardens." The section on Xeriscape is necessary because of water restrictions in central Florida.

One- and two-family residential building sites are exempt from the Xeriscape requirements, but are encouraged to comply. All planned developments fall under the regulations. The ordinance urges the grouping of plants with similar water needs into different zones. Water use zones must be shown on the landscape plans. The irrigation system will then be designed to correlate to the plant zones.

The tree protection portion of the code works on a system of "tree points," with the attainment of a certain number of points required for different types of development. For example, a retained native specimen or historic tree is worth seven (7) points, and a one and one-half (1½)-inch caliper, ten (10)-foot high small tree, either retained or installed, is worth one (1) point. The ordinance includes a lengthy Approved Plant List for Orlando, Florida, that lists the water zones. An Approved Aquatic Plant List is also included.

Ormond Beach

City of Ormond Beach, Article VIII, Land Development Code, January 1, 1992.

The purpose of this ordinance is to beautify the landscape; preserve natural plant growth; regulate the removal and replacement of trees; protect specimen trees; preserve property values; control flooding, soil erosion, and light, wind, dust, heat, air and noise pollution; improve the environment of the urban area; and maintain a sanctuary for birds and animals. The use of "xeric plantings" and native plants is encouraged.

The ordinance includes lists of definitions and trees that are exempt or promoted by the regulations. Ormond Beach has several "canopy roads," on which the removal of specimen trees is prohibited. Under the tree replacement requirements, developers who receive a waiver for their site must install the balance of trees on public properties designated by the Parks Director, or donate money to the city's tree replacement fund according to a formula presented in the ordinance.

Several of the Ormond Beach provisions require the services of a registered Florida landscape architect. For example, a landscape architect must prepare a tree protection plan for development and a landscape plan required under the landscape/irrigation regulations.

The ordinance contains chapters on tree removal/protection for nondevelopment and development areas, landscaping and irrigation plans, buffer area requirements, fences and walls, maintenance of plantings and irrigation systems/enforcement, land clearing permits, grading and filling permits, mining and excavation.

Oviedo

Zoning Ordinance. Article XVII, "Landscaping, Tree Planting, and Buffer Requirements," n.d.

This community finds that it is important to use vegetation to provide food for birds, which will, in turn, reduce the mosquito population. There are other reasons for enacting a landscape ordinance, among them is the desire to buffer land uses, improve the environmental context of the city and provide guidelines for landscape preservation, planting and design. It encourages the use of existing vegetation and native plants and strongly recommends xeriscape design principles.

This ordinance requires landscaping of parking areas and buffers along property edges and along street rights-of-way. Canopy tree plantings, at the rate of so many trees per acre, are required for each land use. Three types of buffer yards are required; these vary in width from ten (10) feet to thirty (30) feet and range in-opacity from impression of separation to partial separation to complete separation.

Maintenance standards, xeriscape standards and plant material standards are included in this ordinance. Alternative compliance provisions apply to this ordinance.

This community is committed to the principles of Xeriscaping, and this theory of practice permeates their ordinance. Anyone interested in developing a water-efficient landscape ordinance should consult this ordinance.

Parkland

Parkland. Landscaping and Vegetation. Chapter 9, Parkland Code, Ord. No. 87-5, December 16, 1987.

The Parkland landscape ordinance consists of three general parts: Tree Removal and Land Clearing, Landscaping and Tree Abuse.

Land clearing that removes trees is a serious issue in this community. In order to clear land and remove trees, a survey prepared by a landscape architect, land surveyor or civil engineer must show all trees over three (3) inches in diameter or six (6) feet in height. The tree survey must show the exact location, size, botanical and common name. Groups of trees of a dominant species may be designated as clumps, exact tree location and size need not be given, only a count of the trees is necessary.

In Parkland no tree of more than three (3) inches in diameter may be removed without a permit except for several listed exotic species. For each tree removed without a permit, a five hundred (500) dollar penalty may be charged. Provision is made in this section for tree removal, relocation, replacement and tree protection during construction.

Parkland has established a "tree Bank " to assist in mitigating the changes that take place when land is cleared and developed. When trees are not relocated or replaced by a developer on-site, trees from the tree bank can be planted on public land at the developer's expense at some future date.

Tree removal permits are obtained from the city building department.

Landscaping to achieve a "parklike setting" is required following construction of all projects in which site plan approval or building permits are required. The landscape design components of this ordinance listed by zoning district type include criteria for lawns, access ways, landscape buffers and screens. Parking, vehicular use areas and storage areas are also included. There are specific requirements for fences, walls, berms, hedges and signage.

Credit is given for preserving existing trees.

Standards are based on linear feet and square footage. For instance, parking lot interiors require thirty-five (35) square feet of planting for each parking space, or one (1) tree for each one thousand (1,000) square feet of landscape, building and pavement or fraction thereof. Standards for plant material are based on size and on grades and standards for nursery stock, promulgated by the Florida Department of Agriculture.

A list of recommended trees is included in the code.

Prior to the issuance of a building permit, a landscape plan prepared by a registered landscape architect must be submitted to and approved by the Director of the Department of Planning. A landscape manual has been prepared to illustrate graphically the proper interpretation of the landscape standards.

The planning and zoning board of the city sits as the Parkland Tree Board and enforces the terms of this article. In addition, the Tree Board oversees the cutting, trimming and pruning of trees in the city, as well as replacement of trees removed by permit.

Tree abuse is defined and prohibited by the Parkland Tree Board.

The Board requires that replacement trees be installed on site or on public lands. All replacement trees are to have the largest diameter available in the trade and in no instance be less than three (3) inches in diameter. Replacement is made on the principle that the aggregate sum of the diameters of the replacement trees shall be equal to or greater than the tree removed.

This is a well-balanced and well thought out landscape ordinance.

Pembroke Pines

Pembroke Pines. Landscaping Code, Sections 153.01 through 153.99,
Code of Ordinances, Proposed Ordinance 95-07, n.d.

The landscape code for this small Florida community is organized efficiently in three parts. Part one of the code contains general provisions; part two, standards and requirements; and part three, administration and enforcement.

Part one defines the purpose of the ordinance and sets forth technical definitions. The second part of the code presents information about the technical aspects of compliance. Requirements are given for plant materials, installation and maintenance, as well as the planting of perimeters, parking lots, medians, waterways and storage areas. The final part of this well-crafted ordinance sets forth administrative and enforcement procedures.

The objective of this ordinance is to preserve land values and the particular characteristics and qualities of the city. In addition to promoting the "public health, safety, and general welfare," this ordinance aims to perpetuate "aesthetic appeal" on a citywide basis.

Plant standards are given for trees, shrubs and ground covers. Fifty (50) percent of all plant materials used are to be native and drought resistant to reduce the amount of water used for irrigation. The principles of Xeriscape and a plant material guide developed by the South Florida Water Management District are to be followed.

Irrigation is from nonpotable water sources and can take place only during certain hours of the day. All irrigation systems must be equipped with rain sensors to conserve water.

Other standards in this ordinance include planting requirements, planting adjacent to public rights-of-way and in "district boundary yards" and perimeter landscaping. Parking lot planting requirements use a formula of one (1) tree for each five (5) parking spaces and at least ten (10) square feet of interior parking lot planting for each parking space.

In this community, residentially zoned districts must be landscaped. Single-family land uses must also be planted with one (1) street tree per forty (40) linear feet of frontage. There are lot planting requirements as well. For instance, a typical unit shall have one (1) tree for every fifteen hundred (1,500) square feet, with a minimum of three (3) trees for each unit or a maximum of ten (10) trees per lot. Two (2) accent plants, thirty (30) shrubs and thirty (30) ground covers must be used for each unit. Common areas and totally enclosed privacy areas are also to be landscaped.

In multifamily housing areas, the complete site is required to be landscaped. Plant quantity requirements are based on number of units and the number of stories. In commercial districts, the complete site must be landscaped and plant quantities are based on square feet of gross area. Sites of more than twenty thousand (20,000) square feet use a five thousand (5,000) square foot factor, and sites of more than one million (1,000,000) gross square feet are to be approved by the Planning and Zoning Board.

This community requires plantings along waterways to be in conformance with requirements set forth by the public drainage district. Specific standards for waterfront zone areas are included in this ordinance, as shown in Figure 2.19.

Administration of this ordinance seems simple. No building permit is issued until site development plans are reviewed by the city, and no Certificate of Occupancy will be granted until all landscape improvements have been made. There is an "application for modification" clause inserted in this ordinance that allows developers to seek alternative compliance approval from the Planning and Zoning Board. Appeals to decisions of the Planning and Zoning Board can be taken to the Board of Adjustment, which may affirm, modify or reverse the ruling of the Planning and Zoning Board.

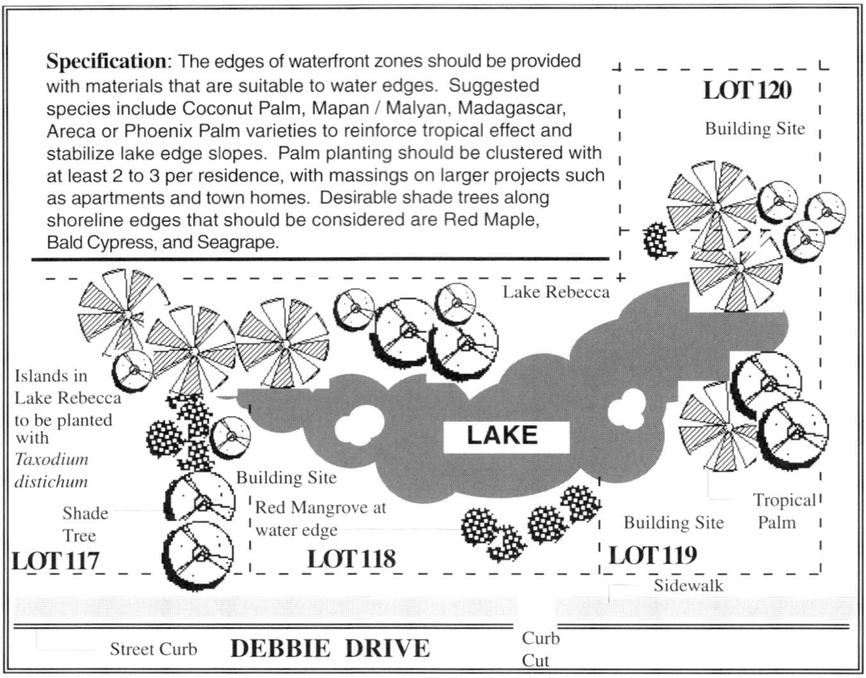

FIGURE 2.19. Waterfront zone planting requirements, Pembroke Pines, Florida.

Certified landscape inspectors employed by the city inspect sites periodically to ensure that proper maintenance is taking place.

Interestingly, this ordinance was recently amended to increase the size of plant materials and the size of areas to be planted in certain land use districts. Few landscape ordinances apply to residential land uses, and fewer require one hundred (100) percent landscaping of a site, and still fewer are as detailed at this.

This ordinance is different in that regard and might well be an example for other communities that want to control landscaping in residential zoning districts.

Plantation

Plantation. "Comprehensive Regulation of Landscaping and Landscaping Requirements." Chapter 13, Code of Ordinances, December 16, 1978, amended January 6, 1988.

The citizens of Plantation, Florida, find that the perpetuation of the special characteristics and aesthetic qualities of the life-style of the community justifies the regulation of landscape treatments and the physical development of the city. To that end, they have enacted through their city council minimum landscape standards, including those that specify landscape materials, installation, maintenance and design requirements.

Design requirements are stated in this ordinance for yard areas, vehicular use areas, parking lots, areas adjacent to public rights-of-way and property perimeters. Points of intersection (sight triangles) and pedestrian zones along building facades are also included as design requirements. Specific reference is made to walls, fences and islands in parking bays.

Specific plant materials are recommended for use in the city, including natives, shade trees, palms and hedge material. Planting standards are based on linear measure, square footage or percent of parking area size. Automatically operated underground irrigation systems are required on all sites except single-family and two-family platted residences.

Permits are required for the removal of any tree with a trunk diameter of more than four (4) inches, except those that are considered prohibited or storm damaged.

Section 13-44 of the ordinance is a comprehensive tree preservation article. It governs the protection of trees and vegetative cover within the city, as well as their replacement. Preserved trees count toward required plantings.

Requirements are given for tree removal. Should trees have to be destroyed for building purposes, the developer may substitute equivalent tree value with an on-site replacement or plant a replacement on public land by contributing to the City of Plantation Tree Program or by contributing to the city's Tree Beautification Program. The latter program allows the developer to contribute an equivalent value in money.

Together these programs constitute the essentials of a tree bank program.

This article also defines accepted standards for tree protection during construction, qualifications of tree services and arborists and removal of damaged, diseased or dead trees.

Tree abuse is defined and prohibited.

Section 13-49 sets forth regulations for city street trees that must conform to the "Master Landscape Plan for the City of Plantation" prepared by Sasaki Associates in 1977. This plan created an Official Street Tree Plan Map, which, by reference, is made part of this ordinance. All commercial and multifamily projects must plant street trees in accordance with the Official Street Tree Plan Map.

The ordinance is enforced by the city code enforcement officer, based on recommendations from the city landscape architect and review by the Landscape Planning and Review Board. Specific drawings and specifications are required at the time that site plan review takes place. The drawings include a layout plan, conceptual grading plan, planting plan, proposed elevations and plans showing overhead utility lines.

Should approval be denied, the City Landscape Planning and Review Board may approve adjustments to the standards if such adjustments would not be contrary to the public interest.

Few cities define design standards and planting requirements for the area between the parking lot and the building. This area, sometimes referred to as the street wall zone or pedestrian planting zone, is meant to prevent paving to the building foundation. This city recognizes that trees and plantings in this area function to visually and aesthetically buffer and enhance the building facade and to reduce air and noise pollution. Plantings in this zone also enhance energy conservation within the structure itself.

The width of this zone is based on the height of the structure. No more than fifty (50) percent of this area may be paved for foot traffic. The use of benches and a seating area is encouraged. The building pedestrian zone is to be planted with a specified number of trees and other nonspecific plantings.

Ordinance No. 1818. Mandatory Tree Planting and Buffering in RS-1EP Zoning Districts, November 13, 1991.

This ordinance adds a new section to the existing landscape code, calling for special tree planting on residential lots in order to preserve the unique residential area of a special interest zoning district in Plantation, Florida.

The purpose of this change to the code is to help maintain a rural appearance, buffering and soil conservation on each residential lot. The owner of each lot is to present a site plan when seeking a building permit, showing a minimum of eight (8) trees if the lot is more than forty thousand (40,000) square feet, and six (6) trees if forty thousand (40,000) square feet or less. Trees are to be planted in the front and side yards to buffer adjacent buildings.

The tree planting plan must be approved by the city landscape architect.

Ordinance No. 1674. Definition, Landscape Architectural Plans, January 10, 1990.

Chapter 481, Part II, Florida Statutes, entitled "Landscape Architecture," was revised, and, subsequently, nurserymen, nursery stock dealers and agents may no longer prepare plans for landscape architecture for approval by local governments. A plan may be prepared only by the person actually owning the property or by a licensed landscape architect, who must sign, date and imprint upon the drawing a seal to certify authenticity and compliance with the city's comprehensive plan.

The definition of "landscape architectural plans" was added to the code. The ordinance reads, in part, "Any landscaped [sic] plans required to be submitted under this Code of Ordinances for governmental approval may only be submitted by the actual person owning the property or by a person registered as a landscape architect in Florida. . . . All plans, specifications, or reports prepared or issued by a registered landscape architect and filed for public record shall be signed by the registered landscape architect, dated and stamped with his seal."

Pompano Beach

Pompano Beach Zoning Code, Section 155.125, "Landscaping," February 6, 1990.

Like many of the landscape ordinances in south Florida, this ordinance combines a postconstruction landscaping ordinance with a tree preservation ordinance and screening and buffering requirements. The intent of the ordinance is to establish standards, such as shown in Figure 2.20, for the installation and maintenance of landscaping and landscaped open green space in the city. By setting these standards, the city hopes to promote environmental quality, preserve and encourage open space and protect the natural beauty of the city through preventing the unnecessary destruction of trees and plant life.

This ordinance applies to all development within the city and will go into effect at such time that a development permit is issued that alters the previous use of any given area of land. All zoning classifications fall under this ordinance, and each classification has slightly different landscaping requirements. Single-family residential zones need not comply with the requirements of this ordinance for vehicular use areas and buffer areas.

Enforcement is achieved through withholding the Certificate of Occupancy until all landscape requirements are met. The Code Enforcement Officer under the Director of Planning and Growth Management is responsible for overseeing compliance with this ordinance.

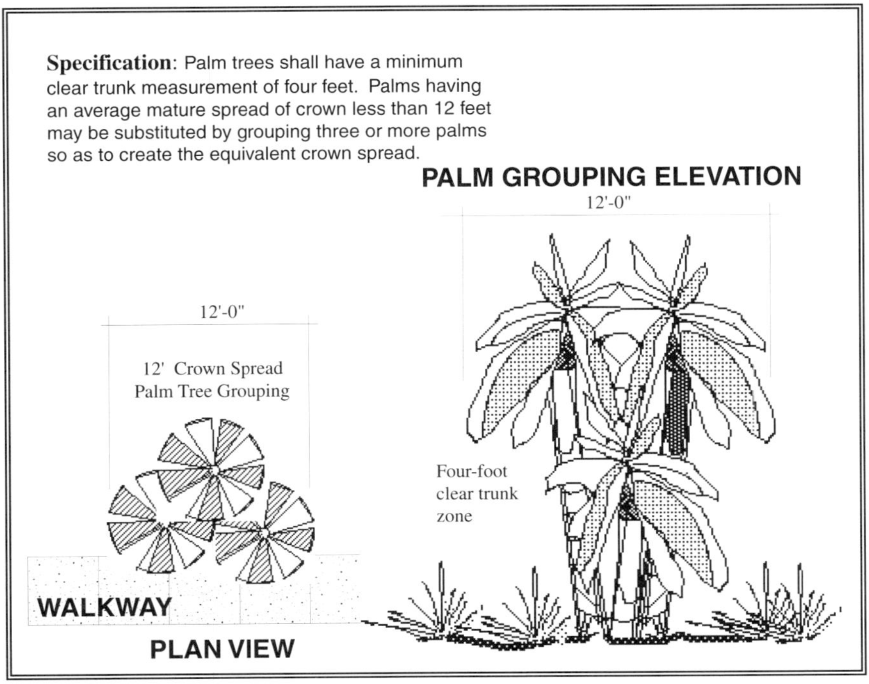

FIGURE 2.20. Palm tree specifications, Pompano Beach, Florida.

Landscape plans illustrating compliance with the ordinance must be submitted for review by the Director of Zoning's office. Quality is ensured by requiring that anyone providing landscape services for hire, especially those who provide inspection, installation, maintenance, design, pruning and removal, be properly licensed. Plans must be prepared, signed and sealed by a Florida registered landscape architect and must include specific technical information in order for the plan reviewers to ascertain whether the design components of the ordinance are being addressed in the design.

Technical standards or performance standards are given for plant materials, installation, maintenance, irrigation, tree protection and tree preservation.

An unusual example of these standards pertains to the size of installed trees. The tree height chart shown in Table 2.35 was developed to ensure that fifty (50) percent of all required trees on a plot be related to the height of the main structure.

By reference, the ordinance indicates that certain accepted principles of practice in south Florida should be followed. These include the use of native vegetation, drought-tolerant plant species and Xeriscape techniques for reducing water consumption and maintenance. Specific components that must be addressed in the design include street trees, open space planting requirements by zoning district, buffer requirements, vehicular use areas, waterway frontage, screening, sight distances at intersections and exterior lighting. These standards are based on linear measure in the case of street trees, unit measure in the case of landscape parking islands, square footage measure in the case of plot size. Plant materials are based on height, spread, caliper, container size and grade. Topsoil and mulch are based on depth, and berms are based upon height and slope. Irrigation is based on percentage of coverage.

Widths of buffers and perimeters are generally ten (10) feet, whereas vehicular use areas must reserve fifteen (15) percent of area for landscaping. Five (5) feet of landscape area will separate vehicular use areas from single-story buildings. An additional five (5) feet must be added for each additional story, up to a maximum landscape width of twenty-five (25) feet. Outdoor storage areas must be screened on seventy-five (75) percent of the perimeter, and trash receptacles must be enclosed with a six (6)-foot masonry wall and an opaque access gate.

TABLE 2.35. Tree Height Chart, Pompano Beach, Florida

Height of Structure	*Shade and Ornamental Tree Height and Spread*	*Palm Height/ Clear Trunk Measurement*
To 15 feet	12 feet; 6 feet	14 feet; 4 feet
15 to 25 feet	14 feet; 7 feet	18 feet; 8 feet
26 feet or more	16 feet; 8 feet	22 feet; 14 feet

This ordinance has special language creating what might be called a "police surveillance view zone." This open view zone is to occur above the top of thirty-six (36)-inch hedges and below the bottom limbs of trees. Limbs cannot be lower than six (6) feet. Landscape architects who prepare the plans must specify the proper plant materials, and property owners must maintain a clear view into a property abutting a public right-of-way. This will enable police officers on patrol to see into the site.

This ordinance is very specific and covers all of the normal concerns of a contemporary landscape ordinance. Reading the ordinance is somewhat difficult because of the way requirements seem to run together. Reorganization into a structure that clearly differentiates the code between the contextual, technical and administrative requirements would be helpful. The city does make available a landscape manual that provides graphic and illustrative interpretation of the code requirements therein.

Sanford

Zoning Ordinance, "Schedule J, Landscape, Buffer and Tree Requirements," n.d.

This community favors trees and landscape features as a necessary part of the built environment. It is important that landscaping provide visual and climatic relief from buildings, urban structures, broad expanses of paving and vehicular traffic. This landscape ordinance, which applies to all premises, is intended to preserve trees, provide shade, scenic beauty and natural habitat. Sanford has developed several performance-based design standards, such as shown in Table 2.36, to assist with this endeavor.

This ordinance requires general canopy plantings, planting of off-street and vehicular use areas, street edges and buffers between properties.

Quantities are based on unit measure, linear feet and square foot measure.

TABLE 2.36. Design Standards, Sanford, Florida

Enhance the urban development by blending natural and man-made environments.
Provide shade for paved surfaces.
Separate vehicular and nonvehicular use areas.
Define vehicular access ways and access points.
Screen vehicular movement, noise and glare from public view.
Provide visual and physical separation of potentially incompatible land uses.
Incorporate water conservation features such as drought-tolerant landscaping and reclaimed water use.

Standards are given for tree protection and preservation, maintenance, installation and drought-tolerant plants. Appendix A to the ordinance provides a list of drought-tolerant species.

A site development permit is required prior to any action to directly, or indirectly, cut down, remove, relocate or damage any living tree situated on sites in the city. Criteria for seeking this permit are explained in the ordinance, as is the procedure to make application.

South Florida

South Florida Water Management District, "Development of a Model Landscape Code for South Florida," Schnelle, J.F., 1986.
South Florida, "Model Landscape Code for South Florida," South Florida Water Management District, 1986.

A model landscape code was created for South Florida late in 1986. The code was created by the Model Landscape Code Advisory Committee, comprised of special-interest groups, governmental units, and recognized professionals interested in water conservation through creative landscaping and irrigation techniques.

It was the initial mission of the Advisory Committee, working with a consultant engineer and landscape architecture firm, to promote economic and efficient water use, protect and conserve water resources, encourage the use of drought- and flood-tolerant plant materials and establish standards for landscape installation and maintenance.

The model landscape code was developed by the twelve (12)-member Advisory Committee meeting on a periodic basis. Its objective was to achieve public participation and to work in a participatory manner with the project consultant. In this capacity, the Committee functioned as a vehicle for incorporating community and special interest values into the landscape code development process. In addition, the Advisory Committee was to provide input to the preparation of standards for landscaping/installation and maintenance and to an implementation methodology for code adoption.

The results of the Advisory Committee's work was a model landscape code and a set of supplemental guidelines.

St. Lucie County

St. Lucie County Code, Section 7.09.00, "Landscaping and Screening," August 1, 1990.

In St. Lucie County the installation and maintenance of landscaping is regulated for a variety of environmental, aesthetic and land value reasons. The ordinance applies to all nonresidential uses as well as mobile home parks and subdivision and multifamily residential districts. Two-family and three-family land developments must comply with selected sections (general open space planting) of the law.

Standards are cited for installation, maintenance and plant materials. Plant material standards cover quality, species mix, prohibited plants, and native plant usage. Further, plant standards cover trees, palms, shrubs, hedges, vines, ground covers, lawn grass and synthetic lawns and plants. Finally, "water wise" site design standards are listed for the use of native and drought-tolerant vegetation, which include those shown in Table 2.37.

Design components include landscaping adjacent to public rights-of-way, perimeters to abutting properties, parking area interiors, visibility points of access and buffers between nonresidential and residential land uses. In addition, off-street loading spaces, waste storage areas and above-ground irrigation fixtures (backflow preventers) are design concerns of this ordinance.

This ordinance contains an alternative compliance provision that calls for one and one-half ($1\frac{1}{2}$) times the amount of landscape area and plant material if the

TABLE 2.37. Water-Wise Site Design Standards, St. Lucie County, Florida

Standard	*Expected Result or Reason*
50% of min. landscaping shall be drought-tolerant vegetation.	Reduces water needs.
100% of lawn grasses shall be drought-tolerant vegetation.	Reduces irrgation of lawns.
Group plant materials by water needs.	Reduces overwatering.
Group plant materials by microclimate needs.	Reduces overwatering.
Illustrate water usage zones on site plan.	Controls water distribution.
Use ground covers in strips eight feet wide or less.	Contols overspray and runoff.
Use three-inch depth of mulch.	Reduces evaporation from soil.
Mulch 100% of planting bed.	Reduces need for grass and water.
Alternative Method of Meeting Standard	
Preservation of 25% or more of existing site	Eliminates water-wise requirements.
Preservation of 15%–25% of existing site	Water-wise requirements limited to 30% of req. plant material.
Preservation of 1%–15% of existing site	Water-wise requirements limited to 40% of req. plant material.

applicant for a landscape permit cannot meet the literal application of this law or its general spirit and intent.

St. Petersburg

St. Petersburg, Chapter 31½, Landscaping for Vehicular Use Areas, July 2, 1992.

The purpose of this ordinance is to improve the appearance, environment, character and value of the urban area; to reduce storm water runoff; to reduce impervious surface area; to implement Xeriscaping; and to protect nearby properties. All vehicular use areas in the City of St. Petersburg, except those serving single-family and duplex residential uses, must conform to these requirements. All new development or redevelopment requires a landscape permit to be obtained from the City Manager prior to the paving of a vehicular use area. Landscaping materials must meet these code requirements before a Certificate of Occupancy can be obtained. No landscape architect or other professional is required to prepare the plans.

The major requirements of this ordinance are perimeter landscaping requirements, interior landscaping requirements, off-site replacement of required trees, Xeriscape requirements, encouraged Xeriscape techniques, sight distance restrictions at intersections, existing plant material, and screening of backflow preventers.

This ordinance is unique in that it does not require different standards for different zones. Requirements for all vehicular use perimeters include a buffer strip averaging three (3) feet in width, except for planting areas, which are to be a minimum of five (5) feet in width. They must include one (1) tree for every three (3) parking spaces or thirty (30) feet along the perimeter. If the strip is adjacent to a residential land use, the buffer strip must include a decorative, painted, masonry wall with hedges or vines in order to screen the vehicular use area.

A "vehicular use area," in this ordinance, is defined as all areas used for the circulation, parking and/or display of any and all types of vehicles, boats or heavy construction equipment, whether self-propelled or not, and all land upon which vehicles transverse as a function of their primary uses, including parking lot driveways. This is to include, but is not limited to, areas of a drive-in nature, such as areas used in connection with but not limited to service stations, convenience stores, banks, restaurants and the like. Only driveways and parking spaces serving single-family and duplex uses will be exceptions to this definition.

Sunrise

Sunrise. Functional Landscaping, Article X, Subpart B, Land Development Code, Ord. No. 402, November 27, 1990.

The Sunrise code was established to promote the functional landscaping of rights-of-way and private sites. The code provides for the protection of existing trees, energy conservation and standards for new landscaping. Tree abuse is defined, and other definitions are given in the code.

All land uses except single family home sites must submit a landscaping plan in conjunction with the site plan by those seeking a building permit. The landscape plan must be rendered by a registered landscape architect.

Specific plant standards, irrigation design requirements and planting procedures are not listed in the code. Rather, mention is made of standards promulgated by others. Planting procedures are prescribed by the American Society of Landscape Architects. Irrigation standards follow minimum requirements set forth by the South Florida Water Management District. Plant material standards follow Grades and Standards for Nursery Plants of the Florida Department of Agriculture. Pruning must follow guidelines of the National Arborists Association.

General design requirements are given for street trees, access ways, landscape strips adjacent to streets, perimeters, canal or road separations, land use buffers between business uses, parking area interiors and pedestrian zones. Special requirements apply to specific zoning districts.

Section 16-166 sets forth tree preservation requirements. In Sunrise, the preservation of trees is integral to the prevention of air and water pollution, in that trees use their leaf surface to trap and filter out ash, dust and pollen in the air. Root systems hold and consolidate soil and other loose earthen materials.

Tree destruction is a public nuisance that must be controlled. Priority is given to preservation, relocation, replacement and payment into the City Reforestation Fund.

In order to get a tree removal permit, the developer or owner must make application, describe the work to be constructed, submit a certified Tree Survey and Site Plan drawing and pay an appropriate permit fee.

This ordinance establishes the City Reforestation Account. This account is set up to accept revenues and pay expenses associated with tree replacement fees and tree removal permits. Funds will be used to obtain trees, landscaping, sprinkler systems and any other items or materials necessary for the preservation, maintenance, relocation or restoration of tree ecosystems for any public lands in the city.

Tamarac

Tamarac Code, Section 11, "Landscaping," n.d.

The ordinance strives to improve the community's appearance by providing for the installation and maintenance of trees and shrubs, and to make urban life more comfortable by providing shade and reducing noise and carbon dioxide. The ordinance states that trees "are known as producers of oxygen as well as beauty in the community."

A brief list of definitions includes such words as *swale* and *encroachment*. Concerning planting, the ordinance accepts the planting procedures of the Florida Cooperative Extension Service, South Florida Water Management District's Xeriscape principles and the "Tree Protection Manual for Builders and Developers" by the Florida Department of Agriculture, Division of Forestry. An approved plant list for the city is included. Developers must submit a landscape plan for approval. Tamarac requires replacement trees and proper maintenance. The ordinance outlines the conditions of "tree abuse," such as hatracking and stripping bark, and sets fines for violations (two hundred fifty (250) dollars and up).

Owners and occupants of single-family and two-family residences in the city must maintain the front yard as a lawn.

Tampa

Land Development Code, Chapter 13, Article 1, Section 13.1. "City of Tampa Landscaping, Tree Removal and Site Clearing Ordinance," Ord. No. 89-262, October 12, 1989.
Originally, Ord. No. 6481-A, adopted September 21, 1976.

This is one of the earliest ordinances in this study. Enacted in 1976 and amended in 1989, it is a good example of a comprehensive landscape ordinance. Comprehensive landscape ordinances regulate not only landscaping but tree removal, land clearing and modification to natural resources. The Tampa landscape ordinance occurs in a Chapter of the Tampa Code which is organized in three (3) distinct parts or "Articles." The articles cover general provisions and authority; administration and appeals; and technical requirements. Each article is further broken down into "Divisions" and "Sections."

The purpose of the ordinance is to protect trees, wetlands and other natural resources by regulating the trimming and removal of trees, tree planting, site clearing and landscaping. Specific standards are presented for site clearing, as can be seen in Figure 2.21.

The ordinance is administered by the Parks Department.

Landscape and tree planting plans must be prepared by registered landscape architects to satisfy the plan preparation requirements of this ordinance. Plans are submitted at several stages of land development. They include the conceptual stage, final plat stage and construction phase. Several design incentives are listed to encourage protection of and preservation of existing native habitat. They include such incentives as given in Table 2.38.

Standards or requirements for various zoning districts include minimum amount of landscape area, minimum number of recommended trees and additional landscape requirements. Other standards cover plant materials, wetlands protection, tree protection and tree removal.

Technical standards are kept to a minimum in this ordinance, most likely as a result of setting high qualifications for the registered landscape architects who prepare the landscape plans, tree surveys and permit applications. In fact, the emphasis of the ordinance seems to be on performance backed by strict enforcement, rather than unduly burdensome detail covering each issue of site design.

This is one of the most well organized ordinances in this study. It is broken down into sections of commonalty, with an index making it very easy to find the

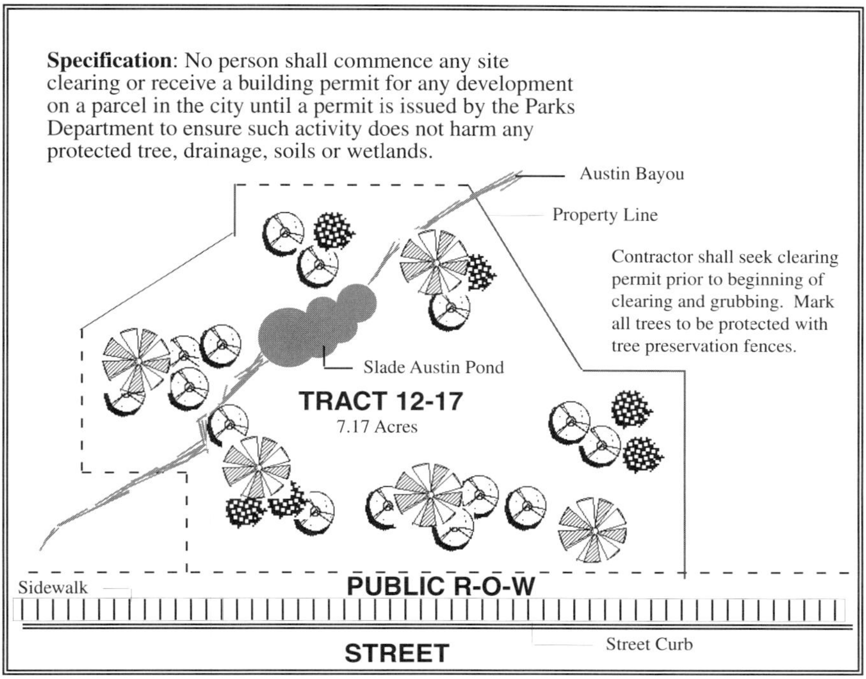

FIGURE 2.21. Site clearing permit and specifications, Tampa, Florida.

TABLE 2.38. Design Incentives, Tampa, Florida

Incentive	*Cost Savings*
Reduction in vehicular use buffers	Reduce screening costs by eliminating materials
Reduction in interior landscape islands	Reduce size and cost of parking areas, easier construction
Full credit toward tree planting requirements	Reduce cost of materials, planting and maintenance
Exemption from permanent irrigation systems	Reduce cost of system, water and maintenance
Other "alternative forms of compliance"	Reductions in other costs, provide attractive alternatives

information you are seeking. The basis of organization covers contextual, technical and administrative aspects of the ordinance. It may also be noted that this ordinance goes into great detail concerning its administration. This ordinance would provide a good model for communities that would like to establish an efficient organization for assisting developers and reviewing, approving and regulating landscaping and land development.

Related Document, Parks Department Manual, "Site Clearing, Tree Removal and Landscape Technical Manual," March 1989.

The Tampa landscape ordinance grants authority to develop technical standards and administrative guidelines when necessary to assist with the orderly administration of this law. The "Site Clearing, Tree Removal and Landscape Technical Manual," referred to here as the "manual," is a compendium of technical ordinance requirements, policy statements and landscape industry accepted standards. The document gives technical information concerning permits, landscaping, right-of-way tree trimming, land clearing, subdivision review and tree protection. The document is illustrated with graphics, tables, diagrams and sample permit applications.

Vero Beach

"Landscaping and Tree Protection, 72.02, City of Vero Beach," 1984.

This ordinance is intended to encourage reduced energy consumption and conservation of water by regulating existing and proposed landscaping. Off-street parking perimeters adjacent to public rights-of-way ten (10) feet in width require one (1) tree for every fifty (50) linear feet, a continuous hedge and ground covers. A strip five (5) feet in width between off-street parking and abutting property requires one (1) tree every forty (40) lineal feet, a continuous hedge and ground covers.

Off-street parking requires a one hundred (100)-square foot planter island at the end of each row in the lot. Fifteen (15) square feet of planter island are required for each parking space, and one (1) tree for every two hundred twenty-five (225) square feet, the remainder covered with ground covers. One (1) tree is required for every twenty-five hundred (2,500) square feet of open space in excess of the aforementioned requirements, as well as a continuous hedge and ground covers. The ordinance defines *large scale canopy tree, hedges* and *ground covers*.

Article III of the ordinance concerns tree protection and its regulatory process. Article IV lists drought-tolerant vegetation, trees to be preserved and undesirable trees.

Volusia County

Appendix B, Zoning Ordinance, Article VII, Supplementary Regulations, Section 808.00, "Landscaping Requirements," 1994.

This is a limited-issue ordinance.

It pertains to off-street parking areas, landscape buffers and refuse screening. Standards and requirements are given in the ordinance, such as shown in Table 2.39, for plant materials, landscape plan and irrigation plan preparation, buffer requirements by land use category and maintenance.

The buffer requirements are illustrated by zoning districts in tabular form. The table shows the zoning classification of the proposed development, the adjoining land use, minimum landscape buffer area in width and required landscape materials. The latter may include perimeter boundary trees and or a visual screen. Special provisions apply to rivers, canal banks, lakes and the Atlantic Ocean.

Planting requirements are minimum and are based on linear, square footage area and unit measure.

The use of native drought resistant plant materials is encouraged. The City Growth Management and Environmental Services Center maintains an approved Plant Materials List.

TABLE 2.39. Design Standards for Off-Street Parking Areas, Volusia County, Florida

Standard	*Requirement*
GENERAL	
Applies	Eight or more parking spaces
Amount of required area	Ten percent of total paved area
Maximum spacing between islands	Two hundred linear feet
ISLANDS	
Minimum size end of row	One hundred seventy-five square feet
Minimum width end of row	Ten feet in width
Minimum length end of row	17. 5 feet abuts one space, 35 feet abuts two spaces
Minimum size internal island	One hundred square feet
MATERIAL REQUIREMENTS	
Trees	Minimum of one 1½ inch caliper, six feet tall
Shrubs	No quanties or other specifications stated
Ground covers or grass	No quanties or other specifications stated
Other materials	Stone, gravel or mulch top dressing

Georgia

Alpharetta

Zoning Ordinance, "Standards for the Protection and Preservation of Trees," April 12,1992.

Tree protection and preservation ordinances are quite common in the metro Atlanta area. Some of the major highways in the area, such as the Turner McDonald Parkway (Georgia 400), have set aside one hundred twenty (120)-foot tree protection zones that give the area that leafy green look that travelers notice when passing through the city.

The community has enacted this ordinance to prevent the indiscriminate removal of trees and to encourage the preservation, planting and replacement of others for the many benefits that are mentioned in the ordinance.

A tree commission of seven (7) citizens is created and tree permits are required. All trees in the city fall under this ordinance except those on single family lots or those on a list of exemptions, which include dead, dangerous or diseased trees, and trees presenting problems to utilities or rights-of-way.

Applications are submitted to the administrator along with a tree survey and inventory and additional information. Among the information required on the drawings is a delineation of tree-save areas, locations of specimen trees, and calculations showing compliance with the required "site density factor." In this community all zoning districts must maintain a tree coverage density of twenty (20) units per acre even if no tree lived on the site prior to development.

The required density can be achieved by preserving existing trees, replacing trees or planting new trees.

To determine whether a site meets the density requirement (twenty (20) units per acre of net site area), one must make an inventory of each existing and proposed tree from the landscape plan, convert their diameters (DBH) to Density Factor Units (DFU) using Table 2.40, and then subtract both Existing Density Units (EDU) and Replacement Density Units (RDU) from the Site Density Factor (SDF). (SDF – EDF – RDF = or >20 units per net acre).

To determine the number of replacement trees needed to replant a site simply subtract the Existing Density Factor from the Site Density Factor (RDF = SDF – EDF). Table 2.41 can be used to determine the number and composition of diameters of trees that must be planted in order to meet the Replacement Density Factor requirement.

If 2.2 DFU are needed to bring the SDF to 20 units per acre, then plant three (3)-inch trees; one two (2)-inch tree; and one one (1)-inch tree for a total of six (6) trees.

$$(3 \times 0.6) + (1 \times 0.3) + (1 \times 0.1) = 2.2$$

The ordinance contains tree preservation standards, replanting standards and sections dealing with permit fees, appeal procedures, and nonliability protection for the city.

TABLE 2.40. Conversion of Tree Diameters (DBH) to Density Factor Units, Alpharetta, Georgia

Size Class	*Diameters*	*Density Factor Unit (DFU) Value*
1	1″–4″	0.1
2	5″–8″	0.3
3	9″–12″	0.6
4	13″–16″	1.2
5	17″–20″	1.9
6	21″–24″	2.8
7	25″–28″	3.8
8	29″–32″	5.1
9	33″–36″	6.5
10	37″–40″	8.1

TABLE 2.41. Conversion of Replacement Tree Caliper to Density Factor Units, Alpharetta, Georgia

Caliper Size in Inches	*Density Factor Unit (DFU) Value*
1″	0.1
2″	0.3
3″	0.6
4″	1.2
5″	1.9
6″	2.8
7″	3.8
8″	5.1
9″	6.5
10″	8.1

The ordinance contains technical appendixes to help the reader calculate tree density, determine whether a tree is specimen, and convert tree diameters to density factors. A list of recommended overstory and understory trees is attached.

Americus

Americus. Article XI, "Landscaping," Americus Zoning Code, as amended September 28, 1992, and December 21, 1995.

This ordinance does not apply to agriculture zoned districts or to single family or duplex family developments. It does apply to all other zoning districts for either new development or redevelopment. As amended, the ordinance does not apply to churches, public, private and parochial schools or federal, state and other governmental entities.

Certain standards, often called design requirements in this document, are specified for the design and installation of landscaping. They include off street parking and vehicular use areas, sight triangles, utility service areas, outdoor storage areas and perimeter planting areas.

The standards are based on percentages, unit numbers, linear measure and square footage. As amended, most of the standards are reduced. This has the effect of making compliance more cost-efficient for developers. For instance, the front perimeter was reduced from ten (10) feet to five (5) feet, and side and rear perimeter strips were reduced from six (6) feet to three (3) feet. Also, as amended, "triggers" were added to further limit compliance. For instance, front perimeters need not be included on off-street parking areas of less than two thousand (2,000) square feet in size or on existing off-street parking areas of less than one hundred fifty (150) spaces or fifty thousand (50,000) square feet.

In some cases more specific design criteria were added. For instance, tree planting in the front perimeter strip uses the ratio of one (1) tree for each thirty (30) linear feet of frontage, or one (1) tree for each four hundred eighty (480) square feet of interior landscape area.

Should meeting these standards not be possible, there is provision in this ordinance for alternative design or installation consistent with the objectives of the ordinance. Alternative compliance must be demonstrated to be consistent with the objectives of the ordinance. Written application for variance must be filed with the City Building Inspector for a hearing before the Zoning Board of Appeals.

In all situations a landscape plan must be submitted for review.

Compliance is ensured by withholding a building permit, Certificate of Occupancy or city business license or by requiring that a performance bond be posted.

It would be interesting to know the complete story about the evolution of this ordinance. From what has been reviewed here, one must conclude that the design standards specified in the original ordinance were reduced in response to pressure from some interest group.

Dalton

Dalton. City of Dalton Tree Ordinance, City Code of Ordinances, December 17, 1990. Amended.

This ordinance is an example of a tree management ordinance later amended and combined with landscaping requirements and tree preservation requirements. It is a hybrid ordinance that combines tree management, tree preservation and post-construction landscaping requirements.

The original ordinance establishes a program regulating the planting, maintenance and removal of plants within the city. The ordinance creates a city Tree

Board and provides for the appointment of a professional to act as City Arborist. Further, the ordinance requires licensing and insuring of persons engaging in the business of planting, pruning, cutting and spraying plant materials within the city. It defines public trees and injury to trees and sets forth penalties for damage or destruction of trees on public land.

An amendment to the ordinance expands the authority of the city to private property. This amendment applies to all property within the city exclusive of single-family and duplex family property and property which, as altered, requires no addition of square footage or exterior renovation. This amendment provides very basic landscaping requirements. They include perimeter planting requirements and internal planting requirements.

Perimeter planting must take place in an eight (8)-foot wide strip abutting the public right-of-way, sometimes known as the "treelawn." Planting requirements call for the planting of one (1) large maturing tree every forty (40) feet or one (1) small maturing tree every thirty (30) feet on center. Existing sites, even if paved, must be brought into compliance when a renovation building permit is required. Cutouts of a minimum of eighty (80) square feet with a minimum dimension of five (5) feet must be provided along an existing paved perimeter.

Internal planting requirements affect parking lots and general site planting. Whenever impervious cover exceeds ten thousand (10,000) square feet, an area equal to five (5) percent of the surface must be provided for landscaping purposes. Internal tree planting must be provided at the rate of one (1) tree per ten thousand (10,000) square feet of impervious cover. Trees must be planted within parking areas so that no parking space is farther from a tree than ninety (90) linear feet.

No tree larger than eight (8) inches diameter at breast height (DBH) may be removed from the tree protection zone of a site without a permit. The tree protection zone is that part of the site defined as a distance equal to a designated zoning district setback. No site grading may take place here without a tree removal permit. In order to receive this permit, the applicant for a building permit must submit a tree survey and a tree protection and planting plan. However, if a permit is granted, there is no requirement in this ordinance for replacement. Specifications for a tree survey are shown in Figure 2.22.

Few specifications are given for plant materials other than caliper and height. The City Arborist provides a list of approved city trees. Fifty (50) percent of all trees planted must be larger maturing trees, and only small maturing trees may be planted within twenty (20) feet of a utility line.

Variances with alternative compliance are allowed under this ordinance. The ordinance is administered by the City Building Inspector, with general oversight provided by the City Tree Board. The City Building Inspector is the enforcement officer and is responsible for inspecting sites and issuing permits. Appeals are heard before the Zoning Board of Appeals.

This ordinance in its inception was clearly adapted from the model Standard Municipal Ordinance published in the classic urban forestry handbook, "Municipal Tree Manual," a publication of the International Society of Arborists and the

Specification: Tree Survey Required. Applications for grading, building and change of use permits on all property, except that which is excluded by Section 3-1, shall provide a tree survey that shall include all trees of eight-inch DBH and larger within the tree protection zone (zoning district setback area) and all trees over one (1) inch caliper and six (6) feet in height on the city right-of-way. Stands of southern yellow pine species may be indicated by groups with average tree DBH.

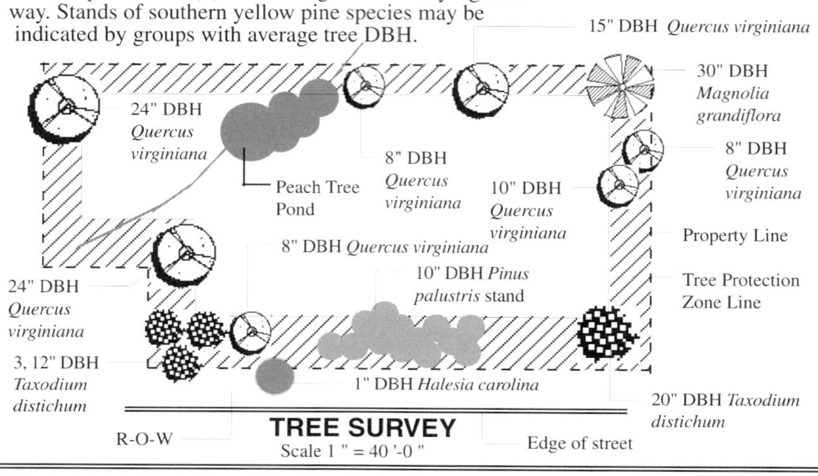

FIGURE 2.22. Tree survey requirements, Dalton, Georgia.

Municipal Arborists and Urban Foresters Society Associations. This model ordinance has been edited for conditions in Dalton and revised to include landscaping and tree preservation.

From the perspective of this book, this is indeed an interesting ordinance. It is interesting because this Georgia city has found a way, primarily by evolution based on need, perhaps, to combine the three types of landscape ordinances into one comprehensive ordinance that provides for tree management, tree preservation and postconstruction landscaping. The ordinance is not well crafted, is not very detailed and has missing elements, but none-the-less it is an example of what may happen in many American communities when they evolve tree management ordinances into postconstruction landscape ordinances, or even into tree preservation or land alteration ordinances.

Gwinnett County

Gwinnett County Zoning Resolution, "Buffer, Landscape and Tree Ordinance," September 22, 1992.

This ordinance is referred to locally as the "BLT ordinance." It regulates buffers, landscape and trees and is administered by the Department of Planning and Development.

The intent of the ordinance is to enhance the county's natural environment though tree protection, tree preservation, the planting of trees and other landscape material and the provision of natural and/or planted buffers between dissimilar uses. A prime goal of this ordinance is to ensure that on all development sites where trees are removed, a uniform standard of tree coverage will be achieved upon project completion.

Tree protection standards are specified in the ordinance, some of which are shown in Figure 2.23.

Design components of this ordinance include buffers, landscape strips along street rights-of-way and off-street parking areas.

Buffers are to be of such nature and density as to screen dissimilar zoning districts. Buffers must meet the minimum width requirements contained in the zoning resolution for each zoning district defined therein. Buffers may be constructed of evergreen trees, shrubs, fences, berms, walls or some combination. Buffer trees

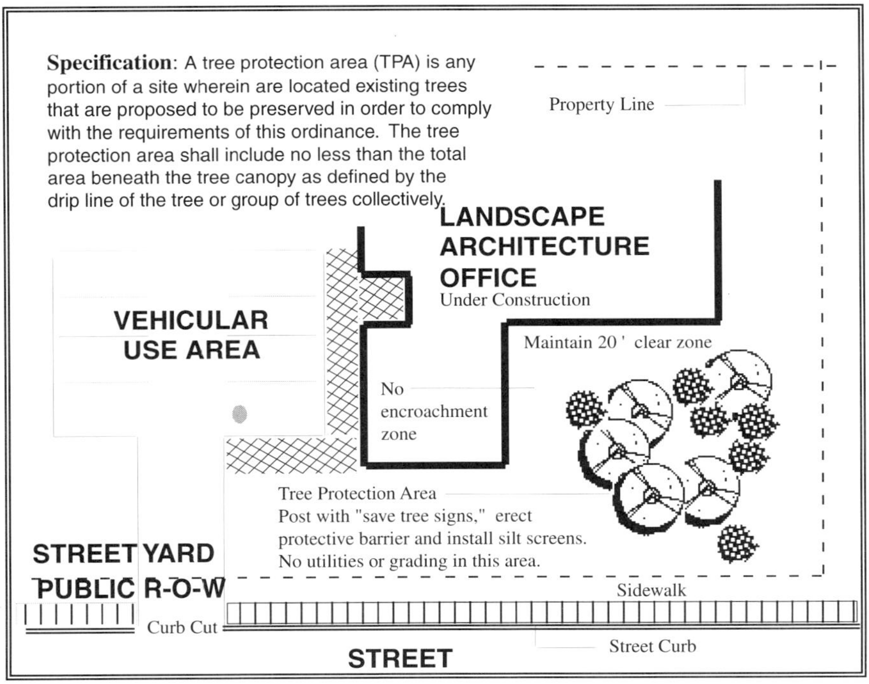

FIGURE 2.23. Tree protection area, Gwinnett County, Georgia.

are to be six (6) feet tall at planting and must grow to a height of twenty (20) feet at maturity.

In parking areas, one (1) tree is to be provided on the perimeter for each five (5) parking spaces, and one (1) tree planted in the interior for each ten (10) parking spaces. Ground areas are to be sodded, planted in ground cover or covered with other landscape materials.

Landscape strips are to be either five (5) or ten (10) feet in width, based on zoning designations. Plantings within these strips are based on a unit per linear foot ratio. The greater part of this ordinance is devoted to tree preservation and tree replacement. Tree preservation requirements apply to all land in which a Land Disturbance Permit is required, with several exceptions. Exceptions include single and duplex family zoning districts, agricultural operations, timber harvesting and dead, diseased and infested trees.

Existing trees and proposed trees in required landscape buffers cannot be credited toward the requirements of the tree density standards. Certain easements may be deducted from the site area requirements as well.

A Tree Preservation/Replacement Plan, herein after called the tree plan, must be submitted for review in order to receive a Clearing, Grubbing, Grading or Development Permit.

Each site must contain suitable tree plantings to achieve the minimum tree density requirement established by this ordinance. Existing trees may be retained and new trees planted so that the property shall attain a Tree Density Standard (TDS) of sixteen (16) Tree Density Units (TDU) per acre of net site area. The trees, both existing and new, are to be distributed throughout the site, grouped where possible to achieve aesthetic effects.

Tree density is calculated by adding all tree credits for new and preserved trees, dividing by the total acreage of the project site, excluding any areas included within zoning buffers. Trees in these areas do not receive credit.

Credit for existing trees is based on DBH, and the Tree Density Unit is determined as shown in Table 2.42. Credit for proposed trees is based on DBH, and the Tree Density Unit is determined as shown in Table 2.43. Trees under one (1) inch in caliper do not receive credit and the largest trunk on a multitrunk tree is used to determine credit units. Additional credits (3 × unit) are given for preserving "specimen trees" having historic value, for rare or unique trees and for trees preserved in floodplains.

Standards are given for establishing tree protection areas and erecting protective barriers. Encroachment is prohibited, and any protected trees that are damaged must be replaced.

Specifications are listed for water-efficient design and for preparation of the required Buffer and Landscape Plan, Tree Preservation/Replacement Plan, Grading Plan and Summary (Plant Schedule). Landscape architects are authorized to prepare these drawings.

This ordinance emphasizes tree preservation rather than design. It could be strengthened by placing additional emphasis on design. Some of the technical

TABLE 2.42. Credit for Existing Trees (conversion from tree diameter in inches to Tree Density Units for tree preserved on-site), Gwinnett County, Georgia

DBH	*Units*	*DBH*	*Units*	*DBH*	*Units*	*DBH*	*Units*
3″	.05	15″	1.2	27″	4.0	39″	8.3
4	.1	16	1.4	28	4.3	40	8.7
5	.15	17	1.6	29	4.6	41	9.2
6	.2	18	1.8	30	4.9	42	9.6
7	.3	19	2.0	31	5.2	43	10.1
8	.4	20	2.2	32	5.6	44	10.6
9	.5	21	2.4	33	5.9	45	11.0
10	.6	22	2.6	34	6.3	46	11.5
11	.7	23	2.9	35	6.7	47	12.0
12	.8	24	3.1	36	7.1	48	12.6
13	.9	25	3.4	37	7.5	49	13.1
14	1.1	26	3.7	38	7.9	50	13.6

TABLE 2.43. Credit for Replacement Trees (conversion from tree diameter in inches to Tree Density Units for proposed replacement trees), Gwinnett County, Georgia

Diameter	*Units*	*Diameter*	*Units*
1″	.4	8″	1.3
2	.5	9	1.5
3	.6	10	1.7
4	.7	11	1.9
5	.9	12	2.1
6	1.0	13	2.3
7	1.2	14	2.5

spacing standards, for instance, are just not correct. The ordinance in total is very well organized and administratively explained.

The tree protection and site density requirement provisions of this ordinance should be considered as a model for other areas that do not set minimum density standards.

Oconee County

Zoning Ordinance, Article X, "Off Street Automobile Parking, Loading and Unloading Spaces," May 2, 1996.

This is a very minimal, limited-issue landscape ordinance requiring planting of parking areas and buffers along major arterial streets and in commercial and industrial developments that abut residential properties. It encourages developers to preserve all trees in these areas with trunks over five (5) inches caliper. No enforcement procedure is indicated, although a landscape and maintenance plan must be submitted to and approved by the Planning Director.

Savannah/Chatham County

Relatively new ordinances are being drafted at this time. The reader is urged to contact these communities directly to secure copies of the new ordinances.

Hawaii

Honolulu

Chapter 21, Revised Ordinances of Honolulu, Land Use Ordinance, § 3.80, "Landscaping and Screening," 1990.

The purpose of zoning in Honolulu is to regulate land use in a manner that will encourage orderly development and protect the public health, safety and welfare. The landscape and screening sections of the ordinance do this, in part, by minimizing adverse effects resulting from location, use, site design and structures. In addition, this ordinance directly contributes to conserving the city's natural and scenic resources, an important need of this community that is visited by thousands upon thousands of tourists each year.

This ordinance applies to a select list of land uses only. All parking lots, automobile service stations, service and loading spaces, trash enclosures, utility substations and rooftop machinery must be landscaped. Special standards are given for providing shade in parking lots, as shown in Figure 2.24.

Design components include VUA interiors, VUA perimeters, service areas, loading areas and refuse storage. All plantings must have permanent irrigation systems. Minimum plant material standards apply.

Honolulu has several special districts that are addressed in its land use ordinance, for instance, Chinatown, the Capitol District, the Punchbowl, Waikiki and Diamond Head. These districts all have special landscape requirements and design controls. For example, in the well-known Waikiki district design controls include street tree plantings, gateways, reserved sight lines, pedestrian circulation systems and miniparks.

There are prohibitions on removal of all trees six (6) inches in caliper in this district, and all trees used must be from an approved list, samples of which are listed in Table 2.44.

There are few other items of merit in this ordinance.

This is the only ordinance in this study that regulates the screening of rooftop machinery.

Specification: To provide shade in open parking lots and minimize visibility of paved surfaces, parking lots with more than 10 parking stalls shall be planted with two-inch caliper trees for each six parking stalls or one six-inch canopy tree for each 12 parking stalls. The tree well should be no less than nine square feet. A five-foot landscape strip with continuous 36-inch hedges shall screen parking from the street.

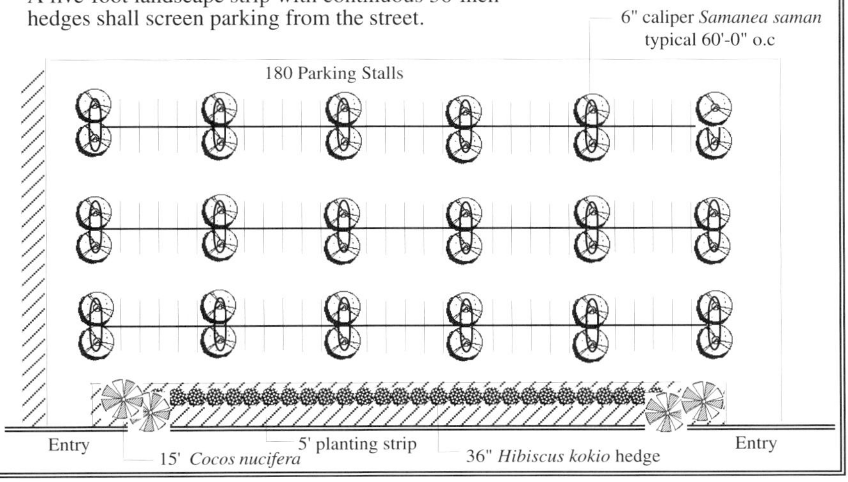

FIGURE 2.24. Parking lot shading and screening, Honolulu, Hawaii.

TABLE 2.44. Acceptable Street Trees—Haleiwa District, Honolulu, Hawaii

African Mimusops	Autograph
Coconut	False Olive
Fern Tree	Golden Rain Tree
Hong Kong Orchid	Indian Coral
Loulu Palm	Madagascar Olive
Mahogany	Monkeypod
Royal Palm	Royal Poinciana
Tamarind	True Kamani
True Kou	Wiliwili

Illinois

Arlington Heights, Village of

Village Code, Excerpts Chapters 20, 28, 29, "Requirements for Landscape Approval," 1991.

Reducing negative impacts is the stated purpose of the landscape ordinance in this community. This ordinance consists of both tree preservation and postconstruction landscaping provisions. The citation preceding this paragraph refers to a landscape manual that summarizes relevant sections of the Village Code.

Ordinance design components in this community include parking lot screening, interior parking lot landscaping, landscaping between zoning districts and landscaping antenna structures and earth stations. A unique design component mentioned in this ordinance are standards for landscaping detention basins as part of a storm water management system. It recommends the standards listed in Table 2.45.

For landscaping between zoning districts, the ordinance recommends the use of either walls, fences, double staggered rows of six (6)-foot evergreen material or planted landscape berms.

Standards are presented for preparation of the landscape plan, tree preservation plan, tree survey, maintenance and administrative procedures. Preservation techniques, including fencing, reducing root impact and transplanting, are to be illustrated on the tree preservation plan.

As a form of enforcement, cash bonds are held by the city until all work on a project has been completed.

TABLE 2.45. Landscape Design Standards for Detention Basins, Arlington Heights, Illinois

Design Standards	*Expected Results*
Landscape to consist of trees, shrubs, emergent vegetation	Natural mix of plant species
Plant material arrangement	Arrange to be aesthetically pleasing
Use aerator device to maintain water quality	Aesthetic appeal of a fountain
Use wetland plants along edges	Soften shoreline and clean water
Install site amenities, walks, paths, gazebos, benches	Make better use of the open space
Post warning signs where water level fluctuates more than 36″	Safety

Perhaps the most novel aspect of this ordinance is the assessment of a "parkway fee." Parkway fees are collected for the purpose of community tree planting when application for a building permit is made. The parkway fee is nonrefundable and pays for tree planting by the Forestry Division of Public Works on public streets. Parkway fees are calculated at the rate of four (4) dollars per linear foot of right-of-way. The fee for a lot frontage of sixty (60) feet would cost two hundred forty (240) dollars. This is enough money to pay for the installation of two trees.

Bannockburn, Village of

Ordinance 88-20, "Bannockburn Tree Ordinance," September 26, 1988.

This ordinance is, in part, the result of provisions of the Illinois Municipal Code, Illinois Revised Statutes Chapter 24 § 1-1-1, that vests with the Village the power to regulate subdivisions, zone land and complement the state's interest and values through the Illinois Environmental Protection Act. This act's purpose is to protect the quality of life and general welfare of the Village.

Specifically, in this community, this ordinance will assist in stabilization of topsoil, control storm water and protect an important link in the hydrological cycle that feeds aquifer recharge while maintaining a healthy food chain. Protection of the rural atmosphere and purification of the air are noted as secondary concerns.

A repealer clause is inserted in this ordinance to delete previous regulations and to establish comprehensive regulations for the protection, preservation, planting and regulation of trees. This ordinance is legally connected to all other codes in the Village, such as the building code, subdivison code and plumbing code so that no city permits will be issued that will result in the destruction of trees.

This ordinance is administered by the Building Commissioner, who is assisted by the Village Forester. No "use change," that is, activity involving a license of permit or any activity involving construction, earth moving or demolition, will be allowed until a tree permit has been issued. An application for a permit must be accompanied with a reforestation plan or, under some conditions a site plan prepared by qualified professionals, both of which may be a condition of receiving a permit. A fifty (50) dollar review fee is collected with the application along with reforestation security in the form of a cash deposit, a bond or a letter of credit equal to the cost of implementing the reforestation plan.

Trees that are removed must be replanted based on an inch-for-inch ratio for the various classes of trees. The sum of all DBH caliper inches removed must be replaced with a similar aggregate amount. New plantings must be maintained for a two (2)-year period according to standards common to the forestry, landscaping and landscape architecture professions.

Standards are cited for planting and maintenance. Dangerous, unhealthy and dead trees must be removed. The Dutch elm fungus (*Ceratostomella ulmi*) and the European elm bark beetle (*Scolytus multistriatus*) are declared public nuisances and are banned in this community. The Village may remove these nuisances on private land if "notice of removal" is ignored or resisted.

The ordinance sets penalties and gives the Village president the authority to appoint a Tree Commission to annually review the performance of this ordinance and other duties related to tree protection, education and administration.

This tree ordinance is a reasonably good small-town ordinance that is easy to understand and administer.

Bartlett

North Suburban Zoning Ordinance, Chapter 11A, "Landscape Requirements," n.d.

Bartlett is a pro-growth village, a suburb of Chicago, that has adopted a landscape ordinance to create uniform screening and tree preservation standards. The ordinance governs all development except detached single- and attached two-family developments.

Landscape plans are required for all projects requiring site plan review and/or special use permits. The landscape plans must show all existing trees over four (4) inches caliper to be preserved, trees credited toward landscape requirements and various site information including structures, quantities, dimensions, grading, specifications and proposed plant materials. Details of all site structures to complement landscaping, as well as elevations, cross sections and the like must be submitted to the Community Development Department for review. Installation of this plan is required prior to receiving an occupancy permit.

This ordinance is one of the few in this study that presents the criteria for review and approval of the landscape plans. Most communities just state that certain information must be illustrated on the plan. They do not say why the information is needed nor how the information is used to make decisions of approval. This community does. It bases its decisions on plant material and installation methods.

This ordinance regulates five (5) different landscape design components: (1) interior parkways (street yards or front perimeter), (2) perimeter areas (screening, several alternatives), (3) foundation areas, (4) parking lots (several alternatives) and (5) site interiors.

Of the five components, the foundation area landscaping is unique in that few communities have this type of component in their ordinances. No specific technical requirements are given, but rather a broad, general design guideline. "Plantings should emphasize softening large expanses of building walls, accenting building entrances and architectural features and screening mechanical equipment." The foundation planting area is to be four (4) feet wide.

Technical requirements in terms of materials, quantities, sizes and spacing are given for each of the landscape components. Table 3 in the ordinance gives a list of recommended trees, shrubs and ground covers.

This ordinance has a tree preservation requirement with standards given for tree credits and protecting existing trees. Six guidelines, as shown in Table 2.46, are given for tree protection.

This is a reasonably well written ordinance that covers most of the essential elements of a landscape ordinance. A lot of well thought out detail is given for

TABLE 2.46. Tree Protection Guidelines, Bartlett, Illinois

Tree Protection Guideline	*Reason*
Protect with fencing during construction.	Prevents mechanical and chemical damage
Do not compact or contaminate soil under tree.	Provides for free flow of air and moisture
Keep sources of heat away from tree.	Prevents damage to leaves and bark
Repair damaged roots and branches.	Maintains water uptake-evapotranspiration ratio
Prune existing trees surrounded by paving.	Reduces evapotranspiration zone
Do not change grade near existing trees.	Maintains drainage, water table level and soil chemistry

some of the requirements. The ordinance could be improved in a number of ways. The community might provide more standards for maintenance, including irrigation, be more specific on administrative procedures, especially enforcement, and increase the size of the nice graphic illustrations in the ordinance so that they are easier to read.

Bensonville

Bensonville Zoning Ordinance, Article 8.04, "Landscaping," n.d.

This community has a very basic landscape ordinance with very general requirements and standards. It requires minimal landscaping of transition strips, frontage strips, and island strips, as well as screening. Landscape plans are submitted to the Director of Building and Zoning.

Credit is given for preserving existing landscaping or saving larger trees. General performance standards are cited for tree protection, installation, maintenance and replacement of dead plant materials. Quality standards are given for plant materials. These standards are accompanied by a table of recommended and prohibited street trees.

Bolingbrook

Bolingbrook, "Article 7, Landscape Ordinance," amending Bolingbrook's Zoning Ordinance of the Municipal Code, n.d.

The purpose of this ordinance is to promote compatibility among land uses through the preservation and installation of vegetation, screening and other landscaping materials.

A preliminary development plan is to be submitted including a list of typical plants and their approximate sizes. A final development plan must be submitted that is not less than the preliminary development plan and must include each proposed plant's botanical and common names, size and installed condition.

Parking lots and vehicular use areas are given much consideration in this ordinance. Three types of parking and building adjacencies are discussed, and requirements are given for each adjacency: vehicular use areas adjacent to front and corner side yards, vehicular use areas adjacent to interior side and rear yards and drive-throughs adjacent to other vehicular use areas. Interior parking requirements include a ratio of one (1) overstory tree for every ten (10) parking spaces, and trees must be evenly distributed through the parking lot. There must be a one hundred eighty (180)-square foot planting bed per tree with a minimum dimension of nine (9) feet in any direction. These beds shall not be used for snow storage. The beds must be curbed with a barrier curb; not be planted within three (3) feet of the curb, except for ground cover; and, other than overstory trees, the plants must not reach a mature height of more than two (2) feet within ten (10) feet of any curb at an intersection. A six (6) foot wide curbed parking island is to be provided at the ends of each row of parking, extending the length of the parking stalls, and landscaped with trees, shrubs, flowers, or ground covers. Minimum requirements are also listed for refuse receptacles, waste removal areas, retention/detention facilities, transition yards, loading docks, service yards, exterior work areas and open storage yards.

The ordinance sets specific minimum requirements for plant quality and quantity. Minimum size requirements are given for each tree and shrub type. The ordinance is based on "plant units" or minimum quantities of specific plants per square footage for different site landscape zones. Planting units are listed for various tree and shrub types. Trees and shrubs must not be located closer than ten (10) feet to any hydrant or other above-ground utility. Existing plants can be counted as credit toward planting requirements.

Several areas of concern are unique to this ordinance. Single-family residential districts must also comply with the ordinance. Private homes that abut primary arterial or major streets are required to install landscaping. Requirements for snow receptacles, "foundation" planting, storm water retention/detention facilities, parking/building adjacencies and various work and service yards are other special provisions unique to this ordinance.

Bolingbrook must be a beautiful city. For a city of only forty-one thousand (41,000) people, this is the most complex ordinance that has been reviewed. The ordinance is very thorough and demanding.

Cherry Valley, Village of

Village of Cherry Valley Zoning Ordinance. "Article XV, Landscaping Restrictions in Parking Areas," 1988.

The landscape ordinance of the Village of Cherry Valley is a single-issue ordinance dealing only with landscape improvements to parking areas. No other design components are involved.

The ordinance calls for the submission of a site plan and a landscape design. Both are to be prepared and submitted to the village Zoning Officer. The ordinance applies to all public and private parking and asphalt-covered areas, including open sales areas, containing more than five (5) parking spaces. Gas stations must also comply, regardless of how many parking spaces they provide. Technical requirements include screening, with landscaping on all sides adjacent to residentially zoned property and sides abutting public rights-of-way. All parking of ten (10) or more spaces must contain dispersed plantings of three (3) trees for the first ten (10) parking spaces and one additional tree for each ten (10) spaces thereafter.

Plant material standards are given for size, grade, spacing, planting area and protective measures. Planting strips are to be a minimum of eight (8) feet in width. Technical standards are given for drawing preparation. Minimal maintenance requirements are given, and enforcement is managed by issuance of or denial of a Certificate of Zoning Compliance.

One wonders why cherry trees are not the recommended trees of choice for this community.

Chicago

City of Chicago Landscape Ordinance, Title 10, Chapter 32, and Title 17, Chapter 194A, of the Chicago Municipal Code.
Guide to the Chicago Landscape Ordinance: Regulations and Guidelines Relating to Title 10, Chapter 32, and Title 17, Chapter 194A, of the Chicago Municipal Code," November 1991.

Mayor Richard M. Daley notes in a letter at the beginning of the Guide that its purpose is to help the city live up to its description, captured in the city seal—*Urbs in Horto*, or the City in a Garden. Daley says the objectives of the ordinances are to ensure attractive tree-lined streets, greener neighborhoods and enhanced property values.

Chicago has no separate landscape ordinance, but a series of additions and amendments to the city's municipal code; so the city commissioned a private landscape architecture firm to prepare a comprehensive guide that would clarify, illustrate and expand the language of the ordinances. The ordinances already authorize such a guide, and it has the force of law. The ordinances themselves are included in Appendix 8 of the Guide.

Chicago traditionally has not demanded landscaping, so the Guide's requirements are considered substantial. The landscape requirements fall into several categories: parkway planting, vehicular use area screening and internal shading of surface parking lots. In addition, the ordinance requires screening for side and rear lot lines and front yard screens for the purpose of screening from street view any parking area of more than twelve hundred (1,200) square feet in extent. Loading areas are screened in a manner similar to vehicular use areas, and space must be set aside for sight triangles.

Certain alternative landscaping or architectural treatments such as hedges, berms, vine trellises, walls, screens and fences are allowed. Generally, Chicago ordinances require one tree per twenty-five (25) linear feet along street frontages; a continuous hedge around the perimeter of parking areas; and planting islands in parking areas that total five (5) percent of the vehicular use area and are at least one hundred sixty-five (165) square feet in size. Minimal standards apply for installation and maintenance. Few specific design standards are given in this ordinance, but many others are listed in the Guide. Those that have been specified are based on linear measure, square foot area or specific unit measure.

Parkway plantings are called street tree plantings in most communities. In this community, "parkway" means "that portion of the public right-of-way between a public street and the nearest parallel property line including sidewalk areas." In this area trees are planted twenty-five (25) feet on center.

Small renovations and residential projects are exempt from the ordinances, but otherwise the ordinances apply to new construction and renovation projects.

The city Guide is more than one hundred (100) bound pages in length and contains photographs, illustrations, diagrams, preferred plant lists and various design standards. "Quote-outs" are used in the document to better explain the landscape requirements and the city's intent.

This is an interesting ordinance in that it is very general yet there are many specific requirements put forth in the Guide administered by the Zoning Administrator.

Chicago's written ordinance itself is rather clumsy and redundant because its language has been assembled from various council amendments. No one could use this ordinance as a model because of its hit-and-miss character. The Guide, however, is a different story. This document is very detailed as to its meaning and carries the weight of law. To understand the landscape requirements for the City of Chicago, just consult the Guide.

Danville

Danville Zoning Ordinance, Chapter 167, "Landscape Ordinance for Parking Lots and Other Vehicular Use Areas," March 1996.

The stated purpose of this recently enacted ordinance is to improve the appearance of certain setback and yard areas, including off-street parking and other vehicular use areas in the city. The city sees this as an important feature of preserving the value of surrounding neighborhoods and perpetuating its aesthetic appeal on a citywide basis.

This ordinance applies to all land uses except single and duplex residential and to all expansions increasing building size by more than fifty (50) percent. It is enforced by controlling paving permits and issuing Certificates of Occupancy.

This is a limited-issue landscape ordinance, administered by the Department of Development Services and applying primarily to accommodating automobiles as a part of site development.

TABLE 2.47. Landscape Plant Units, Danville, Illinois

Plant Type	*No. of Plant Units Each*
Small flowering trees	3 points each
Evergreen shrubs	2 points each
Deciduous shrubs	1 point each

Design components of this landscape ordinance include street right-of-way (r-o-w) edge plantings, perimeters between parking areas and property lines and parking area interiors.

Credits toward landscape requirements are granted for preservation of existing healthy plant materials in parking areas. Upon application by the developer, "adjustments" or alternative compliance provisions may be approved by the city in instances where strict compliance with these requirements and standards present a hardship or would prove to be impractical.

Developer incentives can also be granted in the form of reducing the amount of required parking spaces by up to twenty five (25) percent for compliance with these provisions. Few communities grant this type of developer incentive or have incentive clauses in their ordinances.

Standards are given for installation, maintenance and plant material. Tree spacing and sizing are controlled. Any plantings not matching the requirements must be approved by a landscape architect and the city.

Planting standards for landscape screens or buffers include width requirements, which vary from five (5) to ten (10) feet. A number of specified "plant units," based on the point schedule shown in Table 2.47, determine the number and composition of small trees and shrubs to be used in each screen or buffer planting.

The city maintains an off-street parking landscape manual and has a list of approved plant materials to assist developers.

One of the interesting elements of this ordinance is language requiring a tree root barrier system constructed of four (4)-inch thick reinforced concrete for any tree species with aggressive roots located within twelve feet of a public roadway.

It might also be noted that the language of this ordinance, as well as the name of the city agency that administers this law, is very developer friendly and the ordinance seems more pro-development rather than focused on stopping development.

DuPage County

DuPage County Zoning Ordinance, Chapter 1, and "Landscaping Requirements for the County of DuPage, Illinois," August 1991.

This county, which includes the town of Wheaton, adopted a revised landscape ordinance as a part of its zoning ordinance. The revision was developed by county landscape architects, planners and zoning officials. The county's landscape architects are responsible for administering the landscape requirements. A booklet, titled "Landscaping Requirements for the County of DuPage, Illinois," outlines the zoning ordinance's landscape regulations, although developers are urged to consult the full zoning ordinance for specific requirements.

The ordinance intends to improve the quality of life in the county. The primary goal of the regulations is to provide screening of conflicting land uses from other land uses and public areas.

The county uses a point system to approve landscape plans. Various sizes of "landscape yards" are assigned certain point totals that must be achieved by planting shrubs and trees, which are assigned point values based on their average size and cost. For example, a low shrub is worth ten (10) points, whereas a shade tree is worth one hundred (100) points. The system also includes "Plant Preservation Credits," with the proper retention of existing trees and shrubs also earning points.

Parking lot regulations are included. Interior landscaping must occupy at least ten (10) percent of all lots of ten thousand (10,000) square feet or more.

The landscape booklet includes illustrations, drawings, sample forms and permits and a list of prohibited trees (those that have weak wood, offensive fruit, fatal disease, etc.).

Machesney Park, Village of

Village of Machesney Park Zoning Code, Article I, Section 20-8 (Fences, Walls and Hedges), and Article XI, Section 20-57 (Off-Street Parking and Loading), September 1996.

This small midwestern community does not have a complete freestanding or comprehensive landscape ordinance as is common in many larger communities.

Its landscape ordinance consists of language spread throughout its zoning code. This is quite common for smaller communities. The Village of Machesney Park is new, having been incorporated in 1981. It has assembled its zoning code from surrounding counties and municipalities. Off-street parking and loading landscape requirements are modeled after those of the City of Madison, Wisconsin. The Director of Planning and Zoning intends to build upon this foundation and make the ordinance more comprehensive in the future.

The Village recognizes the public and private benefits of landscaping. Landscaping may serve the public interest by controlling the circulation of cars and pedestrians, help identify entries and exits, provide reference points and allow open space for drainage and snow storage. In addition, community landscaping creates environmental and aesthetic benefits and positive assets for shopping areas and business establishments.

The off-street parking and loading requirements of this ordinance apply to parking areas of five (5) or more spaces, all open off-street loading areas and all open storage areas. These areas must have effective screening on each side adjoining or fronting on any residential district or any private or public street. Effective screening consists of a solid fence, wall or compact hedge not less than three

(3) feet nor more than four (4) feet in height in front yards, and not less than three (3) feet nor more than six (6) feet in side and rear yards.

The owner may choose to "landscape" in lieu of providing effective screens. In this case, in commercial districts there is to be one (1) canopy tree two to two and one-half (2 to 2½) inches in caliper for each twelve (12) parking places. In industrial districts, this changes to one (1) canopy tree two to two and one-half (2 to 2½) inches in caliper for each twenty-four (24) parking places.

All property located in commercial or industrial districts must have effective screens along lot lines adjoining residential districts. These screens shall consist of a solid fence, wall or compact hedge not less than six (6) feet nor more than eight (8) feet in height. Swimming pools and dumpsters must also be screened, and screens may be used along some arterial streets.

Trees, shrubs and other landscaping materials must be depicted on landscaping plans that are approved by the Village.

There are few standards, design components or technical requirements in this ordinance. Enforcement and administration are not clear. Although minimal and brief, this ordinance does set some design requirements that will result in a more livable village.

Mount Prospect

Mount Prospect, Ordinance No. 4202, "An Ordinance Creating Chapter 15 Entitled 'Landscape Ordinance' of the Village Code of Mount Prospect," June 20, 1990.

The stated purpose of the ordinance is to ensure aesthetic compatibility between land uses within the community and reduce the harmful effects, such as noise, dust or light intrusions, caused by adjoining land uses. In addition, the ordinance tries to preserve environmental quality and aesthetic character within the community by limiting the removal and ensuring the replacement of trees on private property.

A list of definitions for such words as *caliper* and *sight triangle* is included. Mount Prospect's regulations require a landscape plan, to be approved by the Director of Planning and Zoning, for most new developments. The plan should be completed by a landscape architect or "a person capable of fulfilling all requirements set forth in this ordinance."

Article IV outlines design criteria, such as the scale, nature, selection and maintenance of planting materials. The ordinance stresses energy conservation by urging the planting of evergreen materials on the north side of structures.

Parking lots of twenty (20) or more spaces must have interior plantings in five (5) percent of the area, not counting perimeter or foundation plantings. Interior landscaping areas must be at least sixty-four (64) square feet. Shade trees must be the primary planting material.

Article VIII addresses vegetative buffers between various land uses. Article IX concerns tree preservation. No trees of a four (4)-inch or greater caliper are to be removed without the city's permission. The ordinance includes a list of approved replacement trees.

Peoria

Peoria Code, Article 16, "Landscaping and Screening," January 18, 1994, Ord. No. 13670 §1.

This ordinance assists in achieving the community-wide goal of developing the visual appeal of public/private open space as directed in the city's comprehensive plan. It is expected that the ordinance will help the community achieve a number of environmental, property and social needs objectives.

The ordinance applies to all land uses except single-family residential. This ordinance can be satisfied by two means. The most common method of meeting the requirements of this ordinance is the use of a point system. This method allows the designer to design the landscape with a great deal of flexibility while achieving a minimum number of required landscape points. The landscape points are based on measurable site attributes, such as listed in Table 2.48. For instance, points for street frontage and transition yards are based on length of property line and required points for a vehicular use area are based on a parking stall count.

Within each planting area, one-half of the points must be used for trees and one-half for shrubs. Of this amount, one-half of the points must be for evergreens.

The other approach to design is through an alternative compliance provision. This approach is to be used when a site is unique, has special problems or when

TABLE 2.48. Landscape Point System Ratings, Peoria, Illinois

Landscape Material	*Point Value*
BASE VALUE POINTS	
Shade Trees	18 points
Evergreen Trees	18 points
Intermediate Trees	12 points
Evergreen Shrubs	3 points
Deciduous Shrubs	2 points
Ground Covers	no points
Other Materials	no points
INCENTIVE POINTS	
Shade Trees 12″ diameter or greater	5 bonus points
Evergreen Trees, 15′ or taller	5 bonus points
Intermediate Trees, 15′ or taller	5 bonus points
Shade Trees 4″ caliper or greater	5 bonus points
Evergreen Trees, 10′ or taller	5 bonus points
Intermediate Trees, 10′ or taller	5 bonus points

extra-special design is wanted. Under this approach the zoning administrator must approve the design. Denial of approval will require the applicant to amend the plan or seek approval using the point system approach.

Design components of this ordinance include front and corner side yards, parking lots, transitional buffer yards and screening for activity areas such as refuse containers, storage areas, loading docks and on site work areas.

Included with the ordinance are a series of design performance standards, landscape design plan preparation standards, plant material standards, ground cover guidelines and landscape maintenance requirements. Technical standards are given for depth of buffers, planting zones and minimum planting spaces. Certain tree species are not welcome in this community, as the tombstone graphic in Figure 2.25 illustrates in such commanding fashion.

Incentives are provided for the applicant. Extra points can be earned by saving existing landscaping and by providing larger-size plant materials.

City of Peoria
Outlawed Trees
Not Wanted in Peoria

Ailanthus (Tree of Heaven)

Box Elder

European Mountain Ash

European White Birch

Mulberry

Poplar

Purple Leaf Plum

Russian Olive

Siberian Elm

Silver Maple

FIGURE 2.25. Prohibited urban trees, Peoria, Illinois.

Enforcement is controlled by withholding of the Zoning Certificate and the Certificate of Occupancy.

This is a sensible little ordinance that benefits from its easy-to-understand nature, its incentive rewards for developers, its landscape plan preparation requirements and its alternative compliance provision that encourages better quality design.

Planning staff have prepared a colorful, reader-friendly design flyer that helps readers calculate landscape points and understand the purpose and context of the ordinance. They report that the community has accepted the ordinance and are pleased with its resultant impact on the appearance of the city. Others interested in how point systems work might consult this ordinance.

Rockford

Rockford Zoning Ordinance, Article XIV, "Landscaping, Buffering and Tree Preservation," July 1993.

The original Rockford landscape ordinance was adopted in 1973 and amended in 1977. This ordinance was vague and poorly written. When rewritten in early 1933, the concept of "landscape units" was added to provide a tool to measure a proposed landscape plan and existing plant materials for compliance with the minimum requirements of the ordinance.

A landscape unit (LU) is a point type of measurement system that determines the amount of landscaping required on a new project site. Landscape units (see Table 2.49) take into consideration the quantity, size and spacing of plant materials. An LU is a value assigned to landscape elements based on their relative cost, land coverage potential and screening characteristics. A certain number of landscape units are required, based on linear footage.

TABLE 2.49. Schedule of Landscape Units, Rockford, Illinois

Landscape Units	*Plant Type*	*Minimum Size (HT)*	*Recommeded Spacing (OC)*	*Other Requirements*
225	Shade Trees	2″ cal.	27′–90′	1/10 spaces
225	Evergreen Trees	6′–7′	9′–54′	
150	Ornamental Trees	6′–7′	9′–94′	
30	Evergreen Shrubs	18″–24″	3′–6′	50% of LUs
15	Deciduous Shrubs	18″–24″	3′–6′	
4	Perennial Plants	1 qt. pot	2′–3′	
1	Ground Cover Plants	2″ pot	1′–2′	
0.2	Earth Berm & Lawn	3′–6″	per SF	3:1/maximum
0.1	Lawn	n/a	per SF	3″–6″ height max.
4	Fence or Wall*			

*Counted as evergreen Landscape Units

The intent of this ordinance is to reduce incompatibility between zoning districts while enhancing the environmental quality and visual character of the city. In addition, the ordinance is intended to encourage tree and shrub planting while reducing the removal of existing indigenous vegetation. Requirements contained in this ordinance apply to all new privately owned multi-family residential, commercial and industrially zoned properties and "kick in" on renovations and additions that add more than ten (10) percent to an existing building, parking or outside storage yard.

Design components in this ordinance include landscape buffers, perimeter landscaping, interior landscaping and shade trees.

Perimeters and buffers are to be planted based on LUs. For example, ten (10) landscape units of landscaping per linear foot of street frontage are required. Interior plantings are based on a percentage of the site requiring interior plantings, generally four (4) percent for areas under fifty thousand (50,000) square feet and eight (8) percent for areas exceeding this amount. Shade trees are to be planted based on one (1) tree for every ten (10) parking spaces or one (1) tree for every twenty-five hundred (2,500) square feet of paved area.

Several alternative design expressions are suggested in this ordinance. Well-articulated graphics in the document encourage expansive lawns, earth berms, fencing and four (4) different buffer types. Each buffer type (A, B, C, D) is based on landscape units per linear foot. The wider the buffer, the more landscape units are required to meet compliance. Fifty (50) percent of all landscape units must be evergreen.

Tree preservation is an important part of this ordinance. Credits are provided for preserving existing trees of six (6)-inch diameter or larger, and fee penalties are assessed for removal of trees designated to remain. A Tree Survey and a Tree Preservation and Protection Plan must be submitted to achieve tree credits. Tree Removal Permits are required prior to destroying trees on public lands and in certain zoning districts.

Minimal maintenance standards and plant material standards are included in this law. A list of recommended plant species, well adapted to public landscapes in the community, is provided.

Site plans and landscaping plans illustrating compliance shall be prepared by landscape architects and submitted to the Zoning Officer. These plans must illustrate specific design and site engineering criteria. Failure to comply with the requirements of this ordinance will result in failure to receive a Certificate of Zoning Compliance.

This is a well organized ordinance that breaks down into three (3) distinct parts. The first part of the ordinance deals with purpose, applicability and general requirements. The second part deals with standards, requirements and specifications, and the third part deals with administrative aspects. Appropriate graphics, tables and lists, such as depicted in the Table 2.49, make this a very readable and user-friendly landscape ordinance.

Rockford would have a very complete and contemporary landscape ordinance if additional design components were added to this document and the issue of alternative compliance was addressed.

Schaumburg

Schaumburg Zoning Ordinance, Article IX, "Tree Preservation, Landscaping and Screening," n.d.

It is important in this community to dissuade unnecessary clearing and to limit the removal and ensure the replacement of trees that safeguard the ecological and aesthetic environment. This ordinance, which consists of both tree preservation and landscaping requirements, applies to both public and private property.

To comply with this ordinance several documents must be submitted to the Engineering Department: a Tree Survey, a Tree Preservation Plan and Statement of Methodology and a Landscape Plan. The Landscape Plan must be submitted with all projects requiring submission of a site plan. Specific design criteria and tree removal criteria are listed in the ordinance. Innovative landscape design is encouraged.

No trees of more than four (4) inches in caliper may be removed prior to final site plan review until a tree removal permit is granted. Any tree that is damaged during construction that is indicated to be preserved on the tree preservation plan will have to be replaced. An exchange rate schedule setting forth the replacement rate is provided in the ordinance. For instance, if a thirty-six (36)-inch protected tree is damaged during construction, it must be replaced with twelve (12) new three (3)-inch caliper trees from a select list of approved species.

Design components include parkway plantings (street r-o-w trees), parking lots, perimeters, foundations and refuse disposal facilities. Standards are given for plant materials, installation and maintenance.

South Holland Village

South Holland Village Code, Article X, as amended, "Landscaping," October 15, 1990.

South Holland Village is a community of twenty-five thousand (25,000) people living south of downtown Chicago, Illinois.

This community requires creative and attractive landscaping of all properties in the Village as a benefit to owners, to neighborhoods and to the identity and pride of the Village. All new development and all renovations or additions adding more than twenty (20) percent to the value of the last assessed tax roll valuation must be landscaped according to this law. The ordinance is specific as to land use zoning classification. Different technical standards apply to different zoning classifications.

The ordinance's Section 6-265, Objectives, sets out objectives that in every sense of the word are design criteria. These criteria must be met and illustrated on a landscape plan for the evaluation of compliance and any requested variations to the requirements set forth in the ordinance. These design criteria are interpreted by the author in Table 2.50 for ease of reading.

Specific design components and minimum standards adopted for specific zoning classifications are set forth in this ordinance.

TABLE 2.50. Selected Design Criteria, South Holland, Illinois

Design Criteria	*Design Response*	*Typical Standard*
Natural-looking effects	Variety of plant material	Appropriately spaced
Principles of design	Balance, unity, color and variety	Unity in design
Visually soften structures	Variety of plant material	Arrange by size and height
Reduce intrusive headlight glare	Develop screening	Use common plants
Trap noise, odor, dust	Develop screening	Use evergreen plants
Provide habitat for wildlife	Mixed plantings	Layer plants
Control erosion	Use ground cover and shrubs	Assess soils and drainage
Allow ground cover recharge	Set appropriate grades and ground covers	Proper coverage
Provide visual separation	Add land use buffers	Screen density
Provide safety barriers	Design curbs and safety restraints	Add parking islands
Shade seating and outdoor areas	Use shade trees	Properly spaced sq. ft.
Deflect winter wind, summer sun	Use evergreen trees and shrubs	Select by plant habit
Preserve existing site features	Perform careful site analysis and land use study	
Ensure long-term maintenance	Variety of plant materials	Well-mixed plantings
Innovation and creativity	Interesting design	
Use Best Professional Practices	Follow standards of ASLA and AAN	See standards
Select native plants	Use plants that do well in area	Use Appendix A

Design components include street side (parkway) plantings, parking islands, parking lot setbacks, parking lot sides, outdoor storage areas, interior trees and abutting side perimeters.

Technical standards are based on square footage, linear measure, single units, size, height, habit and density. Best management practices of the American Society of Landscape Architects and the American Association of Nurserymen are cited. Specific vegetation size standards are mentioned for evergreen plants, deciduous plants, shrubs, shade trees, ornamental trees and existing vegetation to be preserved.

No tree taller than twenty (20) feet in height or larger than four (4) inches in caliper may be removed without a permit from the Village. For those trees that are allowed to be removed, replacement trees shall be installed based on one (1) new tree for approximately each six (6) inches removed.

Installation and maintenance standards pertaining to the soil mix, planting, mulching and maintenance guarantee are listed. Any plant dying within thirty (30) days shall be replaced. This is enforced by requiring that ten (10) percent of the planting budget be placed in escrow payable to the Village to ensure maintenance for a period of at least one (1) growing season.

The ordinance is administered by the Director of Code Enforcement and the Planning Commission. Reviews and approvals are given through the vehicle of the landscape plan, which they suggest be prepared by a landscape architect or licensed landscape contractor. Landscape plans prepared according to a set of specified standards are submitted for zoning approval, special use approval, subdivision approval and to receive a building permit. Appeals are made to the Village Board of Trustees.

For doing more than is required as written in the ordinance, incentives (bonuses) in the form of setback variations, floor area ratios, parking quantities and signage are allowed. Specific reasons for incentives are listed in the ordinance. Cash penalties, although minor, can be assessed on a daily basis for failure to comply.

This ordinance is one of the most distinctive ordinances in this study. The difference? It places emphasis on design. This seems to be the case because of the careful detail in its crafting and organization. One of the reasons this ordinance emphasizes design rather than technical standards, which often are cold and calculated, is because it was written by a planning commission landscape architect who knew how to carefully balance requirements with design subjectivity and creative freedom.

One of the really interesting aspects of this ordinance is that it is one of the few in this study that has incentives as well as requirements.

Many of the terms used in this ordinance are not common to the typical ordinances found elsewhere, leading the annotator to believe that this midwestern town has developed a truly unique ordinance.

This is an ordinance that might be emulated in many smaller communities in which residents can agree to maintain a high level of landscape design and neighborhood livability.

TABLE 2.51. Tree Replacement or Removal Fees, Wheaton, Illinois

Diameter of Tree Removed	*Number of Replacement Trees*	*Fee Amount*
6–9 inches	2–3″ Trees	$ 900.00
9–12 inches	4–3″ Trees	$1,200.00
12–18 inches	6–3″ Trees	$1,800.00
18–24 inches	8–3″ Trees	$2,400.00
24–30 inches	10–3″ Trees	$3,000.00
30–36 inches	12–3″ Trees	$3,600.00
36–42 inches	14–3″ Trees	$4,200.00
42–48 inches	16–3″ Trees	$4,800.00
48 inches plus	18–3″ Trees	$5,500.00

Wheaton

Wheaton City Ordinance No. E-3807, Amending the Wheaton Zoning Ordinance, Article VI "Landscape Requirements," Article XVI "C-1 Local Business District," Article XIX "C-4 CBD Perimeter Commercial District," and Article XXI "Off-Street Parking and Loading," July 7, 1992.

The purpose of this ordinance is to provide buffer zone and screening requirements for adjacent land uses in the City of Wheaton.

Landscape plans are submitted to the City Planner, and certain fees, as shown in Table 2.51, must be paid if trees are to be removed and not replaced. After approval of the plans, the City Planner and a landscape architect inspect the site. The landscape architect provides the City Planner with a written statement certifying that the landscape plan has been implemented in accordance with the city's specifications.

The unique aspects of this ordinance include the design criteria required, such as scale and nature of landscape material, selection of plant material, screening ability, shade trees, softening of walls and fences, planting beds, detention/retention basins and ponds, water conservation and energy conservation. The author of this ordinance does not require an educated professional to develop the landscape plans, but these design criteria ensure that an attractive plan will be submitted.

No specific plant sizes or quantities are given. Requirements are given in percentages and heights for rights-of-way, parking lot interiors, parking lot perimeters with different adjacencies, rear yards, building perimeters, lot perimeters, residential/nonresidential adjacencies, multiple-family residential property, preservation and protection of existing trees and removal of trees. Parking lot perimeter requirements are summarized in Figure 2.26.

This entire ordinance is unique in that it gives the designer requirements in a format that is easy to work with. For example, this city has established a schedule

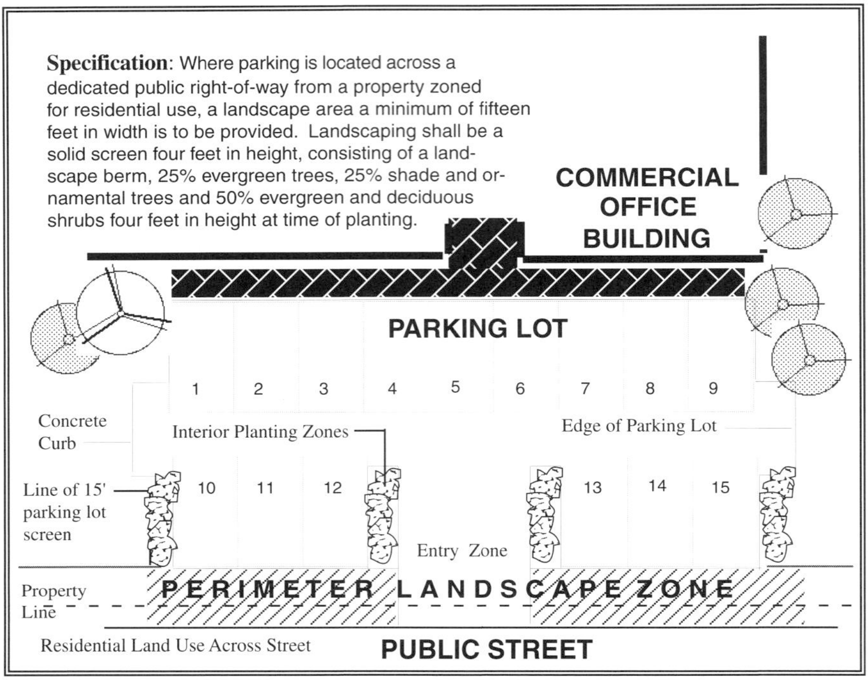

FIGURE 2.26. Parking lot perimeter landscape zone, Wheaton, Illinois.

of fees so that trees that are removed without a permit may be replaced by the developer with a fee paid to the city in lieu of trees. Table 2.51 shows the fee schedule for this city.

Indiana

West Lafayette

West Lafayette City Code, Chapter 26, "Trees," August 1991.

This ordinance addresses trees, including maintenance and permits for trees in public rights-of-way; planting and maintenance of street trees; and landscaping, interior planting, protection and maintenance of trees in off-street parking areas.

The ordinance begins with a list of definitions and several tables of preferred shade trees for various soil and water conditions. Article III, "Street Trees," establishes a Tree Fund, which is supported by voluntary contributions and used for the planting of shade trees along public streets of the community. The ordinance strives for a "unified street vista." New developments adjacent to streets must plant deciduous trees, one (1) per forty (40) feet of frontage.

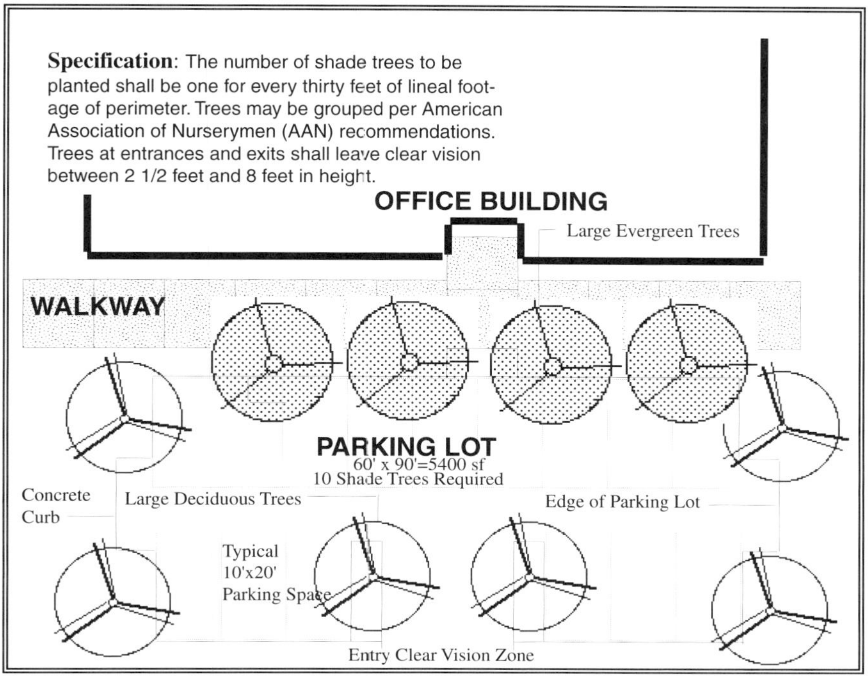

FIGURE 2.27. Shade tree requirements, off-street parking areas, West Lafayette, Indiana.

For parking lots, the ordinance requires perimeter tree plantings of at least one (1) for every (thirty) 30 feet, berms or shrubs as a screen from public streets, and an interior planting of one hundred fifty (150) square feet for every ten (10) parking spaces (see Figure 2.27). Each parking island must have at least one (1) shade tree. The city engineer must approve plant materials.

New developments must meet minimum "green space" requirements established in the Code. For instance, any industrial or commercial use on a lot of more than one (1) acre in an I or I R district must have thirty (30) percent of the area as green space. The total drops to twenty-four (24) percent for sites of less than one (1) acre.

Iowa

Davenport

Title 17 Zoning Ordinance and Related Documents. Section 17.31 Planned Development District, Section 17.35 Planned Commerce Park District,

Section 17.41 Highway Corridor Overlay District, Section 17.56 Site Plans, Chapter 12.52 Trees and Shrubbery and Tree Ordinance, n.d.

The City of Davenport does not have a comprehensive landscape ordinance but instead has landscape requirements that are quite general and scattered throughout the zoning code and other related city ordinances. Under this circumstance, landscaping gets much less recognition, is much more difficult to understand by consultants or developers and is, perhaps, not easily enforced.

Contained within the code are open space requirements, buffer yard requirements, some standards for plant materials and some very general design standards for parking areas. Other standards are included for buffer yards, highway corridors zones, drainage control, topsoil preservation and exterior lighting. The landscaping standards shown in Table 2.52 specify the amount of plant material required, but not the design, for each zoning district.

Buffer yard requirements are stated in terms of the width of the buffer yard and the number of plant units required per one hundred (100) feet. The higher the intensity of land use conflict, the wider the buffer and the denser the screen becomes. Table 2.52 shows the minimal landscape standards required to be met in this Midwestern community. In some buffer yards, berms, fences and walls apply. Graphic diagrams are given, showing general layout and design intent of the buffer yards.

Osage orange hedge fences, once popular in rural areas, are prohibited within the corporate limits of the city.

This is a very general, somewhat dated ordinance, which is difficult to use and places little emphasis on landscape design.

TABLE 2.52. Landscaping Standards, Davenport, Iowa

Landscape Standard		*Required per 10 DU or 300′ Building Perimeter*	
Zoning	*Canopy*	*Understory*	*Shrubs*
R	5	5	0
A	5	5	25
B	3	3	15
C	2	2	10
D	1	1	5
E	0	0	0

Kansas

Kansas City

Article XXII, Zoning Ordinance, § 27-1347, "Landscaping and Screening," September 1, 1993.

This is a simple, limited-issue landscape ordinance pertaining to landscaping of street edges, parking lot screening, screening of outdoor facilities and equipment, night lighting and general site planting.

Landscape plans are required for all new multifamily, office and professional, commercial and industrial development and major additions to such developments. Standards for the preparation of the plan are given. Generally, they include showing all new plant and construction materials to be used, existing trees over twelve (12) inches caliper and topographic, dimensional and location data for all site improvements. Landscape screening and architectural screening details must accompany this plan.

Planting requirements are based on unit numbers, square foot measure and linear measure. In certain districts one (1) shade tree is required for each dwelling unit and each seven thousand (7,000) square feet of site area. In addition, one (1) evergreen tree, one (1) shade tree and three (3) large shrubs are required for each thirty (30) feet of adjacent single-family or two-family property line. Multifamily developments must provide one (1) shade tree for each eight (8) dwelling units. Within industrial districts that front residential areas, plantings and architectural screens must be used. A single row of shade trees forty (40) feet on center and a single row of large shrubs spaced eight (8) feet on center is the standard. In addition, in M-3 industrial districts one (1) tree shall be planted for each fifteen thousand (15,000) square feet. Plant material standards, definitions, maintenance and planting requirements are mentioned.

This is a very general landscape ordinance, restricted to certain zoning districts under certain conditions, and is based primarily on planting formulas rather than design.

Lawrence

The Code of the City of Lawrence, Kansas, 1994 Edition, Zoning Regulations, Section 20-14A04, "Landscaping Requirements," Ordinance 6610, January 24, 1995.

It is important in Lawrence to maintain the city's quality, heritage and character by enhancing the visual appearance of the community and preserving its environmental quality by adding landscaping, protecting existing trees and replenishing the local stock of native plant materials. The landscape ordinance applies to all zoning districts except residential districts RS-1 and RS-2.

Landscape plans must be submitted showing compliance with the various design components, technical standards and requirements of this ordinance.

Design components include minimum tree requirements, protection of existing trees, parking and vehicular use areas, and screening of outdoor storage and loading areas.

Minimum tree requirements are based on street frontage and a ratio of tree per dwelling unit or other measure of site use. For example, in zoning district RM-D (Residence Duplex) one (1) shade tree per forty (40) linear feet of street frontage is required, along with seventy-five hundredths (.75) tree for each dwelling unit thereon. Minimum tree requirements vary by zoning district intensity.

Credit is given for "protecting and preserving" existing trees during construction. However, credit is based on a tree for tree basis and does not reflect the size or species credited. There are no restrictions on removing trees, so this is a tree preservation clause rather than a tree protection clause, for the interest of anyone seeking the difference.

Curiously, this community also has a design component related to at-grade highway, arterial and collector street frontages that restricts how property owners may landscape their frontages and screen the streets. It appears that in this community little thought was given to requiring the highway department to screen its roadways from nearby private property owners. Requirements pertain to berms, walls, fences, plant materials and size and location of planting strips.

Technical standards are given for landscape plan preparation and tree protection, and minimum planting requirements. No standards for maintenance or plant material quality are given.

Suggested requirements include adopting Xeriscape irrigation principles for the conservation of public water supply. The seven principles of Xeriscape culture are cited.

A unique feature of this ordinance is the Alternate Compliance Provision that allows slight modifications to meeting the requirements of the ordinance under certain stated conditions. An alternate requirement proposal must meet or exceed the minimum standards. The ordinance applies primarily to tree plantings and screening, with unspecified directives given for shrub, ground cover and turf plantings.

Leawood

City of Leawood Zoning Ordinance. Article 4, Supplemental Conditions, "Landscaping and Screening Requirements," January 1, 1995.

Leawood does not have a comprehensive freestanding landscape ordinance but includes landscaping language in the zoning ordinance under Special Development Districts (Section 3-12-SD, K) and Supplemental Conditions (Section 4-6). Of the two, the Special Development District is the more detailed and current. The city plans an update of Supplemental Conditions in order to bring them more closely in line with the format and content of Special Development District requirements.

TABLE 2.53. Selected Ordinance Requirements, Leawood, Kansas

Requirement	*Technical Standard*
Street frontage	1 tree per 30 lf, 1 shrub per 15 lf of frontage in 5″ wide strip
Landscape buffer	30″ width, 1 tree per 20 lf, 1 shrub per 10 lf
Open space planting	1 tree per 3,000 sf of landscaped open space
Parking lot screening height	36″ with use of berms, walls or plantings
Parking lot interior planting area	6%, use formula of no. of spaces × 280 sf/.06 to determine total sf
Trash enclosure screening	6′ tall solid fence
Deciduous trees	Average spread of crown > 15′
Shrubs and hedges	24″ in height at planting
Ground cover	Spaced so as to gain complete coverage within 6 months after planting

Application for final development plans for all proposed special development districts must be accompanied with a Landscaping and Screening Plan, with calculations prepared by a registered landscape architect. The plan should illustrate compliance with Section 3-12-SD, K, and Section 4-6.

The Leawood Planning Commission oversees compliance with this ordinance.

The ordinance, which applies to all zoning districts except agricultural, provides for landscaping street frontage, setback/buffer areas, general open space tree planting and parking areas. Standards are listed for plant materials, installation, maintenance and landscape plan preparation. This is a very typical zoning ordinance set of landscape requirements that sets standards based on linear, square foot, and unit measures rather than design. Technical requirements are not very complex or stringent.

A summary of the technical standards for this ordinance is given in Table 2.53.

The community values its trees. Credit toward the landscape requirements is given to developers for preserving four (4)-inch or larger caliper trees.

Lenexa

Lenexa. Unified Development Code, Landscape Requirements, Sections 4-1B-20, 4-1D-2 and 4-6F-63, n.d.

This city has adopted a unified development code to help municipal authorities achieve the desired objectives of its comprehensive plan. Various landscape requirements are found in several sections of the code. Contained within the development code are tree preservation requirements, landscaping requirements and site design standards, all of which preserve vegetation and/or add to the public tree canopy. The Planning Director is largely responsible for ensuring compliance with the ordinance and can withhold the Certificate of Occupancy if the terms of the ordinance are not met.

Within the Planned Unit Development (PUD) district, the city emphasizes the preservation of natural features such as mature trees, vegetative cover and water courses and the creation of common open space for recreation facilities and mini-parks. All development within the PUD must comply with the landscaping, buffering and screening requirements and other site design standards noted in the unified development code.

These requirements apply to all new development in the city.

The Lenexa ordinance is interesting. It includes tree preservation language in its code to require that trees not be removed in certain land use districts. To get approval, site plans and plats must incorporate existing significant stands of trees and be sensitive to site grading, storm drainage, building location and orientation and parking lot configuration. Developers must prepare and submit a Tree Survey, a Vegetation Protection Plan and photogrammetric documentation. The city requires that this information be submitted along with a landscape plan sealed by a registered landscape architect at the time any project is submitted for initial Planning Commission review. Because air photographs, a tree survey and drawings are submitted prior to development, planning staff have an opportunity to review the impact of site design in regard to the loss of existing trees.

Tree credits against new plantings may be granted for preserving existing trees through site design excellence.

Landscaping requirements start with street tree plantings for single-family and duplex family developments. A fifteen (15)-foot "landscape easement" for the purpose of planting street trees is required to abut the street right-of-way. In addition, two (2) yard trees are to be provided for each lot, and perimeter plantings of various widths and planting characters are to be established fronting common street classifications. Other site tree planting requirements are summarized in Figure 2.28.

All parking lots are to be planted in Lenexa. Those lots of more than ten (10) spaces and thirty-five hundred (3,500) square feet are to have internal plantings that range from ten (10) percent of the parking lot site for multi-family projects, seventy-five (75) percent for commercial use and five (5) percent for industrial and warehouse sites.

Buffers are required between various land uses. A formula has been developed to calculate differences in land use intensity (LUI) and determine any effects of intervening roads, drainage or utility easements on site livability. The resulting land use intensity difference is then used to determine the design of the buffer, whose specifications are illustrated in Table 5 of the ordinance. Generally, the greater the difference in LUI, the wider the buffer must be, and its planting palette must contain more shade and evergreen trees and screening shrubs. Reduction in width is allowed with the introduction of fences or walls.

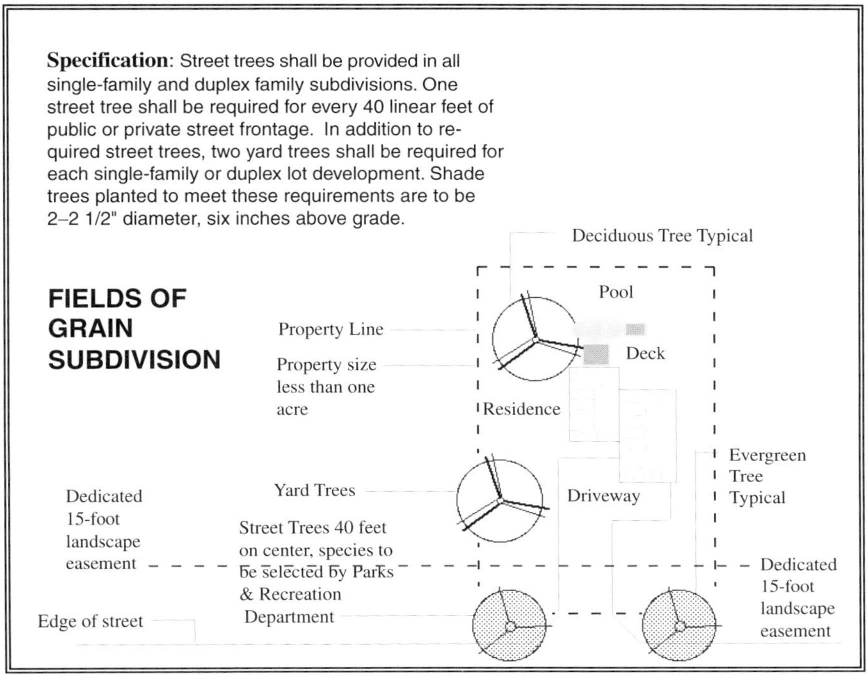

FIGURE 2.28. Site tree planting requirements, Lenexa, Kansas.

Standards are included for landscaping of signs, loading areas, outdoor storage, satellite antennas and ground-mounted utility equipment. Performance standards rather than technical standards are given for plant materials, irrigation, Xeriscape and landscape maintenance.

Among the more interesting landscaping standards in this ordinance is one that specifies requirements for landscaping "sign monuments." An area equal to three (3) times the size of a sign monument is to be planted with ornamental trees, shrubs, ground covers, rock beds or other decorative ground treatments. When new signs are introduced on existing sites with more than three hundred thirty (330) feet of road frontage, the entire front street yard shall be brought up to current standards for planting that part of the site.

Overland Park

Overland Park. Landscaping and Screening,
Chapter 18.450, Zoning Ordinance, n.d.

Overland Park intends to provide greenery to establish optimum environmental conditions for the city. Its ordinance ensures the preservation and replenishment of native trees, the use of screens to hide unsightly views and the use of buffers to shield poor land use relationships. Through the use of vegetation, screens and buffers, the appearance of developed properties will remain at a high level.

This ordinance applies to all zoning districts except residential and agricultural. Landscape plans signed by a registered landscape architect must be submitted in order to achieve a building or land use permit and a Certificate of Occupancy. Compliance with certain technical standards for the preparation of the landscape plans is required in order to allow plan reviewers to easily understand the plans. These standards are outlined in Table 2.54.

Design guidelines for each individual project must consider visual safety, species selection and landscape function. Landscape plans must address minimum tree requirements by zoning district, vehicular use areas and screening requirements. Detailed planting specifications for shrubs, turf and ground cover are not mentioned in the ordinance. Tree planting is based on linear footage of street frontage and a sliding scale percentage per building unit. For instance, seventy-five hundredths (.75) tree is required for each dwelling unit in PR-2 zoning districts.

Parking lot planting is based on the following formula:

$$\text{No. of parking spaces} \times 280 \text{ sq. ft.} \times .0600$$

Standards are given for plant material and maintenance. To ensure maintenance of required plantings, this city requires that a cash escrow or irrevocable letter of credit in the amount of twenty-five (25) percent of the initial landscaping costs

TABLE 2.54. Landscape Plan Requirements, Overland Park, Kansas

a. North point and scale
b. Topographic information and final grading adequate to identify and properly specify planting for areas needing slope protection
c. The location, size and surface of materials of all structures and parking areas
d. The location, size and type and quantity of all underground utilities and structures with proper notation, where appropriate, as to any safety hazards to avoid during installation of landscaping
e. The location, size and type and quantity of all proposed landscaping materials, along with common and botanical names of all plant species
f. The location, size and common name of all existing plant materials to be retained on-site
g. Mature sizes of plant materials, drawn to scale and called out on the plan by a common name or appropriate key
h. Location of hose connections and other watering sources
i. The location of all trees, 12-inch caliper or larger, measured 4½ feet above ground level, that are proposed for removal
j. All screening as required

shall be posted to ensure the needed replacements of materials and continued maintenance for two (2) years after installation.

Screening is to be provided for trash storage areas and ground-mounted or building-mounted equipment such as mechanical equipment, meter banks and utility connections. Six (6)-foot solid wall screen fences or walls are required where commercial or industrial properties abut residential land uses.

There is little unique about this ordinance besides the fact that the community requires that a cash escrow or irrevocable letter of credit be posted to ensure maintenance for the first two (2)-year period of time.

Wichita

Wichita, Ordinance Number 41-510 of the Code of the City of Wichita, Kansas, September 17, 1991.

The purpose of Sections 3 to 20 of the Wichita ordinance is to enhance the attractiveness of the community through establishment of landscape requirements for urban development projects. The sections apply to all new development and certain levels of redevelopment, renovation and/or additions within the corporate boundaries of the City of Wichita, except single-family residences, duplexes, and development occurring on property zoned D, Central Business District.

Section 1 of this ordinance deals with zoning districts in the City of Wichita, and Section 2 deals with community unit plan regulations. Section 2 also covers screening, which may be considered part of the land ordinance. The landscaping requirements begin under Section 3. Section 4 contains definitions important to the ordinance. Section 5 deals with required landscape street yards. Section 6 deals with required buffers. Section 7 deals with parking lot screening. All development, except for the central business district, one-family and two-family residential projects, must provide screening from adjacent residential properties and streets within one hundred fifty (150) feet at least three (3) feet high. Section 8 of the Code deals with percentages of living materials. Section 9 covers "other landscape regulations." Landscaping in the right-of-way of a state highway must be approved by the District Engineer. Planting strips for parking lot buffers must be approved by the City Engineer. Four copies of the plan must be submitted. No professional is required to prepare the plans. Section 10 deals with maintenance, Section 11 deals with exceptions and modifications and Section 12 encourages Xeriscaping. Section 13 explains enforcement/assurances for installation and completion. Section 14 deals with administrative remedies, Section 15 deals with penalties, Section 16 deals with appeals, Section 17 deals with amendments, and Section 18 deals with severability. All landscaping plans must be submitted to the Office of Central Inspection in order to receive a Certificate of Occupancy.

There are many unusual aspects of this ordinance. A sliding scale is used to determine street yard area. Street yard depth requirements change with the size of the development. Lots with an average depth of one hundred seventy-five (175) feet or less require eight (8) square feet of street yard, lots with an average depth of less than three hundred fifty (350) feet require ten (10) square feet of street yard, and lots with an average depth of greater than three hundred fifty (350) feet require twenty (20) square feet of street yard. A formula for this requirement has been designed to calculate the required street yard:

$$W \times X = Y$$

where W= width of the entire lot, X = required square footage per code, Y= the required area for street yard.

This requirement can, however, be reduced by twenty (20) percent if the minimum planting size of materials specified is increased by one hundred (100) percent or more, or by twenty (20) percent if all seven Xeriscaping principles are employed, but no reduction may exceed thirty (30) percent. Planting strips for parking lot buffers may be implemented through approval of the office of the City Engineer. Evergreen and/or deciduous trees in the parking lot buffer area may be planted, provided a solid screening effect is maintained year round for at least two-thirds of the area. The percentage of living materials for the required landscaping area are to contain fifty-five (55) percent ground covering surface, not including the crowns of trees. The other forty-five (45) percent may be covered with bark, wood chips, rock, bricks, stone or similar materials (monolithic paving not included). The planting of female or cotton-bearing cottonwood trees is prohibited. Landscaping within three (3) feet of a fire hydrant, traffic sign, traffic signal or utility structure is limited to eight (8)-inch mature height. Xeriscaping is an unusual feature to find in a city in the center of the continent. This code encourages use of all seven Xeriscape design elements.

The City of Wichita's ordinance is accompanied by a summary of its requirements. The ordinance is very formal with many small requirements.

Kentucky

Lexington

Lexington, Article 18, "Landscape and Land Use Buffers," n.d.

The intent of this article is to improve the appearance of vehicular use areas and property abutting public rights-of-way; to require buffering between incompatible land uses; to protect, preserve and promote the aesthetic appeal, character and value of the surrounding neighborhoods; and to promote public health and safety through the reduction of noise pollution, air pollution, visual pollution, air temperature and artificial light glare. All new development shall meet the requirements of this ordinance. Changes to existing developments of any kind call for at least the perimeter landscaping requirements to be added. The plans for developments including six thousand (6,000) or more square feet of vehicular use area shall be prepared by a licensed architect, landscape architect or engineer.

Property perimeter requirements, vehicular use area perimeter requirements, landscape buffers, easements, joint driveways, interior landscaping for vehicular use areas, service structures and screening are the landscaping topics covered. The perimeter requirements are each given in the form of charts, listed by abutting land uses. Next, the plant materials are discussed. Submittal and approval information is given last. Plans are to be submitted to the Division of Building Inspection in order to receive a Certificate of Occupancy.

Landscape materials shall be installed to provide a minimum of fifty (50) percent winter opacity and a seventy (70) percent summer opacity. Chain link fencing is prohibited for use in order to meet the walls and fences requirement, unless it is surrounded by continuous plantings. A plant materials list is included with this ordinance, which is necessary in order to apply the requirements of the ordinance. The use of any plant materials that are not on this list must be approved by the Division of Building Inspection.

This is a very concise, easily read ordinance.

Louisville and Jefferson County

Louisville and Jefferson County, Article 12, "Landscaping and Land Use Buffers," n.d.

This ordinance has several purposes stated in the contextual section of the document. Town officials seek to improve the appearance of vehicular use areas and property abutting public rights-of-way and to require buffering and screening between incompatible land uses. They are also interested in protecting, preserving and promoting the aesthetic appeal, character and value of neighborhoods while promoting public health and safety through the reduction of noise pollution, air pollution, visual pollution, air temperature and artificial light glare. Parkway standards, such as shown in Figure 2.29, offer an example of the standards contained within this code.

It is important to note that the ordinance does not intend to be restrictive to the point of preventing creativity and innovation in landscape design. The ordinance's "minimum standards" may be varied if plantings and site improvements offer a "substantial improvement" over the minimum standards. The Louisville and Jefferson County Planning Commission administers the ordinance and sees that all requirements are met on each and every new development.

The Planning Commission maintains a "Planting Manual" and a "Plant Materials List" for meeting the requirements of the ordinance.

Louisville and Jefferson County Planning Commission, "Parkway Policies," Resolution, "Interim Policies for Future Development Along Designated Parkways," 1989.

This resolution was developed to provide standardized review criteria for new development along the community's parkways. The Planning Commission will use the resolution until permanent standards are developed.

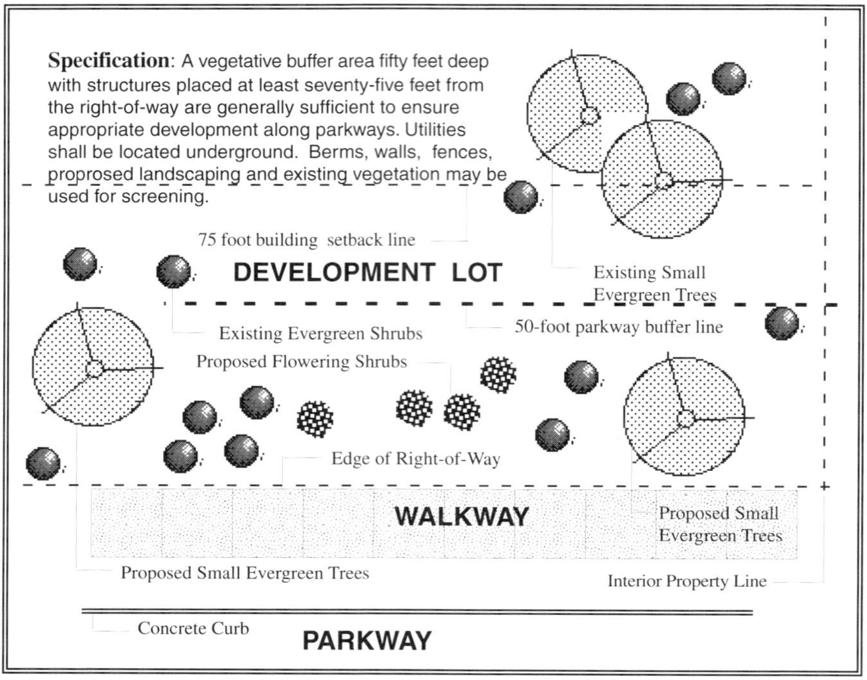

FIGURE 2.29. Parkway setback zone, Jefferson County, Kentucky.

The resolution attempts to protect the beauty of the parkways by establishing standards for buffer zones, fences and walls, entrances to subdivisions, parking areas, business signs and access roads. A vegetative buffer area fifty (50) feet deep and the placement of structures at least seventy-five (75) feet from the right-of-way are encouraged to "ensure appropriate development along parkways."

Louisiana

City and Town Ordinances

Baton Rouge

Baton Rouge, Code of Ordinances, Ordinance 2641, "Care of Trees, Shrubs and Flowers in Public Places," 1968.

The City of Baton Rouge and the Parish of East Baton Rouge are dedicated to prohibiting damage to trees, establishing certain regulations in regard to the care and maintenance of trees, shrubs and flowers in the public ways and providing penalties for violation.

With the ordinance, the city recognizes that trees have real economic value, offer great relief in a southern climate, provide screening of undesirable views and play an important part in soil conservation, noise control and air pollution.

The ordinance falls short of being a "green law," because it is based entirely on the preservation of public plantings, many of which have disappeared over the last few years as a result of road widening, utility clearing, drainage projects, boulevard clearing and storm damage. In short, there are no provisions in the ordinance for new plantings, only penalties for damage to plant materials in public places. Permits are required from the Director of Public Works, Superintendent of Recreation and Parks, or the City-Parish Permit Office to cut, trim, spray, remove, treat or plant any shrub, hedge or other plant on a public right-of-way within the city-parish.

Baton Rouge, Code of Ordinances, "Zoning Ordinance, City of Baton Rouge, Parish of East Baton Rouge," 1985.

This is an ordinance dividing the City of Baton Rouge and the Parish of East Baton Rouge into districts and, within said districts, regulating and restricting the height, number of stories and size of buildings and other structures, the size of yards, courts and other open spaces, the density of population, and the location and use of buildings, structures and land for trade, industry, residence and other purposes. It also establishes a Board of Adjustment, prescribes its powers and duties and provides penalties for violations.

Baton Rouge, Code of Ordinances, Title 7, Chapter 3, Part 13, Section 13.1, "Minimum Landscape Requirements," Ordinance 9808, January 19,1994.

This ordinance requires that new commercial, industrial, multifamily, religious, educational and institutional, and public and semipublic land uses and expansion of certain existing buildings meet minimum landscape standards. Landscape plans, prepared according to the laws administered by the Louisiana Horticulture Commission and presented by developers, must be reviewed and approved by the city-parish in order to receive a building permit. Plans are submitted to the City Parish Inspection Division. The Director of Landscape and Forestry approves all landscape plans and specifications.

Requirements are given for street planting areas, sight triangles, buffer planting areas, vehicular use areas and trash storage areas. Planting requirements are based on several methods of calculation: square footage, linear footage, percentage of use area and numbers of units. Tree requirements for general site planting are based on each ten thousand (10,000) square feet of site area. Street plantings and buffers are based on linear footage. Parking lots and vehicular storage areas are based upon the number of vehicle parking spaces and percentage of total area. Minimal size specifications are given for plant materials, and trees are grouped in two classes. Class A trees are large forest types or shade trees, and Class B trees are small flowering and fruiting ornamentals. No special plant palette is given.

The developer must install and care for plants and other landscape features according to landscape maintenance specifications provided. Clearing permits are required for tracts of land of more than five (5) acres; tree credits will be granted for preserved trees. Alternative compliance provisions within the ordinance may be applied under special circumstances. Minimum landscape standards and definitions are included. A Landscape Review Committee of citizens reviews all appeals. Fines are imposed for failure to comply with provisions of the ordinance.

The structure of this ordinance is a fine example of the proper way to structure a landscape ordinance for maximum readability. The subsections are structured into three distinct parts: the contextual, the technical and the administrative.

The contextual section provides the legal context and background information required to understand the ordinance. In this part are stated the purpose, applicability and definitions. The technical section states the minimum performance requirements or design standards to be met. Subsections here include landscape standards, landscape plan requirements, and alternative compliance. Designers will consult this area for specific design requirements.

The final part of the ordinance covers administrative procedures. This section helps the applicant understand the process necessary to receive a permit. Subsections explain permits and inspection requirements, enforcement, appeals and penalties and administrative guidelines. Of course, one will find the usual "conflicts," "severability," and "effective date" clauses located in this section.

Amended: Ordinance 10516, November 15, 1995, Buffer Yard Requirements.

In this ordinance, buffer yards are added which require specified types and amounts of planting and landscape screens to minimize conflicts in land use. A standard buffer yard width is imposed, with a prescribed number of plants per one hundred (100) linear feet. Different land uses call for various widths of buffer yard that range from fifteen (15) feet to seventy-five (75) feet. A "plant unit multiplier" factor is used to compute the exact number and type of plants required in the buffer. In some instances screens, walls, fences and berms may be substituted for buffer yard width. Height, material and opacity standards are given for fences, screens and walls. Earth berms, at least thirty-six (36) inches high, must be planted with both shrubs and ground covers. Size and height requirements for screening shrubs are specified.

Related: Ordinance 10517, November, 15, 1995, amending Title 7 (Planning and Zoning), Chapters 1 and 3 of the Code of Ordinances Subsection 7:2.215—Plan Review.

This ordinance, referred to as the Site Plan Review ordinance, requires that all high density developments (of more than thirty thousand (30,000) square feet or multifamily projects of seventy-five (75) units or more) be submitted to the Planning Commission for review and/or approval prior to seeking a building permit. Site plan review requires submittal of facts, design data and drawings itemized on a Site Plan Review Checklist contained within the ordinance.

A Tree/Woodland Survey illustrating generalized tree communities and a Landscape Plan, prepared in accordance with Ordinance 9808 (the landscape ordinance), are two items that must be submitted according to the Site Plan Review Checklist.

Baton Rouge, Code of Ordinances, "Creation of the East Baton Rouge Parish Tree Registry Program," Resolution 37341, October 23,1996.

Trees are a legacy for the City of Baton Rouge and the Parish of East Baton Rouge. This community believes that by enactment of this resolution, a greater understanding of trees will provide for the enhanced protection and understanding of the benefits of trees through the enlistment of public participation in the identification of trees which by virtue of their size, age, historic significance, or other uniqueness are worthy of registration. Ancient, Historic and Unique Trees will be entered into an official registry administered by the East Baton Rouge Parish Tree Commission.

This ordinance defines Ancient, Historical and Unique Trees, as well as Bicentennial Oaks and Legacy Oaks. The resolution creates an official register in which these trees will be listed by public nomination during a yearly induction ceremony hosted by the mayor-president in association with Arbor Day.

The Tree Commission will receive nominations by the general public and owners of trees in October of each year. It will then arrange for the Office of Landscape and Forestry staff to review, measure, assess, catalog, photograph and enter into the city's Geographic Information System (GIS) data base the locations and statistics of all inducted trees.

The mayor will present the owner of each registered tree with a Certificate of Registry as public recognition of the value of that tree.

Country Club of Louisiana

Country Club of Louisiana Design Guidelines, a private landscape ordinance, Country Club of Louisiana, Nicholas Development Group, Tampa, Florida, n.d.

One of the most interesting documents to appear recently is that containing the landscape design standards and recommendations for the Country Club of Louisiana. These standards, typical in many other places of the country, have not been recognized for what they really are. These are private green laws prepared and enforced by private developers and a willing neighborhood association.

Contained within the guidelines are recommendations for the siting of structures, dealing with drainage, protecting natural features and planting and site amenities. Also included are a description of the private plan review process, suggested plant materials and guidelines for the preparation of submittals to the Architectural Review Committee.

One could learn much from a visit to the Country Club. There one can see the results of a private landscape ordinance and the visual effect it has on the subdivision.

Covington

Covington, City of Covington Code of Ordinances, Section 4.4, Appendix B, "Minimum Landscape Requirements," Rev. 1989.

Covington, Louisiana, located on the north shore of Lake Pontchartrain, has one of the best landscape ordinances in the state. Known as "Minimum Landscape Requirements," the ordinance was designed to conserve the natural resources and maintain the character of this small Louisiana tourist town.

The ordinance applies to selected land uses. Minimum landscape requirements apply in all instances where a change of use would increase parking requirements. This ordinance consists of provisions for street planting, sight triangles, buffers, parking area plantings, screening, maintenance of plantings and tree preservation. Landscape plans must be submitted, and building permits are required prior to any site clearing or construction.

Denham Springs

Minimum Landscape Requirements, Zoning Code, City of Denham Springs, October 23, 1996.

This ordinance requires that new commercial, industrial, multifamily, religious, educational, and institutional land uses meet minimum landscape standards. Landscape design plans presented by developers must be reviewed and approved by the city in order to receive a Landscape Certificate. The developer must install and care for plants and other landscape features approved by the Landscape Ordinance Review Committee. Landscape plans submitted by developers should show plantings of trees and shrubs in street planting areas, buffer planting areas, vehicular use areas, trash and storage areas and storm water retention areas. Clearing permits are required for tracts of land of more than one (1) acre; tree credits will be granted for preserved trees. Alternative compliance will be granted for special situations.

This ordinance was modeled after one established in nearby Baton Rouge, Louisiana. It was designed to be highly participatory rather than prescriptive. A community review board of citizens works with developers to establish a reasonable landscape design for each new development in this small town. Strict requirements are not prescribed; rather, developers are given general performance standards, according to which they offer solutions in the form of a landscape design that will be installed at the time that building improvements are made.

DeRidder

DeRidder, Section 13-30, DeRidder Code Article III, "Plat Approval Procedure," 1978.

This code covers information regarding the design of subdivisions. It discusses details of information needed for a preliminary plat of a proposed subdivision and mentions the Planning Commission's review and approval procedures for a preliminary plat. Constructed improvements must provide permanent markers and comply with standards for sanitary sewers, water supply and storm drainage. Requirements for the final plat are discussed. The final plat shall be submitted to the city council (with complete construction plans and specifications) in triplicate. Plans should be drawn at a scale of one hundred (100) feet to one (1) inch and shall be of a kind that is reproducible by blueprint machines. A fee of one (1) dollar per lot for each lot in a subdivision is required, with a minimum fee of ten (10) dollars. At least sixteen (16) other requirements are mentioned for final plats in order to obtain approval.

DeRidder, Article 1, In General 12-1-12-19, "Streets and Sidewalks," Article 2 12-20-12-26, "Excavations," 1978.

In these short articles, topics include damage to sidewalks and trees, permits for excavation and their associated fees, specific regulations regarding excavation, restoring soil fill and surface soil requirements after excavation and penalties for violation of the articles.

Hammond

Hammond, "Landscape Ordinance of Hammond," n.d.

A public tree ordinance has recently been adopted by the City of Hammond to regulate and coordinate the planting of trees and shrubbery in the streets and public grounds of the city and to preserve existing trees from indiscriminate removal and damage.

Provisions of the ordinance create the position of Urban Forester and a public body known as the Advisory Committee on Urban Forestry. Permits are required for tree removal, and developers must submit plans showing public trees to be removed during construction activities. Replantings must conform to a list of approved trees, and minimal planting standards and requirements are contained within the ordinance. Fines for violation of the ordinance are specified.

There are few street tree ordinances in Louisiana, but this ordinance is a model for other cities to follow. The Hammond ordinance should be strengthened and made more comprehensive in its scope. Budgeting and administrative responsibility must be assigned, and a master tree planting plan for the city must be prepared.

Jamestown

Jamestown, Ordinance No. 18, "Landscape Ordinance of Jamestown," 1987.

This unusual ordinance places restrictions on the visual appearance of any wrecking yard or holding yard of damaged equipment or other products to be stored or held upon any property within the confines of the village of Jamestown. Failure to abide by the requirements results in a fine, after thirty (30) days' written notice by the representatives of the village, of no less than one hundred (100) dollars or a possible jail term to be set by the district judge.

Jennings

City of Jennings, Ordinance No. 953, September 12, 1978.

Within Ordinance No. 953, the City of Jennings has set up a City Tree Board, which consists of citizens of the city and two professional arborists. They are in charge of studying and developing plans for the care, preservation, pruning, planting and removal of trees and shrubs in public areas. They have set up a mandatory plant list and regulate various aspects of tree care in Jennings. This seems to be the only City Tree Board we know of in the state. Two other ordinances, Nos. 860 and 1049, deal with the removal of weeds in the city.

Kenner

Kenner, Zoning Ordinance No. 2427, Section 20.11, "Landscaping Regulations," 1987.

Kenner adopted Ordinance No. 2427, Section 20.11, in January 1987. This ordinance, although not sophisticated or complex, is one of the most comprehensive landscape ordinances found in the State of Louisiana. It deserves notice as a model ordinance for small towns that are experiencing rapid growth.

The ordinance requires landscaping for all multifamily, office, commercial and industrial developments in the city. Its stated purpose is to provide standards for landscaping and screening in the city, thus aiming to improve the general appearance of the community and diminish the harsh effect of the components of high-density developments such as buildings, parking lots and trash receptacles. The ordinance is designed to do this by specifying the use of plant materials as a unifying element, to define space and articulate the uses of specific areas.

Landscaping, as defined in the Kenner ordinance, is any combination of living plants such as trees, shrubs, vines, ground covers, flowers and lawns. In addition, included within the definition are natural features such as rock, stone and bark and structural features including, but not limited to, fountains, reflecting pools, artworks, screen walls, fences and benches.

The ordinance, administered by the Regulatory Department and the Director of Planning, does not include a plant list in its regulations, but does have standards for plant sizes, the use of plants indigenous to the area, landscape area requirements and maintenance. Landscape area requirements are based on a square or linear footage method.

Compliance with the terms of the ordinance starts with the submission of a landscape plan that illustrates the types and locations of existing vegetation, proposed vegetation, location of dumpsters, and all other site elements such as structures, parking areas and man-made elements. The landscape plan must be approved prior to the issuance of a building permit.

The ordinance does not require the landscape plan to be sealed by a landscape architect. This ordinance withholds the Certificate of Occupancy until all requirements are met; there are no provisions for enforcement or alternate compliance.

Lafayette

Lafayette, Ordinance No. 0-22-1/2, "Tree Ordinance," n.d.

It is unclear whether this amendment to the previous ordinance of the same name has been adopted. The ordinance describes a "City Tree Advisory Committee," its intent and member-appointment procedures. It defines terms such as *street tree, park tree* and *city arborist* and includes a tree list based on size. Small trees may be planted no closer than thirty (30) feet apart, medium trees forty (40) feet and large trees fifty (50) feet, except in special plantings approved by a landscape architect. No tree may be planted closer to any curb or sidewalk than two (2) feet for small trees, three (3) feet for medium trees and four (4) feet for large trees.

This ordinance also makes it unlawful for any person, firm or city department to cut back limbs to stubs any larger than three (3) inches in diameter within the crown, which is disfiguring to any street tree. Owners are required to prune vegetation obstructing light from city street lamps, as well as vegetation creating a hazard for pedestrian or vehicle traffic. Dead or diseased trees must be removed, and stumps must be removed to below the surface of the ground.

The amendment attempts to regulate and restrict the size of all buildings and other structures, the percentage of a lot that may be occupied, the size of yards and other open spaces, the density of population, the location and use of buildings, structures and land for trade, industry, residence or other purposes, and for said purposes divide the city into districts; to regulate and restrict the erection, structural alteration or use of buildings or land therein; to provide for the change of such regulations, restrictions and boundaries of zones; and to provide the enforcement of this code.

Lafayette, Article 1 Section 1-101 to Article 7 Section 7-102, "Tentative Draft No. 6 of the City of Lafayette Development Code," n.d.

In response to the survey recently conducted, Lafayette provided a copy of its zoning ordinance and a draft copy of its development code. The zoning ordinance contains regulations about parking lots and their separation from residential areas, as some green laws do. The laws are not specific enough to function as a comprehensive green law.

The city's development code, which has never been adopted, addresses some of the issues normally covered by green laws. The purpose of establishing minimum standards is to minimize adverse effects of particular uses on adjacent properties and to further the aesthetic quality of the environment. Section 5-110 goes into detail about buffering and does a good job of addressing residential areas that abut commercial areas, but is very weak in its plant materials requirement. No trees are specifically required, only plant materials, which could consist of anything the owner would like to plant.

The proposed code does state that the Department of Planning has a recommended plant list that one should use. Included in this section is a statement about conditional use that calls for a landscaping plan to be approved by the City

Planning and Zoning Commission or the City Council. No landscape plan is required otherwise, and enforcement is not addressed in this section.

Lake Charles

Lake Charles, Ordinance No. 7717, "Zoning Ordinance for the City of Lake Charles, Louisiana," 1984.

The City of Lake Charles has a complete and thorough zoning ordinance. Typical topics are covered, which include the following: title, purpose and applicability, definitions, rules of interpretation, land use policies, administration of development standards, development regulations, enforcement and fees.

Lake Charles, Ordinance No. 7717, Article V, Section 5-209, "Fencing and Perennial (Nondeciduous) Screening Standards for Landscaped, Constructed, or Natural Buffer Yards," n.d.

This city provided a copy of its zoning ordinance. Within it are two sections that address some typical landscaping issues. Section 5-209's purpose is to promote the harmonious use of the land through effective site planning and the use of landscaped, constructed or natural buffer yards; it addresses only buffer yards. Section 5-210 deals with landscaping of off-street parking and loading areas. These parking requirements, though minimal, can be the beginning of a good landscape ordinance. Both of these sections require the use of plant material, yet neither requires a planting plan or has any approval process to regulate this planting. An approved plant list in not included in the law, but is suggested in an insert provided by the Office of City Planning.

Leesville

Leesville, Ordinance No. 276238, "Subdivision Regulations for Leesville, Louisiana," 1968.

Within the city's subdivision regulations, Section 10 deals specifically with street trees. This is a very limited section in that it does not require planting, but recommends it. There is no penalty attached, and no planting plan is required. The best part of this section is the expression of willingness of the Planning Commission to aid in the placement and selection of trees. If a tree is to be planted in a right-of-way, then the proposed location and species must be approved by the Planning Commission.

Mandeville

Mandeville, Ordinance No. 84-14, Sections 4.1100–4.1117 "Landscape Ordinance of Mandeville," 1988.

The requirements of this code generally concentrate on periphery landscape requirements; parking requirements; buffer requirements; screening of trash and garbage cans; trees, vegetation and screening to be preserved/maintained; clearing permit; building permit—landscape ordinance; tree and shrub removal; live oak protection requirements; minimum planting requirements; tree barriers; violation and penalty; emergencies; and fee schedule. A design manual accompanies the ordinance.

Mandeville, Mandeville Code, Article 4, Section 4.11 "Landscape Ordinance of Mandeville," 1985.

The landscape ordinance established in Mandeville in 1983 was revised and adopted as Ordinance No. 84-14, Sec. 4.11, Appendix A, Zoning, in January 1985. This ordinance was found to be comprehensive and a good model for small towns that rely on beauty and "greenness" as a tourist attraction.

The Mandeville law covers issues such as the permitting process, periphery landscape requirements, parking requirements, buffer requirements, screening of trash and garbage cans, and maintenance and preservation of trees, vegetation and screening.

Of unusual interest in this law is the language providing for the preservation of plant materials. In fact, such features as tree and shrub removal permits, live oak protection requirements, tree barriers and vegetation protection zones occur in no other ordinances reviewed.

Mandeville requires a landscape plan, though it does not state who is qualified to prepare it. The ordinance goes into some detail as to clearing, building, and tree and shrub removal permits that are needed prior to developing in the city.

Penalties for violations of this ordinance can run as high as five hundred (500) dollars for each plant that is removed, caused to become diseased or to die. Each separate day of the violation constitutes a separate fine.

For a small north shore resort town, the completeness of the green law is remarkable. This is evidence that the City of Mandeville cherishes and sees the value of plant materials in its community. This ordinance seems to be having a positive effect on the city, and time will show the effect of this green law on the livability of the community.

Monroe

Monroe, Ordinance No. 37-166, "Monroe Code Landscaping Requirement" (i.e., Percent of Landscaping per Area of Parking), n.d.

The Monroe code deals with the landscaping requirements of parking facilities. Very limited requirements are found in this community, based on the information received.

New Orleans

New Orleans, "Draft Landscape Ordinance," 1988.

An asset to Louisiana is the Landscape Ordinance package for the City of New Orleans.

This green law is actually a package that contains the proposed Landscape Ordinances for the City of New Orleans, CBD Parking Lot Design Standards, the Lower Coast Algiers Design Review District, the Bullard Avenue Urban Corridor District, the I-10/510 Urban Corridor District and the General DeGaulle Urban Corridor District. Together, they constitute the most comprehensive landscape ordinance package in Louisiana. The districts cited in the latter four (4) ordinances are overlay zoning districts.

The City Planning Commission is presently considering several "generic urban corridors," which would be administered in the same manner as the existing urban corridors (UCs). The generic UCs would have landscape guidelines with more flexibility and be an improvement over the existing UCs.

The entire package of green laws deserves the full support of the Louisiana Association of Nurserymen (LAN), the American Society of Landscape Architects (ASLA), environmental groups and concerned citizens of Louisiana to ensure their adoption and the favorable impact they will have on historic and developing New Orleans.

Based on critical observation, this package of ordinances, described in the following paragraphs, appears to be on the same plane of excellence as the ordinances of other large cities of America.

City of New Orleans, Draft Landscape Ordinance.

This ordinance is proposed because the City Council finds that the *tout ensemble* (character) of the city is threatened through degradation of the appearance, character, and value of existing land use and by ecological changes such as increases in air temperature, accelerating natural soil erosion, sedimentation, water runoff and hazardous traffic situations. If adopted, the law will safeguard and enhance property values and contribute to the process of air purification, oxygen regeneration, groundwater recharge and storm water runoff retardation.

Specific provisions of the ordinance concern the establishment of compliance districts, perimeter and interior landscaped areas, street yard requirements, screening, preservation of natural landscape character and issuance of permits. Other aspects of the code deal with jurisdiction, administration and enforcement of the law.

Of importance are provisions for alternative compliance to give developers options for individualized landscape design. The City of New Orleans has been divided into three districts according to the growth pattern and historical value of the areas. Each of these areas has a different point value that must be attained by the developer in order to comply with the ordinance.

It is required that the City Landscape Architect implement the review process as required by this ordinance and approve all landscape development plans submitted to the City Planning Commission, the Department of Streets, and the Department of Safety and Permits. The ordinance requires that all plans for developments having a vehicular use area of five thousand (5,000) square feet or greater shall include the stamp or seal of a landscape architect, licensed by the State of Louisiana, and his or her statement certifying that all requirements of the landscape ordinance have been satisfied.

Enforcement is accomplished by the issuance or withholding of the Certificate of Occupancy. This ordinance has not passed yet, but it is already having a positive effect on New Orleans, because developers are voluntarily following the code in regard to preserving nature and building nature in the city with their new developments.

City of New Orleans, Lower Coast Algiers Design Review District.

Presently under consideration for adoption in the City of New Orleans is a revision to the Comprehensive Zoning Law to establish an overlay zoning district, to be known as Lower Coast Algiers Design Review District, for the purpose of preserving and enhancing the woodland character of Lower Coast Algiers and to provide for a superior environment along English Turn Parkway. The overlay district regulations are designed to promote the community health and welfare by protecting and encouraging woodlands, trees, and open space for the unique benefits they provide in enhancing community appearance and assisting in the natural control of solar heat, soil conservation, flooding, air pollution and noise. In addition, the code will provide citizens with psychological relief from the increasing complexities of a man-made urban environment.

Provisions of the proposed ordinance set design standards for landscape buffer zones, interior lot landscaping, woodlands buffer zones, perimeter landscape areas, supplementary planting within buffer yards and planting within vehicular use areas. In addition, the draft ordinance will make it illegal for any site to be indiscriminately cleared of existing vegetation prior to issuance of a building permit from the Department of Safety and Permits and following approval of a site plan by the City Planning Commission. Special provisions of this proposed law include preservation of hedgerows and pecan groves and protection and preservation of natural areas within the district.

Minimal plant material specifications are given, and there are no enforcement provisions other than nonissuance of a building permit. However, an approved species list is available and fifty (50) percent of the plants used must be native plants.

City of New Orleans. Bullard Avenue Urban Corridor District, Section 34, Article 5, Comprehensive Zoning Law, March 20, 1986.

Bullard Avenue is located in New Orleans East in an area that is just now developing. This new urban corridor is a commercial district that connects Lake Pontchartrain with the Mississippi. Nearby is the upscale gated residential community of Eastover. This district is being used as an area to test urban design concepts. The purpose of the ordinance is to provide for a superior environment along a portion of a major urban corridor.

This ordinance is somewhat unusual in that it is an "overlay district landscape ordinance." The overlay district regulations are intended to supplement the regulations of the underlying commercial zoning district.

Design components of the ordinance include a twenty (20)-foot front property line landscape buffer, off-street loading areas, buffer screening and interior landscaping of vehicular use areas. A perimeter landscape strip is to be designed to clearly delineate the boundaries of vehicular use areas. Credit is granted for preserved trees, based on a sliding scale. For example, nine (9) trees are credited for a tree thirty-six (36) inches in diameter while only three (3) trees are credited for a twelve (12)-inch tree.

In addition to most of the usual landscape requirements, this ordinance regulates signage, lighting standards and height requirements. Special provisions are made for automobile dealerships to allow them to have "automobile display pads" within the twenty (20)-foot landscape buffer setback.

The ordinance is administered through site plan review by the City Planning Commission. Appeals may be reviewed and reversed by the City Council.

The concept of an overlay district landscape ordinance is an interesting idea that should be considered in all communities that are about to adopt a landscape ordinance. This green law "trial balloon" can help the public understand the effects of adopting a citywide ordinance prior to the actual political process that must be followed to gain acceptance of a new community law.

City of New Orleans, Comprehensive Zoning Ordinance No. 4264 M.C.S., Section 27.2.32—Article 5, CBD "Parking Lot Design Standards," 1987.

This is a revision to the Comprehensive Zoning Ordinance of the City of New Orleans that became law on September 17, 1987. The ordinance provides for design standards for parking lots in CBD Zoning Districts and makes nonaccessory parking lots in the central business district (CBD) a conditional use for up to a five (5)-year period, and applies the design standards to accessory parking lots. All new parking areas in the CBD will come under the requirements for screening, landscaping, perimeter planting, landscape maintenance, signage, litter receptacles, extended storage, structures, hydraulic lift parking, curb cuts and pavement surfacing.

Plant materials must be of a specified size and species, and a landscape plan must be approved by landscape architects on the City Planning Commission.

Ruston

Ruston, "Landscape Requirements," Ordinance 1044, February 2, 1990.

The focus of this landscape ordinance is on retaining and enhancing the quality of the environment with street trees, screening of objectionable views, and implementation of a minimum standard of landscaping for commercial properties. The ordinance applies to new development with street frontage in commercial zoning districts C1 through C3 only. The ordinance also applies when existing buildings are expanded by more than twenty (20) percent or to redevelopment that increases the nonpermeable coverage by more than two thousand (2,000) square feet. Landscape plans with specifications must be submitted in order to receive an occupancy permit. Requirements set forth in the ordinance include (a) specifications for percentage of green space, (b) percentage of land clearing and tree removal allowed, (c) landscape buffers, (d) fencing, (e) maintenance, (f) irrigation, (g) utility placement and trash storage, (h) vehicular access dimensions and (i) yard size regulations.

This ordinance contains an "alternative compliance" provision that allows the Planning Director to approve the landscape plan if the design achieves the intent and general landscaped open space ratio called for in the ordinance.

Planting requirements are based on what is submitted in the landscape plan. The ordinance requires only that landscaping shall consist of a combination of materials such as grasses, ground covers, shrubs, vines, hedges and trees. No specifics are given as to quantity or size. Plants shall be of high quality, hardy and drought tolerant.

Attached to the ordinance is a listing of recommended trees and shrubs, according to height, that are suitable for Ruston. Example plans of sight triangles for public rights-of-way and building setback/landscape buffers also accompany the ordinance.

In the original ordinance enacted by the City of Ruston, twenty (20) percent of all commercial property must consist of green space and no more than seventy (70) percent of all existing trees six (6) inches DBH could be cleared from the site. The green space requirement was amended and reduced to five (5) percent of the site following protests by developers. The tree preservation language in this ordinance, one of the most stringent in Louisiana, was eliminated completely. No credit is given for preserving existing trees in the revised ordinance.

According to city employees in the permit office, the ordinance works well for this small northern Louisiana city of twenty-five thousand (25,000) people. They see results in the expanding suburban fringe.

Shreveport

Shreveport, Code of Ordinances, Chapter 14 1/2, "Drainage and Erosion Control," 1987.

Two sets of regulations in Shreveport are considered relevant environmental laws. Ordinance No. 34 of 1987 deals with issues related to drainage, storm water runoff and topsoil loss. This is the only ordinance inventoried that deals with drainage, erosion control, water pollution and flooding problems as related to land-altering activity. This ordinance has been included in our analysis because we believe that its pertinent issues can be part of the justifiable basis for green laws in Louisiana.

Site Development Permits are required, and erosion control plans and grading and drainage plans must be submitted to the City Engineer in the Department of Public Works. Other provisions of the ordinance include maintenance, standard definitions, appeal procedures and a penalty clause including a fine of up to five hundred (500) dollars on a day-by-day basis and sixty (60) days in jail.

Guidelines for plan preparation require that a registered professional civil engineer must stamp and sign that the plans are complete and that the technical data they contain is accurate. Landscape architects can prepare grading and drainage plans and erosion control plans for residential single-family detached dwellings. With the problems of drainage and erosion found in Louisiana, more of this type of regulation is needed to protect the environment in developing areas.

Shreveport, Code of Ordinances, Section J, "Landscaping Requirements," 1987.

This second set of regulations is landscaping requirements. This section, a result of Ordinance 136 of 1987, amending the Zoning Ordinance, Section III, Item J, is considered a green law (landscape ordinance). Its intent is very similar to the ordinance found in Austin, Texas. It addresses parking and street yard requirements and requires a landscape plan to be submitted, though it does not state who is qualified to prepare the plan for submittal. This ordinance also addresses alternative compliance, adding flexibility to the regulation.

As to requirements for plant material, this regulation is somewhat weak. No plant list is required; a minimum size, but no control over the quality of the plant material, has been established. This ordinance seems to be fairly successful.

An interesting point determined from the research is that the Shreveport ordinance is almost an exact copy of Ordinance No. 2445 of 1987, the landscape ordinance for Caddo Parish. This indicates that conformity between city and parish law is important for the visual effects upon the community.

Slidell

Slidell, Code of Ordinances Section 2.25, Protection of Existing Trees and Landscaping Requirements, n.d. Slidell, Ordinance No. 2144, "New Addition to Slidell Code of Ordinances, Appendix A–Zoning, Section 2.2502, Land Clearing Permit Required," 1987.

Section 2.25 of the city zoning ordinance addresses tree protection, land clearing and landscaping requirements.

This law is of interest because it requires a land clearing permit, at the cost of ten (10) dollars per acre, prior to the preparation of a landscape plan. Land clearing is defined in the ordinance as the removal of five (5) trees of more than six (6) inches in diameter per platted lot. Live oaks and magnolias over twelve (12) inches in diameter and other species over fifteen (15) inches are highly desirable and are required to be preserved and protected pursuant to revisions enacted in Ordinance No. 2144, 1987, and Ordinance No. 2171, 1988.

The landscape requirements as outlined in the ordinance are limited to a ten (10)-foot wide planting area along public rights-of-way, parking lot planting areas and planted pedestrian access planting areas between buildings and parking areas.

This is summarized in Figure 2.30. Ordinance requirements are restricted to providing landscape zones and do not give detailed planting requirements.

A list of approved plant materials suggested for planting and the minimum sizes acceptable for planting are given. Violation of this ordinance can lead to a five hundred (500) dollar fine per tree removed.

In addition, Slidell has a landscape ordinance found under Section 2.25 that addresses important issues such as parking lot screening, buffering of residential areas and specific plant requirements. The ordinance does require a landscape plan, but does not specify who shall draw up this plan.

To enforce this ordinance, Slidell has given the permit office power to withhold the Certificate of Occupancy until all requirements are met. It would be very informative to find out how well this ordinance is working and the specific effect it is having on the city.

Another section of the code, Section 2.2207, is an ordinance that specifically addresses buffering with the use of opaque six (6) foot tall fences. It states the requirements for all zones and very specifically how this is to be done.

The City of Slidell has available for citizens an illustrated guide to the green law. The document, interestingly enough prepared with a grant from the Louisiana

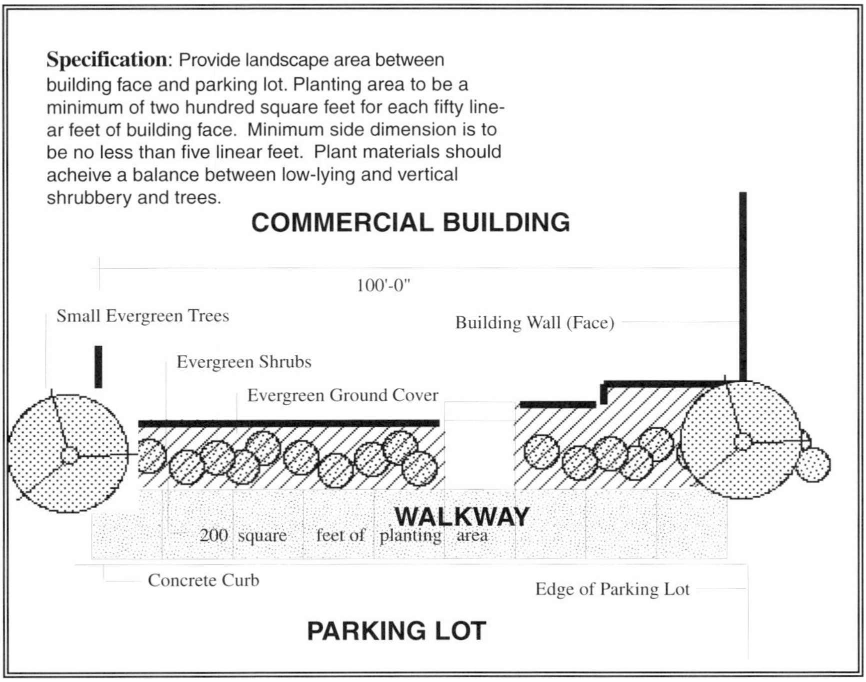

FIGURE 2.30. Pedestrian access planting requirement, Slidell, Louisiana.

Arts Council, is referred to as "The Development and Design Guide" and simplifies the language of the ordinance with drawings and illustrations.

Winnfield

Winnfield, Ordinance No. 3, "Weed Control," 1983.

Basically, this ordinance places responsibility on property owners to cut and remove noxious weeds or grass. Information is given regarding action that may be taken by the municipality in the event of failure of the property owner to perform such acts. Fines to the property owner are also discussed.

Winnfield, Ordinance No. 4, "Nuisances and Offensive Conditions," 1983.

In this code, three sections are covered: nuisances and offensive conditions (defined), noise control and disposal of defective vehicles.

The word *nuisance* is defined in this ordinance as any source of filth, cause of sickness, source of rodent problems or conditions causing a safety hazard.

Topics covered in the section entitled "Nuisance" include exposure of unwholesome matter, emission of smoke and other noxious fumes and materials, termite-infested wood, storage of material, and display of merchandise.

The word *noise* means any unreasonably loud, disturbing or unnecessary noise or any noise of such character, intensity or duration as to be detrimental to the life or health of any individual or which is in disturbance to the life or health of any individual or which is in disturbance of public peace and welfare; any such noise is prohibited. Topics include exceptions; horns and signal devices; playing of radio, phonographs or musical instruments; animals, birds, fowls; unnecessary noises from vehicles; engine mufflers; and use of drums or loudspeakers.

Under "Disposal of Defective Vehicles," no disassembled or inoperable or unlicensed and no junked or wrecked motor vehicle is to be stored or allowed to remain in the open on private property within the city for a period in excess of three (3) days, and vehicles of this type are not allowed to remain on any street within the city for a period in excess of twenty-four (24) continuous hours. Exceptions and penalties are provided.

Parish Ordinances

Sixty-four (64) Louisiana parishes were surveyed. A total of twenty-seven (27) responded. Six (6) parishes indicated that green laws have been adopted on a parish-wide (county) basis. One community, East Baton Rouge Parish, uses the same ordinance for the city as well as the unincorporated areas of the parish, and another parish, Jefferson, has several related ordinances. A brief discussion of each parish ordinance follows.

Ascension Parish

Ascension Parish, Chapter 11, "Health and Sanitation," Article I. Sec. 11-1 to Sec. 11-3, n.d.

Section 11-1 to 11-3 in this ordinance explains the penalty to the owner of a vacant lot who does not cut and remove all grass in excess of eight (8) inches.

Bossier Parish

Chapter 19, "Subchapter A, Zoning and Land Use Regulations, Bossier Parish, Louisiana," 1983. Bossier Parish, Chapter 19, "Subchapter G, Zoning and Land Use Regulations, Bossier Parish Louisiana," 1984.

The zoning ordinance of Bossier Parish does not contain a green law. Section 19:601, (c)4, mentions the value of trees in the environment and the benefits associated with trees. Preservation of trees is encouraged, but no protective measures are taken or enforced.

Caddo Parish

Caddo Parish, "Code of Ordinances, Article IX, Chapter 51, Landscaping Requirements," 1987.

Caddo Parish has an impressive set of detailed green laws, enacted in 1987. The intent, definitions and administration of the green law is defined within Ordinance No. 2445, Article IX of Chapter 51 of the Code of Ordinances.

The law is founded on environmental principles, addressed by stabilizing the ecological balance by contributing to the processes of air movement, air purification, oxygen regeneration, groundwater recharge and storm water runoff control, at the same time aiding in noise, glare, heat and dust abatement. Enhancement of beauty, quality of life, visual buffering between land uses and protection of the public health, safety and general welfare are secondary concerns.

The ordinance purports to safeguard and to protect property values and to protect private and public investment by addressing existing developed areas, street frontage requirements, off-street parking facility requirements, acceptable landscape materials, landscape plan submission and public review requirements.

Alternative compliance and the steps to be taken in complying with the ordinance are discussed. This is a very important section, as green laws must have a range of flexibility; achievement of the intent of the law is more important than the law itself. Caddo Parish also defines the acceptable standards for plant materials. Although requirements for plant materials are minimal, the community requires the use of certain standard sizes and encourages the use of high-quality, hardy and drought-tolerant species.

Enforcement is achieved by withholding the Certificate of Occupancy or granting a temporary certificate good for a six (6)-month period until the landscaping requirements are completed. No penalty provisions are provided.

Maintenance needs and the responsibilities of the property owner are defined in the law. The Metropolitan Planning Commission will provide limited technical assistance to developers and property owners when necessary. The parish does not require the seal of a landscape architect on the landscape plans.

East Baton Rouge Parish (see City of Baton Rouge)

Jefferson Parish

Jefferson Parish, Louisiana. Commercial Parkway Overlay Zone, Section XIII G—Comprehensive Zoning Ordinance, May 11, 1988.

Jefferson Parish adjoins the City of New Orleans and is a highly populated urban center. The parish is located between Lake Pontchartrain, the Mississippi River and nearby coastal wetlands at the margins of the Gulf of Mexico. Much of the land is low and unbuildable. The parish looks very much like a city, although there is no distinct downtown or CBD. Commercial growth has occurred randomly along some of the major canals that drain the parish. All of the major commercial districts seem and look like strip development. To remedy this situation and bring a sense of unity to commercial corridors, Jefferson Parish has enacted a better version of the New Orleans "overlay district landscape ordinance."

Initially developed in New Orleans, this new overlay zoning district superimposes landscape and buffer standards to enhance the general quality of commercial, office development and other structures located on major streets. Commercial Parkway Overlay Zone (CPZ) requirements are imposed in addition to the underlying zoning district regulations. Development in these zones must comply with both the standard zoning requirements and the landscape buffer overlay requirements.

Design components of this ordinance include requirements for site areas, parking lots and buffer zones. A twenty (20)-foot landscaped buffer zone is required in the front of all properties, and a seven (7)-foot landscape buffer is required adjacent to residential districts. Parking lots must be separated from streets and surrounding land uses by buffer strips. Parking lots must have at least ten (10) percent of the interior landscaped with planted islands and medians.

Other design components of this ordinance include perimeters adjacent to public rights-of-way, service drives, landscape lighting and sign regulations.

Standards are given in the ordinance for vegetation, sidewalks, signage and plant material installation.

All development must comply with this ordinance. Existing sites must be brought into compliance when there is a change of use or when renovations or additions are made to the property. An addition of twenty-five hundred (2,500) square feet will result in bringing the land use in compliance with this ordinance.

The ordinance is administered by the Jefferson Parish Planning Department. Preapplication conferences are held prior to the submission of the site plan and CPZ application materials. Specific requirements are listed for the preparation of the site plan and CPZ application. An application fee of one hundred fifty (150) dollars is required along with registration of the CPZ site plan with the Clerk of Court's office. Title restrictions must accompany the plan in favor of the Parish of Jefferson, restricting the use of the property to that approved by the Jefferson Parish Council. The CPZ may be amended or withdrawn by the developer according to the same procedure described in this law.

This overlay zone landscape ordinance should be emulated in many towns and cities in which long commercial strip developments coexist with residential developments.

From personal observation of the author, this type of landscape ordinance pays great dividends in the form of better designed environments. Such ordinances minimize the visual and land use impact of commercial development on drainage by reducing paved areas and by coordinating green spaces, signage, buildings and parking areas.

Jefferson Parish, "The MUCD Handbook: A Comprehensive Guide to Mixed Use Corridor District Development," 1988.

MUCD stands for Mixed Use Corridor District. The intent of MUCD regulations is to improve the quality of development along major streets through site plan analysis and landscape, buffer, sign and design standards.

Site plans, complete with all of the details of a project, including building location and dimensions, parking, traffic circulation, landscaping and so forth, are submitted to the Planning Department. Following a public hearing by the Planning Advisory Board, the plans are forwarded to the Jefferson Parish Council for a final public hearing and approval.

MUCD regulations offer the developments greater flexibility regarding what is permitted on the site, and greater flexibility regarding certain parish regulations. Sites developed under these regulations are generally more attractive and coordinated with surrounding developments than under conventional zoning.

The special provisions built into the MUCD—landscape, buffer, sign and design standards—have been used successfully in other areas to guide development to the benefit of the developers, adjacent property owners and local governments.

Topics of the handbook include MUCD procedures, additions or changes to existing development, and attachments such as an MUCD application form, MUCD sample ordinance and ordinance format guide, site plan review requirements, the MUCD checklist and sample MUCD site plan statistical blocks and standards for sign area measurement.

Ordinance No. 16967, "Mixed Use Corridor District," Jefferson Parish Planning Department, 1986.

A Mixed Use Corridor overlay District (MUCD) has been developed by the Planning Department with landscaping, buffering, sign and design standards geared toward improving the quality of commercial and office corridors. Site plan review is required, a landscaping plan and maintenance plan must be submitted and two public hearings are held. Standards for the MUCD exceed those of the CPZ. Neither requires the seal of a Registered Landscape Architect. A MUCD handbook is available from the Planning Commission.

Lafayette Parish

Lafayette Parish, Ordinance No. 059-93, July 26, 1993.

The purpose of this ordinance is to promote, protect, and preserve the general welfare, safety, health, peace and good order of the citizens of Lafayette Parish by regulating the developments of certain business activities. The ordinance governs the development of borrow pits, dumping pits, scrap and salvage yards, landfills, waste transfer stations, waste pickup stations, disposal facilities, prisons, incinerators, wrecker yards and pipe yards.

No certified planner or landscape architect is required for the planning of these requirements.

The ordinance sets up Category A, a width requirement, to be used for businesses within one-half (½) mile of a residence located in an approved subdivision, one-quarter (¼) mile of a residence not located in an approved subdivision or within one (1) mile of a school. Category B, a smaller width requirement, is to be used when the development is more than one-half (½) mile from an approved residential subdivision, more than one (1) mile from a school, or more than one-quarter (¼) mile from a residence. These measurements are from property line to property line. The ordinance lists the required minimum greenbelts and buffer zones for each restricted land use and states that Category A developments must provide a sight-proof, eight (8)-foot tall fence at the inside perimeter of the greenbelt.

The parish seems to have a problem between industry and residents.

St. Bernard Parish

St. Bernard Parish, Louisiana. Tree Management Ordinance,
Code of Ordinances, Ordinance SBPC #329-04-97, April 21, 1997.

This is one of the newest ordinances in the State of Louisiana. Its prime purpose is to establish a Tree Advisory Committee of citizens to organize community tree planting projects, conduct educational seminars and coordinate annual Arbor Day activities. The Tree Advisory Committee consists of five members who are charged with preparing a community tree plan to organize the work of caring for existing trees on public lands in this semitropical Louisiana parish. Protection is tendered to all trees on private property, and tree abuse is outlawed. Historic trees, such as the magnificent De La Ronde Oaks, are protected. A permit is required for any tree on public land that is to be altered, removed or disturbed.

The ordinance is administered by the Department of Public Works. The ordinance is not very sophisticated but does protect all trees defined as historic, specifically those trees of more than twenty-four (24) inches in diameter. Ancient live oaks adorn this coastal parish, and the Tree Advisory Committee is organized in such a manner that their perpetual care is ensured.

St. John Parish

St. John Parish, Section 27.6.3, "Physical Considerations," 1977.
St. John Parish, Section 27.7.9, "Plans Required for the Control of Erosion and Sedimentation," 1977.

Ordinances concerning land use and planning mention minimizing the destruction of trees and erosion during development. No specific requirements or standards are confirmed.

St. Tammany Parish

St. Tammany presents its landscape ordinance in the Comprehensive Plan, Land Use Regulation Zoning Ordinance No. 523. St. Tammany Parish, Ordinance No. 523-Section 5.14:1984, "Land Use Regulation Zoning Ordinance," revised 1987.

As an aid in understanding the ordinance and for the purpose of communication and education in the field of tree preservation and urban forestry, a St. Tammany Parish Landscape Manual has been prepared that illustrates the requirements of the ordinance in easy-to-understand, graphic form. This manual, covering such topics as the value of trees, minimum landscape requirements, design recommendations, tree and shrub characteristics and the permit process, has addressed the importance of plant material to this "Ozone Belt" parish.

This ordinance, under development since 1981 and in effect since 1984, addresses such issues as front, rear and side yard planting requirements, parking lot planting requirements, screening of trash and garbage cans, credit for tree preservation, sight triangles and requirements for the submittal of landscape plans. Figure 2.31 illustrates that planted berms are acceptable for screening parking areas.

In addition, the procedure for receiving a permit for occupancy, adjustments to the law, enforcement and penalty provisions and tree and shrub selection guides are included in this document.

Plans must be submitted to the Department of Engineering for approval. There are standard requirements for the preparation of the landscape plans; however, the parish does not require the seal of a landscape architect, although landscape architects usually prepare such landscape plans.

This parish ordinance has been found to be the most detailed at the parish level in the State of Louisiana. Of special interest is the fact that St. Tammany has the only parishwide land clearing regulations in the state. Their enforcement is similar to that of Caddo Parish in withholding the Certificate of Occupancy until all requirements of the ordinance have been met. Violations can be cited every fifteen (15) days until compliance, and fines can be as high as five hundred (500) dollars. Unlike that of Caddo Parish, this ordinance does not mention alternative compliance options of plan submittal.

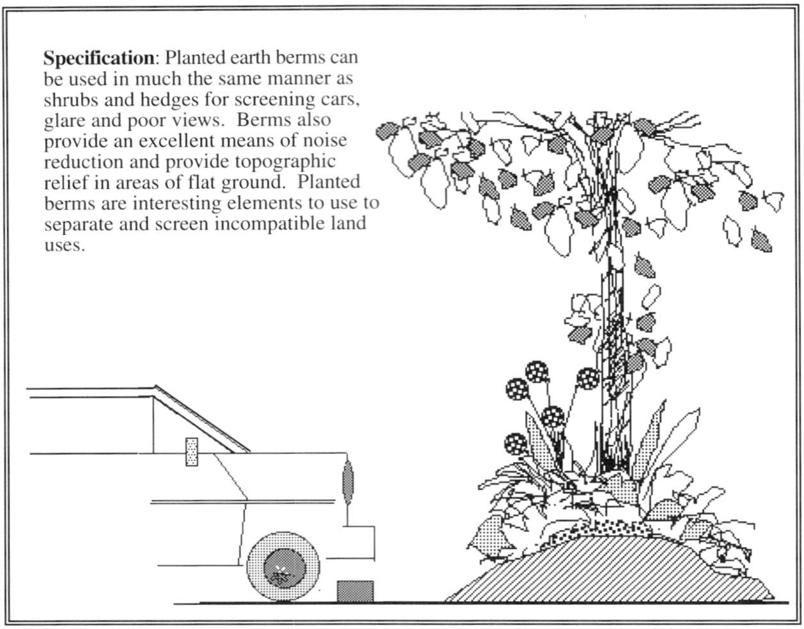

FIGURE 2.31. Earth berm detail, St. Tammany Parish, Louisiana.

This ordinance is a good model parish ordinance meeting the conditions established by the State of Louisiana. Its adoption has led to implementation of city green laws in Slidell, Mandeville, Covington and, soon, in Bogalusa. Interested parties would do well in adapting this ordinance to other parishes of the state. The long-term positive effects of this ordinance will be noticed in a number of years as the parish greens up as a result of the provisions that protect trees and require replacement landscaping for new development.

State Ordinances

Louisiana is the only state that has laws based on the Napoleonic Code, which dates from the 1800s. Under this system, laws are not recognized unless they are written. Court precedents, which are the basis of most other states' law systems, have less weight in Louisiana. Only what is written is considered law.

The following annotations apply to ordinances that are statewide in nature.

State of Louisiana, Model Ordinance

State of Louisiana, "Model Landscape Ordinance for Use in the Parishes and Municipalities of the State of Louisiana," 1989.

A model landscape ordinance has been prepared and included here to assist communities in the preparation of a landscape ordinance. The Model Landscape Ordinance contained herein is abbreviated for clarity. Each community wishing to use this model ordinance should adapt it to circumstances found in that community. A small municipality may want to shorten it, whereas a larger city may want to add special provisions.

Current laws, customs, political constraints, public policies and citizen needs may influence the direction the ordinance will take in any community. Any parish, city or town wishing to enact an ordinance should consult with an attorney and a landscape architect or perhaps contact Louisiana State University for assistance. Special information and assistance can be acquired from the organizations and individuals listed in Appendix A to the ordinance, "A Directory to Landscape Ordinances in Louisiana." The first step for a community might be to establish a Landscape Ordinance Advisory Committee that can review the attached model landscape ordinances (see Appendix A) for applicability.

Model Landscape Ordinance Outline

The Model Landscape Ordinance was developed with the use of the Green Law Database housed at the School of Landscape Architecture at Louisiana State University. The database contains ordinances from throughout the country that were reviewed for usefulness and applicability to the southern Gulf Coast states where climate and landform are consistent.

Of particular usefulness to the study was the monograph "Model Landscape Code for South Florida" prepared by James F. Schnelle Jr. of Environmental Management & Engineering and Bob Smith, ASLA, of Neal Smith & Associates Landscape Architects. This outline code prepared for the South Florida Water Management District has acted as the model for this ordinance because its provisions can pertain to any locale where water conservation, air quality, vegetation management, economic development and beautification are community goals. This model code is the basis of many of the fine landscape ordinances throughout southern Florida.

In addition, the work of landscape architect Keith Villere, ASLA, Ginger Fortson, ASLA, and others in St. Tammany Parish, Louisiana, added content to this ordinance. Landscape architects with the New Orleans City Planning Commission have helped shape the ordinance to the special conditions of Louisiana.

The Model Landscape Ordinance affects real property within incorporated areas of a community. The ordinance provides rules, regulations, controls and procedures for the protection, preservation and modification of nature in the city. It primarily pertains to vegetation and landscaping, but special provisions are contained with the model for dealing with drainage, aquifer recharge, flood control, air quality improvements, sun control, shade protection and any other natural resource the community thinks is important to its well-being, health and safety.

The following outline summarizes the important sections of the Model Landscape Ordinance and can be used by any writer wishing to craft an ordinance for any town or city in America.

PART I—CONTEXTUAL

Section 1—Short Title

This section of the ordinance identifies the law and places it in context of some other community code. Most landscape ordinances are contained within zoning ordinances, subdivision regulations or general municipal codes or regulations.

Section 2—Purpose, Intent and Definitions

It is the purpose of this section to declare the purpose and intent of the ordinance and how it has a bearing on the health, safety and welfare of the community. Definitions are given to clarify the meaning of certain terms and technical language contained within the law.

Section 3—Applicability of Landscape Ordinance

This section describes how the law applies in the community. Generally, landscape ordinances apply to specified zoning districts that are defined within the community's zoning ordinance. For example, in some communities landscape ordinances apply only to commercial districts, whereas in others they apply to all, from residential to industrial.

PART II—TECHNICAL

Section 4—Land Clearing and Modification

It is the intent of this section to protect the natural resources of the community by requiring that a building permit and land clearing permit be acquired prior to the start of construction or modification to land areas.

Section 5—Site and Landscape Design Standards

Within this section of the ordinance are minimum site design and landscape design standards that the community believes are important to protect the public health, safety and welfare of the community. Typical standards address plant and unique natural resource preservation, landscape zone dimensions, plant installation standards and requirements, storm water retention and recharge, irrigation, air cleansing, site distances, maintenance, plant material standards and recommended plant species.

Section 6—Landscape Maintenance

Maintenance is important for all living things, particularly plant materials in their first year of establishment. To ensure that newly planted vegetation survives and serves the purpose of the ordinance and that it be neat, healthy and orderly, it is the intent of this section of the ordinance to specify certain minimum maintenance standards of watering, pruning, fertilizing and plant care. In some instances communities require the posting of bonds to ensure the survival of the plant material.

Section 7—Landscape Plan Required

This section describes the preparation of the landscape plan that is used by the community to evaluate compliance with the terms of the landscape ordinance. The language in this section describes what is to be shown on the plan, what dimensions, quantities and calculations are necessary, and provides drawing standards and conventions so that drawings can be read with clarity. Often this section requires that the person preparing the plan be trained in a professional engineering, architecture or landscape architecture course and be licensed in conformance with appropriate state law and insured for public liability protection.

Section 8—Alternative Compliance and Landscape Credit

Alternative compliance refers to the betterment of the requirements of this ordinance. In addition, because all sites are different, there must be a procedure for encouraging an innovative, unique and site-specific landscape design that exceeds minimum requirements. Alternative compliance will provide a mechanism to exceed these minimum standards, develop a point standard system, and set minimum qualifications of the person designing the landscape plan.

PART III—ADMINISTRATIVE

Section 9—Permit Application Procedures

This section of the ordinance describes the procedure for seeking the required permit, payment of fees and public review policy.

Section 10—Enforcement, Penalties and Appeals

It is the purpose of this section of the ordinance to describe the enforcement procedures to be followed to ensure compliance with the provisions of the law. Penalties for violations of the law and a procedure for appeals for any aggrieved party seeking redress are given. The community generally designates enforcement officials and offices having jurisdiction.

Section 11—Administrative Guidelines

Each community will have special administrative procedures that they will follow to help the public interpret the ordinance. Administrative guidelines can be devised to assist with the administration of this ordinance.

Section 12—Conflicts

This section of the ordinance addresses conflicts between this ordinance and other ordinances within the community.

Section 13—Severability

Severability provisions are usually included to sever and remove any part of the ordinance that may prove to be unconstitutional, in conflict with or in violation of other applicable laws.

Section 14—Effective Date

This is the date on which the law goes into effect.

State of Louisiana, Large Community Model Ordinance

"Standard City Tree Management Ordinance, Large Community Model, for Use in the Parishes and Municipalities of the State of Louisiana," 1993.

This version of the Model Tree Management Ordinance is suitable for larger communities that have existing departments such as parks, planning or public works. This version is more formal in nature and more detailed in extent. This model will work well in urban and suburban areas where government structure is already working to provide community needs.

This ordinance establishes a larger Tree Commission of citizens who are charged with developing policy for managing public trees and communicating to others the importance of trees in the community.

The Tree Commission in this model holds regular town meetings, prepares an annual tree management plan and undertakes programs to improve the town tree canopy. This model calls upon the Tree Commission to develop programs to involve the community, organizations and families in tree preservation, planting and tree care. City Tree Commissions should become prime sponsors of tree planting programs in town parks, schoolyards, cemeteries and other public places.

A City Forester trained in urban forestry, arboriculture, horticulture, landscape architecture or a closely related field is employed by the community to undertake day-to-day tree management responsibilities. Written permits for planting, maintenance or removal of trees from public property are obtained through the City Forester's office.

This ordinance may be enacted by organizing a tree support group, holding public hearings and a vote of the city or town council.

State of Louisiana, Small Community Model Ordinance

"Standard City Tree Management Ordinance, Small Community Model, for Use in the Parishes and Municipalities of the State of Louisiana," 1993.

This version of the Model Tree Management Ordinance is suitable for small communities and/or parish governmental units. Because of the informal nature of this version of the ordinance, this model will work well in rural areas and small communities. This ordinance might also be used by any city that would like to draft an ordinance of minimal requirements and complexity.

This ordinance establishes a Tree Commission of citizens who are charged with the task of managing public trees and communicating to others the importance of trees in the community.

The Tree Commission may hold periodic town meetings to discuss tree care, prepare a tree plan or undertake to improve the town tree canopy. It may develop programs to further the mission of the Tree Commission. It may, for instance, become a prime sponsor of tree planting programs in town parks, schoolyards, cemeteries and other public places where trees are needed.

One of the citizens on the Tree Commission is given added duties as being the volunteer Town or Parish Forester. Permits for planting, maintenance or removal of trees from public property must be obtained from this community volunteer. With this version of the ordinance permits are very easy to apply for and to receive, many being just informal verbal authority from the Town or Parish Forester.

This ordinance may be enacted by public hearing and vote of the town council or parish police jury.

State of Louisiana, Reforestation Ordinance

Louisiana, Act 176 of the 1990 Legislature, Amending and Reenacting R.S. 3:4271, Title 7, Part XXXIX, Forestry, "Chapter 209, Reforestation of Public Lands."

This act requires the planting of two trees (five (5) feet tall and of one (1) inch caliper) for every one (1) (ten (10) inches in diameter breast height or greater) cut down on public lands. There are exceptions, and replacement trees are to be planted in the immediate project area. The Louisiana Department of Agriculture and Forestry may require the use of a landscape architect where it deems necessary in order to ensure adequate attention to sensitive design considerations.

Organizations desiring to remove trees must write to the Louisiana Department of Agriculture and Forestry, Office of Forestry, Attention: State Forester, P.O. Box 1628, Baton Rouge, LA 70821-1628. The request must include location, size, species, a site plan and the intent or reason for the tree removal.

Louisiana Tree Ordinances

There are six (6) tree ordinances in Louisiana that protect and manage city tree resources. These ordinances have been collected and analyzed and have added depth to local conditions in the model ordinances of Louisiana. Each of the ordinances is annotated in the following sections so that the reader may see the extent of variation that presently exists in Louisiana tree ordinances.

Sixty four (64) Louisiana parishes were surveyed. Several cities indicated that this type of green law has been adopted or is under discussion. After reviewing the ordinances collected during the study, it was determined that several are significant enough to be considered in this study as green laws. A brief discussion of each parish ordinance follows:

City of Crowley

Ordinance No. 1040, adopted date unknown, Administered by the Mayor's Office.

This ordinance adds language to the Code of Ordinances by adding Chapter 22, Sections 1–17, which defines and regulates the planting, maintenance, and removal of trees and shrubs on public property, provides for the protection of existing trees, requires the licensing of arborists and establishes a community Tree Board.

A City Tree Board of no less than fifteen (15) nor more than twenty (20) members is to be appointed by the mayor to study and investigate city trees and develop a written tree plan.

The plan, to be submitted annually to the mayor and Board of Aldermen, will provide for the care, preservation, pruning, planting, replanting and removal of trees and shrubs in parks, along streets and in other public places.

This ordinance also regulates spacing, locations and distances for planting along streets and near utility lines. Tree topping is prohibited, and private owners shall keep private trees overhanging public streets pruned and maintained.

In addition, this ordinance provides for public tree care including the planting, maintenance and removal of trees along streets, squares and public grounds.

Licenses are required for those engaged in the business of tree service. The licenses must be renewed yearly, with an annual fee to be paid to the city, evidence of proper insurance and a copy of a current Louisiana Horticulture Commission license.

Street trees and park trees are defined, and a list of Official Street Tree Species is included in this ordinance.

Penalties for violation of this act are given.

City Parish of East Baton Rouge

Ordinance 9360, adopted December 11, 1991. Administered by the East Baton Rouge Parish Tree Commission and Director of Landscape and Forestry.

The Metropolitan Council amended the Code of Ordinances, Section 1, Title 2, Chapter 1, Part V, to establish a Tree Commission and to regulate the planting and removal of trees on public property within the city and parish of Baton Rouge.

A nine (9)-member Tree Commission is appointed who shall study problems involved with city-parish trees, determine needs, compose an annual City-Parish Tree Plan and seek ways to implement needed work.

The legislation also allows for the appointment of a City-Parish Forester who will work with the Tree Commission to develop an orderly process for identifying public tree needs including, but not limited to, inventorying existing tree resources, maintenance, removals, planting, replacement and public education.

The Tree Commission may undertake and participate in cooperative projects such as developing tree planting systems, creating a tree bank, developing a City-Parish Botanical Garden, providing technical advice and engaging in public education programs.

This ordinance specifies minimum regulations for maintenance of trees and plants and requires that a permit be issued to remove, cut, trim or plant trees and shrubs on public property. This permit also applies to public utility companies, which may request area permits for tree work. Permits are issued by the City-Parish Forester. Penalties for violation of this act are no less than twenty-five (25) dollars nor more than one thousand (1,000) dollars or imprisonment for not more than thirty (30) days.

The name of the tree commission was changed by council resolution in December, 1997, to the Tree and Landscape Commission.

City of Hammond

Ordinance No. 2058, January 7, 1986, amended with Ordinance No. 2161, January 3, 1989. Administered by the City Urban Forester.

A public tree ordinance was adopted in 1986 by the City of Hammond to regulate and coordinate the planting of trees and shrubbery in the streets and public grounds of the city and to preserve existing trees from indiscriminate removal and damage.

Provisions of the ordinance create the position of urban forester and a public body known as the Advisory Committee on Urban Forestry. Permits are required for tree removal, and developers must submit plans showing public trees to be removed during construction activities.

New tree plantings and replantings of removed trees must conform to a list of approved trees. The approved tree species list consists of small, medium and large trees that may be used along streets in the City of Hammond.

Minimal planting standards and requirements are contained within the ordinance. Fines for violation of the ordinance are specified.

There are few street tree ordinances in Louisiana, but this ordinance is an example of a very concise version. The Hammond ordinance should be strengthened and made more comprehensive in its scope. Budgeting and administrative responsibility must be assigned, and a master tree planting plan for the city must be prepared.

City of Lafayette

Ordinance 0-1881 establishing Chapter 22 1/2 of the Lafayette Code, Articles I, II and III, adopted January 15, 1980, Administered by the Shade Tree Advisory Committee and the City Arborist.

The city code Chapter 22 1/2, Sections 22 1/2-11 through 22 1/2-27, requires the establishment of a nine (9)-member citizens shade tree advisory committee. The committee, whose role is strictly advisory, may recommend to the city arborist a master street shade tree plan for public property and public rights-of-way. In addition, the committee is empowered to recommend arboricultural specifications governing the planting, maintenance, preservation and removal of all trees and shrubs on public property.

The ordinance creates the position of city arborist, a person who is to be responsible for coordination and review of plans and actions affecting trees and shrubbery on public property. The arborist is responsible for the planting and growing of trees and shrubs on public grounds.

The purpose of the ordinance is to establish a uniform city policy relative to the planting of trees and shrubbery, to regulate activities of persons engaged in servicing trees and to encourage protection of existing trees and shrubs on public property. A policy is included that assigns responsibility to the city arborist for tree care.

Numerous definitions are given, including those for arboricultural specifications, city arborist, drip line, covered area, maintenance, preservation, removal, shrubbery, street tree and tree.

Permits are required of the public for the planting of trees. To remove a tree a citizen must consult with the city arborist and, in some circumstances, submit plans which the city arborist reviews within a stated period of time. Public departments and private utility companies are given blanket approval if their written trenching and pruning specifications are reviewed and approved by the city arborist.

There is an interesting clause in this ordinance that requires tree planting and other landscape factors be given consideration in the design of all major construction projects by the city. All major construction projects are to be designed with regard to minimizing damage to and loss of existing trees and shrubbery.

Penalties for violation of this ordinance are not given, nor does the ordinance regulate the activities of tree service companies or public utilities. No specific tree care or planting requirements are given.

City of Metairie

Comprehensive Zoning Ordinance, Section VII-E, Old Metairie Neighborhood Conservation District (OMNCD) Ordinance, Subsection 7B1, Tree Preservation. Draft Copy, April 14, 1997.

Metairie, Louisiana, is a community adjacent to and upriver of the City of New Orleans, lying between the Mississippi River and Lake Pontchartrain. The community is primarily a middle- to high-income residential community, with many of its residents working in the New Orleans CBD. One of the older sections of the city is referred to as "Old Metairie" because of its many significant and old live oak trees and its fine collection of early twentieth-century architecture. This area has been designated a "neighborhood conservation district," and within this district special zoning provisions apply. One of these special provisions, seen as a tool to preserve neighborhood character, is a restriction on removing ancient trees. In this part of the city some of the live oaks have graced the neighborhood for well over one hundred (100) years. Their replacement would be impossible in the span of a human generation.

The community sees these old trees as valuable assets for reducing ground level temperature, filtering contaminants from the air and as habitat for urban wildlife. Some of the most expensive homes in the city are found in this conservation district, and these trees add value to property.

All development is required, to the greatest extent possible, to preserve trees larger than eight (8) inches in diameter.

The ordinance is presently to be revised to strengthen its tree preservation requirements. The proposed amendments will define the role of the Director of Parkways and establish submittal and review procedures. It increases protection for trees and better defines a significant tree. A specified list of trees eight (8) inches or greater in diameter and known to have long life are considered significant in this neighborhood. Trees maintained as hedges are also considered to be significant trees in this community. When a significant tree is permitted to be removed, it must be replaced by two trees of at least two and one-half ($2\frac{1}{2}$) inches DBH from the selected list.

A tree registry of all significant trees in this neighborhood is maintained. The ordinance encourages replacement plantings of trees from the list of significant trees documented in Table 2.55.

Standards are included for determining tree value. ISA (International Society of Aboriculture) standards are used to calculate tree value. Other standards included in this ordinance define streetscape and specify tree preservation and tree replacement requirements. One site-specific street is given special mention. Fines and penalties are included in this legislation. The ordinance is administered by the Jefferson Parish Director of Parkways.

City of Monroe

Ordinance 9100, adopted October 10, 1989, Administered by the City of Monroe Tree Board.

This ordinance amends Chapter 34 of the City of Monroe Code, adding Article III, Sections 34-31 to 34-44, which creates a seven (7)-member Tree Board and defines public tree care.

TABLE 2.55. Significant Trees—Old Metairie Neighborhood Conservation District, Metairie, Louisiana

American elm	*Ulmus americana*
American holly	*Ilex opaca*
Bald cypress	*Taxodium distichum*
Sycamore	*Platanus occidentalis*
Green ash	*Fraxinus pennsylvanica*
Hickory sp.	*Carya species*
Nuttal oak	*Quercus Nuttallii*
Oak sp.	*Quercus species*
Pecan	*Carya illinoinensis*
Red cedar	*Juniperus virginiana*
Red maple	*Acer rubrum*
Southern live oak	*Quercus virginiana*
Southern magnolia	*Magnolia grandiflora*
Sweet gum	*Liquidambar styraciflua*
Tulip poplar	*Liriodendron tulipifera*
Water oak	*Quercus nigra*
Willow oak	*Quercus phellos*

The duties of the Tree Board are defined in this ordinance. The Tree Board is to study tree needs and develop and annually update and administer a written plan for the care, preservation, pruning, planting and removal of trees, shrubs, bushes or other woody vegetation along streets, in parks and in other public places in the city. The plan must be submitted annually to the City Council in the form of an ordinance to be adopted as the "Official Comprehensive Tree Plan for the City of Monroe."

The ordinance requires adoption of an official list of trees to be planted along city streets. In addition, Ordinance 9100 requires the city to maintain public trees, including planting, pruning, maintaining and removal, to ensure public safety or to preserve or enhance the symmetry and beauty of public grounds. Finally, this ordinance regulates the sizes, placement and spacing of trees near utilities, street corners and fireplugs, prohibits tree topping and requires removal of stumps.

Rules, acts and decisions of the Tree Board may be appealed to the City Council. Violation of this ordinance results in a misdemeanor and fines up to five hundred (500) dollars.

City of New Orleans

Ordinance 365, establishing Zoning Ordinance Article II, Section 43-5 through Section 43-11, and Article IV, Section 43-22 through Section 43-31, adopted 1954, amended 3/16/78. Administered by the Parkway and Park Commission.

This is the oldest existing tree ordinance in Louisiana, having been adopted in 1954.

This ordinance establishes a ten (10)-member Park and Parkway Commission, which controls and manages parks, oversees recreation and installs and maintains plantings in parks, parkways, highways and other public grounds. The Commission employs a superintendent, arborists, landscape architects and gardeners to pursue the activities of the Commission. By ordinance it is allowed to establish a nursery for raising trees, shrubs and other plants to be used in parkways, parks and other public places.

The ordinance makes it unlawful to damage trees, shrubs and other landscape features on "neutral grounds," in parks and in other public places. Written permission is required for any party to install or prune plant material on property controlled by the Commission. The Commission investigates citizen complaints and prunes or removes trees or shrubs that interfere with the lawful use of private land. Private interests pay for the pruning or removal of public trees, but written permission is required and the Commission requires that the consulting arborist be licensed according to state law and follow generally accepted standards of the trade.

Public trees must be protected near construction sites. Bonds are required for replacement of public trees or other damage to public places caused during construction. Appeals to decisions of the Parkway and Park Commission can be made directly to the City Council.

Maine

Bangor

City of Bangor Land Development Code, selected sections, "Screening of Parking," "Parking Lot Improvements," "Buffer Yards," n.d.

This northern city does not have a comprehensive landscape ordinance. Landscape requirements are contained within the city land development code. These requirements cover screening of parking areas, minimal interior parking lot plantings and buffer yards. Several types of buffers are defined in Figure 2.32.

The most complete of these requirements are those concerning buffer yards. There are five (5) different buffer yards, noted as A, B, C, D, and E, which vary in width from ten (10) feet to thirty (30) feet. Within each category the applicant for a building permit has a choice of designs. Figure 2.32 illustrates a typical one hundred (100)-foot section of a Type C buffer yard that would be used to separate retail, auto service, drive-in, light industry or a mini-warehouse from a higher zoning designation, such as single family residential.

The descriptive graphic in Figure 2.32 makes the design requirements of the buffer yard very easy to understand. The ordinance as written does not meet the standards commonly found in other parts of the country.

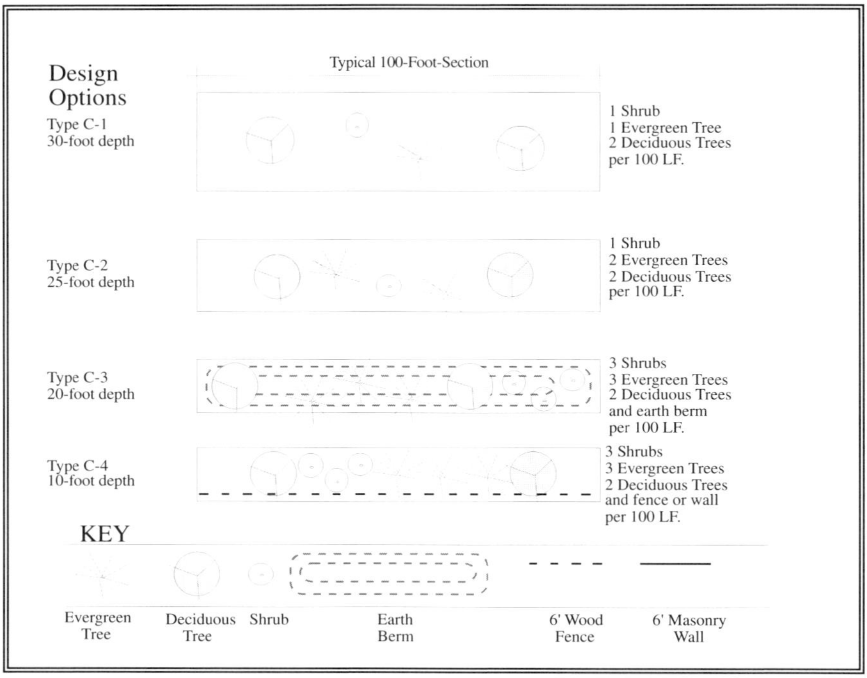

FIGURE 2.32. Buffer types and design standards, Bangor, Maine.

Maryland

Annapolis

Zoning Code, Chapter 17.09, Section 17.09.010, "Trees in Development Areas," 1988, Chapter 21.98, "Site Plan Review," 1987, Special Document, "Parking and Landscaping: A Manual of Landscape Standards for Parking Lots," September 1986.

Annapolis is an old sailing city on the Chesapeake Bay in tidewater Maryland. This important town has a quaint, historic character and pedestrian qualities. Home of the Naval Academy, seat of state government and once the home of the author, this town appreciates quality landscape design, which is evidenced throughout its neighborhoods.

This is one of many towns in the region that participate in the Chesapeake Bay Critical Areas Program aimed toward protecting the natural resources of the Chesapeake Bay. This program is administered by Maryland Department of Natural Resources, Article 8-1808(D). The landscape ordinance is one means by which Annapolis meets the requirements for coordinated, controlled development.

This community does not have a comprehensive landscape ordinance, but rather some connected documents in the zoning code. The various documents appear to do a good job of communicating the design components and standards needed to constitute a successful ordinance.

Chapter 17.09 requires the protection of trees before, during and after construction and sets forth replacement values, mitigation, landscape standards and approvals, waivers and enforcement. The provisions of this article apply to any application for a building permit, grading permit or any application under Chapter 21.98 requiring site plan review. In addition, for development of subdivisions or development projects in excess of forty thousand (40,000) square feet, applicants must comply with a related state code, the Maryland Forest Conservation Act, Article 5.1601. The code applies to all zoning categories.

The latter code is not reviewed here but might be consulted if anyone is interested in landscape ordinances on the state level. This code can be accessed through state statutes by writing directly to the Maryland Department of Natural Resources or conducting a computer search over the West publishing system used exclusively by attorneys to conduct background research.

Lots cannot be cleared prior to sale or development without a permit. No cutting, clearing, digging or grading may be undertaken until a landscape plan has been approved. Trees that are removed for development are to be replaced with two (2)-inch caliper stock according to the schedule shown in Table 2.56.

In a case where it may not be practical to replan on-site, the developer may be required to "mitigate" the tree removal by planting off-site at some approved point in the city, or within the boundary of the "critical zone." Preference is given to the watershed or creek area from which the trees are removed. In cases where mitigation proves unsatisfactory to either the developer or the city, a "fee in lieu" amounting to in-the-ground cost plus ten (10) percent is made payable to the city urban forestry program, to be used exclusively for tree planting and tree maintenance.

Technical standards and guidelines are given for protection of trees during construction and after construction.

Design components of this article include three types of buffers: natural buffers, landscaped buffers and one hundred (100)-foot critical area buffers. The latter are required landward from the mean high water line of tidal waters, tributary

TABLE 2.56. Tree Replacement Schedule, Annapolis, Maryland

Size of Removed Tree	*No. of Replacement Trees*
5″–8″ DBH	1 tree for every 4 removed
8″–12″ DBH	1 tree for every 2 removed
12″–18″ DBH	1 tree for every 1 removed
18″–24″ DBH	2 trees for every 1 removed
>24″ DBH	3 trees for every 1 removed

TABLE 2.57. Buffer Design Technical Standards, Annapolis, Maryland

Technical Standard	*Expected Result*
Shall be in conformance with tree preservation standards	Save existing trees
Protect existing habitat	Save areas for wildlife
Designed with vertical stratification	Increase diversity
Design continuous plantings	Develop visual screen
Respond to local utilities	Coordinate with local utilities
Work with local sedimentation and erosion control plans	Coordinate with local planning agency
Work with local storm water management plans	Coordinate with local DPW

streams and tidal wetlands, which are protected areas. Several technical standards are given for design of the buffers. They include standards for preservation, stratification, erosion control and storm water management, as shown in Table 2.57.

Chapter 21.98 provides for site plan review for all new development of land, new construction, enlargements or substantial alterations of buildings for all zoning categories other than single-family and two-family construction. No zoning certificate, building permit, use permit, grading permit or Certificate of Occupancy will be granted until site plans have been reviewed and approved. Development plans, including landscaping plans, will be reviewed by the Planning, Zoning and Public Works departments using the standards and criteria shown in Table 2.57.

A special document, titled "Parking and Landscaping: A Manual of Landscape Standards for Parking Lots," is available from the Department of Planning and Zoning, Municipal Building, 160 Duke of Gloucester Street, Annapolis, MD 21401, for a fee of five (5) dollars. This document graphically portrays requirements and standards specified in the Annapolis Zoning Code, Section 21.64, Off-Street Parking and Loading Requirements.

The document communicates adopted standards and specific parking and landscaping guidelines for the design of parking areas. The standards apply to all new construction, expansions and changes in use intensity and, in some cases, conditional uses.

The Director of Planning and Zoning may schedule and conduct a public hearing to receive comments from citizens or impacted individuals. Appeals may be made and waivers of required information may be granted under special circumstances. In some instances, the Planning and Zoning Department may initiate a general or specific site plan for a particular piece of property where site plan approval may be needed in the future. Site plan review standards in this community are quite extensive, as can be seen in the summary presented in Table 2.58.

TABLE 2.58. Site Plan Review Standards, Annapolis, Maryland

Standard	*Example Reason*
Ecological Considerations	Minimize degradation of resources
Landscape and Trees	Minimize tree and soil removal, determine planting requirements
Relation of Proposed Buildings	Harmony of construction, reduce adverse impact
Relation of Proposed Structures to Existing	Compatible with surroundings
Scenic, Historic and Archaeological	Protect cultural resources of the city
Surface Water Drainage	Surface water management through controlled drainage
Driveway Connections	Maximum traffic flow and safety, examine sight triangle
Traffic Effects	Maximum traffic flow
Pedestrian Safety	Safe and convenient pedestrian circulation
On-Site Parking and Circulation	To ensure safe, well designed and planted parking areas
Utility Services	Compliance with state public utilities regulations and convenience
Disposal of Waste	To ensure healthy, clean, odor-free developments
Noise	Minimize disturbances
Signage	Control signs and advertising and compliance with sign ordinance
Special Features	Outside storage, loading special use and screening if required
Open Space	To determine visual characteristics and landscaping
Building Area Landscape	Compliance with city landscape standards

Landscape plans must be prepared by a landscape architect or someone with a degree in horticulture or landscape design and with a minimum of five (5) years' experience in commercial planting design. The landscape plans must consist of Planting Plans, an Existing Tree Survey, a Statement of Landscape Maintenance and a Plant Material List. The plans must illustrate the design of parking areas, dumpsters, loading areas, property line buffers and right-of-way buffers. Typical design standards for buffers, interior islands and plant materials for parking area designs include those shown in Table 2.59 and Figure 2.33.

TABLE 2.59. Design Standards for Parking Areas, Annapolis, Maryland

Standard	*Requirement*
BUFFERS	
Property line buffers less than 15 spaces	15′ setback from property line
Property line buffers more than 15 spaces	20′ setback from property line
Property line buffers other than residential	Varies from 5′ to 20′ setback from property line
Right-of-way buffers, less than 60′ ROW	15′ setback from property line
Right-of-way buffers, more than 60′ ROW	20′ setback from property line
Right-of-way buffers, irregular lots	10′ setback from property line
INTERIOR LANDSCAPING	
Size standards, more than 15 spaces, > 6,000 SF	7% of total paved area
Landscape peninsulas and islands < 100 spaces	1 for each 7 parking spaces
Landscape peninsulas and islands > 100 spaces	1 for each 10 parking spaces
Size of peninsulas and islands	$8\frac{1}{2}$ feet by 18 feet inside dimension
PLANT MATERIAL	
Shade trees	12 feet tall, 3 inch caliper

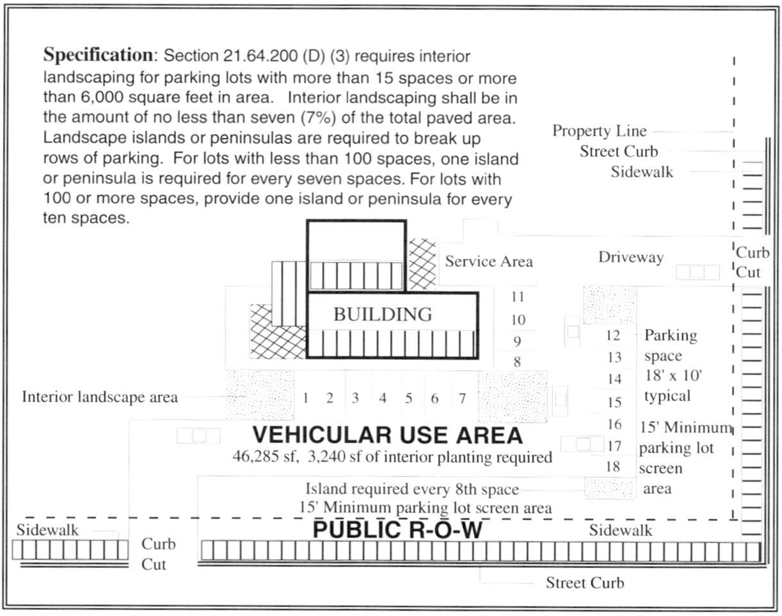

FIGURE 2.33. Interior landscape requirements for parking lots, Annapolis, Maryland.

The Planning and Zoning Department encourages innovative design with plants and other landscape materials. It provides in its manual a complete appendix of approved ornamental trees, shrubs, evergreens, seasonal interest plants and approved planting details. It also approves planting specifications and makes reference to specifications prepared by the Landscape Contractors Association of Metropolitan Washington, the National Arborists Association and the American Association of Nurserymen.

These documents produce a rather complicated ordinance that does not cover in detail several design components and technical standards found in other communities. As an example of this complexity, it took more than five (5) hours for a trained, experienced professional to do a first reading of this ordinance and analyze the document.

Largely as a result of the site plan review process and the Chesapeake Critical Area requirements, these documents are sure to get good results for the community. Perhaps in the future other components normally found in landscape ordinances can be added to make this a comprehensive ordinance.

Prince George's County

Prince George's County, Series No. 9058201522, "Manual for Tree Preservation in Development Areas," 1982.

This manual is designed to offer tree preservation guidelines for development sites. Section 1, Introduction, outlines the purpose and objectives of the manual. Section 2, Discussion of Terms, explains the meaning of terms as used in this document. Section 3, Selection of Trees to Be Preserved, is an aid to developers, planners and designers in determining the vegetation that should be saved on development sites. Section 4, Protection of Trees to be Preserved, illustrates techniques for protecting vegetation once it has been selected for preservation. Numerous sketches and charts aid in explaining the subject material. Appendix A is a tree preservation selection chart showing a sampling of trees commonly found in Prince George's County, species natural habitat, average height at maturity, average growth rate, root form, disease resistance, air pollution resistance, change of environment tolerance, salt resistance, transplanting tolerance, provision for wildlife food or habitat and design objectives. Appendix B is a draft list of identified federal and state rare, threatened and endangered trees of Maryland.

In accordance with CB-143-86, "Building Excellence, " 1987.

There is an extensive guide for the community and developers for initial planning and design of any new project. The nine (9) cell matrix with two (2) axes (residential-commercial-industrial and low-medium-high) appearing on nearly every page allows readers to determine all information applicable to a project by asking (1) What land use type is it in? and, (2) What zoning category is it in? The guide is particularly user-friendly, well organized into six (6) chapters with charts and diagrams, Site Planning, Circulation, Buildings, Landscape Design, Buffering and Screening and Lighting, as well as a glossary and an extensive bibliography.

Site planning policies: Respect and enhance the existing natural and historical qualities of the land. Encourage variety by combining building types and forms. Lot and building orientation should minimize intrusions on adjacent properties and maximize regional and climatic conditions. Common outdoor spaces as well as private outdoor spaces should be incorporated into planning. A hierarchy of open spaces should be planned, including entries, public recreational or gathering areas, semipublic areas and private areas.

Circulation design: Earthwork, fences and walls with or without vegetation can shield parking lots from buildings and break up large paved expanses. Variation in pavement material enhances the pedestrian experience. Cluster lots, separated by vegetation or berms, are preferable to uninterrupted expanses of asphalt.

Circulation policies: Parking should be designed, located and buffered to minimize the negative visual impact. Reinforce street continuity through plant materials. The nine (9)-cell matrix regulates planting. For example, a small commercial lot of high activity requires one (1) tree per five (5) spaces.

Landscape design policies: Preserve, enhance, and manage existing vegetation and natural resources. Use plant material appropriate to region functionally as well as decoratively; delineate pathways and entries, control microclimate and erosion, buffer, soften hard paving or architectural elements.

Buffering and screening: Examples of requirements given by the nine (9)-cell matrix: local street residential high activity requires seventy-five (75) percent screening, whereas the same area in an industrial context requires one hundred (100) percent.

Queen Anne's County

Queen Anne's County, "Landscaping Standard on Lots." Queen Anne's County Zoning Ordinance, Sections 6202-3, 6205, 6300-4, 6400, 6401, n.d.

This ordinance says that the primary attraction to Queen Anne's County is its rural appearance, and that this appearance drives the economy of the county. Thus, the goal of the ordinance is to protect this appearance. The ordinance applies to both residential and nonresidential properties within the county. However, the requirements of the ordinance are not very stringent.

This ordinance is based on specified "plant units." It requires a certain number of plant units for "on-lot plantings" for different sites, exclusive of parking areas and buffers. The most required in any zone is four (4) plant units per acre, and most residential areas do not require any. Section 6201 describes what plant units consist of.

This document also gives landscaping standards for parking lots, woodlands and grassland reforestation. Figure 2.34 represents standards for the design of landscape islands within parking areas. Parking lot plantings are keyed to land uses. As illustrations in the ordinance show, different zoning districts require different amounts of plant units and areas devoted to landscaping.

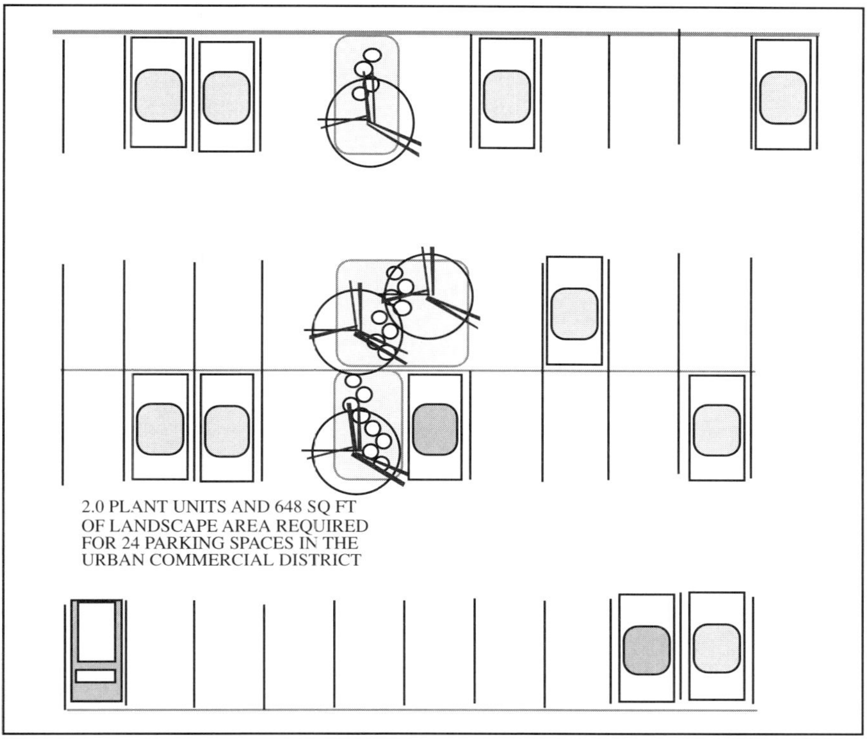

FIGURE 2.34. Landscaping islands, Queen Anne's County, Maryland.

When woodlands are required to be replaced or established, they are planted with a woodland mix available from the Department of Natural Resources, Forestry Program. This mix consists of four hundred (400) eight (8)-inch canopy tree seedlings, six hundred (600) understory trees or wildlife shrubs, and four (4) small trees known as "whips," three (3) to four (4) feet tall, per acre.

However, the main concentration of the ordinance is on the topic of buffer yards. The ordinance describes the buffer yard as a component that is "a combination of setback and visual barrier and is a yard or area together with the planting thereon required." Such buffer yards are intended to mitigate zoning conflicts by creating a barrier between zones. The ordinance requires different size buffer yards for different zones, the largest required being twenty (20) feet wide. Finally, the document lists what can and cannot be located in a buffer yard.

Minimum requirements are given for signage.

What is probably most unusual about this document is how difficult it is to decipher. It contains several charts showing the property owner how many plant units are required for his or her property. Not only are these charts very hard to understand, but exactly what a plant unit is is left to the imagination of the reader.

Very few contemporary cities use this type of landscape ordinance based on quantities. This approach, based on quantities rather than site use, will deliver a planting solution with a mathematical pattern rather than one that might reflect the fabric of nature.

Massachusetts

Fitchburg

Fitchburg Zoning Ordinance, Chapter 181, "Landscaping and Screening," December 1, 1987, Ord. No. 483.87 amended through October 6, 1992.

This ordinance is very brief. It requires landscaping in business, commercial and industrial districts that abut residential districts. Landscape buffers are required consisting of screen plantings not less than three (3) feet in width and six (6) feet in height. Plants are to be planted not more than three (3) feet on center, and at least fifty (50) percent must be evergreen. A planted solid six (6)-foot wall may be substituted. For each three (3) new parking spaces, one (1) two (2)-inch caliper tree and one (1) twenty-four (24) inch shrub are to be planted on the site.

Owners are required to provide, protect and maintain all landscaping in a healthy growing condition.

Sommerville

Sommerville Zoning Ordinance, Article 10, "Landscaping and Screening," March 23, 1990.

This is a modest landscape ordinance, quite typical of those widely used during the 1970s and early 1980s.

The ordinance requires minimal tree planting in required site open space, minimal plantings in parking lots, parking lot screening and minimal screening adjacent to residential land uses. Screening of loading areas, storage areas and site utility equipment is required. Special screening applies to open storage lots in industrial park districts.

A typical screen consists of a strip four (4) feet wide, densely planted with shrubs and/or trees. If the screen is adjacent to a public way, a mixture of plant specimens of less than three (3) feet in height and greater than ten (10) feet in height is recommended. Trees must be pruned or limbed up to a height of six (6) feet so that visual surveillance through and beyond the screen may be possible for passing or approaching vehicles and pedestrians. If a wall or fence is used as a screen, it must be a minimum of four (4) feet tall but not more than six (6) feet tall. If the fence is perforated, no more than fifty (50) percent of the screen shall be open.

Minimal standards are contained within this ordinance for screening, landscaping and fence height and location. Interestingly, the use of barbed wire is controlled in this ordinance.

Credit will be allowed for preserving existing trees. Should existing trees on public rights-of-way be removed in the course of new construction, removed trees will be replaced on the basis of an inch-to-inch ratio.

The ordinance applies to all new construction and expansions, with the exception of sites used for religious or educational purposes. The ordinance is enforced by withholding the Certificate of Occupancy.

This type of landscape ordinance is somewhat dated and represents an early stage in the evolution of public landscape ordinances.

Michigan

Ann Arbor

Zoning Ordinance, Chapter 62, "Landscape and Screening " December 19, 1994. Ord. No. 56-94
Related Law, Chapter 57, "Subdivision and Land Use Control," November 1994; Chapter 60, "Wetland Preservation Ordinance," January 2, 1996.

Ann Arbor, Michigan, home of the University of Michigan, is an environmentally aware community in southern Michigan a little to the west of Detroit. In this community landscape ordinance provisions, green laws, are scattered in several places in the City Code. This discussion will focus on Chapter 62, with passing reference to the other sources of requirements.

The landscape ordinance has been created to reduce urban blight, maintain the value and appearance of neighborhoods and protect specified natural resources. Other significant chapters have been enacted to protect wetland habitat, preserve "natural features" and require site plan review. Natural features include archaeological finds, endangered species habitat, one hundred (100) year floodplains, hedgerows and specified "landmark trees."

Landscape plans showing this information are submitted at two times in the development process. They are first submitted during the Site Plan Review phase, along with a Natural Features Impact Statement. Second, landscape plans along with a Natural Features Impact Plan are submitted during the construction phase in order to get a building permit.

Design components in this ordinance include vehicular use areas, both edge screens and interior plantings, as well as conflicting land use buffers. Refuse container screening, as shown in Figure 2.35, and exterior lighting are also included in this ordinance. Developers pay a street tree escrow fee to provide for street trees that are designed and planted by the Ann Arbor Department of Parks and Recreation, one of the greatest parks departments in the county. This street tree program is administered through the Forestry Division, and the current rate is one (1) dollar thirty (30) cents per linear foot of frontage.

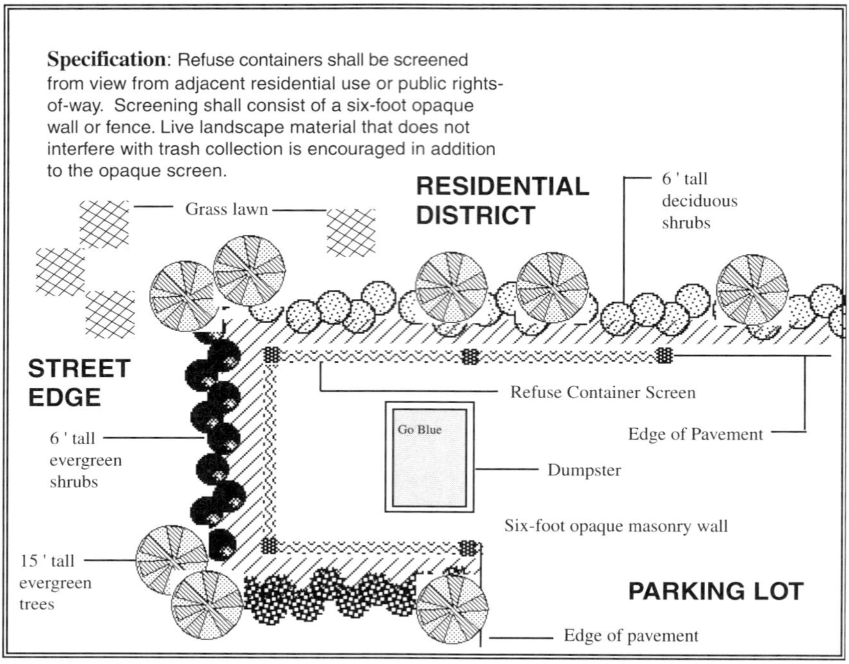

FIGURE 2.35. Refuse container screening, Ann Arbor, Michigan.

Landscape standards are included for landscape materials and preparation of site plans. Maintenance and irrigation are mentioned, with some reference to Xeriscape, although there are no specifications.

All design solutions are based on linear foot or area measure. For vehicular use areas, a ratio is used to calculate the amount of interior landscape zones. This ratio is shown in Table 2.60.

In a one hundred thousand (100,000)-square foot vehicular use area (VUA), for instance, fifteen thousand (15,000) square feet must be set aside and distributed

TABLE 2.60. Interior Parking Lot Landscape Zone Ratio, Ann Arbor, Michigan

Vehicular Use Area Size	*Landscape/Vehicular Use Area Ratio*
3,300 sf to 49,999 sf	1:20 square feet
50,000 sf to 149,999 sf	1:15 square feet
150,000 sf and larger	1:10 square feet

throughout to satisfy this ordinance. The size of the landscape zone must be a minimum of one hundred sixty-five (165) square feet. Using the minimum landscape zone size would require ninety (90) planting zones in the VUA.

Enforcement is controlled through the use of building permits, occupancy permits, civil infraction punishable by five hundred (500)-dollar fines and reinspection fees.

Accompanying the landscape ordinance is Exhibit A of the Land Development Regulations. Exhibit A sets forth guidelines for protecting natural features. Specific guidelines are related to wetlands, vegetation protection, slope protection and historic properties. The Building Department maintains a list of invasive botanical species by class, scientific name, National Wetland Category, and plant type. These plants are to be kept out of all wetland mitigation activities.

This community takes a strong stand on the benefits of landscaping, particularly in preserving existing natural features. Other communities would do well to integrate wetland preservation, natural feature protection, and post-construction landscaping and design in their landscape ordinances.

Emmet County

Zoning Ordinance, Section 2204, "Performance Uses Permitted by Special Permit," May 2, 1996.

Emmet County is located in the far northern part of southern Michigan. The principal city in the county is Petoskey. This green law is a limited-issue landscape ordinance that pertains primarily to the design of greenbelts, walls or fences that separate nonresidential from residential land uses. These features can be designed for either protection or screening. Additional design components mentioned in the law include minimal plantings for parking lots accessory to nonresidential land uses.

Standards are given for plant materials, and a suggested plant materials list is included. Detailed planting plans must be prepared following some general design guidelines included in the ordinance. Maintenance is required for all plantings, and all planting must be must be installed within seven (7) months from date of issue of the Building Permit.

Specific land uses that require planted greenbelts are identified.

Southfield

Title V, Zoning and Planning, Chapter 45, Zoning Ordinance, Article 4, § 5.38, "Landscape Requirements and Plant Materials," June 14, 1992.
Related, Article 4, §5.29, "Off-Street Parking Provisions," June 14, 1992.
Related Ordinance, Ord. No. 1367, "Wetland and Watercourse Protection," January 31, 1991.
Related Law, City Code, Chapter 28, "Tree Regulations," n.d.

In this community the landscape requirements are scattered throughout the zoning ordinance. Landscape requirements can be found in subsections related to site plan review, off-street parking provisions, woodlands and tree preservation and wetlands and watercourse protection. In this discussion they will be treated together.

Landscape requirements generally begin during site plan review. Along with other materials, a landscaping plan prepared by a registered landscape architect must be submitted whenever, according to the zoning ordinance, a site plan is required. Site plan review applies to most zoning districts except single family residential and several special districts.

Landscape requirements are based upon various measures. In certain districts covered by this ordinance, "percent of site" applies to the amount of landscape space, and "percent of area" is the common standard in regard to parking interiors. Linear measure is used in other instances.

Standards are presented for preparation of landscape plans, application for a Tree Permit and plant materials. The standards that must be assembled, prepared and submitted with an application for a Wetlands Use Permit are shown in Table 2.61.

A list of suggested plant materials, as well as a list and description of landmark trees, is included in the ordinance. Limited plant material quality standards and planting standards are also included in this law.

Trees and woodland areas are important to this city. Trees cannot be removed, transplanted or destroyed, nor can grubbing take place in designated woodlands. Designated woodlands are mapped and made part of the zoning ordinance. Trees defined as landmark trees and all trees over eight (8) inches DBH outside of woodlands cannot be removed without a tree permit. Those trees over eight (8) inches that are permitted to be removed must be replaced on an inch-by-

TABLE 2.61. Wetlands Use Permit Application Standards, Southfield, Michigan

Title block showing applicant's name, project name and name of architect, engineer or planner
Identify the environmental specialist who delineated the wetland
Location and extent of wetlands and watercourse
Identify and map types of wetlands
A development site plan, plat or map that overlays the wetlands showing conflict
Cross sections of site showing structures, elevations and wetlands
Descriptions of construction materials to be used, especially fill materials, volume, depth and area impacted
Identify type, location of soil erosion control measures
Identify disposal areas for dredged materials
Show bridge and culvert cross sections and bank stabilization locations
Identification and description of all mitigation areas

TABLE 2.62. Criteria Determining Community Impact, Southfield, Michigan

Criteria	*Point Measures*
Displacement of residents	1 impact point
Site is a diversified habitat for wildlife	1 impact point
Site is a regulatory floodplain	1 impact point
Site is considered a wetland	1 impact point
Site contains a lake, pond or water impoundment	1 impact point
Site is considered a woodland	1 impact point
Site has slopes greater than twenty-five percent	1 impact point
Property is located on other than a major thoroughfare	1 impact point
Development will require street widening	1 impact point
Development will require extension of utilities	1 impact point
Increase in CO_2 concentrations above standard	1 impact point

inch basis. Replacement trees are to be planted on site or at other sites determined by the city. In cases where this proves impractical, "payments in lieu of" can be made to the City Tree Fund for the purpose of maintaining and preserving wooded areas, for planting trees on public lands and for administration and enforcement of this ordinance.

When trees are illegally removed, the city can issue a stop work order, file for injunctive relief and cause the damaging party to replace all trees removed and pay a civil fee in addition, that is added to the City Tree Fund.

A special requirement, seldom seen in landscape ordinances, is the requirement for a Community Impact Statement (CIS) regardless of the size of a property when three (3) or more points from Table 2.62 apply to the circumstances of the site.

Several state regulatory laws* add to the basis of this landscape ordinance. Although the ordinance does not stress design, it does place great emphasis on careful, thoughtful planning. Taken together, all language scattered throughout the zoning ordinance makes this a formidable landscape ordinance that illustrates all contextual, technical and administrative components found in comprehensive landscape ordinances.

The only criticism that might be suggested by the annotator is that it is very difficult and time-consuming to understand this ordinance on first reading. Those

---

*Michigan Landscape Regulatory Enabling Acts

1. Goemaere-Anderson Wetland Protection Act, Act 203, Public Acts of 1979
2. Inland Lakes and Streams Act, Act 346, Public Acts of 1972
3. Soil Erosion and Sedimentation Control Act, Act 347, Public Acts of 1972
4. Floodplain Regulatory Authority, Act 245, Public Acts of 1929, amended
5. Michigan Environmental Protection Act, Act 127, Public Acts of 1970

who attempt to do so should allow about four (4) hours. Many communities have solved similar complexity problems by creating a landscape design manual, bringing all of this information together in an easy-to-read resource.

State of Michigan Model Ordinance

State of Michigan, "Model Tree Protection Ordinance," n.d.

This is a model that lists required tree removal permits, lists exceptions, sets forth application and application review procedures, establishes review standards, and requires tree relocation or replacement and tree protection during construction. It provides for appeals, requires display of permits and inspection, provides enforcement, prescribes penalties for violation and repeals ordinances in conflict therewith.

The ordinance provides for the protection, preservation and proper maintenance and use of trees and woodlands located in the city in order to minimize disturbances to them and prevent damage from erosion and destruction of the natural habitat. It protects the woodlands for economic support of the local property values when allowed to remain uncleared and/or unharvested, and for their natural beauty, wilderness character, or geological, ecological or historical significance. The ordinance addresses the paramount public concern for these natural resources in the interest of the health, safety and general welfare of the city residents.

Sumpter Township

Sumpter Township Zoning Ordinance, "Landscape Design Standards," November 1993.

Sumpter Township regulates the types of plant materials that are used in landscape design only. This ordinance does not have design components or technical standards that must be complied with.

In Sumpter Township all plant material must meet specified minimum requirements of quality and type and must conform to horticultural standards of the American Association of Nurserymen. The ordinance includes a detailed list of plant material species that are approved for use in Sumpter Township. This list, shown in Table 2.63, is based on ecological landscape units that are commonly found in this midwestern glaciated-landscape township.

A list of support plants is given, and additional trees are listed as Landmark Trees with common diameters at maturity. At least sixty (60) percent of all plants used in landscape design must be from one of these associations and be compatible with the specific landscape position and soil type of the site being built upon. No more than forty (40) percent of any landscape design can be composed of a single species.

Additional plant material standards are given in the ordinance. They include minimum plant sizes, spacing requirements, installation practices and prohibited plant materials.

TABLE 2.63. Ecological Associations, Sumpter Township, Michigan

Association	*Common Indicator Species*	*Soil Type*
Deciduous Swamp Species	Blue Beech, *Carpinus caroliniana*	Houghton Hn
Beech/Maple Community	Sugar Maple, *Acer saccharum*	Kibbie KnA
Oak/Hickory Community	White Oak, *Quercus alba*	Metea MhB
Oak/Savanna Community	Northern Pin Oak, *Quercus illiposoidalis*	Sprinks SpB
River Floodplain Bottomlands	Shellbark Hickory, *Carya laciniosa*	Hoytville Ho

This is an unusual landscape ordinance. Few ordinances are based on ecological principles. Most are based solely on horticultural standards and contemporary landscape practices. Other communities may want to consider placing more emphasis on ecology. That being the case, this ordinance can serve as a basic example from which to start. There are many problems with this ordinance that must be overcome. It falls short in dealing with most site design components and the administrative aspects of land development planning. These, however, can easily be overcome.

Minnesota

Saint Paul

City of Saint Paul Zoning Code, "Landscape Standards," n.d.

The City of Saint Paul does not have a stand-alone landscape ordinance. Landscape standards are scattered throughout the code under various sections, such as Parking, Screening and Subdivisions. To facilitate understanding the ordinance, the City Landscape Architect, in the Office of License, Inspections and Environmental Protection, makes available a flier titled "Landscaping Site Plan Review." The flier summarizes the requirements of the ordinance, provides a list of recommended plant materials and illustrates a sample landscape plan. Typical planting details are also provided, and it is recommended that a landscape architect prepare the landscape plan.

The design components in this ordinance include parking lots and screening. Minimal technical requirements and specifications are given. For example, two and one-half ($2\frac{1}{2}$)-inch trees planted thirty (30) feet on center are required. Shrubs must be eighteen (18) inches tall at time of planting, and screens must be eighty (80) percent opaque. Planting strips must be at least forty-eight (48) inches wide.

Ten (10) percent of the parking area must be planted. Tree preservation is encouraged, but there are no real requirements in the ordinance to do so.

This is a very minimal ordinance and does not cover many of the design components or requirements mentioned in contemporary ordinances elsewhere.

White Bear Township

Town Ordinance, "Site and Landscape Requirements," n.d.

White Bear has a simple landscape ordinance that establishes site and landscape requirements for business and industrial developments within the city.

This ordinance requires that the thirty (30) percent of a site that must be devoted to open space be planted in grasses and kept mowed to a height of four (4) inches. Within these landscape zones a minimum number of plants is required. Plant quantities are based on measurable site attributes such as total square footage of building area or length of site perimeters. Refuse containers must be screened with fencing painted to match the color of adjacent structures.

Minimal plant material standards and planting and maintenance requirements are given in the law. Clear-cutting of woodland areas is restricted. Shade trees larger than six (6) inches in caliper are to be saved.

One of the most unusual features seen in this entire study is the "public tree removal clause" that was enacted in this community in 1993. This clause requires that the public be given the option of removing, at public expense, all easily transplantable trees that are to be destroyed as a result of grading or building activities. Removed trees will be replanted on public lands or in public parks.

This is such a simple, cost-effective idea that it is a wonder larger cities have not considered adopting a clause like this.

Mississippi

Biloxi

Biloxi, "Landscape Ordinance," n.d.

Biloxi is Mississippi's premier Gulf Coast tourist area. This area has come under intense pressure from increasing development since gambling was introduced in the state in the early 1990s. The city sits between Biloxi Bay and the Gulf and is subject to the effects of tropical storms and hurricanes.

The Building Permit Office administers the city's ordinance. Clearing permits prior to development are not required in this community. Some credit toward the requirements of the ordinance can be granted for saving certain trees on-site. Each tree to be credited is reviewed on a tree-by-tree basis. The ordinance applies to all zoning districts except single-family and two-family developments. Renovations of more than fifty (50) percent trigger compliance with this ordinance on all existing developments.

Design components include parking lot perimeters, vehicular use area interiors, and front setback areas. Planting within parking lots is based on a percentage of area.

This is a minimum ordinance with minimum planting requirements.

Jackson

Jackson, "Landscape Ordinance of the City of Jackson, Mississippi," 1990.

This ordinance addresses erosion, flooding, buffers, native ecology and the health and general welfare of the people of Jackson. It defines terms such as *buffering, clearing, encroachment*, and *refuse storage*.

Trees used in landscaping should all be of nursery stock quality and are defined as shown in Figure 2.36. Owners are encouraged to maintain nonpaved rights-of-way abutting their land with approval of the city, which will take no responsibility in the event any landscaping is required to be removed. The ordinance also addresses parking lots and commercial loading areas in detail.

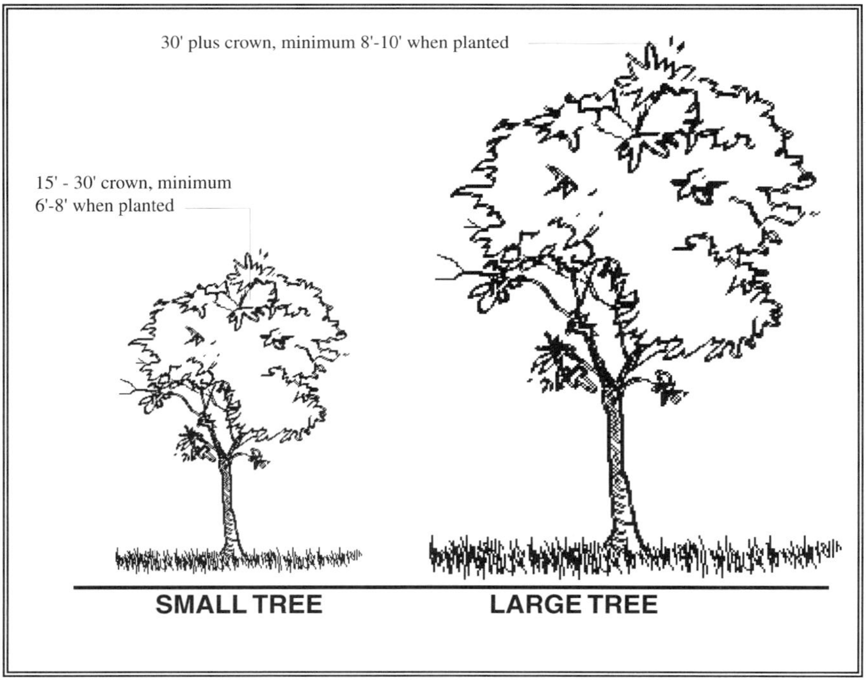

FIGURE 2.36. Tree definitions, Jackson, Mississippi.

Madison

Madison, "Landscape Ordinance," n.d.

In this small Mississippi community, clearing permits must be acquired prior to any site clearing. Credit is given for each tree preserved. This landscape ordinance applies to all developments; there are no exemptions. Design components include interiors of vehicular use areas, parking lot perimeters and street yards. There is no requirement for interior site plantings.

The Planning and Zoning Board administers the ordinance and issues permits.

Ocean Springs

Ocean Springs, "Ocean Springs Landscape Ordinance," Ord. 1-1994. January 4, 1994. Amended July 5, 1995.

Ocean Springs is an old and lovely coastal village overlooking Biloxi Bay and the Mississippi Sound of the Gulf of Mexico. This, the original site of European settlement on the Gulf Coast, is a town dominated by live oaks and other coastal vegetation. Many of the trees in this town have survived numerous hurricanes and offer some protection from high coastal winds. Trees and landscape are highly valued in this town and do much to promote the tourist trade and provide year-round livability.

This ordinance and a related tree removal ordinance were enacted and, after several months, amended to iron out some administrative details causing problems for developers.

This is a very basic ordinance that does not cover many of the items usually found in contemporary landscape ordinances. For instance, minimal planting is required, there are no standards for plant material installation and/or irrigation and there is only passing mention of maintenance. No qualifications are listed for those who are to prepare the required landscape plan. Design components include vehicular use areas, driveway medians, storm water drainage ways and buffers between parking lots and lot lines. General lot planting is based on one (1) tree per square foot measure. For instance, in commercial zoning districts that would be one (1) tree for twelve hundred fifty (1,250), amended to twenty-five hundred (2,500), square feet of lot area. Of these trees, fifty (50) percent must be shade trees. Ten (10) percent of vehicular use areas must be set aside for landscaping.

Landscape areas must be identified on subdivision plats.

All land uses must comply, except single- and two-family residential and existing developments, unless the number of parking spaces increases by fifty (50) percent or exterior additions total fifty (50) percent of original structure or the gross floor area increases by twenty-five (25) percent.

The ordinance is administered by the Planning Commission and the Director of Planning. No Certificate of Occupancy or final subdivision plat can be approved until the landscaping has been installed or a "notarized agreement" of temporary delay has been filed with the city. A method of appeal is described, and variances are allowed under certain circumstances. Alternative plans may be submitted. The alternative plan may take into account other landscaping features not mentioned in the ordinance, such as fountains, pools, waterfalls and the like.

Few landscape ordinances require planting of drainage ways. In Ocean Springs, for all drainage ways with slopes of 3:1 or greater and/or where design depth of maximum water retained exceeds two (2) feet, a two (2)-foot wide planting strip must be provided at the outer perimeter. Also of interest is the alternative compliance provision that allows a registered landscape architect to certify that a plan is better than the minimal requirements of this ordinance.

Ocean Springs. "Cutting and Removal of Trees," Ord. 16-1987, December 15, 1987. Amended Ord. 1-1990.

This related ordinance makes it illegal to remove live oak, magnolia, cypress, sycamore or cedar trees from all lands public and private within the city limits.

Missouri

Blue Springs

Blue Springs, "Landscaping and Screening Regulations," n.d.

The City of Blue Springs is concerned about the disappearance of native trees from the region and believes that conflicts in land use should be resolved with screens and buffers. For these reasons, it has enacted this ordinance to require landscaping and screening for all new construction or expansion of existing uses.

Landscape requirements are given for various zoning categories. For instance, each residential lot must be planted with one (1) tree for every four thousand (4,000) square feet of lot area, not to exceed three (3) trees per lot. In other districts the number of trees is based on linear footage of frontage. Plantings of medium or large deciduous shade trees are encouraged for the "landscape setback" zone of each lot.

Parking lots also fall under this ordinance. Not less than six (6) percent of the interior of a parking lot is to be landscaped, using a formula—number of spaces × 270 square feet—to determine the interior area of the parking lot. Standards are given for minimum size of planting medians, planting locations in parking lots, type of plant materials and zones of ingress and egress. Screening standards require screening parking lots, trash bins and residential districts from nonresidential uses. Screens are to consist of a wall, berm, fence, planting or a combination of these. Definitions in terms of opacity and height are given for each screen type. Evergreen trees are the preferred screening material for landscaping screened areas.

Plant materials standards describe medium and large deciduous shade trees, small ornamental trees, conifers, upright evergreen trees, shrubs, ground cover plants and grass.

All landscaping must be in place prior to issuance of an Occupancy Permit. Landscaping must be maintained and is subject to periodic inspections by the city.

The City Zoning Administrator requires that landscape plans be submitted in support of a final development plan or building permit application. There is no requirement that the plan be sealed by a registered landscape architect. The Administrator has authority for approving all landscape plans, subject to any additional requirements deemed necessary by the Planning Commission or Board of Aldermen. Failure to comply with the ordinance will be considered a violation of the terms of the Building or Occupancy Permit.

The ordinance is very general in nature and must result in enhanced landscapes in the City of Blue Springs without putting undue burden on developers of commercial properties.

Independence

Independence. Landscape Requirements, Article 2 and Article 8, Section 14.540, Chapter 14, City Code, July 1, 1996.

The City of Independence has one of the most recent ordinances in the country. This ordinance repeals an earlier landscape ordinance that merely set standards for trees and planting of trees in various zoning districts within the city. The new ordinance is similar to most contemporary ordinances in that it places emphasis on the public safety concerns of land use rather than the aesthetic concerns of planting, which was more common ten (10) or twenty (20) years ago. However, this ordinance does not emphasize tree or natural landscape preservation as do other contemporary ordinances.

Independence has adopted this ordinance to minimize the environmental effect of development by enhancing shade, erosion control, air purification, groundwater recharge, oxygen regeneration, and abatement of noise, glare and heat. In doing so it hopes to protect and preserve the appearance, character, and value of property, enhance architecture, soften paved areas, buffer uncomplementary land uses and thereby promote the general welfare of the city.

The Community Development Director administers the provisions of this article and may impose fines of not more than one thousand (1,000) dollars for failure to comply. This office reviews landscape plans submitted in support of a final Site Development Plan, Final Planned Unit Development Plan or Building Permit. Landscape plans must be submitted for all uses other than agricultural districts and single- and two-family residential districts. Site plans for multifamily, commercial and industrial sites are to be prepared by a registered landscape architect, architect, horticulturist or landscape designer with an established firm or nursery.

Multifamily, commercial and industrial land uses must come into compliance with the landscape provisions of this ordinance according to a sliding scale whenever a renovation or expansion of the structure or site occurs. The sliding scale is based on total cost market evaluations of a 1996 base year. For instance, when renovations amount to thirty (30) to sixty (60) percent of the base year evaluation, certain listed landscape requirements apply. When renovations amount to over sixty (60) percent of the base year evaluation, all landscape requirements apply.

Design components of this ordinance consist of tree planting per zoning district, streetside tree planting, parking lot perimeter and interior parking lot planting. In addition, there are buffer yard requirements, utility line planting requirements and specifications for tree protection in construction zones that must be included in the design. There is a provision within the design components for "neighborhood landscape plans" that may be submitted where canopy tree-lined streets are desired by all residents. Storage yards are to be screened, as graphically portrayed in Figure 2.37.

Design specifications are given, including width and length of buffer zone, size of interior parking islands, height of walls, fences, berms and screens, as well as the percentage of evergreen trees within a plant screen. Street trees are to be installed every fifty (50) feet of public or private street frontage within certain zoning districts. Other districts require forty (40)-foot spacing. Parking lot setbacks are a minimum ten (10) feet and must be planted with one (1) tree and three (3) shrubs for every forty (40) feet.

Standards, mostly performance rather than technical, have been included for installation, maintenance, irrigation, planting, plant materials and recommended

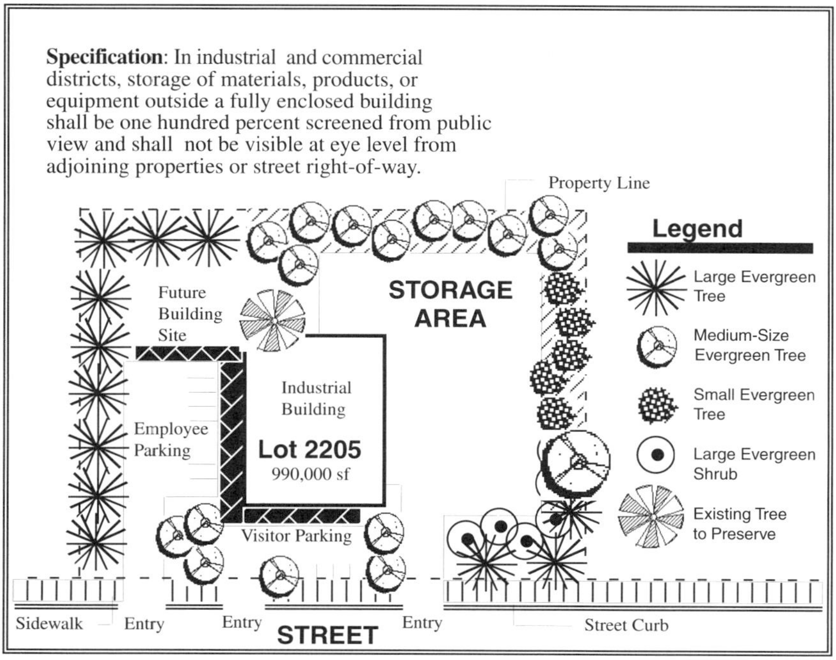

FIGURE 2.37. Storage yard landscaping, Independence, Missouri.

plant lists. Plant lists, for instance, include recommended species for canopy trees, evergreen trees, ornamental trees, evergreen shrubs, flowering shrubs, ground covers and trees prohibited in street rights-of-way.

Screening standards are based on land use relationships and visual impact.

Independence has developed a chart showing the screening impacts of one land use on another. This information is shown in Table 2.64.

For instance, a single-family residential district adjacent to an industrial area would cause "high visual impact" and would require "high-impact screening standards." Likewise, an office district adjacent to a more compatible industrial district would cause "low visual impact" and would require "low-impact screening standards."

Specific screening standards for the various impacts are:

> *High-Impact Screening Standards*: A one hundred (100) percent opaque screen is required between dissimilar land uses. Both of the following elements are required to be installed within the buffer yard: (a) a masonry wall or wood fence and (b) low-impact screening planted on both sides the wall or fence.
>
> *Medium-Impact Screening Standards*: A seventy (70) percent semiopaque screen is required between dissimilar land uses. Semiopaque screening should partially block views from adjoining land uses and create a separation between the adjoining land uses. For medium-impact screening, either a landscape screen or fencing is required. A landscape screen consists of a specified number of canopy trees, ornamental trees, evergreen trees and shrubs.
>
> *Low-Impact Screening Standards*: A relatively open screen is required between somewhat similar land uses. Open screening should provide an attractive separation between land uses. A landscape screen consisting of a specified number of canopy trees, ornamental trees, evergreen trees and shrubs is recommended.

Appeals for variances to the requirements of this ordinance may be made to the Community Development Department and to the Board of Adjustment.

TABLE 2.64. Visual Impact Requirements, Independence, Missouri

	Adjoining Use and Impact Level				
Proposed Use	*Single-Family*	*Multifamily*	*Commercial*	*Office*	*Industrial*
Single-Family	None	High	High	High	High
Multifamily	High	None	High	Medium	High
Commercial	High	High	None	None	Low
Office	High	Medium	None	None	Low
Industrial	High	High	Low	Low	None

Among the interesting things found in this ordinance are some standards more often associated with land subdivision. These include street, lot boundary, sidewalk and utility connection installation regulations. Before a Certificate of Occupancy is issued for a building or structure, each lot must be properly drained and be accessed by a street with curbs, gutters, streetlights, two street trees, drainage structures, storm and sanitary sewers and fire hydrants. Municipal, public and private utilities must also be in place.

Finally, it should be mentioned that this ordinance has a wide range of titular qualifications necessary to prepare the landscape plans that must be submitted at the time the developer seeks a development or building permit. Few cities or states allow the wide range of qualified professions to prepare landscape plans as represented in this ordinance.

Lee's Summit

"Landscaping and Screening," Section 330, Ord. 715,3-27-62;
Ord. 2266, 11-3-81, n.d.

The neighborhoods of Lee's Summit are an asset to the community. Their aesthetic qualities and appearance are the reason for the landscape ordinance, which is administered by the Planning Officer on behalf of the Board of Aldermen.

Landscaping and screening are to be designed, installed and maintained.

The ordinance requires that a Landscape and Screening Plan be prepared and submitted when application is made for a building permit for all new construction exclusive of single and duplex family properties. The landscape plan, drawn to a set of specified conventions, must include a detail drawing of the trash bin enclosure and screen planting. Permits for construction beyond the footings and foundations will not be granted until the landscaping and screening plans are approved. The building permit and occupational license will not be granted without compliance with this ordinance.

All properties must be brought into compliance when changes of ownership occur to commercial and industrial land uses.

The minimum landscaping requirements for all land uses covered by the ordinance shall be one (1) tree and two (2) shrubs per five thousand (5,000) square feet of total lot area. All portions of the site not covered by paving or buildings must be landscaped. Slopes of more than twenty-five (25) percent must be planted with ground covers. Parking lot interiors must be landscaped with not less than two and one-half ($2\frac{1}{2}$) percent of the total parking lot devoted to landscaping. Each curbed landscape area within the parking lot must contain at least one (1) tree adaptable to parking lot environments.

Standards are given for screening and lines of sight. All buildings must be screened, on side and rear, from residential land uses, with six (6)-foot solid screens or walls. Parking lots in all zoning districts shall be screened from residences too. Sight lines at intersections must be carefully considered. Typical details to this effect are included in the ordinance as figures.

Plant material standards follow those given in the book *American Standards for Nursery Stock* and are incorporated by reference. Credit will be given for preserving existing on site trees if they meet certain size and condition specifications and are protected during construction. Certain plant materials are excluded from use in this city.

The long list of excluded plant materials in the ordinance is of interest. On the list are species that are subject to storm damage, pests, disease and excessive maintenance. Some of the plants are considered by many to be desirable and of ornamental value. Controlling the negative aspects of vegetation by providing an exclusion list is certainly within the police power granted by zoning ordinances in the United States and is largely one of the reasons for having landscape ordinances in the first place. This city recognizes this fact.

Nebraska

Lincoln

Design Standards for Zoning Regulations, "Screening and Landscaping and Street Trees and Parking Lots," October 8, 1979, amended 1996. Related document, Design Standards for Subdivision Regulations, "Landscape Screens and Landscaping and Trees," January 18, 1982, amended 1996.

In this northern community, landscape requirements are included within both the zoning and subdivision regulations. They are presented as design standards and, in fact, are included within booklets devoted to the design of such diverse community features as neighborhoods, hiker-biker trails, and storm sewers. Principal landscape requirements are contained in the sections of this ordinance cited. Other minor landscaping requirements are found in other sections of the zoning regulations, such as in design standards for the Capital environs, corporate office parks, and mobile home courts.

This ordinance presents some very specific technical standards for the design of fences, berms, screen plantings and snow control. Plantings must be so positioned that in the winter months the sun can shine on habitable structures, roadways, walks, parking surfaces and recreational areas to melt snow and ice. Plantings cannot increase the drifting of snow onto roadways, walks and streets. These same plantings must also be positioned so as to provide shade and glare reduction to the same facilities in the summer months.

Other standards are given for opacity of screens. Generally, the closer the disruptive land, the denser the screen. Mention is made of the effects of wind loads on fences. They must be designed and installed to withstand wind pressure according to standards set by the city. Fence color is also controlled by this ordinance.

Street trees species, spacing and size at the time of planting are controlled. Detailed specifications are given for plant quality, handling, planting, staking, pruning and maintenance during a one (1)-year "establishment" period. One (1) tree per lot planted along the street is required of all developments.

The City of Lincoln has adopted a list of approved street trees and trees that are prohibited along streets. Approved trees are specified by height, width, shape and color. Plantings must conform to an official Master Street Tree Plan, and combinations of species are controlled. For a tree to be listed as an official street tree, it must meet specific performance standards, such as being free of litter and offensive odors and being storm resistant and long lived. Other standards are presented in Table 2.65.

Standard City of Lincoln installation detail drawings are given in this ordinance for planting, soil preparation, staking and pruning. The intent of the details is to provide very specific design standards and technical requirements for landscape architects.

The emphasis placed on design is this community is commendable. Landscape design standards are presented in such a manner that they are elevated to the same level of importance as street, sewer, drainage and building layout design. This community does address the effects of climate, and its landscape ordinance justifies itself by reflecting this important civic concern.

If improvements to this ordinance could be made, the first step would be to pull all of the landscape requirements together in one comprehensive landscape ordinance where all would be easier to find.

TABLE 2.65 Performance Standards for Acceptable Plants, Lincoln, Nebraska

Standard	*Reason*
Free from litter	Reduced cleanup and more tidyness
Free from offensive odors	Reduces complaints, promotes sweet flowering species
Resistant to breakage	Reduces cleanup cost after wind and ice storms
Resistant to disease and insect pests	Reduces annual maintenance spraying
Resistant to weather stresses	Plants must thrive without extra care
Long-lived	Reduces replanting to once a generation
Adaptable to city conditions	Able to withstand salt, oil, drought and domestic animals
Easily transplanted and grown	Reduces maintenance during the establishment period

Omaha

Omaha, Article XIII, "Landscaping and Screening," Sections 55-711 to 55-722, n.d.

The purpose of this ordinance is to improve the physical appearance and environmental performance of the community; to improve the environmental performance of new development; to buffer potentially incompatible land uses from one another; and to protect property values. This ordinance applies to any new development upon application for a building permit, except for reconstruction of a lawfully existing use after a casualty, remodeling that does not substantially change the location of structures and additions less than twenty (20) percent of the existing floor area.

This ordinance includes sections addressing the following topics: purpose, applicability, definitions, street yard landscaping, buffer yard provisions, screening standards, landscaping provisions, performance bonding, obstruction of view, parking lot landscaping, and buffer yard and screening exceptions. Figure 2.38 depicts the sight triangle requirement for this community.

The street yard landscaping section includes many charts and illustrations, making the section brief and easy to read. The charts list the required percentage of the street yard to be landscaped and the minimum depth of the street yard by zoning districts. The illustrations provided explain where the street yard begins

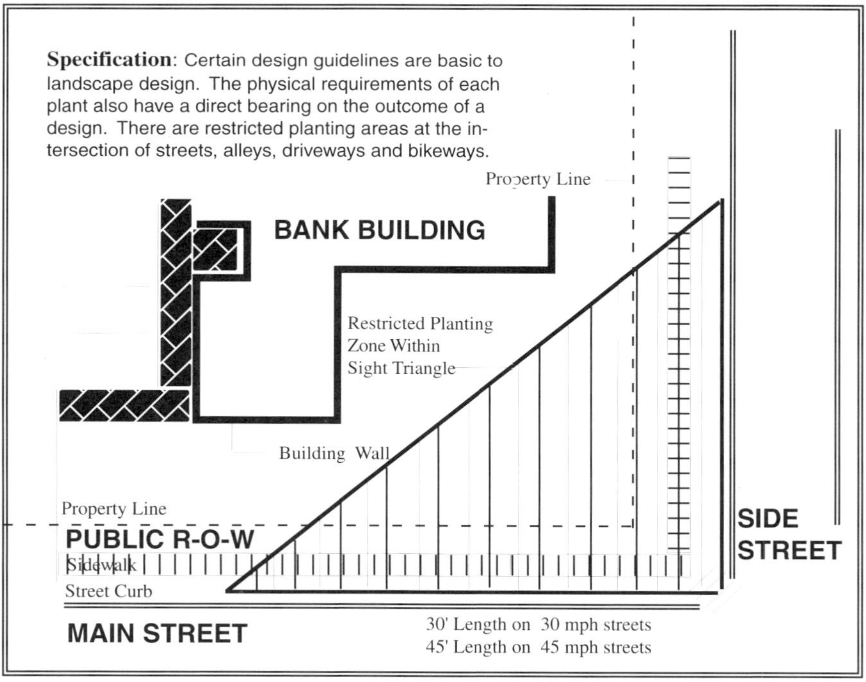

FIGURE 2.38. Sight triangle, Omaha, Nebraska.

and ends, the minimum depth of landscaping, and where the curb and street are located. Also included in this section are some possible solutions for hypothetical street yard problems.

The buffer yard section explains the requirements for development adjacent to districts with common lot lines, intervening alleys, intervening major streets, intervening local streets, and railroad rights-of-way. A table charting the required footage for buffer yards between incompatible zones is given. Illustrations are provided showing the buffer yard requirements between the aforementioned zones.

The screening standards section lists the circumstances under which screening must be provided and gives specifications for the required screening. The landscaping provisions section includes a number of topics: common development, previously-approved sites, tree spacing, bonus provisions and maintenance. Figure 2.38 illustrates the sight triangle requirements for Omaha.

The performance bonding section describes the process a developer must follow in order to occupy the development before the requirements of this ordinance are complete. The sections pertaining to obstruction of view, parking lot landscaping, and buffer yard and screening exceptions refer to additional requirements not provided in this ordinance.

Omaha, Article XIV, Off-Street Parking and Loading Regulations, Sections 55-731 to 55-743, n.d.

The purpose of this ordinance is to provide the number of parking spaces and loading facilities necessary for a particular development, and to provide them in a functional, aesthetically pleasing manner. New developments in the Central Business District or the Neighborhood Business District are regulated by separate standards set forth in Section 55-740.

The first section lists the developments subjected to these requirements, the exceptions under which the required minimum number of parking spaces can be reduced, the requirements for sites with multiple uses and maintenance, and use of off-street parking facilities. The section entitled "Schedule of Off-Street Parking Requirements" provides a table indicating the number of parking spaces required by use types. Horticultural use types require one (1) space per one thousand (1,000) square feet of total sales area. Residential use type requirements vary, but depend on dwelling units within the residence. Many more use types are listed, most of which depend on the square footage of the building. Some use type requirements are described under Schedules A, B, and C.

Other subsections include parking facility location, adjustments for mixed-use developments, compact parking, handicapped parking, bonus provisions, off-street parking design standards, off-street loading requirements, special parking provisions, and permit procedure. Off-street parking design standards address the subjects of vehicle overhang, design requirements for parking reserved for disabled persons, paving and drainage, landscape requirements, screening requirements, entrances and exits, lighting, safety features, maintenance and adjustments.

Omaha, "Standards for Urban Landscaping for the City of Omaha," Nebraska, Report No. 238, February 1987.

This document is a well-prepared design manual combining the Omaha requirements from various ordinances. It lists all the ordinances that require application and explains the application and plan submittal requirements in general. The document does not require the services of a professional, but it does recommend retaining the services of a landscape architect.

The section on standards is the meat of this document. It includes design standards and guidelines, zoning ordinance requirements, general requirements, plant arrangement and screening guidelines, maintenance guidelines, preservation guidelines, grading guidelines and recommended plants. These requirements are in text, chart, and illustration form. The recommended plant section includes trees, shrubs, ground covers, vines, sods and grasses and undesirable plants. This section makes up most of the design manual and is in chart form. Appendixes illustrate sample details and specifications.

This is a very attractive, informative, and easy-to-read manual. The only problem is, as stated earlier, it is a general accumulation of many ordinances and does not contain the specific requirements for each new development type.

State of Nebraska "Model Landscape Ordinance," n.d.

This is a very generalized sample ordinance for the establishment of a management program for the community forest resource. Section 1 suggests definitions of tree types. Sections 2 to 6 outline duties and operational procedures of a tree board. Sections 7 to 16 outline general landscape requirements. Sections 17 to 21 outline enforcement procedures.

Nevada

Clark County-Las Vegas

Clark County Development Code, Chapter 6, "Landscaping," June 21, 1988, amended 1990, 1991.

It often takes many years to draft an effective landscape ordinance. This ordinance is a case in point. It was originally drafted in 1988 as a set of voluntary design guidelines for landscaping, irrigation and suggested plant materials for multifamily and nonresidential uses. In 1991 the design guidelines were evaluated and changed to reflect greater efficiency in water use. Revisions were made, and Chapter 6 and Appendix B, "Suggested Plant Materials," were enacted by ordinance into the Clark County Development Code under §29.44.085.

Chapter 6 cites requirements for preparation and review of the landscape plan, landscaping requirements, landscape design objectives and irrigation plan preparation. Few design components are mentioned. Rather, is it left more to the

TABLE 2.66. Landscape Design Objectives, Clark County, Nevada

Design Objective	*Goal*
Minimize health, pedestrian, and traffic hazards.	Protect the public health and safety.
Minimize water uses.	Reduce demand on water supply.
Promote the visual image desired by the community.	Maintain property values, promote tourism.
Minimize off-site problems.	Reduce conflict between land uses.
Improve site environment, provide comfort to users.	Make sites cleaner and better for people.
Minimize disturbance of walkways and utilities.	Reduce costs to city and utility companies.
Minimize maintenance problems.	Reduce the amount of maintenance, sustainability.

designer to define and satisfy the requirements. The design objectives listed in Table 2.66 are included in the ordinance.

Chapter 7 of the design manual from the Clark County Development Code addresses buffering and defines three types: "maximum," "moderate" and "minimal," depending on density, materials used and amount of conflict between land uses. Options for each are illustrated with sketches.

One of the interesting things noted in this community is that plants have been rated for "allergenic potential" by an allergist. Plants are rated from 4 (highly allergenic) to 1 (slightly allergenic). Certain plants are prohibited by law.

The ordinance gives few technical standards other than those illustrated in Figure 2.39.

Both of these chapters of the design manual, as well as its Appendix B, go into little detail. It requires careful reading, and a good education, to understand the requirements. Graphics, somewhat cartoonish, have been used to highlight the requirements and explain them in general terms. A lot of "do" and "don't" graphics are included. Of the many design manuals reviewed as part of this study, this seems to be one of the most graphically oriented. You have to interpret the ordinance from the graphics. If you cannot figure out the relationship between the design manual graphics and the actual site being developed, you have somewhat of a problem.

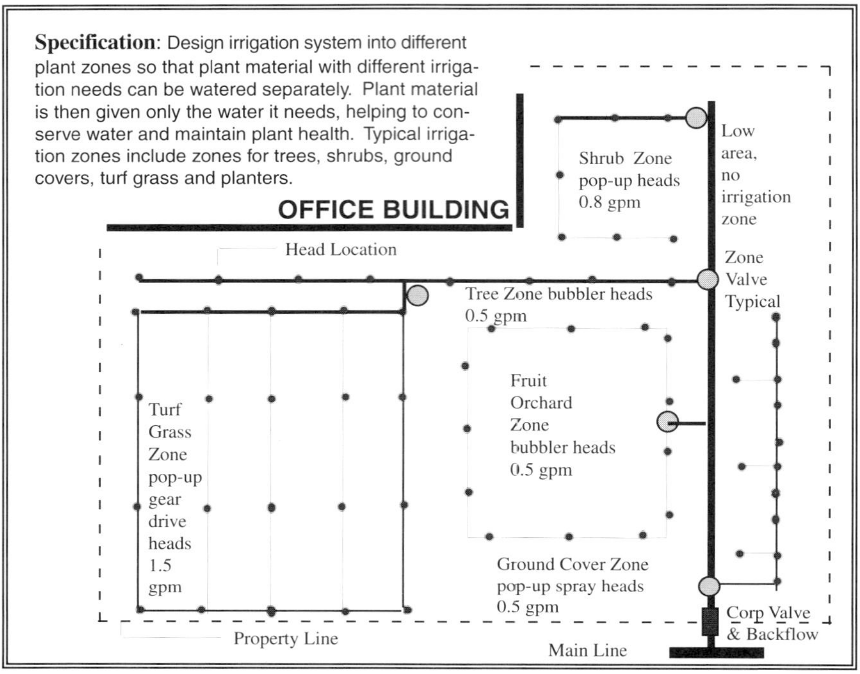

FIGURE 2.39. Irrigation zone design standards, Clark County, Nevada.

This annotator has a suggestion that would make the design manual easier to follow. The page numbers should be centered so that when staff sends out copies of the ordinance, all pages will be in order and page numbers will be visible even if poorly placed on the copying machine.

Sparks

Zoning Ordinance, Chapter 20.32, "Resource Efficient Landscaping," 1992.

This community updated an older ordinance and redesigned it to be more conserving of water supplies, as a result of many years of drought in this region. One of the main purposes of this ordinance is to conserve water, natural resources, and energy by encouraging the community to use resource-efficient guidelines and principles in the establishment of landscapes and gardens.

The ordinance applies to all new development and to renovation, based on a percentage of new construction consistent with the zoning district. Landscape plans prepared by a landscape architect registered in the State of Nevada must be filed with the City Administrator prior to site plan approval or issuance of a building permit. These plans must be drawn with an explicit list of information and installation details attached. A postconstruction certification statement must be filed with the city by the landscape architect who prepares the design.

The design must encompass several components, including percentage of site area landscaping, required number of trees and shrubs, parking area landscaping, VUA screening along streets, and water-conserving irrigation systems. Standards are given for maintenance, resource-efficient landscaping and plan preparation. Certain species of trees are to be excluded from the design.

Planning staff in Sparks, Nevada have developed a checklist to assist with the review process. This checklist, summarized in Table 2.67, contains ninety (90) items that are to be reviewed for compliance with the ordinance. The items range from simply checking the North arrow to checking to see that Sc. 40 PVC pipe is used under all paved areas, or calculating gradients to see that lawn areas do not exceed 4-to-1 slopes.

This checklist, useful to planning staff, gives some indication of how many professional decisions have to be made in the preparation or review of the required landscape plans.

It is obvious from an examination of the sample items from the checklist that adequate training is required in landscape architecture and site engineering in order to skillfully and artfully prepare landscape designs in this city.

TABLE 2.67. Excerpts of the Landscape and Irrigation Plan Checklist, Sparks, Nevada

Yes	*No*	*Landscape Plan/Irrigation Plan Requirements*
___	___	Percent of area landscaped, R1–R5 (residential) = 20%
___	___	Percent of area landscaped, PO (professional office) = 20%
___	___	Percent of area landscaped, C2 (general commercial) = 15%
___	___	Botanical names of plants
___	___	Number of plants
___	___	System point of connection, size, water pressure, available demand gpm
___	___	Equipment identified by manufacturer and model number
___	___	Adequate freeze protection
___	___	Tree requirement, 1 per 300 sf, residential areas
___	___	Tree requirement, 1 per 500 sf, industrial areas
___	___	50% of trees 1″ caliper, 50% of trees 2″ caliper
___	___	Parking lots under 100 spaces, 1 tree each 7 spaces
___	___	Turf area not to exceed 80% of total landscape area
___	___	Planter islands minimum 100 sf, minimum width 5 ft inside dimension
___	___	60% of container-grown shrubs must be 5 gallon at time of planting

This ordinance is typical of those that are based on compliance with predetermined measures such as percentages, quantities, areas and linear feet. The resource-efficient landscaping concept behind this ordinance is a good idea but falls a little short of being truly sustainable landscaping. Most resource-efficient principles mentioned are referred to as Xeriscape in other parts of the country. No mention is made of habitat protection, plant material preservation or use of native ground cover.

Washoe County

Washoe County. Landscaping, Section 110.412.15, Washoe Zoning Ordinance, 1994.

This ordinance seems to be typical of many of the earlier ordinances. The early ordinances generally inserted text into the zoning ordinance at some point that seemed appropriate. In this ordinance, landscaping requirements are included in the section that mandates that certain plans be submitted during the design and development phase.

In Washoe County, site plans, planting plans and irrigation plans must be submitted in order to get zoning and/or building approval. All of these plans must be prepared by a licensed landscape architect pursuant to Nevada Revised Statutes, Chapter 623A. The Director of Development Review must approve the plans. The site plan is needed to ensure that the proposed landscape improvements are in conformance with the landscape ordinance. The planting plan is needed to ensure that the proposed plantings are in conformance with the planting standards. The irrigation plan is required to ensure sufficient artificial watering of newly installed plantings. A soil analysis study is highly recommended prior to the preparation of the plans.

This ordinance requires landscaping of parking and loading areas; buffers and screening between adjoining residential districts; and screening for open storage areas. Equipment and swimming pool areas must be screened as well.

There are specific planting standards for the planting of each of these areas. The ordinance includes standards for plant material as well as for screen opaqueness. One standard that makes a lot of sense is that planting plans should be sensitive to water use. It requires that all plants having similar climatic, water, soil and maintenance requirements be planted together.

All plants should be placed in compatible water use zones.

New Hampshire

Bedford

Bedford. Minimum Landscape Performance Standards, Bedford Zoning Ordinance, 1994.

This landscape ordinance can be considered an overlay district ordinance, in that it applies to properties abutting a major cross-town thoroughfare. One of the stated objectives of this ordinance is to reinforce the visual image of the Route 3 corridor as a tree-lined street, perhaps recalling an earlier day in New England.

Through its provisions, this ordinance attempts to establish a palette of landscape design options to work in relationship to the intensity of the land uses along the path of the street. By doing so, the Bedford Planning Department hopes to promote a pedestrian-friendly streetscape.

The palette of options and incentives spelled out in this ordinance constitute the design components. These include general site landscape area, street tree strips, front landscape strip, side and rear landscape strips, exterior pavement landscape strips, interior pavement landscape strips and signage landscape strip. Obviously, what might be called planting beds, planting buffers or planting areas in other parts of the nation are referred to as "strips" in Bedford.

Other components include open space, screening, preservation of existing trees and parking area arrangement or design.

Each of these components is defined, justified, located and given specific planting standards. Several are given incentive bonuses that do such things as substitute mandated plantings for preserved healthy vegetation. Another example: within parking area interiors, each preserved tree of more than four (4) inches in caliper may be substituted for three (3) new mandated trees.

The signage landscape strip is somewhat unusual. This design component calls for the establishment of four (4) feet of ground cover plantings to screen sign foundations, monuments or pedestals.

Concord

Chapter 28, Zoning Ordinance, Section 28-1 § 28-12-5 and related, "Parking Lot Landscaping Requirements," April 1994. Related document, "Architectural Design Guidelines," n.d.

In Concord the landscape ordinance requirements are scattered throughout sections of the zoning ordinance pertaining to permitted land uses and special (overlay) zoning districts. In an attempt to simplify this matter, the city has retained a consultant to develop Architectural Design Guidelines to apply to an Architectural Design District, a special zoning district under the code of this community. The Architectural Design Guidelines are being used for all districts and projects where site plan review is required.

Therefore, this discussion will focus on the design guidelines as this city's attempt to bring all of the scattered information together. Detailed requirements and many technical standards will be found in subsections that deal with floodplains, stream banks and shorelines, wetland districts, conservation districts, off-street parking and loading and other special zoning districts.

The Architectural Design District has been created to ensure harmony between land uses in the city. Land placed in this district (the AD District) will also be in another district. The AD designation is a form of overlay district created to control design and require planning board review and approval of all development projects.

TABLE 2.68. Architectural Design Standards, Concord, New Hampshire

Design Standard	*Reason*
Site Development	Control site organization, layout, setback distances, building siting and visual continuity of neighborhoods.
Landscaping and Site Treatment	This section regulates and sets design standards for plantings, plant material sizes, screening, parking, site structures, views and existing site conditions.
Building Design and Materials	Requirements and standards guide harmonious design of roof forms, material selection, color, mechanical equipment, architectural features and details.
Signage	Regulate sign sizes, materials, illumination, character and sign graphics.
Special District Standards	These include design guidelines for buffers, landscaping, parking, building features, acceptable materials, flags, signage and natural environments.

The design guidelines of this city build on the "master plan" for the City of Concord created in 1726 and other design considerations developed in the 1930s and updated in 1967 and 1977. The guidelines provide written and graphic standards for the appearance of all new development in the city. They are established to inform applicants of the expectations of the city and how to seek a building permit. Plans prepared for submission to the city showing architectural design, landscaping and other important features of site development must follow the current guidelines as set forth in Table 2.68.

The design guidelines for landscaping are very general and performance based rather than mandatory. Although the city should be commended for placing emphasis on design and sensitivity to historic place, many site scale issues addressed in contemporary landscape ordinances, such as tree protection, go unnoted in this city.

Durham

Article 9, "Landscaping," n.d.

Trees and other vegetation are recognized as a valid asset to the community for health and aesthetics, providing oxygen, shade, wind protection, view barriers, and a priceless psychological counterpoint to the urban environment. This ordinance intends to aid in stabilizing the environment's ecological balance by contributing to the processes of air purification, oxygen regeneration, ground water recharge and storm water runoff retardation and aiding in abatement of noise, glare and heat. This landscape ordinance will ensure that the local stock of native vegetation is protected and replenished.

Landscape plans must be submitted for all commercial and residential uses. The plans must contain a detailed snow removal plan and underground sprinkling systems. Landscaping is required for landscape yards, roadway slopes and buffers/ barriers. Clearing and stripping of natural vegetation is prohibited prior to obtaining approval for a landscape plan. Wooded natural areas are to be preserved when practical, and the landscape plan is to include a reforestation plan to establish and enhance forest cover in certain areas of each development site.

Trees must be protected during construction following specifications in the *Tree Protection Manual for Builders and Developers*, Florida Department of Agriculture, and *Protecting Shade Trees During Home Construction*, published by the U.S. Department of Agriculture. Standards are included in this ordinance for maintenance and landscape materials.

The ordinance defines several terms, such as *specimen tree, damage, historic or special interest tree* and *tree warden*. It is the duty of the tree warden to inspect all landscape installation in the city.

This is an example of an ordinance that was located on and downloaded from the Internet. To get a copy of the ordinance, go to this address: http://nhresnet.sr.unh.edu/granit Net/planning/guide/docs/ldoc1.txt.

In the future, the author expects to see other cities place their landscape ordinance on the Internet, where they will be accessible to any researcher or planner seeking background information on landscape ordinances.

New Jersey

East Windsor

East Windsor, Section 22-27 of the Technical Standards Ordinance, "Landscape Architectural Standards," n.d.

The intent of this ordinance is to improve visual quality and unity; promote safe vehicular and pedestrian circulation; protect against hazards; enhance the microclimate of activity areas; and promote the health, safety and welfare of the community.

This ordinance outlines the requirements for streetscapes, cul-de-sacs and traffic islands, storm water areas, open space, landscape buffers and strips, parking areas, green space, pedestrian space, amenities/resources and landscape maintenance. Special emphasis is given to storm water management, as shown in Figure 2.40.

A certified landscape architect is required to prepare and submit all plans regarding the development project.

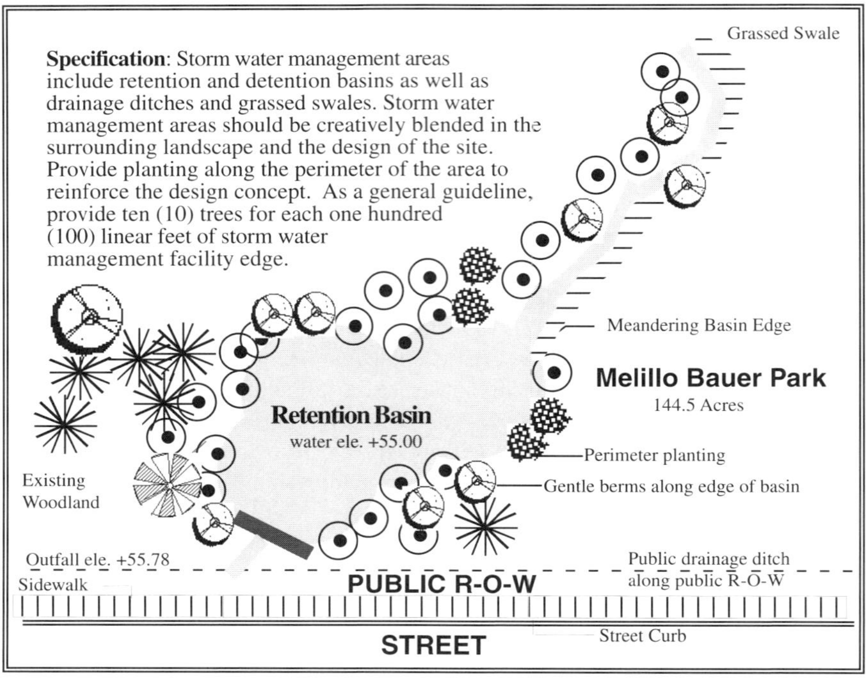

FIGURE 2.40. Storm water management facility design standards, East Windsor, New Jersey.

The topics of this ordinance are its distinctive aspects. Streetscapes, of either a formal or informal tree-lined avenue, are detailed and required for all new development. Cul de sac, traffic island, and storm water area requirements are also detailed. An open space requirement is a unique aspect of this ordinance. Buffer area requirements are given according to levels of nuisance, rather than land use abutment. Requirements for green spaces, areas not developed in an impervious manner and not covered by other requirements of the ordinance, and pedestrian spaces are also singular aspects of the ordinance.

This ordinance is unusual in that it deals more with residential areas and pedestrians than any other ordinance reviewed so far. The ordinance explains what a landscaping element should be used for, not just what the requirement demands. Illustrations are placed throughout the ordinance and at its end to facilitate and add to the understanding of the requirements.

Mendham

"Tree Removal Ordinance for Mendham Township," Ordinance 11-90, Chapter XXIII, n.d.

This ordinance protects trees and plants on municipal lands and easements within the Township of Mendham and regulates, by a tree removal permit, the removal of trees on undeveloped lots. It also establishes a Township Tree Protection Committee.

Initially, the ordinance recognizes the value of trees to the community, citing beauty, property value, shade and wind protection. For regulation purposes, a tree is defined as any woody perennial plant with a main stem or trunk exceeding four (4) inches in diameter, measured at a point four (4) feet above the existing ground level. An exception is made for dogwood, birch and American hornbeam, which can have only a two (2)-inch trunk to qualify for the ordinance.

On municipal lands, trees and shrubs must not be harmed in any way, and no machinery, equipment or heavy objects, including rocks and cement, can be placed within a tree's drip line or within (6) six feet of shrubs. For undeveloped lots, a tree removal permit must be issued before the lot can be "brushed out" or any trees or vegetation removed. The ordinance sets standards for erecting protective barriers, tree wells and extension tiling around trees to be saved.

The Tree Protection Committee established by the ordinance consists of five regular members and two alternate members. A township construction official and environmental commission member are on the committee, along with others appointed for one (1)-year terms by the township committee. The Tree Protection Committee oversees provisions of the ordinance, formulates plans for planting and care of trees and shrubs on municipal lands, recommends to the zoning board adjustments of plans for subdivisions and construction sites and initiates court proceedings against violators.

In reviewing permits, the Tree Protection Committee considers historic, endangered or specimen trees, mature and healthy trees with "desirable characteristics," natural screening between buildings and the condition of the trees. Removal applications cost thirty-five (35) dollars, and the ordinance sets fines for noncompliance up to five hundred (500) dollars.

Paramus, Borough of

Ordinance 83-10, Article 16, "Greenery," 1983.

This ordinance with the unusual name "Greenery" was enacted in the early 1980s. It sets conditions that are intended to maintain a reasonable amount of landscaping, (greenery?) on every lot in the city.

A "percentage of lot" criterion is used for determining the amount of landscaping, as well as a percentage of lot size to determine the extent of landscape buffers. Commonly twenty (20) percent of a lot in most zoning districts must be set aside for landscaping. Buffer areas of various dimensions are capped at twelve (12) percent of a site. The maximum amount of a site devoted to greenery, landscape area plus buffer area, need not exceed thirty (30) percent of site.

This design criterion is considered by the Planning Board in determining the location, shape, size and content of planted areas on each site. Landscaping should serve the functions delineated in Table 2.69.

TABLE 2.69. Criteria to Consider in Design of Landscape Areas, Borough of Paramus, New Jersey

Drainage Control
Traffic and Pedestrian Safety
Conservation of Economic Values, Property Values
Proper Vehicular and Traffic Sight Lines
Shade and Pollution Control
Screening and Privacy of Adjacent Residential Areas
The Configuration and Relationship of Planting Area to Total Plan Submitted
The Reduction of Noise and Lights Disturbing Nearby Residential Property
The Objectives of Good Planning and Zoning
The Preservation of Healthy, Substantial Trees Whenever Reasonable

Minimum design standards for planted areas and buffer areas are presented in the ordinance, along with guidelines for selections of plant materials. A list of recommended evergreens, trees, shrubs and ground covers is included.

The law is administered by the borough's Planning Board. Landscape plans prepared by a licensed landscape architect, architect or professional engineer must be submitted for site plan approval, for subdivision approval when buffers are required and for planting on dedicated public land. The Shade Tree and Park Commission inspects and approves final installation.

This ordinance with a most unusual name is vague and does not communicate exactly what is expected of the landscape designer. It seems that quality control and design are in the hands of the review agencies rather than the site developers. The "percentage of lot" criterion does seem to be ample as compared with those used by other cities to establish site landscaping.

Piscataway, Township of

Piscataway Revised Ordinances, as amended. Site Plan Review Ordinance, Article No. 24 -704.2, "Landscaping Standards," Land Subdivision Ordinance, Article No. 20-5, "Shade Trees, Landscaping and Landscaped Islands," n.d.

Piscataway, New Jersey, has had a landscape ordinance for almost twenty (20) years. At this time it is in the process of upgrading and modernizing the ordinance. This ordinance may be considered typical of the early landscape ordinances in this country. Ordinance requirements are scattered throughout the city code. Most landscape information is contained within the Land Subdivision Ordinance and the Site Plan Review Ordinance.

A landscaping plan prepared by a licensed landscape architect is submitted with each site plan application. This plan must be drawn to scale and identify all existing and proposed landscape materials. The plan must be accompanied with planting details, such as shown in Figure 2.41, along with a planting schedule and notes. The plan must show all required buffers and landscaping of parking areas, as well as related concerns.

Buffers are required between residential and industrial or commercial land uses. No specifications or technical design standards are given, however. Standards are given for parking lot design. Ten (10) percent (in front yards, twenty (20) percent) of parking areas, in the form of curbed islands, must be reserved for landscaping. One (1) deciduous tree must be installed for each one thousand (1,000) square feet of parking area (five hundred (500) in front parking areas). Front yard parking must be screened from the street and adjacent residential zones. Loading, storage, dumpsters and other such facilities must be landscaped. No specifics are given.

Shade trees are to be planted within street rights-of-way. They are to be planted not less than thirty-five (35) feet nor more than seventy-five (75) feet on center. Certain species and planting specs are required by the township landscape architect. They are illustrated in the descriptive drawing shown in Figure 2.41.

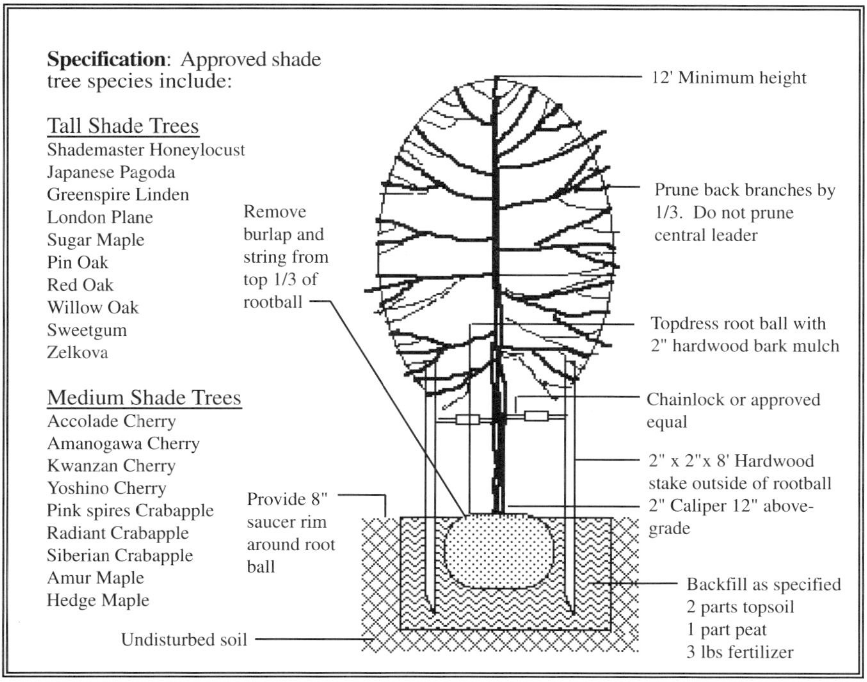

FIGURE 2.41. Shade tree planting detail, Piscataway Township, New Jersey.

Standards and specifications pertain to plant materials and installation. Standards are also given for digging, size, planting, staking, wrapping, bed edging and mulching.

Topsoil is not to be allowed to erode and is to be stored on-site and reused and seeded following construction. No soil can be removed from the site without a Soil Removal Permit from the township. Landscaping of all areas of cuts and fills and terraces are to be sufficient to prevent erosion and must be approved by the municipal agency. All slopes steeper than one (1) foot vertically to two (2) feet horizontally (1:2 slopes) are to be planted with suitable cover plants. Grasses or sodding alone is not an acceptable erosion control device.

Lighting should be provided according to the design standards shown in Table 2.70.

The land subdivision ordinance contains additional landscape requirements. Its provisions require plantings on slopes greater than 1:2 or fifty (50) percent. All subdivision cul-de-sac streets must be designed, planted and maintained according to township design standards contained in Plate 6 of the ordinance. This plate shows a mixed planting of shade trees, evergreen trees, flowering trees, evergreen shrubs and shrubby ground covers. Granite block curbs and gutters and concrete paving over crushed stone and quarry process tailings must also be incorporated into the design.

A landscape plan for the subdivision along with necessary details, drawn by a licensed landscape architect, must be submitted along with application for preliminary approval of the subdivision.

The significance of this ordinance is based on the fact that licensed professionals are required to prepare the landscape designs, both for site plan approval and subdivision approval. In the early days of landscape ordinance development, some municipalities relied on the experience of design professionals rather than writing cumbersome, detailed design guidelines as many communities do today. There are advantages to requiring licensed design professionals, foremost of which is acknowledgment of the public liability involved with landscaping along streets and near homes.

When the ordinance is updated, this provision should be retained.

TABLE 2.70. Lighting Design Standards, Piscataway Township, New Jersey

Site Feature	*Lighting Intensity*
Parking lots	0.5 footcandles throughout
Intersections	3 footcandles
Maximum at property lines	1.1 footcandles
In residential areas	0.6 footcandles

Randolph

"Revised Ordinances of Randolph," Article 9, Section 33, "Randolph Center—Mixed Use," n.d., and proposed amendments for "Design Standards Within the Town Center Zone."

The ordinance for the Town Center Zone of Randolph Township strives for a planned development concept with a mixture of land uses. It requires integration and compatible design for buildings, public open spaces, roads and drives, walkways, utilities, parking, access to the existing road system, drainage basins, landscaping, buffers and environmentally sensitive areas. Site landscaping must be done by a registered landscape architect, the ordinance states.

Of special note in this ordinance are requirements for transition buffers between multifamily and single-family residences, and between commercial and residential lots.

The proposed amendments to the Township Code set specific design standards for such things as street trees, paving, street furniture, lighting, parking and signage. Probably the most interesting aspect of Randolph Township's proposed amendments is the limited used of graphics to direct and control design. For instance, a "Streetscape Detail" illustration is included in the amendments.

In Randolph, the Planning Department inspects all commercial landscape construction.

New Mexico

Albuquerque

City Code, Article No. 1, "Water Conservation Landscaping and Water Waste," 1995.

Landscape ordinances do vary from region to region, primarily because natural systems vary from place to place. This ordinance is a good example of one in which a scarce natural resource is the centerpiece.

This ordinance was proposed by a Water Conservation Task Force in order to reduce yard irrigation and irrigation-related water waste, which comprise over forty (40) percent of the City of Albuquerque's annual usage. Further, the task force sought to prepare an ordinance that would reduce inefficient watering, overwatering and excess water waste while encouraging voluntary water conservation on all properties.

The ordinance applies to all properties served by the municipal water utility, regardless of zoning district. It also applies to public properties, parks and golf courses. Planting Restrictions, Design Regulations, Irrigation System Standards and landscape plan requirements apply to all properties. Occupancy permits are contingent upon compliance with this ordinance.

This ordinance affects those who prepare landscape designs, those who build landscapes and property owners who control water usage. Landscape architects must design landscapes to be water efficient with low water use plants; contractors must build water systems that eliminate fugitive water and carefully control precipitation rates and volumes.

Owners are restricted as to the time of day and the days of the week they can apply water to their landscapes. Each irrigation system must be equipped with a flow meter that will measure how much water is used for irrigation during a twelve (12)-month period. Any excess use over a water budget of forty two (42) inches a year will result in an excess surcharge.

A designer must use one of two design approaches for preparing landscape plans. The first approach requires that the landscaping be designed to meet the water budget. The formula used is:

$$WB = (42)\,(.6)\,(LA)\,(.62)$$

where WB is yearly water usage for landscaping, 42 is average annual water requirements in inches per year, .6 is the adjustment factor to be used to reduce or moderate water usage, LA is landscape area in square feet and .62 is the conversion factor from inches per year to gallons per year.

The second approach involves restricting the types and quantities of plants used in the landscape design. For instance, this requires that on public properties other than parks and golf courses, medium and low water usage plants must be used on one hundred (100) percent of the landscaped area. On privately owned properties other than golf courses, medium and low water usage plants must be used on eighty (80) percent of the landscaped areas.

Specific design regulations and irrigation system standards apply. They affect the types of plant materials, slope plantings, fountains, surface water ponds and irrigation system standards for water use efficiency. The latter includes standards for controllers, valves, heads and limitations to waste, overwatering and overspray. All landscaped areas over ten (10) acres must have a performance audit conducted periodically to ensure uniformity of water use.

Landscape planting plans and irrigation system design plans are required for all building additions of more than two hundred (200) square feet with over ten thousand (10,000) square feet of landscaped area. Plans must be prepared showing all relevant site data as well as grading, planting and irrigation. The standards are listed in Table 2.71.

Appeals, variances, assessments and penalties are specified in the ordinance.

This ordinance is a special type of landscape ordinance that places most emphasis on water use and conservation. Little additional design information is included. Perhaps more Xeriscape principles and requirements for use of native plants and planting strategy could be included.

TABLE 2.71. Technical Drawing Requirements, Albuquerque, New Mexico

Technical Information	*Example*	*Purpose*
Site Information	Site areas, structures, features	Determine extent of landscaping
Site Grading	Contour lines, slopes, elevations	Determine percolation/ runoff rates
Planting Information	Types, quantities, locations of plants	Determine extent of water needs
Irrigation System Data	Pressure, zones, precipitation rates, parts	Determine function of system
Irrigation Management	Timing, frequency, amounts of use	Determine water use

New York

Calgary

Calgary, Section 33, "General Rules for Commercial Buildings" (i.e., landscaping, screening, building design, and garbage storage), 1988.

This brief ordinance lists requirements for general landscaping, soft landscaping, building design, screening and garbage storage.

Clifton Park

Zoning Ordinance, § 86-10 "Trees," n.d.

Clifton Park is typical of many communities across the country, particularly in the North, that have not developed a comprehensive landscape ordinance but, rather, have minimal standards "scattered" through various parts of the zoning ordinance, subdivision ordinance or general city code.

Subsection 86-10, regulating trees, contains language typical of that found in many of those communities with minimal landscape ordinance requirements. This part attempts to preserve trees in the community by restricting tree removal to only those areas "necessary for approved construction." However, no definition of the "necessary" limits of construction are given. It recommends tree wells where grade changes occur. If trees that are designated to be saved are removed, each is to be replaced with three (3) new trees.

Planting requirements include two (2) new trees for each new living unit. Specifications are given for the size, species, habit and planting season. The Town Board, through the Department of Planning, regulates the law and makes available a recommended tree selection list.

Hempstead

Town of Hempstead Town Code, Chapter 184, Section 184-1, "Tree Preservation," October 6, 1987.

This community has enacted a tree preservation ordinance to establish reasonable guidelines for tree preservation and to sensibly regulate tree removal when necessary and warranted. The community believes that an ordinance such as this will stabilize the soil, reduce traffic noise, clean the air of pollutants and reduce energy consumption. No tree can be destroyed, removed, planted or have its habit substantially altered without a permit from the Hempstead Commissioner of Highways. A permit is required by landowners, town agencies and utilities alike. The ordinance applies to trees on public rights-of-way primarily, although it was amended in July 1988 to give some oversight to tree preservation on private land.

There are twelve (12) sections in this ordinance. They describe permit application, right-of-way plantings, tree removal prohibited, notices, tree protection, maintenance, review of site plans, penalties for offenses and public utility trimming. The ordinance applies to trees that occur in what is called the curbside area, that area between the curb and property line. This area may not be paved except under certain permissible conditions.

No tree is to be planted in the curbside area other than trees whose root systems will not cause damage to sidewalks, curbs or utility installations. Hempstead requires that plantings for curbside areas be planted with selections from the palette of trees highlighted in Table 2.72.

It is the responsibility of the adjacent landowner to maintain curbside trees. Public utilities may prune trees within parameters of accepted horticultural practice. These practices are not defined.

The Town Board will not approve any subdivision, lot reapportionment, zoning change or site plan unless a plan containing a tree legend is submitted for the

TABLE 2.72. Trees for Curbside Areas, Hempstead, New York

Scientific Name	*Common Name*	*Recommended Spacing*
Acer rubrum	Red maple	45 feet on center
Acer saccharum "October Glory"	October Glory sugar maple	45
Gleditsia triacanthos "inermis"	Thornless honey locust	45
Platanus acerifolia	London plane tree	45
Pyrus calleryana "Bradford"	Bradford pear	35
Quercus borealis	Northern red oak	50
Quercus coccinea	Scarlet oak	50
Tilia cordata	Little-leaf linden	40
Tilia tomentosa	Silver linden	40

purpose of considering the preservation of existing trees. The plan and tree legend should show all trees to be preserved, removed or replaced, as well as number, sizes, caliper and location of all trees four (4) inches in caliper or greater.

The ordinance can be enforced by civil action, fines (two hundred fifty (250) dollars) and imprisonment (fifteen (15) days). Building permits and Certificates of Occupancy can also be withheld. The ordinance is administered by the Town Board, Department of Buildings and Commissioner of Highways.

This ordinance is somewhat dated in its organization and content. Some of the more contemporary tree preservation ordinances define arboricultural practices, define the duties of the arborist and give specific tree care requirements. Community Tree Boards are often appointed to administer these ordinances in other communities.

New York City

New York City, Ordinance No. 28-03, "Quality Housing," 1987.

The Quality Housing program consists of four components: neighborhood impact; building interior; recreation space and planting; and safety and security.

The neighborhood impact component controls the effect of the Quality Housing building on the neighborhood and includes bulk regulations, street planting and requirements for ground floor glazing in commercial districts, all of which are mandatory.

The building interior component sets minimum and preferred levels for the average size of residential units, establishes minimum amounts of glazed area for each residential unit, mandates laundry facilities and special refuse storage and disposal systems and encourages daylight corridors.

The recreation and planting component establishes minimum and preferred space standards for indoor and outdoor recreation space, requires planting for indoor and outdoor recreation space, requires planting of open areas on the site and encourages the use of balconies.

The safety and security component sets minimum and preferred standards for the number of residential units per corridor, requires elevators, or main stairways in walk-up buildings, that are visible from both the street and the door of each residential unit, mandates security devices for entrances to the building from the accessory parking and requires secure open areas visible from common spaces within the building.

Watertown

Zoning Code, Article IX, Section 345-55, as amended, "Site Plan Review and Approval," May 12, 1975.

Watertown does not have a comprehensive landscape ordinance, and there is not much information scattered through the zoning code pertaining to design or horticulture. Language was added more than twenty (20) years ago to empower the city to review and approve all site plans for commercial, industrial, planned use and certain residential districts.

Site plans can be prepared by landscape architects, architects, engineers or land surveyors. The ordinance requires that "landscape plans" be submitted along with other information for review and approval by the City Engineer.

Review criteria for the landscape plan consists of site grading, landscape design and open areas. Planning staff realize that this ordinance is vague and not very enforceable and have prepared some "guidelines" specifically for buffer zones. The guidelines specify width, landscaping within buffer zones and recommended plant materials.

Specific standards apply to neighborhood commercial districts, as shown in Figure 2.42.

The design guidelines require a maximum buffer width of fifteen (15) feet. Landscaping technical standards based on plant material spacing are given for various zoning districts; for example, where residential adjoins industrial property, small trees planted twenty (20) feet on center, shrubs planted three (3) feet on center, large trees planted forty (40) feet on center in front of a six (6) foot opaque fence. Large evergreen trees are to be "stagger planted" fifteen (15) feet on center.

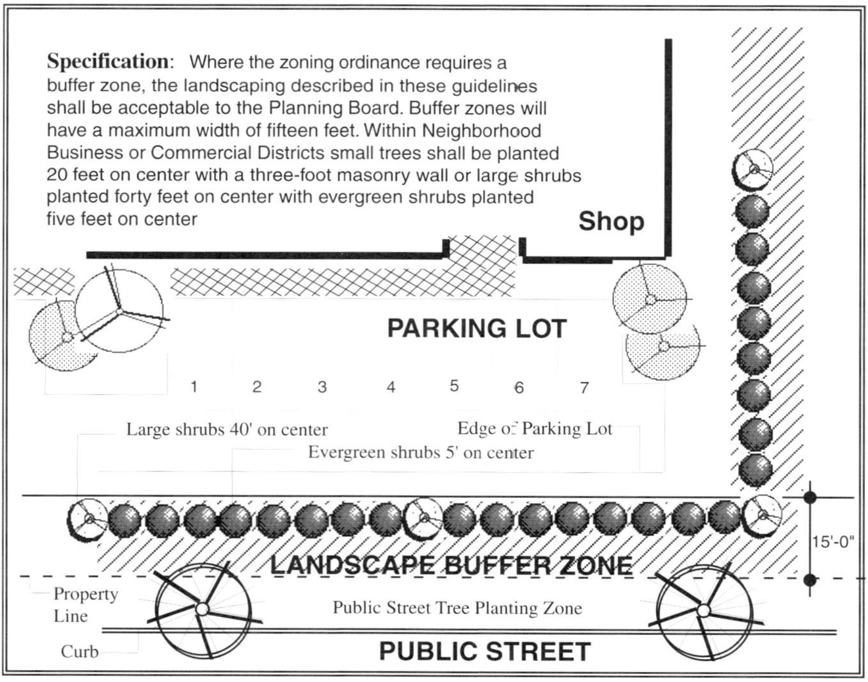

FIGURE 2.42. Neighborhood commercial district landscape requirements, Watertown, New York.

Large trees are to be one and one-half (1½) caliper, small trees one (1) inch caliper and evergreens six (6) to eight (8) feet in height. These are very minimal standards.

It is interesting to see more standards for "adult use" areas in Watertown's Zoning Code than for landscape areas. The city intends to add to and strengthen the landscape requirements when the Zoning Code comes under review in the future.

North Carolina

Cary

Town of Cary Planning and Zoning Ordinance, Article II, Division 2, Section 25, "Appearance and Landscape Ordinance," amended 1988.

The general appearance, style and design of "streetscapes" and developments are addressed in this ordinance, which states that it stresses good design without setting stifling or rigid standards for developers and property owners. It is to be used with a companion volume of town policies titled "The Town of Cary Standard Appearance Specifications Manual." The Code contains all of the legal requirements for appearance and landscaping, and the manual contains design details and examples.

The ordinance includes a list of definitions, requirements for "appearance plans" (conceptual layout, staking plan, topographic map, lighting plan, grading/utilities plan and landscaping plan), regulations for preservation and replacement of existing vegetation, streetscape and buffer regulations, parking lot restrictions, regulations on the location and design of trash containment areas and information on compliance and violations. The Code contains a "Buffer Chart" explaining the type of buffer (opaque, semiopaque, aesthetic or streetfront) to be used for various adjacent land uses.

Town of Cary, "Standard Appearance Specifications Manual," March 23, 1989.

The manual "goes beyond the letter of the Code by describing Cary's minimum desired standards of environmental, aesthetic and functional design quality." It encourages flexibility in design. The manual is divided into three main sections. The first provides detailed information on the required appearance plans. The second section addresses buffers and the third (and longest) covers good planting and horticultural practices. It also contains a list of recommended plants of various sizes, habits and attributes. The manual contains drawings and illustrations for examples.

Chapel Hill

Chapel Hill, "Chapel Hill Tree Protection Ordinance," 1990.

Trees and other landscape elements help to naturally control flooding and erosion, moderate noise pollution, dust and other airborne pollutants, moderate the town climate and shelter and feed wildlife. It is necessary to protect and manage these assets for the welfare of the citizens of Chapel Hill and its extraterritorial jurisdiction. This ordinance regulates installation, protection and removal of trees, shrubs and soils and encourages proper care of existing trees, shrubs and soils on all public and some private lands. It charges the Town Manager with the task of prescribing these processes and establishes a system of displayed permits to ensure correct maintenance, planting, protection and removal of trees and soil.

The ordinance makes issue of protecting rare and specimen trees and inspecting buffers and defines terms such as *tree, undeveloped land, woodlands, life of design, healthy living tree,* and *critical root zone*. Administrative mechanisms are featured.

Chapel Hill Development Ordinance Design Manual, Section 9, Landscaping, n.d.

The Chapel Hill Development Ordinance regulates and sets standards for landscaping, screening and providing shaded parking lots. The ordinance also makes mention of buffers and screening between various zoning districts. The Design Manual explains with text and graphics how to calculate projected shading, configure buffer options and determine which shade trees and screening plants are best used in this community. Finally, the manual illustrates planting options and tree protection methods.

Buffer requirements are well presented. Graphic diagrams are used showing five (5) types of buffers that vary in width, number of plants and screening density. Buffers vary in width from ten (10) to one hundred twenty five (125) feet. Graphics are also used to calculate shade determination for parking lots. Shade projection diagrams are created and a planimeter, dot grid or calculations of rectangular areas are made to determine total parking area and percentages that are shaded.

Charlotte

City Code, Chapter 21, § 21-1, "Trees," September 1996.

The Charlotte ordinance was first written in 1977 and revised in 1989. The current edition is the third generation of this landscape ordinance and dates to September 1996. The changes that have been made over this long period of time are typical of the direct evolution of a good ordinance. The incorporation of minor changes that led to a sounder, fairer, more easily understood law is how this evolution might be described. In the words of one of the authors of this ordinance, it can be "interesting to watch these ordinances grow, change, and work with the realities of enforcement over the years." Original properties that were grandfathered in as nonconforming land uses in 1977 are now being brought into compliance with this current edition as those properties change hands or are renovated or expanded.

In Charlotte the landscape ordinance is perceived as a tree ordinance that applies to trees on both public land and private land. It also pertains to both landscape design and tree preservation. It provides a rich mix of horticulture and community attractiveness.

What makes this ordinance exceptional is that it combines several of the various types of landscape ordinance discussed in the document into one coordinated and comprehensive document.

This ordinance sets up a public tree program, defines postconstruction landscaping requirements, sets standards for tree preservation (Figure 2.43) and suggests several land alteration issues such as erosion control and storm water management.

This ordinance provides for a Tree Advisory Commission of twelve (12) citizens to make recommendations relative to trees and shrubbery in the city and to act as a Board of Appeal in the case of a party's being dissatisfied with a decision of the arborist or engineer. In addition, the ordinance establishes the duties of various city agencies and defines their authority in regard to trees on both private and public land. The City Arborist, City Engineer, City Attorney, City Clerk and City Council are specifically mentioned in this law.

The ordinance sets forth policy and specifications for the protection, planting and maintenance of vegetation. Removal, pruning and private planting on public lands are also regulated by requirements set forth in this document.

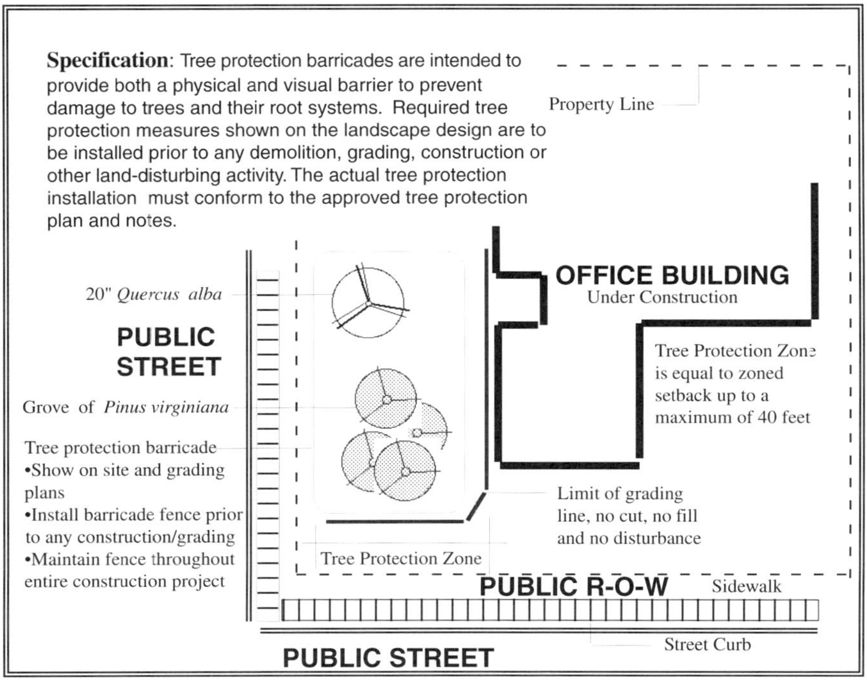

FIGURE 2.43. Tree protection specifications, Charlotte, North Carolina.

TABLE 2.73. Tree Mitigation Standards, Charlotte, North Carolina

Diameter of Removed Tree	*No. of Replacement Trees, 3–3½" Cal.*
8–14" diameters	1
15–24" diameters	2
25–34" diameters	3
35" and greater diameter	Review on case-by-case basis

Design components in the ordinance include perimeter plantings, visibility corridors and internal VUA plantings. No mention is made of screening of site mechanical equipment, loading docks or refuse containers.

Trees eight (8) inches in diameter cannot be removed in tree protection zones without a permit. In cases where trees must be removed or are damaged during construction, "tree mitigation" may be required, according to the standards shown in Table 2.73.

Standards are given for plant materials, tree or root protection and tree mitigation. Credit toward landscape requirements is given for preserving healthy trees. Specific standards apply to the preparation of the Tree Planting Plan, Landscape Plan, Tree Survey and Tree Protection Plan, all necessary for project approval.

The ordinance contains a discussion on administrative procedures. It makes mention of alternative compliance, site inspection, variance, appeal and enforcement. Penalties may be assessed for noncompliance. No permit fees are mentioned.

This ordinance is printed in an attractively printed design manual that presents, side by side, the official ordinance and an easy-to-read version. It makes liberal use of graphics to convey design ideas and simplify complex spatial matters involving trees, utilities and jurisdiction lines. Eighteen (18) appendices are included that offer helpful information on subjects ranging from a proper soil preparation mixture to how to use an old barrel as an irrigation device. Also included are approved species lists, standard planting details, construction details and a variety of administrative forms that are used to implement tree work.

In terms of organization, completeness and attractiveness in packaging, this is without doubt one of the better ordinances in this study. The city should be commended for its leadership in the development of landscape ordinance legislation and efforts toward the protection of trees and promotion of good community landscape design.

Forsyth County, Winston-Salem

Unified Development Ordinance, Chapter B, Article III, "Landscaping Standards," March 7, 1988.

In Forsyth, you must follow written regulations when building a vehicular use area. Developers are not allowed to "pave to the property line" or create ugly masses of paved surface. This limited-issue ordinance pertains primarily to vehicular use areas. It has been enacted to improve the appearance of street rights-of-way, control drainage and erosion, enhance property values and increase the environmental quality (in regard to air, water, temperature, noise and glare) of vehicular use areas.

The ordinance applies to all zoning districts except single-family properties and dwelling units on private lots. Design components in the ordinance cover motor vehicle surface areas, outdoor storage areas, street yards, utility areas and parking buildings and structures. Motor vehicular display areas are also included in this ordinance. Standards and criteria are described for tree credits, planting area size, plant material protection, landscape incentives and suggested plant materials. Units of measure for this ordinance include linear, square footage, caliper, height and individual units as shown in Table 2.74.

A section of this ordinance also includes standards for planting adjacent to overhead utility lines.

There is an alternative compliance provision for parking areas of more than five hundred (500) automobiles, and applications for variance will be accepted by the Board of Adjustment.

Related ordinance Section 3-5 covers buffer yard design requirements. This ordinance is very general, with little emphasis on design. However, the ordinance is well thought out and covers many minor details of parking area design, such as safety, utilities and pedestrian circulation, not mentioned in other ordinances.

TABLE 2.74. Vehicular Use Area Technical Requirements, Forsyth County, North Carolina

Standard	*Unit of Measure*
Minimum planting area existing trees	Edge of tree's drip line
Minimum street yard plantings	One tree every 75 lf, minimum
Required plantings	Two trees deciduous/evergreen each 100 lf
Street yard width	10 feet wide between parking and street
Standard tree size	8 feet tall, 2 inch caliper
Standard shrub size	18 inches tall at planting, 36 inches after 3 years
Street yard fence or wall	36 inches tall of masonry, stone or wood
Street yard berms	18 inches high, minimum crown 24 inches, 2:1 side slopes
Interior planting area size	150 sf minimum of one tree
Parking distance	No more than 50 feet to nearest tree
Tree planting ratio	One deciduous or evergreen tree for each 2,500 sf

Greensboro, Guilford County and Highpoint

Greensboro Development Ordinance, § 30-5-4, "Landscape Regulations," July 1, 1992.

Three North Carolina communities in close proximity have adopted a unified development code with similar landscape regulations. This is a concept that makes a great deal of sense for tightly fit geographic areas with similar habitat, soils, water and climate. This approach makes it much easier for developers to understand the requirements and know what is expected of them in a larger urban setting.

The ordinance applies to all land uses with the exception of single-family, duplex family, community CBD and several minor exceptions. It applies to all new principal buildings or principal uses, substantial changes in use and expansions of more than three thousand (3,000) square feet.

Design components include street planting yards, parking lot perimeters and interiors and general planting yards of four types. Technical standards are mentioned for design, installation and maintenance. Maintenance requirements are summarized in Figure 2.44.

Planting Yard A is a high-density screen intended to block visual contact between adjacent uses and create spatial separation between conflicting land uses.

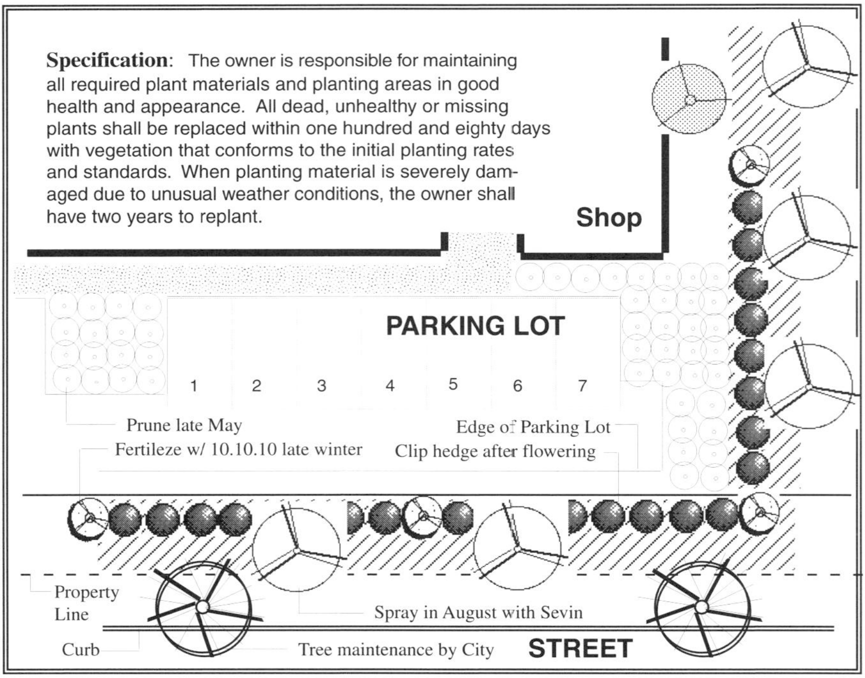

FIGURE 2.44. Maintenance requirements, Greensboro, North Carolina.

Planting Yard B is a medium-density screen intended to partially block visual contact between uses and create spatial separation. Planting Yard C is a low-density screen intended to partially block visual contact between uses and create spatial separation. Planting Yard D is a peripheral planting strip intended to separate uses, provide vegetation in densely developed areas and enhance the appearance of individual properties.

The ordinance contains a table of planting yard requirements for the various zoned land uses in the community. Table 2.75 shows planting area width and rate.

Yard width can be reduced by ten (10) feet if walls or fences five (5) feet tall are utilized. In street yards, two understory trees may be substituted for one (1) canopy tree.

Standards are presented in the ordinance for landscape design, maintenance, installation, plant materials and minimum planting area size. Other standards include landscape plan preparation and protection of existing trees.

This ordinance contains an alternative compliance provision that allows the proposal of a different design solution with different plants materials or methods that exhibit increased quality effectiveness, durability and performance.

The ordinance contains several graphic details that explain the geometry of the various yards, a sample landscape plan and a parking lot planting detail.

This North Carolina ordinance can be found as Appendix 1 in a skillfully prepared design manual titled "City of Greensboro Landscape Manual." The manual is very graphic in organization and design and offers at least a bachelor's degree in horticulture or landscape design. Contained within the manual are planting tips, plant descriptions and selection lists and information about tree preservation and tree protection. It is illustrated liberally with line drawings, explanatory sketches and attractive plant material graphics.

In summary, this ordinance is well thought out and well presented. It is easy to understand and covers most essential site planning concerns. If improvement could be made to the ordinance or to the design manual, it may be in the area of more fully explaining the administrative aspects of the ordinance.

TABLE 2.75. Planting Yard Technical Standards, Greensboro, Guilford County and Highpoint, North Carolina

Yard Type	*Min. Width*	*Min. Ave. Width*	*Max. Width*	*Canopy Rate*	*Understory*	*Shrub Rate*
Street Yard	8	8	25	2/100 lf	n/a	17/100 lf
Type A Yard	40	50	75	4/100 lf	10/100 lf	33/100 lf
Type B Yard	25	30	50	3/100 lf	5/100 lf	25/100 lf
Type C Yard	15	20	40	2/100 lf	3/100 lf	17/100 lf
Type D Yard	5	5	10	n/a	2/100 lf	18/100 lf
Parking Lot	n/a	n/a	n/a	1/12 spaces	n/a	n/a

Hickory

Zoning Ordinance, Section 10.9, "Landscaping Standards for Off-Street Parking," May 21, 1996.

This community recently enacted a limited issue landscape ordinance pertaining to off-street parking areas, primarily the interiors of these areas. The purpose of the ordinance is to moderate temperatures, abate glare and filter automotive exhaust and to encourage the preservation of existing stands of trees in and near parking facilities.

The technical standards in this ordinance include provision for plant materials, spacing, quantities, planting area requirements, percentage of evergreens and distance to shade. There is to be one (1) eight (8) foot tall, two and one-half (2½) inch caliper tree for every twenty (20) parking spaces, planted in an area at least two hundred twenty-five (225) square feet in size and located no more than sixty (60) feet from cars. The ordinance applies to all parking in nonresidential districts with twenty (20) or more parking spaces.

Reference is made to below-ground and above-ground parking structure screening. Five (5)-foot buffers are required to separate parking from buildings, driveways into parking areas and street edges. Specific design requirements are not given for these buffers, however.

Credit is allowed for preserving trees, at the ratio of two (2) for one (1) preserved. The owner of the property is responsible to maintain and ensure the survival of the plant materials into perpetuity.

This ordinance was proposed by the Hickory Regional Planning Commission and the Community Appearance Commission, with input from a consulting landscape architect.

Kinston

Unified Development Ordinance, Article XIX, "Screening and Trees," 1992.

Kinston has adopted a Unified Development Ordinance for its community. The ordinance is based on a standard model that has been used in many communities to tailor a public landscape ordinance.

This ordinance covers several topics that have been referred to in this document as "design components." These include screening, shading, parking and loading area landscaping and screening of dumpsters. This is not an unusually long list of concerns as compared with those of many communities.

The ordinance defines three types of screens. Type A screen is an opaque screen composed of plantings and structures from the ground to at least six (6) feet, with intermittent screening to at least twenty (20) feet. This type of screen is intended to exclude all contact between land uses and completely separate spaces.

Type B screen is semiopaque. It is intended to partially block views and create an impression that adjacent land uses are separated. This screen must be at least three (3) feet high and can include elements up to twenty (20) feet tall. These screening elements must be spaced at least ten (10) feet on center.

TABLE 2.76. Calculating Shade in Vehicular Use Areas, Kinston, North Carolina

1.	Calculate area devoted to parking, including all hardscape.		______	sf
2.	Multiply by shading requirement (20 percent)	×	0.20	
3.	Area to be shaded		______	sf
	Add			
4.	Areas shaded by existing trees to be retained	+	______	sf
5.	Area shaded by required screening, if any	+	______	sf
6.	Area shaded by required street trees, if any	+	______	sf
7.	Subtotal		______	sf
	(If line (7) is greater than line (3), then shading requirement has been met; if not, go to line (8).)			
8.	Enter the difference between line (7) and line (3).		______	sf
9.	Divide line (8) by amount of shade produced by one tree.		707	
10.	Total number of shade trees required within vehicular use area		______	trees

The third screen type, Type C, is a broken screen. Its purpose is to give the impression of separated land uses. This screen can extend from the ground to a height of twenty (20) feet.

One of the interesting parts of this ordinance is the shading requirement, which is intended to preserve as many trees as practical, maintain tree cover for its many environmental benefits and shade parking areas. Twenty (20) percent of all parking areas, including parking spaces, drives, walks and loading areas, are to be shaded.

There are few technical standards and no administrative standards mentioned in this ordinance. Many of the common standards found in other ordinances are not found here. No mention is made of preparation, review and approval of landscape plans. Some standards are mentioned for protection of existing trees, planting and maintaining trees and using trees in parking lots and along streets.

This ordinance has numerous tables, graphics, and an appendix to help the reader understand its contents. Among these are a table of screening requirements, screening diagrams and lists of recommended plant material.

The emphasis in this ordinance is on screening. This may be a good model to examine if one is greatly concerned with the screening of views, noise, dust and glare, and separating land uses for increased privacy and reducing external effects.

The mathematical procedure outlined in Table 2.76 is given for determining the amount of shade in parking areas.

Orange County

Orange County Zoning Ordinance, Article 12, "Landscaping and Buffer Requirements," amended August 1, 1989.

This is a typical postconstruction landscape ordinance with a tree preservation component.

Landscaping and screening are required for vehicular use areas, land abutting public rights-of-way and between noncompatible land uses. The purpose of the ordinance is to protect, preserve and promote the visual appeal, character and value of the county's neighborhoods. The intent of the ordinance will be met by the preservation of existing vegetation and additional plantings in all zoning districts, excluding single-family dwellings and duplexes. No building, structure or vehicular use area may be expanded without compliance with the minimum standards of this ordinance. No vegetation may be removed except in accordance with approved plans.

Two (2) tree protection zones are created. Primary tree protection zones include areas to be used for recreation or open space, front, side and rear setback areas and land use buffer zones as defined in this ordinance. Secondary tree protection zones include all other portions of a lot. Trees over twelve (12) inches in diameter cannot be cut except for certain stated reasons.

Design components include street frontage, lot perimeters, land use buffers and parking or vehicular use areas.

Design standards for each design component vary. For street frontage, tree types have been assigned a value in linear feet. Along side and rear perimeters, trees are planted in ten (10)-foot zones, based on one (1) tree for each one thousand (1,000) square feet. For screening, opaque barriers or continuous hedges are required. For vehicular use areas a percentage of the interior (five (5) percent) must be set aside for median strips and islands. The parking lot design standard is one (1) tree for each sixty (60) linear feet.

Design standards for buffers also vary. Four different types of buffers that establish various levels of screening, based on average height and density of plant material have been defined. These are presented in an illustrated table matrix and are noted as Buffer Types A, B, C, D, E and F. Each buffer type is based on the proximity of adjacent land uses and intensity of land use conflict. The buffers vary in width from thirty (30) feet to one hundred (100) feet, and density increases with incompatibility. Table 2.77 summarizes the types of buffers recommended in this community.

TABLE 2.77. Suggested Buffers, Orange County, North Carolina

Land Use	*Buffer Type*	*Min. Width (ft)*
Military Installation	B	30
Parking Structure	C	40
Assembly Facility	A	30
Club or Lodge	A	30
Drive-in Theater	A	30
Nightclub or Bar	B	30
Sawmill	D	50
Bus Terminal	E	75
Extraction Industry	F	100
Landfill	F	100

No planting is allowed in drainage, access or utility easements, under power lines or within the sight triangle area of a site.

Standards are given within this ordinance for tree protection measures, installation, maintenance and landscape plan preparation.

No building permit can be issued until the landscape design has been submitted, and no Certificate of Occupancy granted until the provisions of this ordinance have been satisfied. The ordinance is managed by the Zoning Officer.

Simple, clear graphics complement the ordinance. Included are elevation screening details, as well as planting and staking details. Plant lists of suitable vines, shrubs, small trees and large trees are included.

This ordinance is interesting to the reader as a result of its wide application to most land uses and to all expansions and renovations. It is also interesting because it places restrictions on tree removal and creates two (2) tree preservation zones that apply to each property. This feature is somewhat original and not common to many communities.

It is clear that this community values trees. It has crafted an ordinance that places emphasis on maintenance of community character and visual appeal. The ordinance could be strengthened by increasing the number of design components and requiring professional registration for those who prepare the landscape plans.

Orange County Subdivision Regulations, Article IV-B-8, "Landscape and Buffer Requirements," amended August 4, 1986 .

Few communities do what Orange County, North Carolina, does. It has drafted a companion ordinance to the aforementioned postconstruction landscape ordinance. This ordinance inserts landscape and buffer requirements into the county subdivision ordinance.

Its intent is to prevent damage from erosion, siltation, flooding and destruction of wildlife habitat while diminishing the impacts of adjacent incompatible land use. A secondary intent is to provide important physical, aesthetic, recreation and economic assets to present and future residents of Orange County.

This ordinance requires every subdivision to make provision for the protection, preservation, maintenance and use of trees and woodlands. Landscaping and screening are to be part of every subdivision.

Landscape plans are submitted at two stages of the subdivision building process. The first submission takes place at the time the preliminary or final plat is turned over to the Orange County Planning and Inspection Department for review. This preliminary landscape plan must show the nature of the property being subdivided, locations of existing trees, proposed tree protection areas, land use buffer zones and all proposed plantings necessary to fulfill the landscape and buffer requirements. Certain calculations, dimensions and quantities are required at this time.

No subdivision will be approved and no building permit will be issued until a final landscape plan is prepared. A Certificate of Occupancy will be withheld until such time as all landscape and buffer zones have been installed.

Two (2) tree protection areas are created. Existing trees, regardless of size, are not to be removed within a primary tree protection area. Trees with a diameter of twelve (12) inches or greater cannot be removed from secondary tree protection areas. A primary tree protection area includes that portion of a lot that is used for required recreation/open space, land use buffers and yard setback areas. A secondary tree protection area is any part of a site that is not defined as a primary tree protection area.

Some exceptions are allowed. Trees may be removed from designated street rights-of-way and utility and storm water drainage easements. Trees may be removed if they are diseased or weakened by age or if special construction access is required.

This ordinance also requires that tree protection measures be implemented during construction activities. Recommendations are given for caring for trees affected by grading operations.

Subdivision developers are required to install landscaping along street frontage, lot perimeters and land use buffers on sites with no vegetation.

Street frontage tree plantings are calculated according to a formula derived from the mature canopy spread of both large and small trees. One large tree (forty (40)-foot canopy) is required on each lot. Small trees are figured with a twenty-five (25) linear foot canopy. The formula shown in Table 2.78 is used to determine the proper number of trees required.

In addition to the trees required along the frontage, a hedge or other durable landscape material such as a fence or berm at least three (3) feet in height is to be installed to provide a continuous opaque hedge.

On lot perimeters, one (1) tree is to be provided for each one thousand (1,000) square feet of land contained within a minimum twenty (20) foot wide landscape area.

Land use buffers are required to separate a proposed subdivision from adjacent major streets and different land use or zoning designations. A table matrix identified as IV-B-8-e-3, Schedule of Required Land Use Buffers, is used to determine the proper buffer.

TABLE 2.78. Street Frontage Calculation for Subdivisions, Orange County, North Carolina

Given	
Required large tree canopy	40 lf value
Small tree canopy	25 lf value
Total lot frontage	130 lf
Less value of required tree	40 feet
Equals: Remaining lot frontage	90 feet
Or 130 lf – 40 lf = 90 lf	
90 lf/40 lf = 2.3 large trees or 3.6 small trees or a combination	

TABLE 2.79. Suggested Buffers for Residential Districts, Orange County, North Carolina

Adjacent Land Use	*Buffer Type*	*Min. Width (ft)*
Arterial Street	D	50
Collector Street	B	30
Interstate Highway	F	100
Office	C	40
Neighborhood Commercial	C	40
R-5 Residential	A	30
R-3 Residential	A	30
Industrial	D	50
Agriculture	F	100
Landfill	F	100

In some instances, buffers are required next to areas of cultural, historic or natural significance identified in an Orange County inventory of natural areas and wildlife habitat.

Finally, individual lots are to be planted according to the companion ordinance described earlier.

Standards are given for installation and maintenance of landscaping. Waivers of landscaping and buffer requirements may be allowed under certain conditions, subject to approval of the Planning Director or the Board of County Commissioners.

Table 2.79 gives a good idea of the types of buffer required for R-4 residential uses with lots of ten thousand (10,000) to fifteen thousand (15,000) square feet.

This is one of the most interesting ordinances in this study. This community places a high value on subdivisions with natural vegetation and has implemented this very restrictive subdivision ordinance. Most communities do not put landscape requirements in their subdivision ordinances because of the fact that most developers like to clear and grade sites prior to infrastructure construction and home building. Other communities could profit by studying this ordinance.

Raleigh

City of Raleigh Landscape Ordinance, Second Edition. Revised April 1, 1990.

The purpose of this ordinance is to encourage the preservation of vegetation; to provide adequate light and air; to provide visual buffering; to preserve, protect, and restore the unique identity and environment of the City of Raleigh; to conserve energy; and to provide habitat for living things that might not otherwise be found in urban and suburban environs. The ordinance requirements focus on a number of areas: street yards, vehicular surface areas, display areas, loading areas, utility service areas and transitional yards.

The intent of the street yard requirements (Figure 2.45) is to provide pleasing views, provide continuity of vegetation, reduce amount of runoff and impervious surface, filter air, provide shade and improve the microclimate and preserve Raleigh's natural vegetative cover. These requirements are given in average, maximum and minimum square footage of street frontage. All street yard types require at least one (1) tree per fifty (50) linear feet of street frontage.

The intent of the vehicular surface area requirements is to protect the public from headlight glare, noise, fumes and dust; prevent overcrowding of land; modify the rate of storm water runoff; provide shade; increase the capability of ground water recharge; and distribute planting around and within parking areas. There must be one (1) interior parking lot tree for every two thousand (2,000) square feet, and one (1) shrub for every five hundred (500) square feet, of vehicular surface area. Parking areas within fifty (50) feet of the right-of-way must have a three and one-half ($3^1/2$) foot tall screen.

The intent of the loading, display, and utility service area requirements is to screen undesirable views. Loading areas must include a six (6) foot tall screen.

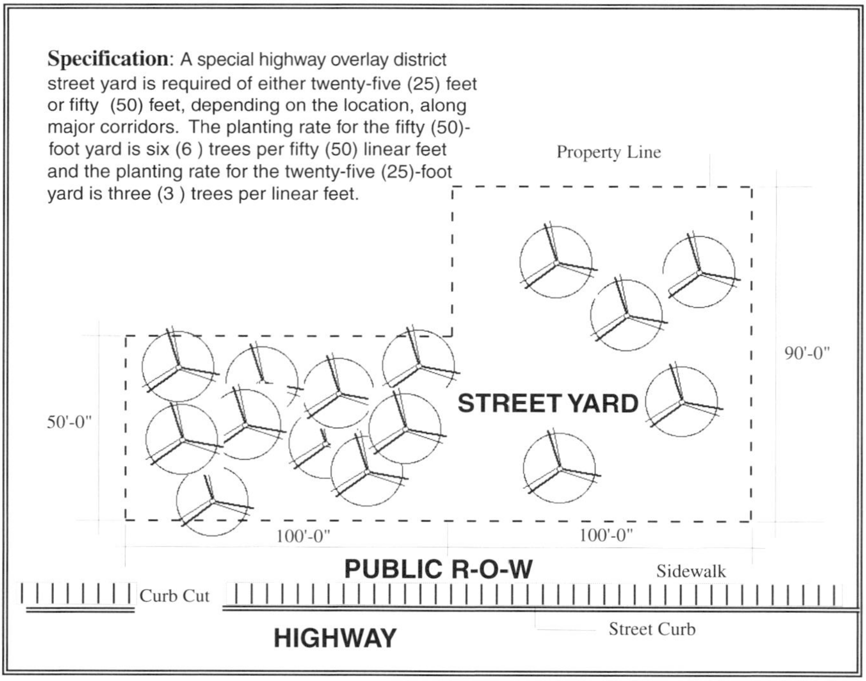

FIGURE 2.45. Highway overlay district street yard, Raleigh, North Carolina.

Display areas must include a two (2) foot six (6) inch tall screen. Utility service areas must be screened with plantings eighteen (18) inches tall that reach a mature height equal to that of the utility service area.

The purpose of the transitional protective yard requirements is to protect adjacent uses from traffic, noise, glare, trash, activity, vibration, odor, visual disorder, and other noxious, harmful effects; prevent adverse community appearance; protect the character of the area; conserve the values of buildings and land; and provide adequate light and air. Yard width requirements are given in the form of a chart. The chart includes high residential density, low-impact uses, medium-impact uses and high-impact uses. The width of the transitional yard depends on the density of the vegetation inside the yard.

This is a very well designed ordinance. The layout of each page contains the ordinance text in legal terms, an easy-to-read summary of the ordinance, and a diagram explaining the ordinance.

Ohio

Cleveland

Cleveland Zoning Code, Chapter No. 352, Section 352.01, "Landscaping and Screening," July 27, 1991.

Cleveland recognizes that cities change and evolve over time. Its landscape ordinance was passed partially in recognition that modern cities do not have the benefit of wide yards and open space to buffer land uses, improve the environment, preserve privacy and enhance community appearance. This landscape ordinance was enacted in response to the changing American city.

The city defines four types of landscape zones. They include "transition strips" between adverse zoning districts, "frontage strips" along yards that contain parking or outdoor storage, "island strips" within off-street parking areas, and "screen barriers" hiding specified incompatible uses such as junk yards, utility stations and the like.

Minimum parking lot planting is five (5) percent of the area.

In addition to these basic design components, several standards are mentioned in the ordinance. These include tree credits for preserving existing landscaping, tree protection during construction, installation and maintenance, and landscape plan preparation. No significant plant material standards are given. Several tables are presented in the code that clarify options and list requirements. They include tables showing "Zoning District Compatibility," "Transition Strip Requirements," "Other Screening or Landscaping," "Screening Intensity," and "Required Contents of Landscape Plan."

The Commissioner of Building and Housing and the Director of the City Planning Commission are the primary enforcers of this ordinance.

The ordinance is somewhat dated and does not include some of the current language found in more contemporary ordinances that are more detailed in regard to design and horticulture.

Dublin

Dublin Codified Ordinances, Chapter 1187, "Landscaping," 1983, amended in 1988.

The stated purpose of the Dublin ordinance is to improve the appearance of vehicular use areas and land abutting rights-of-way; to require buffering between incompatible land uses; to preserve the character and value of neighborhoods; and to reduce noise pollution, air pollution, visual pollution, air temperature and artificial light glare. The ordinance specifically promotes the preservation and replacement of trees and significant vegetation.

Several appendices, through the use of charts and illustrations, outline the requirements for property perimeters, vehicular use areas, driveway plantings, street intersections, vehicle overhangs and recommended trees. The tree list also includes unacceptable trees for the Ohio community.

The Dublin ordinance encourages that heavily wooded areas be preserved "whenever possible" as "park reserves." As a guideline in meeting the requirements of the ordinance, the Dublin Planning and Zoning Department maintains a planting manual and plant list.

"Planting Manual for Dublin Street Trees," September 1988.

The manual, a companion to the city ordinance, describes planting techniques that will increase the success of street tree establishment. It provides information for landscape contractors, nurserymen, horticulturists, residents, developers and landscape architects.

The manual includes recommendations on time for planting, plant quality, tree placement, notifying utilities, planting techniques, guarantees and plant care and maintenance. Illustrations explain proper street tree planting, tree guying, pruning and street tree spacing.

Also included in the manual is an outline of the city's street tree protection procedure. Trees not exhibiting a healthy growing condition at the end of the one (1)-year guarantee period must be replaced at the expense of the developer.

Amendment to Sections 1187.09 and 1187.10 of the Dublin Codified Ordinances to Regulate Street Trees and Other Trees on City Property, July 15, 1991.

This amendment states that "public concern has been expressed about the nature and extent of the pruning performed by some utility companies, commercial landscaping contractors and private citizens." New provisions of the amendment establish requirements for a public tree permit, administered by the Urban Forester, for planting, removal, pruning or growth-inhibiting measures to trees or shrubs in public rights-of-way. Utility companies must provide written evidence of adherence to the National Arborists Association guidelines for line clearance work. The amendment also sets regulations on removal, replanting, abuse and care of trees in public areas, and for licensing and bonding of arborists working in the city.

Section 2 of the amendment adds to the original ordinance's list of definitions.

Hilliard

Ordinance of the City of Hilliard, Ordinance No. 88-25, Amending Hilliard City Code to Adopt Chapter 156, Landscaping Ordinance, May 25, 1988.

The purpose of the ordinance is to protect public health, safety and welfare through the preservation and protection of the environment, especially trees and plant growth. The ordinance specifically promotes the preservation and replacement of trees during land development, the use of landscaping as a buffer between various land uses and the protection of the character of neighborhoods.

A list of definitions includes such words as *opacity* and *major tree* (trunk diameter of six (6) inches or greater). Developers, with a few listed exceptions, must attempt to preserve existing trees. A medium or major tree removed must be replaced by a tree having a trunk diameter of at least two and one-half ($2\frac{1}{2}$) inches. Landscaping plans must be submitted to and approved by the Planning and Zoning Officer. Hilliard generally uses a formula for tree plantings of one-half ($\frac{1}{2}$) inch in tree trunk size for every two hundred (200) square feet in ground covered by a structure. Credit is given for existing trees if they are appropriately distributed about the site. Builders must plant large or medium trees along public streets.

Parking areas of (twelve) 12 spaces or four thousand (4,000) square feet must have interior plantings of not less than five (5) percent of the total area. The ordinance also establishes screening standards for service areas, loading docks, trash container receptacles and adjacent land uses.

Kettering

City of Kettering Zoning Code, Chapter No. 1169, amended, "Buffer Yards and Landscaping," July 26, 1994.

This is a well-organized and well-presented limited landscape ordinance included within the general zoning ordinance of this city. The ordinance requires that each property be provided with buffer yards and landscaping at the rear and side of each lot. The provisions of the ordinance control the quantity, type and location of screening and landscape material in all zoning classifications except single-family residential.

The ordinance provides, for quick reference, a Table of Buffer Yard Requirements for various zoning classifications. Buffer yard specifications and technical requirements are given for such landscape features as plant materials, walls, fences, topography, installation and landscape maintenance. Existing plant materials are mentioned, but no specific requirements are given for preserving existing site vegetation. No credit toward the planting requirements of this ordinance are given for preserving existing plants.

Included within the ordinance are design components for features other than buffer yards. They include design requirements for screening, vehicular use areas, storage areas, signs and loading docks.

The buffer yard requirements apply to the first party to develop a vacant parcel of land. The buffer yard is to be designed as if the adjoining parcel of vacant zoned land has been developed. Six different buffer yards are defined (A, B, C, D, E, and F) in this code. Each buffer yard varies as to width and number of Group A, B, or C trees and shrubs for each one hundred (100) feet of buffer yard. For instance, a Type C buffer yard requires three (3) Group A trees, three (3) Group B trees, three (3) Group C trees, and one (1) shrub for each ten (10) linear feet of buffer yard. The following formula can be used to calculate the number of trees required in a Type C buffer yard :

$$L / 100 \times T$$

where L equals the length of buffer yard, one hundred (100) is the one hundred (100)-foot unit and T is the number of trees required for one hundred (100) feet of buffer. For example, eleven hundred seventeen (1,117) feet of Type C buffer would require:

$$1{,}117 / 100 \times 9 = 101 \text{ trees}$$

To determine the number of shrubs in this buffer yard, use:

$$L / 10 = S$$

where L equals the length of buffer yard, 10 is the ten (10)-foot unit and S is the number of trees required for one hundred (100) feet of buffer. For example, eleven hundred seventeen (1,117) feet of Type C buffer would require:

$$1{,}117 / 10 = 112 \text{ shrubs}$$

Some buffer yards require six (6)-foot-high hedges, walls, fences or earth mounds. Table 2.80 shows the specifications for trees for all buffer yards.

All vehicular use areas of over six thousand (6,000) square feet or more than fifteen (15) parking spaces must set aside five (5) percent for interior landscaping

TABLE 2.80. Plant Material Tree Classification, Kettering, Ohio

Tree Group	*Type*	*Height*	*Caliper*	*Mature Crown*
A	Deciduous	10 feet tall	2 inches	25 feet
B	Deciduous	8 feet tall	1½ inches	< 25 feet
C	Evergreen	5 feet tall	1¼ inches	3 feet when planted

in peninsulas or islands. One tree from Group A or two trees from Group B is required for every one thousand (1,000) square feet of vehicular use areas. The remaining planting area is to be planted with shrubs or ground covers not to exceed twenty four (24) inches in height.

A continuous hedge, fence, wall or earth mound is to enclose all service or storage areas.

Landscape plans are submitted to the Zoning Administrator for review and approval. This office will furnish a document titled "Planting Details for Shrubs and Trees."

Vandalia

City of Vandalia, "Landscaping Requirements," Chapter 1189, December 1986.

The purpose of the ordinance is to preserve and replace major trees and to promote landscaping as a buffer between different land uses. A list of definitions is included.

One interesting part of the Vandalia ordinance is a "Planting Time Schedule," which lists preferred dates for planting to ensure quality control and better landscaping results. For instance, balled and burlapped material is to be planted from March 1 to June 1, or October 1 to December 1, and evergreen material from September 1 to October 15. Lists of recommended plant materials and prohibited plant materials are included in the regulations. The regulations require tree plantings of one-half ($\frac{1}{2}$) inch in trunk size for every one hundred fifty (150) square feet in ground coverage for individual lots in residential districts; and tree plantings equal to one-half ($\frac{1}{2}$) inch in trunk size for every one thousand (1,000) square feet of ground coverage for all other uses. Preserved trees may be counted as part of the total caliper requirements. Interior landscaping must be provided at the ratio of one (1) shade tree for every twenty-five (25) parking spaces. Islands must be at least sixteen (16) square feet.

Tree replacement is an important part of this ordinance as can be seen from Figure 2.46. Trees that are removed over a specified diameter must be replaced with younger trees.

Oklahoma

Oklahoma City

Zoning Code, Chapter No. 59, Section 59-6600, "Sightproof Screening and Landscaping," 1989.

In Oklahoma City the landscape ordinance is very general, covering only four (4) design components: site planting, screening, outdoor storage and parking areas. Landscape standards vary by zoning district, with increased requirements for higher density land uses such as industrial. General site landscape requirements are shown in Figure 2.47.

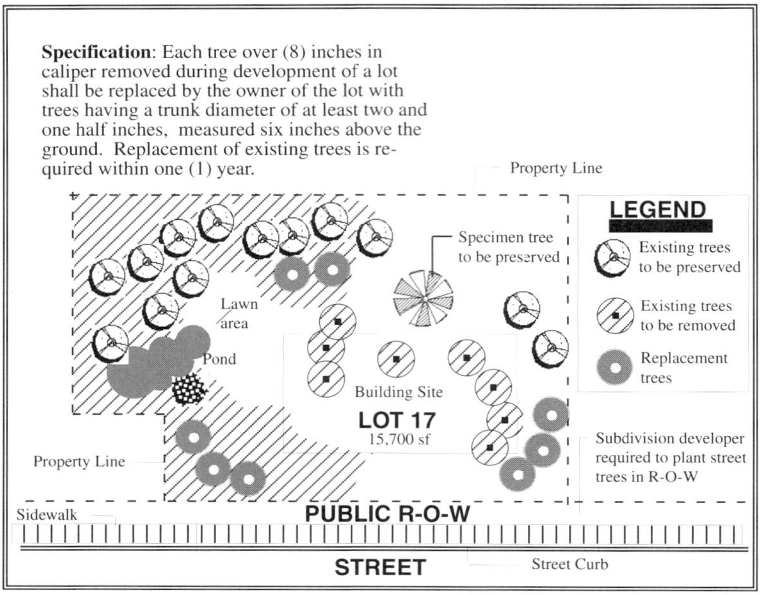

FIGURE 2.46. Tree replacement standards, Vandalia, Ohio.

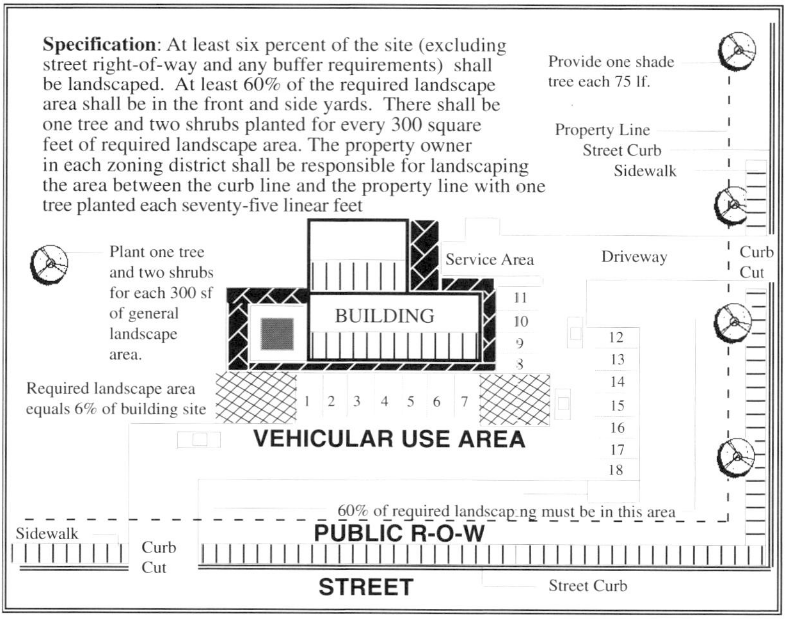

FIGURE 2.47. General site landscape requirements, Oklahoma City, Oklahoma.

This ordinance places emphasis on the design of "sightproof" screening, consisting of fencing or landscaping consisting of evergreen vegetation and berms, or some combination of any of these. Credit against planting requirements is given for preserving existing trees. The few technical standards in this ordinance are listed in Table 2.81.

The Director of Planning administers this ordinance. The Director is responsible for plan review, administrative adjustments, enforcement, receiving appeals and issuing temporary and permanent Certificates of Occupancy.

This is a very general ordinance with no special or unique language. One wonders whether the ordinance is sufficiently complete to gain the community benefits cited in the general description of its intent and purpose.

TABLE 2.81. Technical Standards, Oklahoma City, Oklahoma

Design Component	*Technical Standard*
	Design Component Standards
Sightproof Fence Design	Withstand wind force 15 lb per sf
Sightproof Fence Height	6 feet to 8 feet
Sightproof Fence Materials	Wood, metal, masonry, stockade poles
Acceptable Irrigation Methods	Sprinklers, drip system, hose attachment within 200 lf
Plant Materials	Trees, 1½ inch caliper, shrubs 1 gallon, ground cover
	Planting Standards
Site Area Planting, measure 1	6 percent of site, 60 percent in front or sides
Site Area Planting, measure 2	1 tree and 2 shrubs for every 300 sf of area
Single Family	One tree 75 feet on center
Parking Lot Plantings, most districts	All parking within 75 feet of a tree
Parking Islands	50 sf, one tree minimum
Industrial Districts	1 tree for each 20 feet abutting freeway
Industrial Districts	1 tree for each 40 feet abutting street right-of-way
	Administrative Standards
Plan Submittals	Sightproof Fence Plan, Sightproof Landscaping Plan
Licensing Requirements	None mentioned

Stillwater

Appendix I, Zoning Ordinance, § 11.50, "Landscaping and Screening," n.d.

Stillwater regulates landscaping and screening through the power of its zoning ordinance. This is an example of a limited-issue ordinance that regulates landscaping and screening for specific purposes. The community intends to ensure minimal conflict between utilities and land uses and hopes that plantings will be used to shade buildings and parking areas.

The ordinance applies primarily to multifamily housing, commercial districts and industrial park landscaping.

Standards are developed for the proper location of plant materials, site plan preparation, planting area size requirements and tree classifications.

Design components vary somewhat but include only parking areas and transitional yards between specified land uses. Several standard graphic details are included within the ordinance.

Specific planting requirements are not provided; rather, there is a "point system" requiring fifty (50) points per one hundred square feet of landscape area, which may be achieved by the use of some combination of the design elements shown in Table 2.82.

Planting requirements and standards are zoning district-sensitive.

This ordinance is typical of older ordinances that placed more emphasis on controlling poor landscaping practices, like planting large trees under power lines, than on promoting good design. In fact, the general tone of this ordinance seems to be one

TABLE 2.82. Landscape Requirements Point System, Stillwater, Oklahoma

Design Element	*Points*	*Site Plan Symbol*
Earthen Berm	5 points per 10 linear feet	Berm
Turf	10 points per 100 square feet	TF
Vegetative Ground Cover	25 points per 100 square feet	GC
Small Shrubs	25 points each	SS
Large Shrubs	75 points each	LS
Small Tree 1 inch caliper	100 points each	ST
Medium Tree 1 inch caliper	150 points each	MT
Large Tree 1 inch caliper	200 points each	LT
Preserved Existing Trees	Same as above, plus 20 points per inch over 4 inch caliper, not to exceed double the points for a new tree	

of restriction rather than opportunity. Landscaping and maintenance standards contained within this ordinance are more interested in controlling the placement and care of plant material than the type or quality.

Oregon

Ashland

City of Ashland, "Site Design and Use Guidelines," June 4, 1985.

Ashland's ordinance is set up to demonstrate principles for the design and planning of sound development. The city has published a useful handbook describing its landscape ordinance and related site planning requirements, such as site design concepts, public policy and historic district development. This document is a guide for developers in pursuing quality development practices.

The document (handbook) is quite informative and illustrative and would be a worthwhile read for any landscape designer. It is divided into three sections: Site Design Concepts, Guidelines and Policies and Historic District Development. The Site Design Concepts section includes such topics as Site Analysis, Functional Landscaping, Outdoor Space and Crime Prevention and Design. This entire first section is aimed at assisting developers in sound designing. It contains no actual landscape requirements but gives advice on making the best use of a landscape and illustrates the positive impact of the approach on Ashland's environment.

The second section contains the actual requirements. The ordinance requires that a site- and species-specific landscape plan be submitted to the Planning Division. Planting standards of the ordinance are based on percentage and linear feet. Other portions of this section include Landscaping and Site Design Guidelines, Parking Lot Landscaping and Screening Standards and Street Tree Standards. These parts address multifamily residential, commercial and industrial developments and contain illustrative sketches and examples of each. This section also includes a recommended street tree list.

The final section addresses development in Ashland's historic district. It states that the historic commission will make recommendations to developers, but they are not required to follow them. However, one has to think that these recommendations would be influential, as they are easily understood and make good sense.

Ashland is unique in that it takes a less legislative view toward landscape ordinances. The handbook contains few real requirements and focuses its attention on assisting developers in good design rather than threatening them. Overall, this is a very helpful resource and would be a nice addition to any landscape architect's library.

Water Conserving Landscaping Guidelines and Policies, Section 3, August 4, 1992.

This set of guidelines proposes to reduce water demand through water conservation strategies. The ordinance contains no actual requirements, but makes recommendations on plants, irrigation, turf and topography. This document's lack of actual requirements once again illustrates Ashland's unique approach to landscape ordinances.

Grant's Pass

Grant's Pass. "Landscape and Buffering Standards," Article 23, Zoning Code, revised November 17, 1993.

The legislators of Grant's Pass understand that "landscaping is a significant factor in maintaining the livability and economic viability of the community." Thus this ordinance's purpose is to provide standards for landscaping and buffering within Grant's Pass.

Sections of this ordinance address landscaping requirements, landscaping and buffering development standards, landscape construction standards, completion and occupancy, submittal requirements and street tree standards. Planting standards are based on square footage for yards and linear footage for street trees. These standards apply to residential, commercial and industrial areas with differing criteria for each. The ordinance also provides for buffering between different zones.

Grant's Pass does not require that all landscaping be preceded by a landscape plan. However, without a plan, approval of installation is required prior to occupancy. Those plans that do have to be submitted must be very detailed. For example, they must include "percentage of impervious area, landscaped area and recreation open space as a percentage of usable sight area." This document also contains a listing of approved street trees.

This is another Oregon ordinance that is highly detailed, easy to understand and well illustrated. These ordinances are very thorough and leave almost no stone unturned.

Medford

Medford. "General Landscape and Irrigation Requirements," Section 10.780, Medford Code, December 15, 1995.

The Medford landscape ordinance was recently updated and amended through a public participation process that involved agency staff, the local landscape architecture community and the general public. Amendments clarified certain sections of the code that had operated for eight (8) years with mixed results.

The revised ordinance helps to maintain the aesthetic qualities of the entire community and the individual living conditions of all citizens. Water conservation and plant material diversity are encouraged for aesthetic and environmental reasons.

The ordinance sets standards for site coverage, minimum plant material sizes, screening, efficient automatic irrigation systems, parking lot planters, driveways, curb cuts and disabled parking zones. In greater detail, standards are provided for street frontage requirements, pedestrian walkway design and buffer yards between adjacent parcels of land.

Buffer yards standards apply to each zoning district. Each buffer yard is defined according to width and number of required plants per one hundred (100) linear feet. Two (2) types of buffer yards are required in this community. Type A is ten (10) feet in width and requires three (3) canopy trees, two (2) conifer trees, three (3) understory trees, twenty (20) shrubs and a six (6)-foot wooden fence per one hundred (100) linear feet. Type B is twenty (20) feet in width and requires four (4) canopy trees, three (3) conifer trees, four (4) understory trees, twenty (20) shrubs and an eight (8)-foot concrete or masonry wall per one hundred (100) linear feet.

For instance, Type A is used between commercial and residential land uses, whereas Type B is used between industrial and multifamily residential. Plants are to be evenly spaced so as to provide a continuous buffer throughout all seasons. The specific location of all plants is left up to the developer.

Specific requirements are presented for agricultural buffers and landscaping along street frontage.

The code provides for submission of a planting plan and a site plan. Alternative compliance is possible by petition for a special public hearing.

Phoenix

Phoenix. "Site Review," Section 8. Related "Street Trees," Section 6, n.d.

Phoenix's ordinance is divided into two sections: Site Review and Street Trees. The Site Review section covers topics such as Site Approval Required, Plans Required, Site Review Board, General Standards, Review Procedure, Compliance, Application Fee, Rehearings and Appeals. This law requires that a plan be submitted before issuance of a building permit. It does not apply to single family developments nor to any old developments unless a greater than fifty (50) percent of present value renovation is done.

Detailed plans are to be submitted to the Site Review Board, which will make a decision within seven (7) days. The Site Review Board is made up of at least three (3) members of the Planning Commission. This ordinance contains a set of conditions that must be met, several of which are rather unique. One requires the value of landscaping to be between one and one-half ($1\frac{1}{2}$) and five (5) percent of total construction cost. Another unusual condition allows the board to restrict the height of buildings to thirty-five (35) feet if necessary.

The second section of the ordinance is a basic tree ordinance, which sets up street tree requirements and guidelines. Overall, this ordinance imposes few actual requirements. Instead, it says that the Site Review Board may require a developer to do certain things. Thus, a great deal of power and responsibility is given to the Planning Commission. This makes the ordinance a difficult one for developers in that they are not sure what they will be required to do.

Portland

Title 33, Planning and Zoning, Chapter 33.248, "Landscaping and Screening," Ordinance No. 166572, June 25, 1993.
Related Ordinance, Title 33, Planning and Zoning, Chapter 33.266, "Parking and Loading," October 12, 1995.
Related Ordinance, Title 33, Planning and Zoning, Chapter 20.42, "Tree Cutting Ordinance," Ordinance No. 168486, February 2, 1995.

The city of Portland recognizes the value of landscaping and promotes its use. It does this to reestablish vegetation in urban areas, enhance the area's visual character, promote compatibility, unify development, retain existing vegetation and aid in energy conservation.

In this community the landscape ordinance is scattered in several other sections of the Planning and Zoning ordinance. They will be treated together in this instance.

The documents contain three main design components: general landscaping and screening standards, motor vehicle parking and loading areas and corner lots (sight triangles) and mitigation plantings. Standards are given for plant materials, installation, maintenance, tree cutting on developed property and notice of tree cutting permits.

Planting standards are based on square footage. However, most of the ordinance is dedicated to screening. Six types of screen are defined, based generally on height, density and material composition. All plant materials used must be listed in the Portland Plant List.

This ordinance also requires the use of an irrigation system until the plantings have become established. This information must be shown on a landscape plan to be submitted. Street trees are not regulated under this ordinance and cannot be counted toward landscaping. Street trees are regulated under Chapter 20.40.

Its unique feature is that it is so concise an ordinance for such a large municipality. However, this is because Portland has other ordinances that address specific districts and/or environmental zones that are intended to protect the city's natural resources. It has a chapter on Greenway Zones, which attempts to protect areas along Portland's rivers and provide public access to them. Finally, Portland also has a chapter on the Columbia South Shore Plan District, which attempts to "maintain the capacity of the area infrastructure" and set up landscape standards to enhance the image of the plan district. The set of ordinances taken as a whole serve to make Portland one of the more proactive cities in terms of landscape ordinances.

Portland planning staff are presently looking into some innovative changes to their landscape ordinance. They are seeking storm water solutions and rooftop gardens as possible additions to the ordinance. The concept of "building green" is being expressed by many as a method of developing a cleaner urban environment, and the landscape ordinance is adaptable to these types of interesting changes. Other concepts anticipated include greater emphasis on using native plants and loosening the regulations to allow for more variation in edge design (such as hedgerows) rather than the monoculture look that is presently being achieved in hedges, buffers and screens.

Pennsylvania

Findlay Township

Subdivision and Land Development Ordinance, Article 6, "Buffers and Off-Street Parking, and Related Elements," n.d.

This community has landscape requirements contained within its subdivision and land development code. It does not have a comprehensive landscape ordinance. Within this ordinance there are design components for the design of buffer yards, off-street parking facilities, storm water management and erosion control.

Standards are given for plant material sizes, slopes and storm water control devices and detention/retention basin design.

Buffer yards, for lots or sites, are defined by their width and a required number of "plant units" for each one hundred (100) feet of buffer yard. Plant units consist of canopy trees, understory trees and shrubs. Shrubs may be deciduous or evergreen. For buffer yards surrounding parking facilities, low earthen mounds four (4) feet in height are to be used to complement the plantings and block headlight beam penetration. Existing plants in buffer zones must be retained. All trees in this location over four (4) inches caliper may be credited toward the tree planting requirements.

Storm water management provisions are referenced to criteria established in the Township Storm Water Management Ordinance (Ord. #195), or the Pennsylvania Storm Water Management Act (Act 167). Landscape architects may prepare storm water management plans for "minor subdivisions" only.

More communities should consider adding storm water management and erosion control standards to their landscape ordinances.

Upper Macungie Township

Zoning Ordinance, Part 10, Article 1000, "Landscape Improvement Standards," March 1990.

This ordinance applies to all subdivisions, land developments and any uses requiring site plan review that fall under Section 1400 of the Zoning Ordinance.

A landscape plan is required at the preliminary plan review stage. The ordinance lists criteria or standards that must be included in the plan. These include site layout of proposed lots, buildings, street buffers and paving, as well as additional information on such features as existing trees, tree preservation methods, all proposed planting materials, and dimensions. Tree planting requirements are given in the ordinance and are summarized in Figure 2.48.

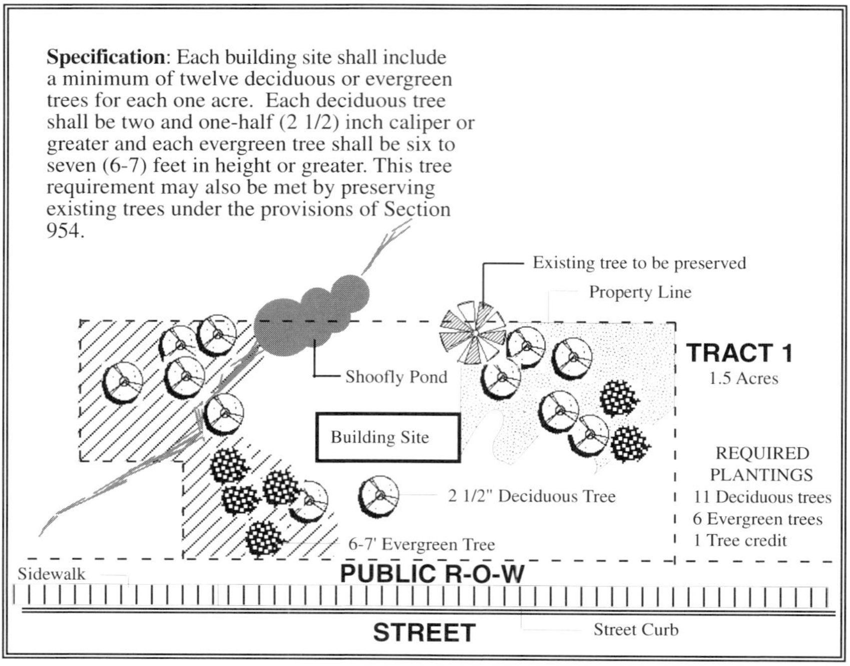

FIGURE 2.48. Tree planting requirements, Upper Macungie Township, Pennsylvania.

Landscape plans must be prepared and sealed by a registered landscape architect. This requirement applies to all commercial, industrial, single-family attached and multifamily properties and lots of more than thirty (30) acres.

Several technical standards are included in this ordinance. These include preserving all healthy trees over six (6) inches, ground cover on at least twenty-five (25) percent of each lot, topsoil not to be removed, twelve (12) trees per acre (deciduous trees two and one-half (2½) inches, evergreens six (6) to seven (7) feet in height), one (1) street tree per sixty (60) linear feet of frontage, and one (1) tree for each three thousand (3,000) square feet of paved area. Islands are required for parking areas over twenty thousand (20,000) square feet, and they must occur between every twenty (20) spaces. All paved areas over twenty thousand (20,000) square feet shall devote a minimum of five (5) percent to landscaping. Existing street trees may not be removed for construction without a permit.

Buffer yards are required according to Section 1300.I, and buffer strips consisting of fifty (50) percent evergreen material are to be used to screen parking, loading, refuse and storage areas. No size requirement is listed for buffer strips, but plant materials selected for a buffer strip must achieve a size greater than the height of the activity being screened. Buffer yard standards have not been annotated here.

Credit is given for the preservation of existing trees based on a sliding scale of caliper inches to number of credits.

Minimal attention is given to plant material requirements, installation standards and maintenance. The ordinance is enforced by the Planning Commission and the Township Board of Supervisors, although effective enforcement is not spelled out.

South Carolina

Aiken

City of Aiken, "Landscaping and Tree Ordinance," 1984.

Section 2 of this ordinance defines such terms as *buildable area, building inspector, building site*, and *vehicular use area*. Section 3 outlines landscaping requirements. Landscaped areas can be no less than twelve (12) percent of total available area. At least one (1) planter island is required for every twelve (12) parking spaces. Vehicular use areas must have planted borders not less than five (5) feet in width, with one (1) tree per thirty (30) linear feet. Sections 5–11 outline application, penalty and appeals processes.

Anderson, County of

Anderson County Land Use and Development Standards Ordinance, § 38-122, "Buffer Yards," n.d.

Anderson County utilizes performance-based zoning rather than standard zoning. It works with developers to help them understand the performance requirements.

Buffer yards are required to ameliorate nuisances between adjacent land uses and promote compatibility. Buffer yards are required along property lines, at outside storage areas on nonresidential lots and around containers and dumpsters. Buffer yards are to be designed with some combination of plant materials, fences, berms, walls and other screening devices. Six (6) types of buffer yards with options are defined. The types vary as to width and planting requirements. A "plant unit multiplier" factor is used to adjust the planting requirement for changes in the width of a buffer yard. The wider the buffer yard, the fewer number of plant materials required.

The ordinance contains buffer yard specifications, minimum plant sizes and a table of buffer yard requirements. The city strongly encourages the use of existing and native plant material.

This community uses some interesting drawings, planting diagrams and cartoons to help developers understand the buffer yard requirements. A landscape design drawing is included as an example, and it is suggested that all developers consult a professional landscape designer in order to maximize the open space potential of each site.

Beaufort

Code of Ordinances, Part 5—Planning and Development, Chapter 6, Zoning, Article H, "Landscaping and Tree Conservation," May 9, 1995. Related document, "City of Beaufort Landscaping and Tree Conservation Manual," n.d.

The South Carolina Local Government Comprehensive Planning Enabling Act of 1994, South Carolina Code of Laws Section 6-29-340 (B) (2) (d), prompted Beaufort to establish this ordinance. The primary purpose of enacting it was to achieve a high level of quality in the development of land and to maintain a strong economy and high property values. Together, these objectives will assist the community in maintaining an attractive locale for residents and a retirement and tourist destination for others.

This ordinance regulating tree conservation, tree removal and landscaping applies to all land uses with few exceptions. Single-family and two-family developments, as well as plant nurseries and silvaculture operations, are exempt. Special provisions apply to utility companies and city agencies.

No tree with a DBH of eight (8) inches or greater may be removed or damaged unless a tree removal application has been filed and approved by the Building Official. Building permits will not be granted without submission and approval of a Landscaping and Tree Conservation Plan and, in some instances, a Tree Survey. These are filed with the Building Official when making application for a building permit.

These plans may be prepared by a landscape architect, who is required to affix his or her seal and attach name, signature, and address along with additional prescribed information. A Certificate of Occupancy will not be issued until all required landscaping is installed.

The Building Official may reduce or eliminate landscaping and tree conservation requirements at his or her discretion.

All design components, standards and other requirements are addressed in the Appendix to Article H, "City of Beaufort Landscaping and Tree Conservation Manual." Definitions are found within the body of the ordinance.

The manual was enacted as part and parcel of the ordinance for the purpose of implementing the provisions of the law. The manual divides the city into three zones, A, B and C. Technical standards and requirements vary to some extent by zone and by zoning district. An outline of the manual, shown in Table 2.83, provides insight into the requirements of the community.

One of the most interesting aspects of this ordinance is the requirement that each site have a certain threshold of tree coverage expressed in Adjusted Caliper Inches (ACI). ACI is the measure of all trees (sum of the diameters of preserved and planted) to be on site after development is complete. Various sites have different ACI standards, and various types of trees are weighted in value. The formula for calculating ACI is as follows:

TABLE 2.83. Landscaping and Tree Conservation Manual, Beaufort, South Carolina

Manual Section	*Effects*
Tree Removal Criteria	Determines value of trees
Landscape Zones Established	Divides community into zones
Perimeter Buffer Requirements	Gives standards for sizing of buffers
Landscaping Perimeter Buffers	Gives standards for buffer zone planting
Tidal Area Buffer	Sets standards for tidal wetland zones
Screening Requirements	Standards for screening between land uses
Parking Area Screening	Defines screening along r-o-w and historic districts
Parking Area Interiors	Defines tree distance and planting of islands, peninsulas and medians
Foundation Beds	Sets dimensions and planting requirements for building foundations
Utility Screening	Regulates screening requirements for trash, equipment and storage
Tree Removal	Regulates criteria for removal of protected trees and "grand" trees
Tree Coverage Requirements	Specifies tree coverage for each development site
Tree Protection Zone Requirements	Sets area standards around trees to be preserved
Installation and Maintenance	Gives criteria for proper installation and maintenance of plantings
Replacement Plantings	Defines tree mitigation requirements for removed trees
Topsoil Preservation	Regulates guidelines for use and preservation of topsoil
General	Regulates general site requirements
Nonconforming Property	Regulates rules for property not in compliance with ordinance
Significant Species and Tree Lists	Regulates recommended lists of trees and shrubs for use

$$\text{ACI} = (\text{number of trees}) \times (\text{diameter of trees}) \times (\text{species factor}) \times (\text{new tree factor})$$

where sites less than 3/4 acre = 125 ACI per acre, sites more than 3/4 acre = 200 ACI per acre, and core commercial districts = 0 ACI per acre. Tree Species Factor (TSF): broad leafed overstory trees = 2; coniferous overstory and understory trees = 1. New Tree Factor (NTF): preserved trees have a value of 1; planted trees have a value of 3.

TABLE 2.84. Calculation of ACI (Adjusted Caliper Inches), Beaufort, South Carolina

Quantity	*Size—Plant—Type*	*No. of Trees × Diameter × TSF × NTF = ACI*					
5	4″ *Quercus virginiana*, preserved	5	4″	2	1	=	40
2	16″ *Quercus virginiana*, preserved	2	16	2	1	=	64
1	48″ *Quercus rubra*, preserved	1	48	2	1	=	96
3	8″ *Pinus elliottii*, preserved	3	8	1	1	=	24
6	4″ *Melia azedarach*, preserved	6	4	1	1	=	24
8	3″ *Quercus michauxii*, planted	8	3	2	3	=	144
3	2″ *Malus angustifolia*, planted	3	2	1	3	=	18
					Total ACI		410

Sample ACI Calculation

Given, a two-acre parcel of land to be developed. The required ACI equals 400, or two acres at 200 ACI per acre. The proposed landscape plan and plant material schedule would normally illustrate the information shown in Table 2.84 to achieve the required ACI for this site.

Any combination of plant materials, either preserved or planted, totaling at least four hundred (400) ACI would satisfy the tree cover requirements of this community.

Interestingly, the ordinance contains an annual review clause. This clause requires that the Building Official and the DAC (Development Advisory Committee) review the ordinance yearly and report to the City Council on its effectiveness. Review clauses or sunset clauses are not often found in these ordinances.

This ordinance places emphasis on trees, tree preservation and, to some extent, site planning. Design, however, is not emphasized.

Charleston

Charleston. Landscape Requirements, No. 1994-71, February 22, 1994.

This ordinance applies to all property in Charleston except for single-family and two-family residential. Buffer requirements contained within the ordinance apply to all land uses. When there is expansion or renovation of real property that increases the valuation of that property over fifty (50) percent, the property must be brought into compliance with this ordinance.

For all renovations, and for all new uses that fall under this ordinance, a permit is required. A landscape plan shall be submitted to the Zoning Administrator. The landscape plan must show the extent of the project, including all landscaping, site improvements and details illustrating installation, irrigation and materials.

No building permit will be issued until the landscape plan is approved, and no Certificate of Occupancy will be issued until the landscaping is completed and certified by on-site inspection.

Landscape improvements to be designed under the requirements of this ordinance include street frontage, parking lot buffers, interior parking areas, visual screens and refuse collection facilities.

Landscape requirements specify minimum widths and length as well as minimum quantities and sizes needed to satisfy the objectives of this ordinance.

This is a minimal ordinance, which adds some planting to each site. It does not attempt to preserve trees, nor does it address site construction or installation, irrigation or maintenance. There is nothing in the ordinance pertaining to Charleston's historic waterfront district.

Hilton Head Island

Hilton Head Island Ordinance 93-17, Part D, Section 16-7-930, "Trees," August 2, 1993.

Hilton Head Island lies off the coast of South Carolina on a barrier island and is a prime retirement-recreation-tourist mecca for the entire East Coast of the United States. The island is heavily wooded, and home sites, golf courses and walking trails seem to blend together to produce a town with significant ambiance.

This ordinance is a tree protection ordinance and is included in this discussion because Hilton Head is well known for its beautiful coastal live oaks, sea pines and subtle seaside understory plants.

The ordinance sets forth a purpose, standard definitions and requirements for tree preservation, tree approval application procedures and tree protection. Specifications are given for tree replanting and tree selection. Tree damage is defined, and penalties can be assessed for failure to comply with the terms of this law.

No person may engage in any development activity without first obtaining approval for removing trees. All requests must be submitted to the Natural Resources Administrator along with a written narrative, photographs, a tree survey, site plan and tree tally sheet with associated calculations. Central to this procedure is determining the total DBH existing on the site prior to development.

The administrator may approve, approve with conditions or disapprove. Trees are inspected and marked in the field prior to any removal. All sites with trees removed must have new trees planted to bring the site back into compliance with the standard of "nine hundred (900) caliper inches per acre" at maturity, based on the total site acreage less the maximum impervious surface required for the permitted land use. For example, supplemental planting shall be at fifteen (15) percent of the difference between the minimum adjusted caliper inches and the predevelopment DBH on the site. If a site has a total of eight hundred (800) inches of trees before development, subtract 800 from 900 (the standard per acre) for a difference of 100 inches. Multiply $100 \times .15$ to get 15 inches of trees to be replanted to raise the site to the minimum standard.

TABLE 2.85. Tree Replacement Requirements, Hilton Head Island, South Carolina

Tree Category Removed	*Example*	*Tree Replacement Requirement*
Category I Tree	30″ Live Oak	Inch-for-inch ratio, replace with 30″ of live oaks
Category II Tree	20″ Hickory	.75 inch-for-inch ratio, replace with 15″ of hickories
Category III Tree	10″ Red Cedar	.50 inch-for-inch ratio, replace with 5″ of red cedars
Category IV Tree	12″ Cabbage Palmetto	.25 inch-for-inch ratio, replace with 4″ of palmettos

This ordinance makes it clear that trees are important in this community and that the city has developed a scientific basis for measuring the value of a tree removed and its replacement value. Table 2.85 shows the tree replacement procedure used in this community.

Mount Pleasant

Mount Pleasant. Chapter 155, "Tree Protection Ordinance," Mount Pleasant Zoning Code. Related, Section 155.99, "Buffer Yard Requirements," Section 155.88, "Landscaping," n.d.

This community has minimal postconstruction landscaping requirements but does have a very thorough tree protection ordinance. This discussion will focus on the tree protection provisions with only passing mention of some of the interesting parts of the postconstruction requirements.

The South Carolina Code of Laws confers upon the citizens of Mount Pleasant the authority to preserve the natural landscape and protect existing trees in a manner to promote the public health, safety and general welfare. The community has decided to do this by regulating the removal of trees, establishing standards for tree protection during land clearing and construction and providing for replacement trees. The ordinance applies to all real property within the town limits, with certain exemptions. These include residential lots, commercial timber operations and commercial nurseries. Utility companies, electric suppliers and governmental agencies also have certain exemptions.

Definitions, standards and administrative procedures are included in this ordinance.

No "protected tree," defined as a tree eight (8) inches at DBH, may be removed in this community without approval of the Design Review Board. This specifically applies to historic trees and a minimum number of protected trees, to equal twenty (20) protected trees per acre. For parcels containing fewer than twenty (20) protected trees per acre, the total number of protected trees required to be saved must equal the total number of protected trees on the site prior to development. Simply, no tree of more than eight (8) inches may be removed on those parcels with fewer than twenty (20) trees per acre.

During development trees must be protected through a variety of means, which may include barricades, rope flagging and tunneling. Grade changes are restricted; trenching and other forms of encroachment are discouraged. Some damage is tolerated for young trees, and remedial procedures are specified. These may include pruning, fertilizing, root development and root zone capacity amendments that promote air exchange, nutrient buildup and moisture retention. Increased root growth, soil fertility and improved soil structure are key criteria for maintaining healthy growth.

Removal of trees without approval of the Tree Commission or Zoning Administrator is a violation that may result in a two hundred dollar (200) fine or imprisonment. Tree replacement is required for all approved takedowns.

Several tree replacement ratios are used. The formula followed for commercial sites is that the number of inches DBH replaced is to be equal to the number of inches DBH removed. This applies to property between zero (0) and two (2) acres. For larger tracts, replacement inches will be counted as eight (8) inches per tree regardless of size. For example, this would translate into four (4) two (2)-inch replacement trees, or one (1) six (6)-inch tree and one (1) two (2)-inch tree. Replanting should avoid monoculture by mixing species for diversity. Table 2.86 illustrates the species diversity ratio used in this community.

The city does not have standards for vehicular use areas or on-site screening, but it has adopted standards for buffer yards. Buffer yards are required to separate different land uses from each other in order to eliminate or minimize potential nuisances such as dirt, litter, noise, glare of lights, signs and unsightly parking areas or to reduce adverse impacts of odor, fire or explosion.

In this community both the amount of land set aside and the type of planting required are based on the land uses involved.

A buffer yard matrix showing proposed land use and existing adjacent land use is used to determine buffer yard specifications. Several buffer yard types are created in this ordinance, referred to as Types A, B, C, D, E and F. Buffer width

TABLE 2.86. Species Diversity Standards, Mount Pleasant, South Carolina

Number of Plants Required	*Number of Species*
5–10 Trees	Minimum of two species
10–20 Trees	Minimum of four species
20–100 Trees	Minimum of five species
100+ Trees	Minimum of seven species

ranges from seven and one-half ($7\frac{1}{2}$) feet deep (A) to one hundred twenty-five (125) feet deep (F). Planting within the buffer yard types varies as well, according to a "plant unit multiplier." This allows for a high density of planting in a thinner buffer zone or a more spacious planting in a wider buffer zone. The developer is allowed to make the choice.

For instance, according to the matrix, a proposed commercial development building adjacent to a single-family residence would have to design a Type E buffer, varying in width from twenty-five (25) feet to seventy-five (75) feet, with a plant multiplier factor varying from .6 to 1.00. In this buffer there would be planted for each one hundred (100) feet six (6) canopy trees, nine (9) understory trees, thirty-six (36) shrubs and eighteen (18) evergreen conifers. The plant multiplier would be used with this number of plants to determine the proper density for the buffer yard width selected. Structures in the form of wood fences, masonry walls or earth berms may be added to increase density.

A list of recommended plants for buffer yard planting and plant size specifications is provided.

Myrtle Beach

Appendix A, Zoning, Section 901, "Landscaping Regulations," n.d.
Related ordinance, Appendix A, Zoning, Section 903, "Tree Protection," September 24, 1996.

One of the newest places to find information about landscape ordinances is on the Internet. Information about landscape requirements in this community is available on the City of Myrtle Beach Web Page. Do a search for Myrtle Beach with any major search engine and you will find this information. Myrtle Beach has both a landscape ordinance and a tree protection ordinance in its zoning code. In this discussion they will be treated together.

The landscape ordinance applies to all new construction and any developments that increase total gross floor area by ten (10) percent or more.

Requirements pertain to vehicular use areas, property abutting public rights-of-way, buffering between noncompatible land uses, screening of refuse containers and general tree planting, at the rate of one (1) tree for each dwelling unit in multifamily developments. This ordinance has specific design standards for earth berms, as shown in Table 2.87.

A five (5)-foot planted strip is common for most buffers and screens in most zoning districts. Planting of these strips generally consists of specified numbers of trees and shrubs, calculated according to linear measure. These plants, along with ground covers on exposed ground, may be planted by formula or grouped for special effects. For storage and refuse areas opaque walls or fences are required.

Planting for vehicular use areas of lots of more than four thousand (4,000) square feet is based on five (5) percent of the area devoted to vehicular use, loading and storage. This planting area is to be planted with a minimum of two (2) trees and four (4) shrubs for each one hundred fifty (150) square feet of interior

TABLE 2.87. Berm Design Specifications, Myrtle Beach, South Carolina

Design Feature	*Specification*
Height of landscape berm	Three feet
Slope of landscape berm	Three to one, or 33%
Trees per 100 linear feet	Three canopy trees, 3 inches caliper
Understory trees per 100 linear feet	Six understory trees, 1½ inches caliper
Evergreen shrubs	Nine 10-gallon containers

landscape zone. Special provisions apply to small lots of less than sixty (60) feet in width and to certain zoning districts.

In certain zoning districts special requirements mandate preservation of existing trees, reforestation based on eight (8) percent of vehicular use area and nondisturbance of at least twenty (20) percent of the site. Credit is given for saving trees in these districts. The credit is twice the number of trees required for reforestation times the percentage of undisturbed area exceeding the minimum twenty (20) percent. This is calculated as follows:

$$50{,}000 \text{ sq ft of VUA} \times 8\% / 100 \text{ sq ft} = 40 \text{ reforestation trees required}$$
$$30\% \text{ of site undisturbed} - 20\% \text{ minimum requirement} = 10\% \text{ in excess of minimum}$$
$$\text{Therefore, } 2 \times 40 \text{ trees} \times 10\% = 8 \text{ trees credit}$$

Performance standards are given for plant materials, landscape plan preparation, maintenance and installation. There is also a list of required plants, recommended by the planning department as acceptable for meeting the conditions of the ordinance, as well as a list of prohibited plants.

The ordinance is enforced through the use of building permits, occupancy permits, revocation of business license and monetary fines.

The South Carolina Code of Laws and the City Council of Myrtle Beach hold tree protection as an important function of public health, safety and welfare. The tree protection ordinance was enacted for a variety of land use, environmental, aesthetic and property value reasons. Primarily, the ordinance was enacted to protect certain classes, sizes and species of trees and other trees known as "landmark" trees of a specified caliper DBH. Interestingly, added to this list of protected trees are all trees over six (6) feet tall on public land and all trees preserved or planted to meet the requirements of the landscape ordinance. Landmark trees in this community include the species listed in Table 2.88.

Protected trees cannot be damaged, removed or transplanted without receiving a permit from the zoning administrator of the city. Certain criteria are listed for granting permits. All approved removals of protected trees must be mitigated with replacement trees. Protected trees removed without a permit will be replaced

TABLE 2.88. Protected Landmark Trees, Myrtle Beach, South Carolina

Species	*Common Name*	*DBH*
Juniperus virginiana	Eastern Red Cedar	30″
Magnolia grandiflora	Southern Magnolia	30″
Quercus virginiana	Live Oak	30″
Quercus laurifolia	Laurel Oak	36″
Quercus phellos	Willow Oak	36″
Acer rubrum	Red Maple	36″
Taxodium distichum	Bald Cypress	30″
Ilex opaca	American Holly	20″
Cornus florida	Flowering Dogwood	15″
Carya species	Hickories	36″

with trees whose total basal area equals the basal area of the tree removed. All replacement trees will be four (4) inches in caliper. In a case where replacement is not practical, the equivalent value of the tree plus installation and maintenance will be assessed and placed in the City of Myrtle Beach Tree Preservation Fund.

This fund is spent in implementing the Master Street Tree Planting Plan, which encompasses all city rights-of-way and develops themes for each area of the city.

Standards are given for tree pruning, licensing of arborists and tree protection during construction. Particular reference is made to 1995 ANSI A300 pruning standards and an exhaustive list of definitions.

Together, the landscape ordinance and the tree protection ordinance make the City of Myrtle Beach, among all cities in the South, one of the most committed to the quality of life that attractive landscapes can create. One curious feature is that there is no mention of the relationship of trees to hurricanes in either of these ordinances. One wonders why.

South Dakota

Rapid City

Rapid City, Ordinance 2873, Amending Section 14 of Article V of Appendix A of the Revised Ordinances of the City of Rapid City, "Landscape Regulations," April 12, 1991.

The purpose of this ordinance is to control vehicular and pedestrian circulation in parking areas; clarify off-street paved ground areas and adjacent rights-of-way; screen trash; enhance the Black Hills area; protect and conserve property values; reduce water runoff; return pure oxygen; reduce heat, noise, wind turbulence and glare; and provide efficient irrigation waters.

This ordinance explains the amount of plant material and landscaping required, the general installation requirements, site distances for landscaping adjacent to rights-of-way and points of access, maintenance, planting criteria and plan approval. Landscaping is required in all industrial, commercial, and multifamily zoning districts. Landscaping is not required in general agricultural, park forest, low-density Residential I, and low-density Residential II zoning districts. No landscape architect or other professional is required to prepare the plans. The plans are submitted to the Building Inspector, who issues a building permit upon approval of the plans.

The amount of landscaping material needed is based on the point system. Large trees equal two thousand (2,000) points; medium trees equal one thousand (1,000) points, small trees equal five hundred (500) points, an opaque hedge equals five hundred (500) points, shrubs equal two hundred fifty (250) points, one (1) square yard of ground cover equals one hundred (100) points, and one (1) square yard of grass equals ten (10) points. The square footage of the site not covered by a building shall be the number of points required. The amount of landscaping area is dependent on the specific zone. Heavy industrial zones require fifty percent of the area to be landscaped, whereas high-density residential require only ten (10) percent. A minimum of fifty (50) percent of the required landscaping is to be located within twenty (20) feet of the parking area.

The format of this ordinance is formal, but the information is informal and practical.

Sioux Falls

Zoning Ordinance, § 15.49.060, "Landscape Standards," March 1995.

Sioux Falls has prepared a Landscape Design Manual to assist developers, owners, city officials and landscape architects in understanding the provisions of its landscape ordinance.

The Landscape Design Manual contains excerpts from the city zoning ordinance and information concerning planting in public rights-of-way and at intersections and driveway safety zones. Explanatory graphics and text are used to describe landscaping of front yard setbacks, required trees, screening of parking lots and dumpsters and installation requirements. The screening hedge seen in Figure 2.49 is typical of the design standards included in this ordinance.

The manual contains a list of recommended plants suitable for planting in Sioux Falls, as well as a list of prohibited species for street tree planting, as shown in Table 2.89.

Heights, spacing standards and select varieties are listed by both common name and scientific name.

The ordinance sets forth plant material standards and provides two (2) tree credits for all preserved trees over ten (10) inches in caliper. Most planting requirements are based on linear foot measure or percentage of area. No mention is made of administrative standards.

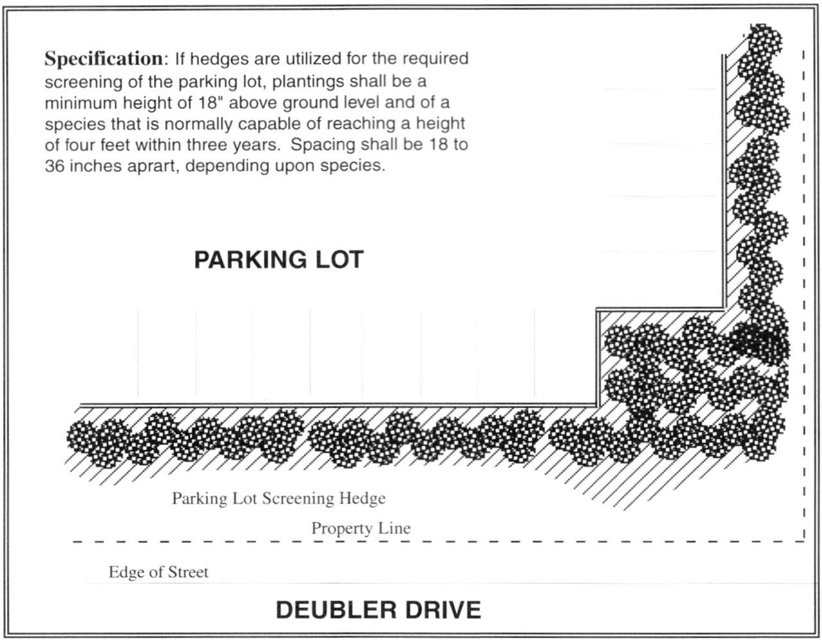

FIGURE 2.49. Screening hedge specifications, Sioux Falls, South Dakota.

TABLE 2.89. Prohibited Streetscape Plants, Sioux Falls, South Dakota

Species	*Reason for Prohibition*
Acer saccharinum	Shallow-rooted, break up walkways, brittle wood
Betula species	Susceptible to bronze birch borer
Gliditsia triacanthos	Dangerous thorns and messy seedpods
Juglans species	Produce "jugalone" growth retardants, messy fruits
Malus species	Dropping fruits cause maintenance problems
Populus species	Susceptible to wind damage, weak-wooded
Salix species	Weak-wooded, susceptible to wind damage
Ulmas americana	Dutch elm disease limits use
Ulmus pumila	Short-lived due to canker
General shrub plantings	All shrubs over 12" can block views and cause safety problems
Evergreen trees	Create traffic hazards, may impede pedestrian movement

Tennessee

Bartlett

Article VI, Section 21, "Tree Planting and Protection," 1989.

This tree ordinance is designed to regulate and control planting of trees and woody vegetation in Bartlett. It encourages the protection of existing trees and root systems, regulates the preservation, replacement and removal of trees and establishes procedures, practices and minimum design standards for fulfilling these purposes. A glossary defines such terms as *tree, tree protection zone* and *tree value factor*.

The city's tree program is administered by the Building Department, with the Planning and Engineering Departments, Parks and Recreation and the City Beautiful Commission reviewing development plans.

Besides setting standards for tree maintenance and planting on public lands, the ordinance, in Part II, establishes regulations for commercial and residential developments. Developers are urged to preserve existing trees whenever practical, and they must obtain a permit for any construction work that will have an impact on existing trees. Even species selection is subject to site plan review by the Design Review Commission. The ordinance includes a "minimum tree density" formula, based on "tree value factor," "diameter at breast height" and the number of trees, for anyone who must have site plan approval from the Planning Commission and Design Review Commission.

Attachment A to the ordinance is the city's recommended tree list.

Chattanooga

"Landscaping Requirements," n.d.

This ordinance pertains primarily to parking lots, vehicular use areas and landscape buffers that screen on-site automobiles. Screening of mechanical equipment and trash receptacles is required, and very minimal buffers between land uses are required in certain circumstances. The ordinance applies to all land uses except single- and two-family residential properties.

Performance standards, such as shown in Figure 2.50, are given for installation and maintenance of landscaping. Specific technical standards are given for plant materials. These standards are based on recommendations of the American Association of Nurserymen. Design standards are included for screening fences and buffers. Ten (10)-foot buffers are required between parking areas and public rights-of-way, and thirty (30)-inch planting strips are required along perimeters of abutting properties. Planting of perimeter buffer strips and right-of-way buffers is based on linear foot measure. Along streets, trees are planted over fifty (50) feet on center, and along adjacent properties trees are planted each seventy-five (75) feet on center.

Credit is granted for existing trees, hedges, walls and other durable landscape barriers.

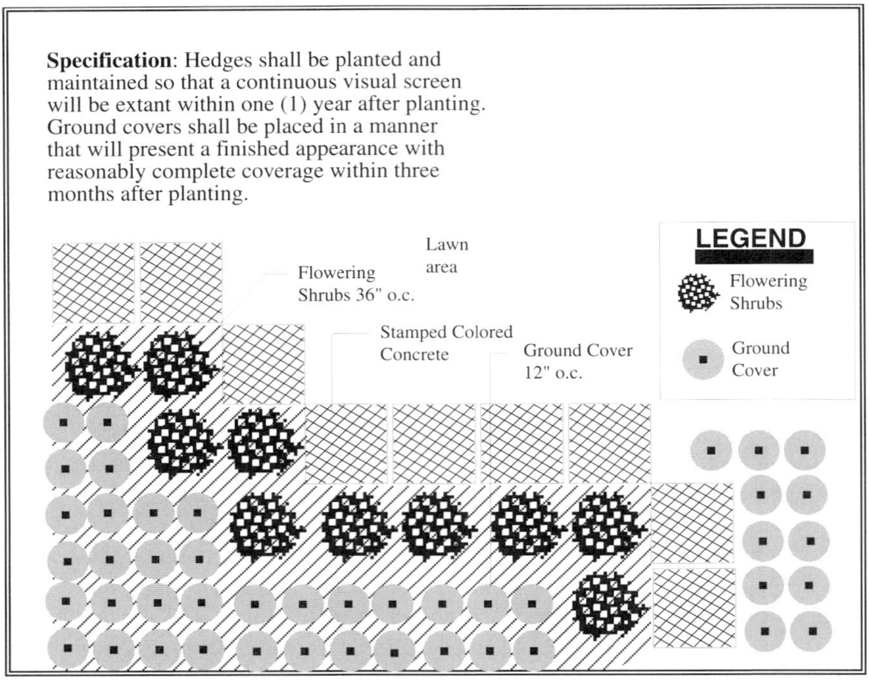

FIGURE 2.50. Plant material installation standards, Chattanooga, Tennessee.

Planting requirements for interior parking areas include at least five (5) square feet of interior parking space for each parking place. The total number of trees is to be not less than one (1) tree for each one hundred (100) square feet. A thirty-five hundred (3,500) square foot parking area will have four (4) trees planted within, for example. Curbs, tree guards and other devices are required to protect planting areas.

No irrigation requirements are given, although there must be one (1) water outlet (hose bib) within one hundred fifty (150) feet of all plant materials.

Somewhat unusual for a landscape ordinance, this law has provisions covering outdoor lighting. Lighting requirements pertain to parking areas. Lighting should be designed to provide good visibility with a minimum of glare to abutting properties. Specific recommended illumination levels are given.

Collierville

Town Ordinance, § 11-1501, "Design and Environmental Review Ordinance," January 1994.

Collierville has formed a Design and Environmental Review Commission to work with the Town Department of Planning for the purpose of proper development of the town in respect to attractiveness, maintenance of property values and quality of environment. Its citizens want to live in a community that is attractive as well as functional and maintains a balance between land uses and development.

It has prepared an attractive, easy-to-understand, graphically illustrated "Design Guidelines Manual" to interpret the zoning ordinance and subdivision and help developers, citizens and designers understand the goals of the town. The manual covers design standards for the site design components listed in Table 2.90.

TABLE 2.90. Design Standards, Collierville, Tennessee

Design Standard	*Reason*
Site Layout	To take advantage of site features, limit amount of site that can be developed, set limits for amount of landscape space.
Site Grading	To control erosion and drainage, and regulate cut and fill and slope gradients.
Preservation of Existing Site Features	To save all trees of 8″ DBH and natural features such as streams, wetlands, fence rows, stands of native vegetation.
Architectural Character	To ensure compatibility with surroundings, maintain character.
Parking Areas	To minimize negative impact of parking areas, maintain streetscape character, set forth detailed screening and planting standards to soften visual effects.
Landscaping	To mirror the surrounding region in terms of design concept. To regulate maintenance, irrigation and plantings in landscape areas, and along streets. To set standards for plant material species, types, spacing, height and quality.
Fences and Screening	To control transition between land uses and screen offensive site nuisances. Several types of screens are defined. They include transitional screening, privacy screening and nuisance screening. Suggested plant materials for screening are listed.
Pedestrian Circulation	To set standards for connecting walkways to buildings, parking, open space.
Signage	To regulate sign types, sizes, character and siting of signage.
Historic District Standards Zoning	All development must meet standards presented in Chapter 13 of the Ordinance.

Also contained in the manual are the administrative procedures for submitting plans, making application for public design review and seeking building permits. A Design Review Checklist is included to summarize the technical information that will be needed by the Design and Environmental Review Commission and the Planning Commission to render a fair judgment of the merits of a project.

This community has framed its landscape ordinance in context with other related design concerns in a very convincing manner that communicates to town officials, citizens and developers what designers have known for a long time: Good planning and design leads to livable communities.

Franklin

Franklin, Zoning Ordinance, Section 8.4, "Landscaping Plan," n.d.

Franklin, Tennessee, a small historic town near Nashville, was the site of a bloody battle during the Civil War between General John Bell Hood's Texas Corps and Sherman's division under General John Schofield. This unique southern community has a minimal landscape ordinance, primarily based on meeting certain performance requirements and specific unit standards.

This community requires that landscaping be integrated into building arrangements, topography, parking and property buffer zones. Landscaping shall include, in addition to trees, shrubs and ground covers, annuals, perennials, plant sculpture and art.

Specific requirements are stated in the ordinance for open space, plant material sizes and minimum landscape surface ratio. Landscape surface ratios are based on land use category and the amount of land area that must be set aside for landscaping. For instance, forty (40) percent of "estate residential district" areas must be landscaped and twenty (20) percent of "heavy industrial" districts must be planted. Landscape surface ratios are not specifically defined in the ordinance but are assumed to mean a ratio of open space to planting areas.

Planting standards are based on units. Each acre of designated open space or landscape surface area not presently forested is to be planted with a specific number and size of trees and shrubs. For instance, for each acre twenty-six (26) trees and fifty (50) shrubs must be planted. The trees are to be either of canopy or understory stature and should range in size from two (2)-inch caliper to five (5)-inch caliper. Two (2) three (3)-inch caliper canopy trees must be planted on each residential lot. Nonresidential developments must plant additional units of plants consisting of six (6) trees and fifteen (15) shrubs per acre. Parking lots must set aside seven hundred twenty (720) square feet of planting for each twenty-four (24) parking spaces. This works out to be thirty (30) square feet per parking slot.

Typical cross sections and elevation drawings must be submitted along with the screening plan. Performance standards rather than specific standards are used to describe the required screening and buffering requirements. Generally, screening is needed for parking areas, mechanical equipment, and buffers between adjacent properties. Screens are to be not less than six (6) feet in height. Buffers and screens may be either earth berms, fencing, plant material or some combination. Most planted buffers are ten (10) feet wide. Along street rights-of-way buffer areas vary between twenty (20) feet and forty (40) feet. The larger are required along interstate highways and the smaller along arterials.

The administrative aspects of this ordinance are not clear.

Hendersonville

Hendersonville, Landscape Ordinance, n.d.

The information concerning Hendersonville reviewed here is not identified in the ordinance itself. The assumption is made that the ordinance is contained within community design guidelines published by the Hendersonville Regional Planning Commission (HRPC).

As a set of design guidelines, this ordinance is fairly comprehensive, covering landscaping as well as closely related site development issues. Included in the design guidelines are design standards covering tree preservation, retention of site features, preservation of old structures, architectural character, parking lot design and streetscape. Some of the standards are performance based and others are specific. For example, that the use of full chroma colors on buildings is discouraged on buildings is a performance-based standard, and that the minimum size of any landscape area is to be seventy-five (75) square feet is a specific requirement.

The landscape standards are primarily performance based. They require landscaping located along public boundaries, within parking areas, around buildings and at entries of buildings. Specific standards are given for streetscape design along certain streets. Standards are also given for plant sizes, plant spacing and screening. Various screen types are presented in Table 2.91.

Other design standards cover the number of contiguous parking spaces, minimum width of landscape beds, number of trees per two hundred (200) square feet of bed area and tree replacement ratio. All trees over ten (10) inch caliper must be replaced on an inch-by-inch basis when removed because of construction activities.

Specific species of trees are listed for use along designated city streets. Irrigation is not required, and very little is contained within these guidelines in regard to maintenance.

TABLE 2. 91. Screening Conditions and Types, Hendersonville, Tennessee

Screen Type	*Purpose*	*Conditions*
Type 1	Transitions	Between land uses
Type 2	Privacy separations	Streets, lot edges, family yards
Type 3	Nuisance screening	Service, loading, storage, utilities

One of the really interesting things addressed in this ordinance is topography and how it affects site development and compliance with the landscape standards. In Hendersonville the planting areas in parking lots are to be used to "take up excessive slope."

This city uses design guidelines rather than specific language to define how sites are to be designed in respect to landscaping. Perhaps less defensible in court than strict ordinance requirements, these design guidelines, if followed by developers, will lead to better-designed sites in which new development is integrated into the natural features of a site.

Knoxville

Knoxville, Zoning Ordinance, Section 14.26, "Horticulture," n.d.

Knoxville appreciates the unique benefits of trees and has enacted into law a tree protection ordinance protecting trees in all land uses except single-family and duplex residential. All trees over six (6) inches in diameter one (1) foot above ground are included, as are certain highly ornamental trees over three (3) inches in diameter. Highly ornamental trees include dogwood, redbud, crabapple, sourwood, flowering cherry, peach, magnolia and holly.

This ordinance prevents the complete destruction or removal of trees prior to seeking a building permit and during construction. No more than twenty five (25) percent of the trees on any parcel of land can be removed within a five (5)-year period without approval of the city horticulturists. A minimum of six (6) trees per acre must be retained on all building sites if cut-and-fill operations allow.

Trees of historical and botanical importance, although not defined, must also be preserved. No tree with a trunk diameter over twenty (20) inches located within one hundred fifty (150) feet of a building erected prior to 1860 may be removed or altered by pruning.

Where significant trees cannot be retained on site, they may be replaced at the rate of eight (8) trees per acre.

The ordinance is administered by the city horticulturist, who issues tree removal permits. Site plans must be submitted by the developer to the horticulturist showing existing trees, predominant species and those trees that are to be cleared.

Memphis and Shelby County

Memphis and Shelby County, Zoning Ordinance Section No. 32, "Landscape and Screening Ordinance," n.d.

A landscape and screening ordinance is part of the general zoning ordinance for the City of Memphis and surrounding Shelby County.

The ordinance was written to preserve the tree cover of the community, while encouraging sensitive site grading and planting to minimize erosion. Landscape plans are submitted during the initial building permit application procedure. The ordinance consists of requirements for streetscape planting (Figure 2.51), edge

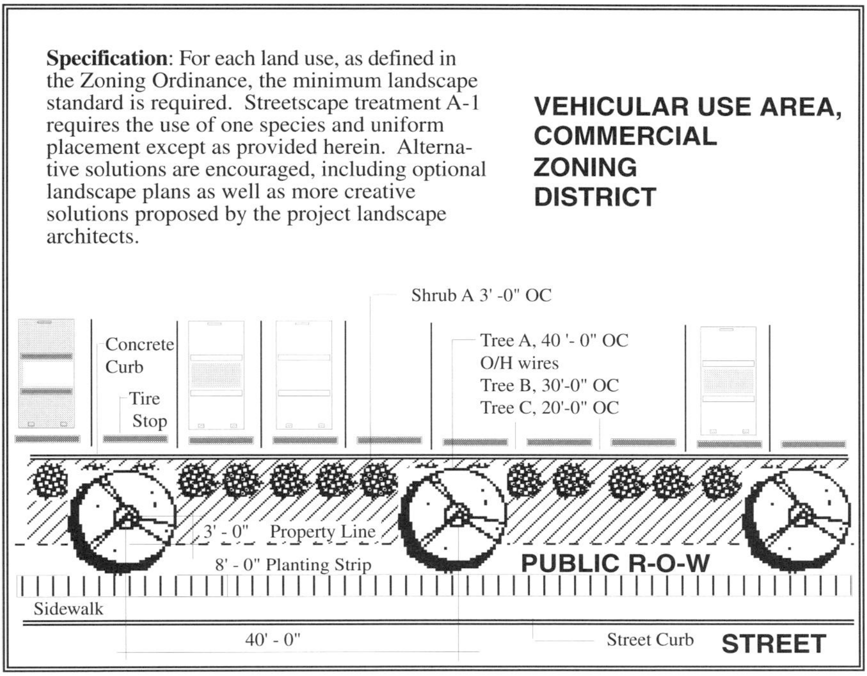

FIGURE 2.51. Commercial zoning district streetscape, Memphis, Tennessee.

screening and interior parking lot planting. Illustrative planting diagrams are given along with an approved plant list.

The purpose of this ordinance is to utilize landscape elements, particularly plant material, in an organized and harmonious fashion to enhance the physical environment of Memphis and Shelby County for the comfort, safety and enjoyment of their citizens.

The ordinance includes: purpose; submittal and approval process; landscape/screening requirements (edge screening and interior landscape requirements); substitutions; alternative treatment; installation and maintenance; quality standards; existing tree cover suggestions; landscape/screening plants; approved plant list; native plant list; and definitions. Many plan sketches of parking lot planting designs are attached, as are a few planting details. Charts of deciduous and evergreen tree heights and rates of growth are also included.

Nashville and Davidson County

Zoning Code Article 6, "Landscaping, Buffering and Tree Replacement," June 27, 1996.

Metropolitan Nashville and Davidson County have recently revised their entire zoning code. One of the major changes in the revised edition is the culmination of the work of the Metropolitan Tree Board, which has been working for several years to establish guidelines for the removal and replacement of trees within Metropolitan Davidson County.

Before discussing Ordinance 094-1104, which addresses tree protection requirements, we will consider the landscaping and buffering requirements of the zoning ordinance.

This ordinance applies to all land uses except single-family and two-family land uses.

Article 6 sets standards for screening and landscaping of parking areas to reduce their impact on adjacent properties and public thoroughfares, as well as to mitigate the visual impact of large areas of unbroken paving. Parking lots are screened from adjacent streets, major thoroughfares and side or rear property lines. In addition, interior plantings must comprise eight (8) percent of the parking area. One (1) tree is to be provided for each fifteen (15) parking spaces.

In addition, this article sets standards for buffering adjacent land uses to reduce the effects of differing activities. Several types of buffers are created, based on density, width and plant material composition.

Standards are contained within this article for plant materials, maintenance, planting scenic easements (designated streets) and screening unsightly areas.

Landscape plans are required as part of the administrative process leading to acquisition of a building permit or a tree removal permit. Detailed administrative procedures, including a listing of permits, fees, and enforcement policies, are contained in Section 10 of this ordinance.

Nashville and Davidson County, Title 17, Zoning Regulations, Chapter 17.18, "Tree Protection," Ord. No. 094-1104, n.d.

This is a basic tree protection ordinance designed to preserve two (2) classes of trees in the metropolitan governmental area of Nashville and Davidson County. It is the intent of the ordinance to minimize the removal of protected trees and to ensure that developers take reasonable measures to design and locate proposed improvements so that the number of protected trees removed is minimized. Incentives are provided for developers who comply.

Tree protection extends to all land within the zoning jurisdiction; the few exceptions include single-family platted lots and emergency situations caused by storms or other natural disasters.

Two types of trees are protected: historic and specimen trees. A "historic tree" is one designated by the Metropolitan Beautification and Environment Commission as a tree of notable historical interest and value. "Specimen trees" are deemed so as a result of their type, size, age or other relevant criteria. Trees are protected on private as well as public properties. Public hearings are held prior to designation. Permits are required for the removal of all protected trees, except for commercial growers, land surveyors and engineers.

A removal permit begins with an application, a tree survey and proposed site development plans along with a ten (10)-dollar fee. Public utilities are given yearly permits. The city urban forester or the Planning Commission reviews permit applications and, in some instances, actual sites. Eight (8) criteria are given for allowing tree removal, as shown in Table 2.92.

Trees that are removed must be replaced in order to maintain a tree density of fourteen (14) units per acre. Acreage is net of land proposed to be covered by structures. Specific units per size of tree are specified in the ordinance. For instance, an eight (8)-inch DBH protected tree is valued at 0.40 units, and the value of a forty-two (42)-inch DBH tree is 9.6 units of density per acre. Replacement trees are calculated in the same manner. A two (2)-inch DBH protected tree is valued at 0.50 units, a twelve (12)-inch DBH tree at 2.1 units of density per acre.

In addition to tree density, standards are given for the sizes of replacement trees, protection of trees during development activities and fencing of "tree protection zones." The tree protection zone generally aligns with the drip line of the tree or a twenty (20)-foot radius. Only certain activities, such as sodding, ground cover planting and tunneling utilities are permitted within this zone. Any protected tree showing damage after one (1) year must be replaced at the developer's expense.

Developers are given incentives to preserve trees. First, preserved trees and relocated trees are granted credit toward tree density requirements. Second, developers are given reductions in parking requirements if this will prevent the removal of protected trees. For example, in a parking lot of twenty (20) or more spaces, up to ten (10) percent of the parking requirement may be eliminated for preserving trees growing in that area of the site.

TABLE 2.92. Protected Tree Removal Conditions, Nashville, Tennessee

1. Permissible use of the site cannot reasonably be undertaken.
2. The tree is located so close to an existing structure that the integrity of the structure is impaired.
3. The tree interferes with the installation and servicing of infrastructure for which there is no feasible alternative.
4. There is created a hazard to motor, bicycle and pedestrian traffic.
5. The tree is diseased, insect ridden or weakened by age, abuse, storm or fire.
6. The removal of the tree is necessary to promote the growth of surrounding protected trees.
7. There is a law or regulation that requires the removal.
8. The site will maintain the required tree density with either protected trees or the installation of new trees.

This is a minimal tree preservation ordinance that brings significant community trees into the planning process. The ordinance allows public input and decision making and give incentives to developers to preserve, relocate or plant new trees.

Texas

Addison

Addison, Ordinance Number 817, Article VIII Section 7, "Required Site Landscaping," August 4, 1982.

The purpose of this ordinance is to require design and construction of landscaped islands in areas of parking lots not suitable for parking or maneuvering space. Prior to the issuance of any building permit a landscape plan shall be permitted in compliance with the following regulations.

This ordinance consists of five Articles, including Local Retail District, Industrial Districts 2 and 3 and Commercial District. All have the same information, but with different percentages. For each zoning district, the following topics are covered: landscaped area, irrigation, parking and maneuvering space, city right-of-way area, permitted uses, the Landscape Development Department, and prohibited actions. The percentages that change are included in the Permitted Uses section, which specifies the percentage of a lot that shall be maintained as open landscaped area.

If a right-of-way has been landscaped in accordance with the Streetscape Plan of Addison, the landscaped portion will be credited toward the required twenty (20)-foot buffer.

All required landscaped open space shall be provided with an adequate and inconspicuous irrigation system and shall be properly maintained.

If the parking and maneuvering space exceeds twenty thousand (20,000) square feet, at least five (5) percent thereof shall be maintained as landscaped area. In order to get credit toward the overall calculated required landscaped area, a tree either fifteen (15) feet in height or three (3) inches in diameter will be required for each two thousand (2,000) square feet of required landscaped parking area. It is the intent of this section to ensure design and construction of parking areas in a manner whereby areas unusable for parking or maneuvering space are landscaped.

If all of the city r-o-w is landscaped and maintained to comply with the Streetscape Plan of Addison, such landscaped portion will reduce the amount of required landscaped area of the lot by that amount (square foot for square foot).

In commercial permitted uses, ten (10) percent of the lot shall be maintained as an open landscaped area. A landscaped buffer of twenty (20) feet will be required along all street frontage. City r-o-w may be included in the aforementioned buffer, and a reduction of three (3) percent will be allowed when the r-o-w is landscaped and maintained according to the Streetscape Plan of Addison.

In reviewing the preceding information, it is obvious that this ordinance is four (4) times too long. A simple chart could have been incorporated in order to make these changes.

Austin

"Guidelines and Procedures for Implementing the Tree Ordinance," 1983.

This document outlines the application process for removal and replacement of trees having trunks sixty (60) inches or more circumference and establishes the new administrative post of City Arborist. The document also outlines enforcement, application and appeals processes for the removal and replacement of trees.

Austin, Ordinance No. 840209-K, 1984.

This is an interim ordinance requiring site plan approval by the planning commission for alteration or removal of certain structures in protected inner-city neighborhoods and declaring this an emergency situation. Site plans accompanying applications must include a landscaping plan and a grading and drainage plan. Land ownership maps of the areas are included.

"Standard Tree Protection Notes," 1985.

Specific procedures and specifications as to tree protection during construction are addressed in this document. Temporary fencing around trees in construction zones is required. Grading within the protected root zone must be done by hand or small equipment, and roots may not be exposed for more than two (2) days. Dust accumulation on leaves is to be washed away. Topsoil dressing within the drip lines of trees may not exceed four (4) inches.

Austin, Ordinance No. L830408-E , Chapter 13-2A, Sections 5600–5635, 1988.

Sections of this ordinance, which provides for ecological balance as affected by vegetation and replenishing of native vegetation, address such issues as land value, aesthetics and energy. It defines terms such as *landscaped area, street yard*, and *downtown area*. At least one (1) tree of six (6) feet must exist or be planted per one thousand (1,000) square feet of street yards less than ten thousand (10,000) square feet in size; one (1) per twenty-five hundred (2,500) square feet in yards between ten thousand (10,000) and one hundred ten thousand (110,000) square feet; and one (1) per five thousand (5,000) square feet in yards over one hundred ten thousand (110,000) square feet. Landowners are encouraged to maintain rights-of-way abutting their land, although the final authority belongs to the city. Small trees may be given double credit, thereby encouraging the preservation of small trees.

College Station

Zoning Ordinance No. 1638, Section 11, "Landscaping," March 13, 1986, revised 1994.

The requirements of this ordinance are fixed to the deed for all lots and are applicable to all land in the city with the exception of single-family and duplex family properties and floodplains.

This is an uncomplicated ordinance that requires landscaping on each lot. Landscape design must address parking area screening, buffer yard screening and street frontage plantings. The latter must follow the design requirements set forth in the College Station Streetscape Plan. This plan requires specific plantings along major and minor arterial streets and special corridors. In addition, the landscape design must prepare screening solutions for trash receptacles, off-street loading areas and utility connections. This ordinance uses a landscape point system. Points are calculated according to measurable site features. Points are assessed based on square footage of site and number of parking spaces. Based on site area, thirty (30) points are required for each one thousand (1,000) square feet. Points based on the number of parking spaces are shown in Table 2.93. Points based on plant materials sizes and types are given in Table 2.94.

The minimum number of points for any site is set by the city at five hundred (500). An additional three hundred (300) points for each fifty (50) linear feet of frontage is required if the site is located on a major, minor or special corridor. Driveway cuts are excluded from this calculation. A minimum of fifty (50) percent of the points must be expended on canopy trees.

Incentives are allowed in the form of point credits for building with enhanced paving or adding special site attractions such as water features.

There are standards in this law for plant materials, site plan preparation, and planting guidelines. The City Forester has prepared a list of recommended plants.

The Zoning Official reviews all landscape plans, irrigation plans and tree surveys. Following approval of final installation of the work, the Certificate of Occupancy is issued. A committee composed of the City Planner, the City Engineer and the Chairman of the Planning and Zoning Committee is the project review committee.

The ordinance is complemented by graphic exhibits that explain visibility triangles, parking screens and landscape reserves.

This ordinance allows maximum design flexibility. As long as the necessary points are achieved, the designer can create any composition of choice.

TABLE 2.93. Landscape Points Based on Parking, College Station, Texas

Number of Spaces	*Required Points*
0 to 50 spaces	16 points per space
51 to 100 spaces	12 points per space
101 to 200 spaces	10 points per space
200+ spaces	8 points per space

TABLE 2.94. Landscape Point System Rating, College Station, Texas

Landscape Material	*Specification*	*Point Value*
Unprotected Existing Canopy Tree	2″ to 14.5″ caliper	35 points
Protected Existing Canopy Tree	2″ to 14.5″ caliper	50 points
Protected Existing Canopy Tree	min. 4.5″ caliper	300 points
New Canopy Tree, containerized or boxed	1.5″ to 2″ caliper	75 points
	2.1″ to 3.4″ caliper	150 points
	3.5″ caliper or larger	300 points
New Canopy Tree, balled and burlapped	1.5″ to 2″ caliper	40 points
	2.1″ to 3.4″ caliper	75 points
	3.5″ caliper or larger	150 points
New Canopy Tree, containerized	min. 1½″ caliper	75 points
Existing Trees, if barricaded at 1 foot per caliper inch of tree	between 4″ and 8″	200 points
Existing Trees, if barricaded at 1 foot per caliper inch of tree	larger than 8″	300 points
Noncanopy Tree	min. 5 feet to 6 feet	40 points
Shrubs	min. 5 gal., 1 gal. dwarfs	10 points
Ground Cover or Grasses		0 points
Vines		0 points

Corpus Christi

Corpus Christi, Ordinance No. 20076, Article 27B, "Landscape Requirements of Corpus Christi, Texas," 1987.

The purpose and intent of this article is to improve the appearance, quality, and quantity of landscaping visible from public rights-of-way.

The ordinance sets minimum standards for development of a site, particularly the "street yard" or that portion that lies in front of site buildings. The ordinance requires three elements: minimum landscape area, minimum landscape material and parking lot screening.

Topics covered in the ordinance include application procedures; definitions; requirements for all street yards; requirements for buffering; incompatible uses; landscaping specifications for all applicable zones (parking areas, dimensional criteria, maintenance and irrigation); measured compliance; enforcement; landscape ordinance required update; and an extensive recommended plans list.

The amount of landscape area and plant materials are zoning area specific and are based on the size of the street yard. The larger the street yard, the more plant materials are needed to install as buffers and screens. Calculations are made to determine the quantity of landscape materials required, based on a point system; various points are allowed for different types and sizes of plant materials.

This community has a highly illustrated "Landscape Handbook," dated June 1991, showing details of the ordinance, specifications, standards and a preferred plants list. The handbook contains useful information in regard to calculating point requirements, proper planting procedures and maintenance. You can even learn to calculate the amount of 15.5.5 fertilizer required to achieve two and one-half (2½) pounds of nitrogen per one thousand (1,000) square feet! The handbook should be consulted in the early stages of the site planning process inasmuch as required landscape areas will affect the entire site development pattern.

This is not an unduly restrictive landscape ordinance, but the point system that is used to quantify design makes it appear more complicated than it really is.

Dallas

Dallas, Article X, Section 51 of the Dallas Development Code of the City of Dallas, Texas, Ordinance No. 18968, "City of Dallas Department of Planning and Development," 1986.
Dallas, Ordinance 19237, Section 51-10.101, "Landscape Regulations of the Dallas Development Code," 1986.

These ordinances cover in detail the following topics: definitions, application of Article X, artificial lot delineation and landscape plan submission (any person may prepare the landscape plan required in this section—there is no requirement that the plan be prepared by a landscape architect or by a person engaged in the landscape business), mandatory provisions, design standards (i.e., landscape screening, parking lot landscaping, buffer strip(s)) enhancement, landscape plan review, and penalty for violating this ordinance. Attached is an explanation of minimum point requirements for incorporating specific landscape features and elements into the landscape plan. The number of points required for landscape plan approval varies, depending on the zoning classification of the lot and its adjacent properties.

Denton

Denton Landscape Code (Ord. No. 88-104, I(101), 6-21-88), August 1988.

The purpose of this ordinance is to provide for the preservation of native trees, prevent the clear cutting of land and provide for minimum landscaping and screening requirements, in recognition that trees, landscaping, and screening protect the health and welfare of the community.

Tree removal has been made difficult through the requirement of a tree removal permit, in order to preserve the native trees. Street yards, as shown in Figure 2.52, tree requirements, parking lots, screening, public parkways and easements, traffic barriers and view obstructions are given specific requirements in this ordinance. Permits for the removal of trees are required for the removal of any tree, with a few exceptions. Properties subject to this ordinance include multifamily and nonresidential land uses, with some exceptions. Landscape plans must be submitted to the building official or his or her designated agent.

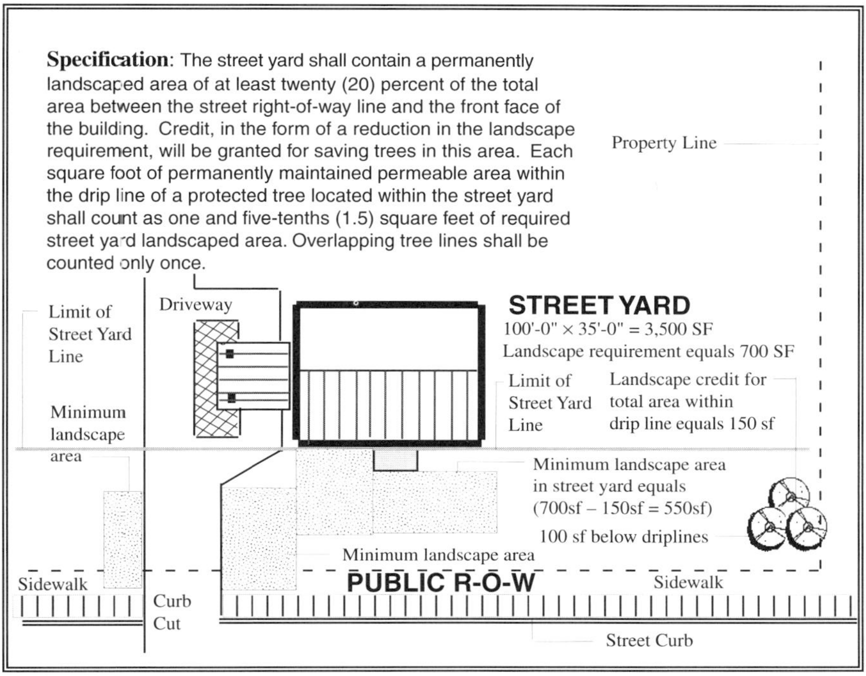

FIGURE 2.52. Street yard landscape area credits, Denton, Texas.

No professionally trained landscape architect is required to develop the landscape plan.

One area of interest in this ordinance is the emphasis on street yards. A street yard is the area of a lot that lies between the street right-of-way line and the front wall building line. Illustrations of street yards are given in the last article of this ordinance. This ordinance does not differentiate between different land uses; the entire ordinance applies to multifamily and nonresidential land uses.

The requirements in this ordinance are straightforward and very easy to apply. The illustrations at the end of the ordinance facilitate the requirements set forth.

Farmers Branch

Farmers Branch, Ordinance 1228, "Landscaping Requirements," Zoning Ordinance, City of Farmers Branch, Texas, January 15, 1979. Amended with Ordinance 1510, August 20, 1984.

This ordinance requires setback zones and yard areas as well as vehicular use areas to be planted and maintained so as to preserve the appearance, character and land values of surrounding neighborhoods. The ordinance also requires that a landscape plan and specifications be submitted for all projects other than residential and multifamily housing, to the Public Works Department, which approves the plan.

Landscape requirements call for five (5) percent of a site not covered by buildings to be landscaped. "Modular units" are described in order to distribute the five (5) percent landscaped area throughout the site. A minimum of five (5) percent of all land between buildings and street rights-of way must be landscaped. Parking areas visible from the street shall be "broken up with vertical landscaping."

The ordinance also gives definitions, plant material sizes and details as to how the ordinance is administered. Occupancy permits are denied or revoked to enforce the provisions of this ordinance.

Ordinance 1510 was added to clarify maintenance of landscaping.

This ordinance has been on the books for more than ten (10) years, placing it within the older generation of landscape ordinances.

Fort Worth

Fort Worth Landscape Ordinance, "Landscape Guide," November 1982.

The purpose of this ordinance is to preserve the existing landscape and protect future changes in the landscape. The ordinance requires the saving of as many existing trees as possible.

Four copies of landscape and irrigation plans, prepared by a Texas registered landscape architect, must be submitted to the Department of Development. The common and scientific names, sizes, quantity, and spacing between plants must be listed on the landscape plan. Any irrigation system within a parkway or median must be submitted for approval by the Building Official for an Encroachment Permit. Plant material for the parkway or median must be in accordance with the Forestry Ordinance of Fort Worth.

The landscape guide also covers landscaping requirements for parkways, medians, easements, parking areas, buffers, structural elements, and maintenance. This ordinance was updated and revised in 1998.

Galveston

Zoning Regulations, Section 29-67, "Vehicle Parking Regulations," n.d.

Galveston is located on the southeastern Texas coast of the Gulf of Mexico. This resort town was visited early in the century by a hurricane that reportedly cost more than six thousand (6,000) lives. Presently, officials in the City of Galveston are reviewing this ordinance with thoughts of making needed revisions.

This is a limited-issue landscape ordinance. It pertains primarily to parking lots, although some mention is made of trash container screening, right-of-way plantings and parking lot screening. All properties must come into compliance upon extension, reconstruction, resurfacing or structural alteration.

Minimal standards are given. Planting strips for screens must be four (4) feet wide, planted with five (5) foot tall shrubs, at maturity, and trees located fifty (50) feet on center. Parking lot plantings for commercial districts with two (2) or more vehicles, and residential districts with ten (10) or more vehicles, must be landscaped. Fifteen (15) square feet for each space or five (5) percent of the paved area must be set aside to be planted with one (1) tree or one (1) shrub. All parking lot planting zones must be at least sixteen (16) square feet.

Very minimal standards are given for plant materials, installation and maintenance. Site plans must be submitted, but minimal information is required.

It is curious that this gulf coast town does not make any mention of hurricane resistance standards or the value of community landscape as property protection devices in its landscape ordinance. We know that during Hurricane Andrew almost all destruction of trees was the result of their being poorly located, poor species selection or improper maintenance.

Perhaps when this ordinance is revised, some thought could be given to the relationship of landscape ordinances and hurricanes. It might make this city's ordinance one of the most geographically unique in the country.

Garland

Garland, "City of Garland Screening and Landscape Standards," February 3, 1987.

The purpose of this ordinance is to establish the installation and maintenance of landscaping and screening to protect and enhance the community's environmental, economic, and aesthetic quality, thereby contributing to the overall objective of promoting the public health, safety, and general welfare. This ordinance applies to the zoning districts of the City of Garland.

The Director of Planning is responsible for the review of landscaping and screening plans. The Environmental Code Enforcement Division is responsible for the enforcement of these standards. The plans are to be prepared by a licensed landscape architect, professional engineer, or architect registered in the State of Texas. The design of masonry walls must be sealed by a professional engineer. The major topics discussed are methods and materials, screening and landscaping of nonresidential yards from residential districts, screening and landscaping, preservation of existing trees and natural landscape, visibility, alternative compliance, maintenance and appeals. This ordinance also contains illustrations, similar to Figure 2.53, which facilitate the understanding of the technical requirements of the ordinance.

The stringent requirements for masonry walls are an aspect unique to this ordinance. Masonry walls and living screens are given two very different descriptions and uses.

This ordinance emphasizes a high-quality design by requiring many licensed professionals to prepare the development plans for all projects.

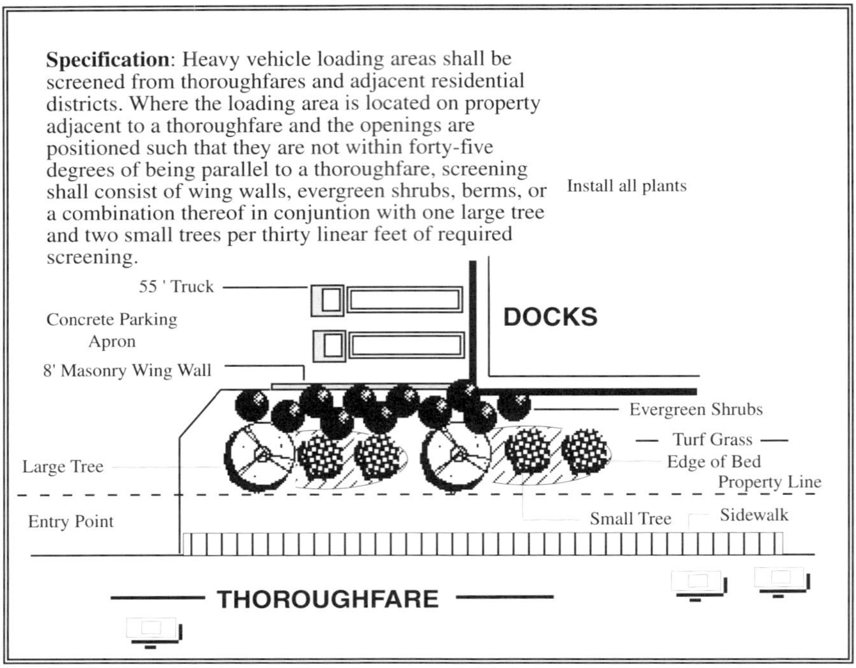

FIGURE 2.53. Screening of loading docks, Garland, Texas.

Grand Prairie

Grand Prairie, "Landscaping and Screening," Article VIII, Unified Development Code, November 20, 1990.

The purpose of this article is to ensure adequate landscaping and screening and to provide a pleasant visual environment for the city. This ordinance applies, within the corporate limits of Grand Prairie, to new developments and old ones that have additions of more than fifty (50) percent. The ordinance requires the submittal of a plan and all landscaping to be shown on the plan. The Chief Building Official, and in some instances the Planning and Zoning Commission and City Council, is charged with the administration of this law.

The ordinance focuses mainly on screening of undesirable views. It requires plant screening at parking areas next to public rights-of-way and areas parallel to arterial and collector streets. Fence screening is required at outdoor storage areas, mechanical and electrical equipment areas, refuse containers, alleyways and where residential areas meet nonresidential. This document also requires the planting of two (2) or more of grass, trees, shrubs, ground covers or other plant materials; protection of plantings from vehicles; and street tree plantings on arterial and collector streets in single-family or double-occupancy areas. Furthermore, it requires that developments of more than one thousand (1,000) square feet have an irrigation system, that upkeep of landscaping be done with a one (1)-year inspection after installation and that landscaping be in accordance with the Master Thoroughfare Plan.

Specific standards are given for plant material sizes, fence construction and street tree planting.

This ordinance has several features not usually found in a community landscape ordinance. It allows and encourages the planting of perennials along public rights of way by clubs, organizations, corporations and neighborhood associations. Assistance with the growing of plants for these areas is available at the city greenhouse, with the help of the Parks and Recreation Department and the city.

This article has rather stringent fencing construction requirements and allows only seventeen (17) species to be used for street trees.

Overall, this ordinance is clear, concise and easy to read, but it is not very ambitious and says nothing about the issue of enforcement.

Houston

City of Houston Ordinance No. 91-1701, Amending Chapter 33 of the Code of Ordinances of the City of Houston and the Building Code of the City of Houston, December 10, 1991.

The purpose of this ordinance is to improve air quality, reduce noise, glare, and reflected heat, mitigate adverse environmental effects of development and provide screening. This ordinance applies to any new development requiring a building permit, or any new additions to existing development greater than one thousand (1,000) square feet. The requirements apply to the entire building site, but can be installed in increments proportional to the progress of the building development. Landscape plans are to be submitted when applying for a building permit. No landscape architect or other professional is required to prepare the plans.

Credit for trees can be earned in the following three ways: by planting trees with a larger caliper than required, by preserving existing on-site trees and by paying a deposit to the city's Department of Parks and Recreation. Where credit for the preservation of existing trees is desired, a separate landscape plan must be submitted. This additional plan must include all information necessary to meet the required tree number and to complete any transplantation of existing trees. The number of street trees required depends on how many linear feet a property abuts a public street. The spacing intervals at which the trees must be planted are also regulated according to large trees, medium trees, or small trees. There is to be one (1) tree for every ten (10) parking spaces located within the interior of a parking area. Screening is required when any nonresidential or multifamily residential development abuts a single-family residence. The screening must be opaque, six (6) feet tall, fifteen (15) feet wide and extend along the entire property line (excluding driveways). Application submissions for a variance must include an application supplied by the city and a nonrefundable fee of two hundred (200) dollars.

Approval of the variance depends on its conformance to the intent of this ordinance and on a majority vote of "the commission." A waiver can be applied for if the area in which planting is required is too small to accommodate the required planting without damage to utilities, curbs, sidewalks, roadways, street lights or drainage facilities. A parking plan must be prepared and submitted to the building official and the traffic engineer. No trees may be located on, extend into or intrude upon any portion of the roadway or sidewalk.

Artificial lot, an interesting term used in this ordinance, does not mean that artificial plantings can be used. It refers to a parcel of land on the developing site that is set aside to contain the plantings required by this ordinance. *Documented assurance*, also used often, refers to a copy of an executed contract for the proper installation of the required landscaping in accordance with the approved landscape plan. This documentation must be submitted when applying for a Certificate of Occupancy before the landscaping requirements are complete. A Certificate of Occupancy granted before the planting requirements are complete is strictly conditional upon the completion of the requirements within a six (6)-month period. If documented assurance is not available, a refundable bond worth 1.25 times the proposed cost to install the required landscaping must be submitted.

This ordinance also contains many appendixes. Appendix A-1 includes the botanical names, common names, and comments on large trees for Houston. Appendix A-2 includes the botanical names, common names, and comments on small trees for Houston. Appendix A-3 includes the common names and botanical names for the Department of Parks and Recreation street trees. Appendix B lists tree selection, tree planting and watering procedures for Houston. Appendix C lists general procedures, tree protection zones, and maintenance for tree protection. Appendix D lists the expected heights after three (3) years, the common names and botanical names for shrubs. Appendix E explains shrub selection, shrub planting and shrub watering. Appendix F lists the costs for various sized trees, shrubs and vines, mulch and fences.

There are also many diagrams illustrating the requirements within the ordinance. Figure A illustrates site visibility triangles. Figure B illustrates street tree planting. Figure C illustrates esplanade planting, and Figure D illustrates screening.

Irving

Irving, Community Development: Building Setbacks and Landscape Ordinance, Ordinance Number 4967, Amending Chapter 33A of the Code of Civil and Criminal Ordinances of the City of Irving, Texas, "Landscape and Setback," March 5, 1992.

The main emphasis of this ordinance is setbacks and streetscapes. The ordinance is chiefly oriented toward commercial and industrial uses. Setback size areas are determined by specific streets listed. Developments adjacent to interstate highways require a forty (40) foot setback. Tree preservation is also a concern. This ordinance is enforced through the issuing of a building permit. No landscape architect or other professional is required to prepare the plans for development.

A unique aspect of the ordinance is a section describing how calculations are to be made. This section gives more detail on exactly where calculations should start and end. Illustrations are given to facilitate the understanding of the ordinance.

This is a very formal ordinance, making it unlawful to violate any of the requirements. Even the building inspector is prohibited from issuing a building permit for a development in violation of the requirements. If the building inspector does issue such a permit, the permit is considered void.

Irving, Ordinance Number 6095, Amending Chapter 33A of the Code of Civil and Criminal Ordinances of the City of Irving, Texas, March 5, 1992.

The purpose of this ordinance is to clarify the Landscape and Setback Ordinance and add pedestrian walkways to the definition of *landscaped*.

This ordinance establishes a minimum fifteen (15)-foot interior parkway required for pedestrian circulation. Pedestrian walkways are not to exceed four (4) feet in width. This area must be kept clean. The ordinance ends with requirements for enforcement and maintenance.

Plano

Plano, "Landscaping Requirements," 3-1200, May 27, 1992.

The purpose of this ordinance is to provide landscape screening for parking lots and rights-of-way and to outline the maintenance requirements for these landscaped areas. The rights-of-way and parking lot requirements apply to all nonresidential districts except CB and CB-1, and there are a few requirements for single- and multifamily residences.

Landscape/irrigation plans must be submitted to the Planning and Transportation and Engineering Departments. No professional training is required to prepare these plans.

This ordinance does not call for much that is unusual. One unique aspect is that any building existing before the adoption of this ordinance that is being redeveloped more than thirty (30) percent must adhere to the requirements of the ordinance.

Richardson

Richardson, Article XIII-A, Section 4, "Richardson, Texas, Code, Appendix A—Zoning," 1988.

This three (3)-page article primarily addresses apartment complex design standards and requirements. Subjects included in the article include apartment parking area specification and maintenance requirements; parking area lighting; accessory building requirements; apartment structure coverage requirements per total areas of the lot tract; landscape and site plan approval; ingress and egress to parking and service areas; and refuse and waste storage.

Round Rock

Round Rock City Code, Ordinance No. 2290, "Landscape Ordinance," n.d.

This landscape ordinance was adopted for several reasons, foremost of which was the desire to replenish the local stock of native vegetation, protect the unique identity and environment of Round Rock and safeguard and protect property values. The ordinance applies to all zoning classifications other than single-family residential and land in the central business district of the city. Landscaping requirements become applicable to each individual lot at the time application for a building permit is made. Substantial restoration of buildings constructed prior to the adoption of the ordinance, and all building permits issued prior to the effective date of the ordinance, are exempt.

A site plan prepared by a landscape architect, architect, engineer or licensed nurseryman must accompany any application for a building permit. For all projects in excess of two (2) acres in size, plans and certifications must be made by a landscape architect or architect only. Specific standards are given for what shall be shown on the site plan, most essential of which are calculations to show that all design components are included and all technical requirements have been met. Additional information is needed to seek approval to remove certain trees.

Design components in the City of Round Rock include street yard plantings, vehicular use areas and parking lots. Minimal design standards apply, which include:

a. Twenty (20) percent of the street yard is to be landscaped. Part of the right-of-way may be used to satisfy this requirement. Fifty (50) percent of this requirement applies to lots of less than ten thousand (10,000) square feet. Certain credits are given for preserving existing landscape.

b. Tree planting requirements: In street yards up to ten thousand (10,000) square feet, one (1) tree per one thousand (1,000) square feet; in street yards up to one hundred ten thousand (110,000) square feet, one (1) tree per twenty-five hundred (2,500) square feet; in street yards over one hundred ten thousand (110,000) square feet, one (1) tree per five thousand (5,000) square feet, plus fifty (50) additional trees.

c. All parked vehicles are to be effectively buffered from street view with two (2) gallon plants, three (3) feet on center or with berms or walls.

d. For all parking areas in the street yard, a minimum of ninety (90) square feet must be set aside for each twelve (12) parking spaces. No parking space shall be located farther away than fifty (50) feet from a tree.

e. All required landscaping must be irrigated with sprinklers, strip irrigation or hose attachment.

This city encourages the preservation of its existing natural character and classifies certain trees as "protected." Protected trees cannot be removed without a permit from the Director of Planning and Community Development. All oaks,

American elms, cedar elms, pecans, cottonwoods and sycamores with circumferences over twenty-five (25) inches are protected.

The ordinance is administered by the Building Inspection Division, and enforcement is ensured by withholding the Certificate of Occupancy. An inspection fee of five (5) cents per square foot for the required landscape area is assessed. This fee will not be more than three hundred (300) dollars or less than twenty-five (25) dollars and will be collected at the time at which the building permit application is made. The Inspection Division uses a Landscape Checklist to determine whether all requirements of the ordinance are met. The checklist helps the inspection officer to determine: (1) site plan requirements; (2) compliance with landscape regulations; (3) landscape credits and noncredits; and (4) to calculate inspection fees and ascertain protected trees.

This is one of the few ordinances in this study in which inspection fees are calculated on a square-foot basis.

San Marcos

Zoning Ordinance, Article No. 8, Section 114-671, "Landscaping, and Buffering," August 1985.

Preserving and improving the natural environment and maintaining a working ecological balance are of increasing concern to the citizens of San Marcos. They believe that the use of landscape elements can contribute to the processes of air purification, oxygen regeneration, water absorption and noise, glare and heat abatement, as well as the preservation of the community's aesthetic qualities. They have enacted requirements and standards for the installation and maintenance of landscape elements and site improvements to apply to all developed areas within the city, with the exception of the tightly organized central business district.

All properties must come under compliance when new building permits are taken out for expansion or renovations amounting to (50) fifty percent of the current replacement cost. A minimum percentage of lot area must be landscaped. The schedule shown in Table 2.95 indicates the requirements for each of several land uses.

TABLE 2.95. Required Landscaping Schedule, San Marcos, Texas

Land Use	*% Landscaping Required*
Town Houses	20 percent of site
Duplexes, Triplexes	20 percent of site
Apartments	20 percent of site
Office and Professional	15 percent of site
Commercial	10 percent of site
Industrial and Manufacturing	10 percent of site

Seventy (70) percent of the area requirement must be placed between the building and the front or side property lines. Undeveloped portions of the site do not count toward this amount.

This percentage amount is credited for preserving existing trees. For example, preserving a tree greater than twelve (12) inch caliper will reduce this area by two hundred (200) square feet. Extra credit (one hundred (100) square feet) is given for preserving select species of trees listed in Exhibit A on file in the city secretary's office.

Existing trees along the San Marcos and Blanco Rivers and within any floodway are to be maintained .

Design parameters are pretty much left up to whoever prepares the required landscape plans for review by Planning and Development Review Department. Some reference is made to parking lot plantings, screenings and buffering, but no really specific design standards are listed. Minimal installation, maintenance and plant material standards are included. Buffer yard requirements are referenced to Article 5, Chapter 94, pertaining to planned development districts. There is no mention of irrigation or licensing requirements.

The greater part of the ordinance is devoted to its administrative aspects. Included are sections dealing with enforcement, plan approval, variances, appeals and assessing credits for preserving existing trees and drainage ways. The City Manager is the enforcing agent, and the Director of Planning and Development Review is charged with all planning decisions. They have the authority to place noncompliance notices, as shown in the graphic tombstone facsimile in Figure 2.54.

> These premises are in violation of the requirements of the City of San Marcos Landscaping and Buffering Ordinance. This notice is to remain as placed here until the requirements of the ordinance have been complied with. It is unlawful to remove this notice until the requirements have been complied with.
>
> San Marcos, Texas
> City Manager

FIGURE 2.54. Facsimile of notice of noncompliance, San Marcos, Texas.

Because of the lack of design specificity and extra concern with administrative matters in this ordinance, one might assume that the document was drafted by someone more familiar with legal details than with design. The ordinance falls short of language that might lead to better community design. However, this ordinance might serve as a good model for someone wishing extra information about enforcement, variances and appeals.

Southlake

Southlake, Landscape Ordinance No. 544, January 21, 1992.

The purpose of this ordinance is to balance the need for landscape treatment and the need for commercial growth in the city through mutually beneficial incentives rather than penalties.

This ordinance does not have a major area of emphasis. It lists landscape and irrigation requirements, which explain that the ordinance applies to all nonresidential and multifamily developments. Each zoning area is given a percentage of required landscape area and planting requirements per square footage. Parking area requirements for landscape islands, existing trees, visibility, irrigation, plant material, improvements in public rights-of-way, and maintenance are provided. Screening, outside storage and buffer yards specified in Ordinance No. 480 are required to be shown on landscape and irrigation plans. These requirements must also be shown on the landscape plans required by this (No. 544) ordinance. All plantings, screening, berms and other requirements of this ordinance must be installed prior to the issuance of a Certificate of Occupancy.

All irrigation plans are to be prepared by a licensed landscape architect or other professional. Lots greater than thirty thousand (30,000) square feet require a registered landscape architect to prepare the plans. In the instance that improvements to the right-of-way irrigation system are made, the city may prohibit installation of the irrigation system until improvements have been installed. If improvements to the right-of-way irrigation are made after the installation of the development's irrigation, it will not be the responsibility of the city or the owner to replace these improvements.

This ordinance is formal, yet noncommittal. It gives a requirement, then gives an exception for each requirement.

Victoria

Victoria. Landscaping, Subdivision and Development Code, 1992.

Victoria believes that it is the duty of the community to establish requirements for the installation and maintenance of landscaping on developed properties to improve, protect and preserve the appearance, character and value of neighborhoods. This ordinance applies to all new construction and to remodeling of an existing structure that increases the gross floor area or off-street parking facility by twenty-five (25) percent or more. Single-family and two-family projects do not have to comply with the provisions of this ordinance.

The ordinance applies to the design of several site features that have been referred to earlier as design components. They include general site landscape area, off-street parking areas, screening fences and planting zones within public rights-of-way. The latter space is usually planted with street trees.

The site landscape area must be a minimum of ten (10) percent of the total building site, less the area of buildings and secured storage area. At least fifty (50) percent of this amount, five (5) percent of site, must be within the street yard. The percentage may be reduced by the Planning Director in the case of multifamily developments so that a larger amount of open space can occur between buildings.

Within the site landscape area a combination of trees, shrubs, annuals, perennials, vines, grass and ground cover may be used to satisfy this ordinance. Nonliving materials such as stone, organic mulch, walls, fences and sand may be used as well. Walkways and driveways made of pervious material within this area shall not count toward total landscape area. The minimum dimension of a landscape area shall be nine (9) square feet.

Within parking areas, islands are to be used as landscape zones. At least one (1) tree must be provided for each nine hundred (900) square feet of landscape zone.

Credit will be given toward the planting requirements of this ordinance for the preservation of existing trees.

Performance standards are listed in this ordinance for plant material installation, irrigation and maintenance. The use of Xeriscape principles published by the Texas Agricultural Extension Services is encouraged. Technical standards are given for plant materials and specific reference is made to a list of trees recommended by the County Agricultural Extension Service.

The administrative components of this ordinance are quite clear. In order to get a building permit for any site, a landscape plan is required as part of the site plan submittal process. The plan must provide sufficient information, including site improvement facilities, plant materials and calculations showing that the plan meets the requirements of this part. The Director of Planning reviews and approves the plan.

In an instance in which following the letter of this ordinance becomes a hardship, owing to several listed factors, an "alternative compliance" plan may be submitted along with written justification. Should approval be denied, the applicant for a building permit may appeal the decision of the Director of Planning to the Planning Commission.

The Director of Building and Environmental Inspection is charged with enforcing this ordinance and will not issue a Certificate of Occupancy until such time as all landscaping has been installed in accordance with the approved landscape plan.

The administrative procedures, especially the alternative compliance provision, of this ordinance make this a well thought out, well-organized, workable ordinance.

Virginia

Chesapeake

Land Use Code, § 22.20-520, "Tree Preservation and Landscape Development," March 1996.

Chesapeake has summarized its landscape ordinance in a design manual titled "Chesapeake Landscape Specifications Manual."

This document contains sections on definitions, tree preservation and planting, tree selection and standards of field practice. The latter cover implementation work, including grade changes, trenching, tree removal, pruning and repair. In addition, the design manual contains ten (10) appendices that pertain to plant material selection, tree care and typical construction details.

Contained within this document is a discussion of the landscape and tree preservation review procedures. It describes preparation and submittal of a landscape plan, field inspection and issuance of the Certificate of Occupancy. This process is used for commercial, multifamily and residential projects.

Standards are given for tree protection during construction, preservation and retention of natural areas, as well as canopy calculations to meet the minimum coverage requirement of the ordinance. To determine canopy coverage requirements, the formula illustrated in Table 2.96 is used.

TABLE 2.96. Calculating Tree Canopy Coverage, Chesapeake, Virginia

Given:

A = Percent of site requiring coverage set by ordinance, example 30%
B = Plantable area (calculation area from site plan) in square feet, example 20,000 sf
C = Total number of square feet of new canopy, following clearing, example 3,000 sf
D = Number of trees to be provided

$$\frac{A \times B}{C} = D \qquad \frac{.30 \times 20{,}000}{3{,}000} \qquad \frac{6{,}000}{3{,}000} = 20$$

The total square footage of new canopy provided must equal the required percentage of of the site calculation area, or 6,000 sf.

Therefore, 20 trees are required that total

10 large canopy trees at 400 square feet each =	4,000 sf
5 medium canopy trees at 300 square feet each =	1,500 sf
5 small canopy trees at 150 square feet each =	750 sf
	6,250 sf

The design manual concentrates on the tree preservation and care and implementation of the landscape plan. Little emphasis is placed on design, although this community takes great care to require that landscape architects or other experienced landscape designers be involved with the preparation of landscape designs.

A designer must consult appropriate sections of the zoning or subdivision ordinance in order to determine the design components of this ordinance. The design manual does not summarize them, and this is perceived as a weakness.

Fairfax County

Fairfax County, "Vegetation Preservation and Planting," 1986.

This ordinance, large enough to be considered a booklet, represents the consolidation into one publication of all the regulations of Fairfax County concerning site plans; vegetation, preservation and planting; and parking lot landscaping and screening. Included in the ordinance are a sample conservation agreement; construction detail sketches; a tree selection chart (includes moisture requirements, soil requirements, type of root system, salt tolerance, air pollution sensitivity and Virginia Department of Highways and Transportation approved street trees); and a transitional screening and barrier matrix.

Having had green laws since the late 1960s, Fairfax County is far ahead of other areas in defining the importance of plant materials in the community. Within one of several community codes (zoning, subdivision and conservation ordinances and a Public Facilities Manual) there is "green legislation" for everything from plant selection guidelines, to special tree preservation, to the duties of the local tree commission and the county arborist. This plant-sensitive county deserves attention and could be a model for our future.

Norfolk

Norfolk, Zoning Ordinances: Articles I–V, Chapter 17, "Landscaping and Buffers," March 3, 1992.

The purpose of this ordinance is to provide for the landscaping and buffering of all building sites and parking areas. The regulations are intended to promote the public health, safety and general welfare by preventing soil erosion; providing shade; protecting from excess noise, glare, and heat; conserving the natural resources of air and water; enhancing the appearance of developed sites; and facilitating a harmonious, attractive streetscape.

This ordinance applies to all zoning cases in which site plan review is required. The Department of Parks and Recreation and the Department of City Planning and Codes Administration will review landscape plans, which must be prepared by a certified nurseryman or landscape architect. Specific items and specifications to be shown on the landscape plan are listed.

Planting requirements for buildings and yards, parking lots, parking garages and buffer yards are given. Submittal conditions for alternative plans are described.

Planting season, maintenance and installation methods are detailed. The ordinance states that existing trees shall be preserved whenever possible, and, when in doubt, young trees are to be favored. All landscaping material must meet the minimum specifications described in the "American Standard of Nursery Stock," 1986.

The ordinance requires that ten (10) percent of the site, exclusive of paved areas, be landscaped and that eight (8) percent of all parking lots be landscaped. Area-specific requirements are given for numbers of trees or shrubs and sizes of planting areas.

Also included in this ordinance are provisions for site elements, facade planting, planting season, tree preservation, enforcement, alternative landscape plan submittal and maintenance.

This ordinance appears to be written from a nurseryman's perspective.

Spotsylvania

Spotsylvania County Code, Chapter 23, Division 5, "Landscaping and Screening," and related documents. Ord. No. 23-66, October 24, 1995.

Spotsylvania is located in eastern Virginia near the old antebellum city of Fredericksburg, not far from the area where Custer's 7th Michigan Calvary Brigade whipped the dashing J. E. B. Stuart and his 1st Virginia cavalry. This community has enacted a modest landscape ordinance, appended with a very detailed County Design Standards Manual. The intent of the ordinance is to make incompatible land use compatible, improve parking lots, preserve groundwater supplies and ameliorate storm water drainage problems. The ordinance applies to all development in which site plans are reviewed.

Standards have been developed for the preservation, installation and maintenance of landscaping as well as for adding required tree cover and screening. Specific sections of the ordinance address parking lot interiors, parking lot peripherals, transitional screening and planted trees. Figure 2.55 shows one example of transitional screening allowed in this community.

The tree planting standard calls for a certain percentage (ten (10) to twenty (20) percent) of site coverage for each zoning district within a period of twenty (20) years. A nine (9)-step formula for calculating this percentage is given in the design manual and is shown in Table 2.97.

Other standards are based on linear foot measure, area measure and specified quantities. Requirements are also given for preparation of the landscape plan, planting and maintenance.

Direct reference is made to the County Design Standards Manual. This document goes into considerable detail, giving background information and specifications for the design standards mentioned in the ordinance. In fact, this document is quite detailed and would lead any developer to think that a landscape architect would be required to unravel the intricacies of the code.

The manual is divided into several sections, which cover all of the aforementioned design components as well as standards, specifications, tree selection,

Specification: Transitional screening shall consist of an unbroken strip of open space a minimum of 25 feet wide and planted with one large evergreen tree with an ultimate height of 40 feet or greater planted 10 feet on center. In addition, plant one medium evergreen tree with an ultimate height of 20 to 40 feet for every five linear feet.

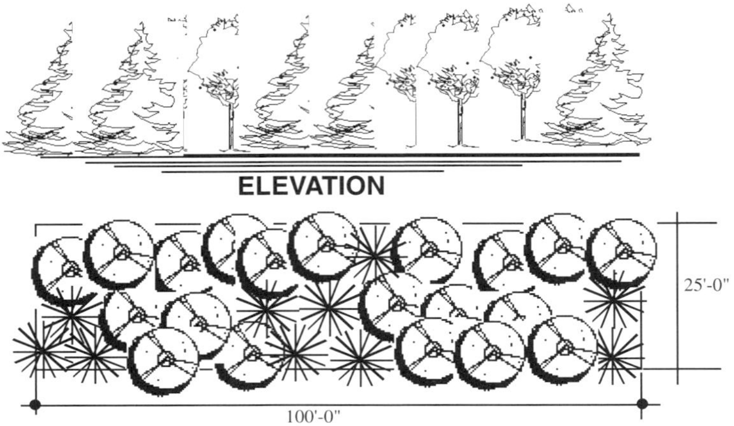

FIGURE 2.55. Transitional screening Type 1, Spotsylvania County, Virginia.

TABLE 2.97. Tree Cover Calculation Formula—Commercial Industrial Districts, Spotsylvania, Virginia

1. Calculate gross site area (GSA) in square feet	30,000 sf
2. Calculate footprint of building, subtract from GSA	5,000 sf
3. Calculate area of 2% grade away from buildings, add to (2) above	2,000 sf
4. Adjusted gross site area (AGSA)	23,000 sf
5. Multiply AGSA by required percent of tree cover area (10%)* (23,000 × .10)	2,300 sf
6. Required tree cover	2,300 sf
7. Calculate percent of cover for preserved existing × 1.5† (1,000 sf × 1.5 = 1,500)	1,500 sf
8. Tree cover deficiency	800 sf
9. Determine 20 yr coverage for proposed trees (ex. *Carpinus caroliniana* 125 sf)	6.4 trees

* From Table 6.3, Required Tree Cover Percentage

† Growth rate factor for 20 years of tree growth

waivers and administration. Graphics, including many tables and plates, illustrate and assist in the explanation of the standards and specifications. Plates or specifications sheets show everything from how to build a retaining wall, to site grading around trees, to how to plant one of three types of buffers. These plates contain drawings, notes and dimensions.

One of the most interesting things about this ordinance is the requirement, mentioned earlier, for a percentage of tree coverage in each zoning district. This encourages developers to save trees. If they do not, they will have to add trees to the site to meet the required percentages over a twenty (20)-year period.

This ordinance is well presented and encourages tree preservation. The County Design Standards Manual makes it easy for trained individuals to determine the requirements.

Suffolk

Zoning Ordinance, § 590.8, "Draft Landscape," December 1995.

In Suffolk, the City Planning Commission and Beautification and Litter Commission are working together to write, implement and refine a landscape ordinance. The draft ordinance will be added to the Zoning Ordinance as §590.8.

This ordinance sets forth minimum planting requirements for screening, perimeter buffers, visibility triangles, street edge plantings and vehicular use area plantings. In addition, and quite unique for a landscape ordinance, a sign landscaping design component is included in this ordinance. A landscape plan and a sign landscape plan must be submitted for review as the first step in satisfying the requirements of this law. Standards are contained within the ordinance for preparation of these plans.

Other standards are presented for plant materials, plant selection and installation, tree preservation, tree protection and tree canopy coverage. Standards for tree canopy coverage in this community are shown in Table 2.98. Existing trees that are preserved and new trees that are to be planted are to comprise the tree canopy.

The Planning Commission is considering the preparation of a design manual, "Guidelines for Landscape Planting in the City of Suffolk," to supplement the ordinance as a guide for developers and designers who may be unfamiliar with standard planting/design/horticultural practices.

TABLE 2.98. Tree Canopy Coverage Standards, Suffolk, Virginia

Zoning District	*Standard*
Business Districts	10 percent coverage
Industrial Districts	10 percent coverage
Residential Districts 10–20 units per acre	15 percent coverage
Residential Districts less than 10 units per acre	20 percent coverage

Virginia Beach

Zoning Ordinance, Section 5A, "Parking Lots and Foundation Landscaping," June 11, 1990, Ord. No. 486. Related Law, Zoning Ordinance, Appendix E, "Tree Planting, Preservation and Replacement," June 11, 1990, Ord. No. 1965.

Virginia Beach has great natural beauty, and its landscape contributes to the ecological well-being, aesthetic sensibilities and economic prosperity of the city and its citizens. The City Council has adopted a limited-issue landscape ordinance for the purpose of maintaining this rich landscape heritage while safeguarding and enhancing property values and public and private investments.

This ordinance consists of design components, as seen in Table 2.99.

The ordinance defines intent, applicability, administrative procedures, and requirements for VUA interior areas, parking lot street edge screens, screening requirements and foundation requirements.

Specifications, standards and technical requirements are placed in Exhibit A and attached to the ordinance. Exhibit A, Parking Lot and Foundation Landscaping Specifications and Standards, sets forth size, spacing and material standards for landscape materials. Tree credits are explained, as is the landscape plan preparation process. In this community landscape designs must be prepared by certified or licensed landscape architects or well-experienced and trained landscape designers. Tree lists, plant material installation details and written standards for protecting trees on development sites are included in Exhibit A.

The ordinance applies to all new development in the city.

The Landscape Services Division of the city has prepared a design manual, "A User's Guide for the City of Virginia Beach Parking Lot and Foundation Landscaping Ordinance," to complement the ordinance. The manual is illustrated with graphics, tables, diagrams, specifications and helpful appendixes to make it easy to understand all design components, requirements and standards. The guide was written, in part, to answer frequently asked questions about the law.

TABLE 2.99. Landscape Design Components, Virginia Beach, Virginia

Component	*VUA Interiors*	*Street Frontage*	*Foundations*	*Screening*
Parking Lots	yes	yes	n/a	n/a
Display Areas	yes	yes	n/a	n/a
Buildings	n/a	n/a	yes	n/a
Parking Garage 1	n/a	n/a	yes	n/a
Parking Garage 2	n/a	yes	n/a	n/a
Loading Docks	n/a	n/a	n/a	yes
Trash Receptacles	n/a	n/a	n/a	yes

Parking Garage 1 has business use on first floor.
Parking Garage 2 has parking on first floor.

Planting requirements and specifications are based on unit, linear and area measure.

The Virginia Beach tree ordinance is a limited issue ordinance pertaining specifically to the preservation, planting and replacement of trees. The ordinance sets forth the intent, standard definitions, application of the law, violations, penalties, variances and appeals procedures.

The ordinance sets tree canopy standards based on land use and area coverage, standards for tree protection during construction and street tree planting procedures. Master Street Tree Plans must be drawn and approved for each subdivision development in the city.

No Certificates of Occupancy will be granted until all required plantings are inspected and approved by the Permits and Inspection Division.

Virginia Beach has a landscape ordinance and companion tree documents that are well organized and fairly easy to understand. The foundation planting requirements are somewhat unique, even though they are not very comprehensive from a design point of view. The design manual and Exhibit A do a good job of explaining highly complex technical data.

Williamsburg

Zoning Ordinance, Environmental Protection, Article IV, "Trees," August 12, 1993, Ord. No. 22-93. Related Law, Chapter 21, Zoning, § 21-614 "Tree Regulations."

This community takes great pride in its trees. In the Chesapeake Bay region tree preservation is seen as a major tool in preserving the environmental quality of the rivers, streams and tidal lands of the Chesapeake Bay.

This ordinance is intended to preserve several classes of trees, protect existing trees on public property and manage tree planting projects along public streets and in public parks.

Heritage, memorial, specimen and street trees are defined and can be so designated by act of the city council. These trees are protected and cannot be removed, damaged or destroyed. All pruning of public trees is to be undertaken by city tree crews.

Trees on private land may be designated in one of these categories after notification of the landowner, public hearing and appeal. A "takings clause" is inserted into this ordinance: "In the event that this section results in any taking of private property for public purpose or use, the city council shall compensate the property owner for such taking by fee or other consideration."

The ordinance does not apply to federal or state property, routine public utility maintenance, activities with minor effects on trees and commercial silviculture or horticultural operations.

Tree regulations set forth in § 21-614 apply to trees located in Chesapeake Bay Preservation Areas.

Yorktown

Yorktown, Ordinance, Zoning, Amending Articles I, II, III, IV, V, VI and VII of Chapter 24 of the York County Code, May 18, 1989.

The intent of this ordinance is to preserve trees in order to control soil erosion and the transport of sediment, protect and improve the quality of surface water and groundwater, screen noise and dust and preserve, protect and enhance the natural environment. The intent of the transitional buffer regulations established in this ordinance are to minimize potential conflicts between potentially incompatible land uses located in abutting zones.

The landscape plan required for a Certificate of Zoning Compliance or a Certificate of Occupancy is to be prepared by a design professional. A landscape architect is required to select appropriate plant species for the intended use.

This ordinance emphasizes designs that appear natural, such as the berms shown in Figure 2.56, and designs that preserve the existing vegetation. The ordinance divides plant materials into six different categories, lists those species appropriate for the Yorktown area and gives minimum heights and branching spreads for each. Transitional buffer zones are given type numbers, and each type number has different requirements. For example, Transitional Buffer Type 25 shall consist of a strip of open space, a minimum of twenty-five (25) feet wide, landscaped to

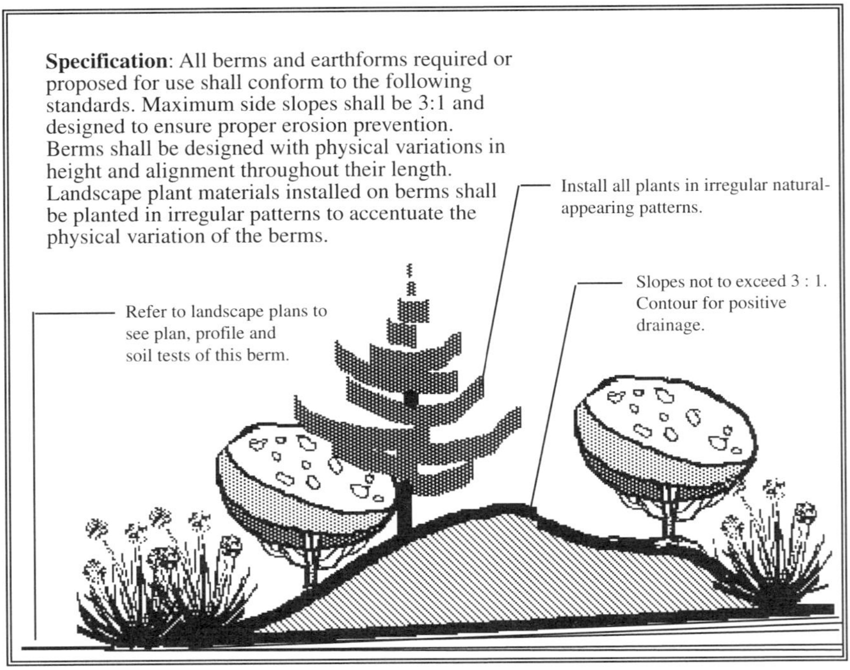

FIGURE 2.56. Standards for berms and earthforms, Yorktown, Virginia.

achieve the following ratio, at minimum: one (1) large evergreen tree (ultimate height forty (40) feet) *or* one (1) large deciduous shade tree (ultimate height fifty (50) feet) for every ten (10) linear feet measured along the outside edge of the transitional buffer, plus one medium evergreen tree (ultimate height twenty (20) to forty (40) feet) for every five (5) linear feet measured along the outside edge of the transitional buffer, *plus* one medium evergreen tree (ultimate height twenty (20) to forty (40) feet for every five (5) linear feet measured along the outside edge of the transitional buffer. Then a chart is provided, showing the buffer type numbers for the various zones required between abutting land uses. General site requirements for buffer/setback zones and special requirements are given for each land use. Infiltration yards are to be located on all sides of every development. General screening/landscape standards for shopping centers and off-street parking are given. Four (4) square feet of landscaping must be provided for every one (1) square foot of signage.

Where any soil-disturbing activities are proposed in conjunction with tree harvesting, except in preparations for reforestation, an erosion and sedimentation control plan must be submitted to and approved by the county prior to commencement of soil disturbance.

In its efforts to preserve as much as possible the existing natural environment, this ordinance includes unique definitions for *mature, heritage, memorial* and *specimen* trees. A mature tree is any deciduous or coniferous tree with a minimum diameter (caliper) of fourteen (14) inches when measured four and one-half (4½) feet above ground level. A heritage tree is any tree that has been designated by ordinance of the Board of Supervisors as having notable historic or cultural significance to any site, or that has been so designated in accordance with an ordinance adopted pursuant to Section 15.1-503.2 of the Code of Virginia. A memorial tree is any tree that has been designated by ordinance of the Board of Supervisors to be a special commemorating memorial. A specimen tree is any tree that has been designated by ordinance of the Board of Supervisors to be notable by virtue of its outstanding size and quality for its particular species.

Yorktown, Ordinance, Amending Sections 2, 4, 5-1, and to add Section 4-21 of Appendix B to the Subdivision Ordinance of the Yorktown County Code, May 18, 1989.

The purpose of this ordinance is to preserve a rural wooded atmosphere; all significant and historic trees located within the area encompassed by development shall be preserved and protected. The removal of trees or clearing of land is prohibited, except to accommodate the construction and installation of the improvements required by the ordinance. The definitions for this section are the same as in the aforementioned ordinance. The definitions, purpose and plat requirements are the only contents of this ordinance.

Yorktown, Ordinance, Amending Sections 10-3, 10-5, 10-6, 10-26 and 10-29 of Chapter 10, Erosion and Sediment Control, of the Yorktown County Code, May 18, 1989.

The purpose of this ordinance is to control the land-disturbing activities regulated and approved under the requirements of this chapter, in order to ensure a minimum of disturbance of the natural environment and vegetation, and in a manner that will prevent indiscriminate or excessive clearing of trees or undue damage caused by erosion or sedimentation.

This ordinance also has the same definitions as those of the Yorktown Zoning Ordinance. The following specific uses and activities are excluded from the terms of the chapter: tilling, planting or harvesting of agricultural or horticultural crops; and forestry where a Forest Management Plan has been prepared and/or approved by the Virginia Department of Forestry and all operations are in accordance with the approved plan. This ordinance contains important definitions, its purpose and the requirements for the plans to be submitted for the approval of development.

Washington

Auburn

Zoning Code, City of Auburn, as amended, Chapter 18.50, "Landscaping and Screening," n.d.

Washington State has strong environmental laws that pertain to development. In some instances, landscape requirements for getting state approval for development far exceed local ordinances.

Some of the provisions of the existing landscape ordinance do not apply well to some of the "superdevelopments" now occurring across the states. When the ordinance was written, this type of large development was not conceived. Many of the requirements, such as spacing, plant size and screening, written for small- to medium-size commercial landscapes, do not work well for these large developments.

Cases in point are such recently completed projects as the Super Mall of the Great Northwest and Emerald Downs Racetrack. In these instances, many of the landscaping requirements were somewhat negotiated between the city and the developers.

This may be something to consider in writing a community ordinance. Landscape ordinances should react to project scale. What might work well for a mom-and-pop retail outlet may not work in new types of land use of greater scale and complexity.

The intent of Auburn's ordinance is to reduce erosion and storm water runoff while enhancing appearance and to protect property values and unify the various sections of the city. The landscape ordinance applies to all zoning categories, excluding single-family and duplex family. The renovation, expansion and alterations clause is set at fifty (50) percent of the value of the building.

This ordinance is land-use-designation specific, meaning that different requirements apply to different land use categories, which are far too many and too complex to describe here. Generally, the design components of this ordinance include

TABLE 2.100. Screen Types, City of Auburn, Washington

Type	*Design Mix*	*Opacity*
I	Evergreen trees, tall shrubs, low shrubs, ground cover, fence	Solid screen 100%
II	50% evergreen trees, 50% deciduous trees, shrubs, ground cover	Visual screen
III	75% deciduous trees, 25% evergreen, shrubs, ground cover	Visual buffer
IV	100% deciduous trees, shrubs, ground cover	See-through buffer

street frontage, screening (four (4) types), outdoor storage areas, parking lots, fences and berms. Minimal requirements are given for irrigation, sodding, maintenance and sight hazards. Screen types are shown in Table 2.100.

Specially mentioned in this ordinance are business parks. For this land use fifteen (15) percent of the site must be set aside for landscaping. No real specifications are given beyond the requirement to follow standards for an M-1 district.

Enforcement is contingent upon withholding the Certificate of Occupancy. For projects not completed prior to occupancy, the city requires a "performance assurance agreement" in the amount of one hundred (100) percent of the value of the landscaping. The duration of the agreement is one hundred twenty (120) days.

Trees defined as significant (evergreen over six (6) inches caliper, deciduous over four (4) inches caliper) cannot be removed and must be made part of the landscape design.

It is apparent that the provisions contained in this ordinance do not apply easily to new or special developments such as some of the newer superdevelopments or power malls. The City of Auburn intends to make revisions in the future.

Bellevue

Land Use Code, § 22.20-520, "Tree Preservation and Landscape Development," March 1996.

The citizens of Bellevue believe that preservation of significant trees and landscape development are necessary to protect property values and retain the natural wooded character of the Pacific Northwest. Well-designed or preserved natural landscapes reduce the impact of storm drainage, maintain water quality and provide better transition between land uses in the city.

The land use code landscape requirement applies to all development except single-family residential. For all sites larger than five hundred (500) square feet, the city requires certification from qualified landscape professionals such as registered landscape architects.

TABLE 2.101. Types of Landscaping, Bellevue, Washington

Type	*Purpose*	*Materials*
I	Very dense sight barrier	Evergreen trees, sight-obscuring fence
II	Visual separation between uses	Evergreen and deciduous trees, shrubs
III	Visual separation of uses	Evergreen and deciduous trees, shrubs, earth mounding
IV	Provide visual relief	Ground covers and shrubs lower than 36″
V	Visual relief/shade in parking areas	Tree, ground cover, decorative mulch, pavers

Significant trees within site perimeters and site interiors must be preserved. One hundred (100) percent of diameter inches within perimeters must be retained, and fifteen (15) percent must be retained within the interior of a site. Types of landscaping are defined in Table 2.101.

An incentive in the form of a ten (10) percent reduction in parking requirements will be allowed for preserving more than the minimum percentage of significant trees.

The ordinance contains design standards for perimeter landscaping, planting for specific uses, site landscaping and parking area landscaping. Landscaping is defined as one (1) of five (5) types, each accomplishing a different site planning purpose. Table 2.101 lists the five (5) types of landscaping recommended in this ordinance.

This ordinance has an alternative compliance clause, allowing the applicant to request modification of the landscaping requirements under certain conditions that will result in increased preservation of existing trees, greater solar access or increased winter wind protection.

Standards for plant material species selection and maintenance are included. Additional detailed landscape standards can be found for special overlay districts described in the land use code. Further landscape standards, related to development of transportation and park-related facilities, are found in a companion document titled the "Bellevue Development Manual." Included are typical planting standards, right-of-way design details and a list of approved street trees.

Federal Way

Zoning Ordinance, Article XVII, "Landscaping," Ordinance No. 93-170, April 20, 1993.

This ordinance was enacted to encourage creative landscaping designs that utilize native, drought-tolerant vegetation, retain existing vegetation and respond to state mandates for water conservation, energy use reduction and enhancement of water quality.

All zoning districts except single-family residential must comply with this ordinance. No permits shall be issued for any construction or development without submittal of a landscape plan subject to the city site plan review process.

All landscape plans must be prepared and bear the seal of a Washington State-licensed landscape architect.

Landscape components in this ordinance include the design of undisturbed open space, general open space, storage areas, trash enclosures, street tree plantings, sight distance zones, blank building walls, loading areas, landscape screens and parking lots.

Technical standards for landscape islands are depicted in Figure 2.57. Blank building walls uninterrupted by architectural features in excess of two hundred forty (240) square feet must be planted and screened with trees, shrubs and ground covers. Foundation landscaping is encouraged, but no design standards are given.

Design standards for landscape components are zoning district specific. Very specific standards are given for four (4) types of landscaping (primarily screens) and parking lot landscaping.

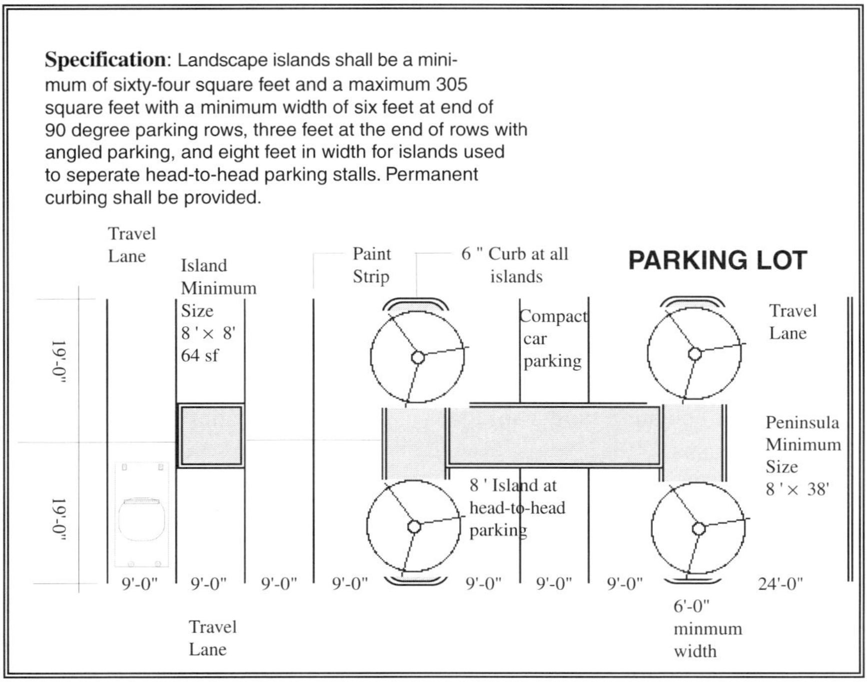

FIGURE 2.57. Interior landscape islands, Federal Way, Washington.

A very sensible tree preservation standard, protecting significant trees, is included in this ordinance. It is sensible because it recognizes that not all trees can be retained and that developers will retain trees if it is practical and credit is given for retaining significant trees. According to this clause, if more than seventy-five (75) percent of the significant trees are removed, up to twenty-five (25) percent must be replaced. This amount can be reduced further if large trees are used.

One of the nice things about this clause is that it fits well within the community's landscape ordinance. This might be a model for many other communities struggling to find a way to protect existing trees without seriously impacting development.

Requirements and standards are presented for protection of significant trees, plant materials, irrigation, performance and maintenance. Performance standards describe the administrative process involved which, upon completion, results in the award of a Certificate of Occupancy (CO).

An alternative compliance clause, termed Modification Options, as shown in Table 2.102, allows slight modifications to meeting the requirements of the ordinance under certain stated conditions and as approved by the Director of Community Development. Modification option proposals must meet or exceed the minimum standards. Some incentives apply to this section of the ordinance that can reduce the required perimeter landscape up to twenty five (25) percent.

Two interesting features of this ordinance are the standards for blank building walls mentioned earlier and the possible use of biofiltration swales and surface water quality structures incorporated into the landscape design. The latter design

TABLE 2.102. Alternative Compliance (Modification Options), Federal Way, Washington

Special Condition	*Results*
Preservation of wildlife habitat	Protects wildlife
Preservation of natural areas	Reduces destruction of nature
Compliance with special easements	Special conditions of land use
Renovation of existing landscaping	Preserves existing character
Unique site uses	Allow innovative design solutions
Proposed modifications represent a superior solution	Extra-special design
Proposed modifications meet intent of the ordinance	Special design beyond minimum standards
Would result in increased retention of existing trees	Prevents erosion, retains existing habitat
Special site conditions, shape, topography, surroundings	Specific circumstances add to uniqueness

requirement is something that should be incorporated into landscape ordinances in areas in which erosion and water quality are at issue.

Finally, the tree protection clause in this ordinance is very well done and could act as a model for other communities.

Medina

City of Medina, Ordinance No. 521, "An Ordinance Establishing Tree Preservation and Landscaping Requirements During Development," December 10, 1990.

The stated purpose of this ordinance is the retention of significant trees in relation to property development, and the installation of landscaping to enhance the visual appearance and "natural character" of the city. The ordinance also tries to reduce the environmental impact of development, stabilize slopes, improve the storm drainage system, provide a buffer between city streets and residential property and maintain the value of property.

Significant trees are defined as "any evergreen tree of eight inches in diameter or greater and any deciduous tree, other than red alder, willow, poplar and cottonwood trees, 10 inches in diameter or greater, measured from 4′6″ above the root crown." A chart is included in the ordinance, outlining the types of permits required for the various types of development. Permits are required for lot line adjustment, street right-of-way, building, and so on. A site survey, a tree retention plan, a landscape plan, and a tree preservation program are also required. The city's "Designated Official," defined as a landscape architect, arborist, building official or other person designated by the city from time to time, must review and approve these plans. In general, the standards intend to protect trees within rights-of-way, easements and building areas, or require replacement trees for those removed.

The ordinance includes lists of "Trees Generally Suitable for the City of Medina" and "Low Growing Trees Generally Suitable for the City of Medina."

Pullman

Title 17 Zoning Code, City of Pullman, Chapter 17.45, "Landscaping and Screening," March 31, 1987.

This ordinance applies to all new developments, including mobile home park expansion, and any additions to existing structures when the cost of the addition exceeds fifty (50) percent of the current assessed valuation. There are several stated purposes of this ordinance, but they are essentially meant to buffer adjacent land uses, improve the quality of the environment and make the city a more aesthetically pleasing place to live.

The ordinance does not explain the exact process for seeking approvals. The City Planner is indicated as the responsible party unless an aggrieved person appeals a decision to the Board of Adjustment. The City Planner reviews all written statements as well as a plan of proposed landscaping and screening submitted at the time of preliminary plat review, site plan review or building permit review. The plan must be drawn to scale and show dimensions, distances, grades, details and existing vegetation. Proposed landscaping and locations of all structures such as buildings, driveways, parking lots, sidewalks, curbs and the proposed irrigation system must also be depicted.

Design components in this ordinance include parking areas, loading berths, open space, land use buffers (screening), storage-scrap-waste areas and existing tree preservation. No planting area is to be less than twenty-four (24) square feet and must be protected with a four (4)-inch curb. In parking areas the ten (10) percent rule applies; that is, ten (10) percent of the parking lot must be devoted to landscaping. In addition, there is a standard for one (1) tree for every ten (10) parking spaces. Planting beds carry a minimum dimension of five (5) feet. Four (4) types of landscape screens are defined and graphically depicted for ease of understanding. Opacity is not defined except for Type I, which requires a density of plant material, primarily evergreens, sufficient to block sight through the screen.

Tree preservation is important in this community. Pullman defines significant trees as all healthy trees over twenty-five (25) feet in height or trees over ten (10) feet in height that form a continuous canopy. It requests that significant trees be retained; however, no real incentive or penalty is given in the ordinance in this regard. If more than fifty (50) percent of all significant trees are removed, the city may require that they be replaced. Several techniques are given for protecting trees during construction.

Contained within the code are acceptable reasons for modification of the landscape requirements. These include unique topography, views, change in use, excessive requirements that cannot be met, and existing vegetation. The decision of the City Planner is final unless an appeal is made.

Technical standards are given for screening, landscape plan preparation, tree protection and retention, as well as installation and maintenance standards. The standards are very minimal and not adequately defined.

This ordinance is similar to others in Washington. They must all have evolved together in the mid 1980s. As a group, they are somewhat dated, and some of the material does not reflect current thinking on the subject. Additional features of a more contemporary nature might be added to upgrade these ordinances to current standards.

Seattle

City of Seattle, Department of Construction and Land Use, Director's Rule 41-88, "Landscaping Standards for Compliance with the Land Use Code and Environmental Review (State Environmental Policy Act) Requirements," August 15, 1988.

The rule provides information for applicants who are required to submit a landscape plan. It is a supplement to the city's Land Use Code (Chapter 23) requirements for landscaping in multifamily, commercial, industrial and downtown zones.

The purpose of Seattle's landscaping ordinances is to lessen adverse impacts of a project, buffer incompatible land uses, block undesirable views, increase amount of permeable surfacing and reduce erosion and drainage problems. Visual beauty is a benefit, the rule states, along with the lessening of reflective glare, the visual breaking up of long walls and parking areas, the provision of shade and cooling, protection from wind and rain, reduction of dust, the provision of homes and food for wildlife, reduction in pollution, buffering of sound and creation of privacy.

The city requires three (3) sets of landscape plans at the time of Master Use Permit application. All landscape plans must include a mix of trees, shrubs and ground cover. The rule provides a minimum tree requirement for single-family and multifamily zones. For example, properties of less than seventy-five hundred (7,500) square feet must have one (1) tree for every eight hundred (800) square feet. Properties of seventy-five hundred (7,500) to fifteen thousand (15,000) square feet must have nine (9) trees, or one (1) per nine hundred (900) square feet—whichever is greater. Twice as many shrubs as required trees must be provided. The Director may require preservation of existing vegetation when it mitigates the impacts of the design proposal.

All landscape plans must show calculations of square footage, number of trees and spacing and use of existing plants; the species of all trees, shrubs and ground cover (common and botanical names); street trees; and an irrigation and drainage plan for rooftop or container landscaping. The rule includes an illustrated, five (5)-page "Landscape Applications" section.

Spokane

City of Spokane Zoning Code, Section 11.19.290, "Guidelines to Landscape Requirements," n.d.

The City of Spokane has adopted a landscape ordinance for special land uses within specific zoning classifications. All property within the following classifications is mentioned: Limited Zones (L Zones), Design Districts (D Zones), R Zones, B Zones and RO Zones.

The ordinance applies to new construction and renovation. The illustrated "Guidelines" have been written to serve as an information source for property owners, developers and design professionals. They cover landscaping requirements, screening, property perimeters, street frontage, parking areas and swale percolation areas (two hundred eight (208) areas). Very few technical specifications are given in the design guidelines.

The Zoning Code identifies three (3) types of landscaping that may be required in various situations:

> Type I—Visual Screen, consisting of a mix of evergreen and deciduous plantings including trees, shrubs and ground covers

Type II—See-Through Buffer, consisting of a mix of evergreen shrubs and ground covers

Type III—Open Area Landscaping, consisting of canopy deciduous trees and spreading evergreen trees with a mix of living evergreen and deciduous ground covers.

Maintenance is the responsibility of the owner. Automatic sprinkler systems are required.

Three types of landscape plans are submitted to the City of Spokane. Conceptual Plans are submitted with zoning applications and special permit applications; these indicate the type of required landscaping and the general location of landscape components. Irrigation Plans are submitted to show location of irrigation systems. Planting Plans are required at the building permit application stage. These plans show all site grading, structures, parking, boundaries, dimensions, quantities, plant materials and locations of all fences, walls, driveways and sidewalks.

The design guidelines include definitions and illustrative drawings in plan and elevation format. The drawings show various landscape arrangements, provide lists of suggested plant materials and make reference to the City of Spokane "Street Tree Guide."

This ordinance does not follow some of the contemporary organizational methods used in ordinance development in other places. In fact, the design guidelines representing the ordinance are somewhat disorganized and not very specific. This ordinance seems to be unique and an example of an ordinance that evolved organically in a localized area.

Wisconsin

Brookfield

Municipal Code Sections 17.035(3)8 and 18.04(6)(e)11, "Site Development Standards for Nonresidential Uses," October 1997.

This is a new type of landscape ordinance that may herald the next generation of postconstruction landscape ordinances based on design rather than quantities.

Recently, the City of Brookfield rewrote their old landscape ordinance, which was based on requirements for an allotted amount of trees or shrubs per linear foot of street yard. The city felt that the old method tended to make designers think in a "linear fashion" and the most designs ended up with plants evenly spaced in row. The new approach, which is one of the few design-based approaches in this study, creates greater ecological and aesthetic flexibility for the designer. The new ordinance requires minimum plant material selections and quantities based on square footage of street yard. Brookfield's new landscape standards require mandatory and advisory maintenance for at least three years.

The design standards cover seven elements that must be considered for all landscape plans prepared for approval by the city. The seven elements or design standards must address street yards; side and rear buffer strips; parking lot interiors; site building entrances and service utility yards; preservation of natural features and plant material selection, installation and maintenance. The ordinance is amply illustrated with drawings that explain the design standards and their calculation procedure. A list of acceptable plant materials and their coverage potential—used in the coverage calculations—is appended to this ordinance.

Landscape plans submitted to the Plan Commission for approval must now be stamped by registered landscape architects, another innovation in this ordinance.

In the future, more landscape ordinances may very well be written using the "design standards approach" exemplified in Brookfield's ordinance. As evidence that landscape standards for site development represent an innovative approach to landscape ordinances, this city received an award for this new city planning tool from the Wisconsin Chapter of the American Society of Landscape Architects.

Madison

Madison General Ordinances, Section 28.04, "Parking Lots, Storage Areas and Loading Areas," February 15, 1992.

Madison has set a framework to improve the appearance of the city with the enactment of its landscape ordinance. This community believes that the ordinance will soften the visual impact of vehicular uses areas, on-site storage areas and loading areas and will protect and enhance the visual environment within the limits of the city. Building site landscape zones, a principal component of this ordinance, are delineated in Figure 2.58.

The city has an Urban Design Commission that understands the importance of design. As a result the landscape ordinance take a strong approach to design. Building site landscape, areas such as shown in Figure 2.58, are covered in this ordinance. The ordinance includes a point system that allows maximum flexibility in design solutions. Unlike many of the communities in this study, which have developed a "formula-based method" of design, Madison has developed a system that allows unlimited use of canopy trees and other landscape elements. Unlike a formula-based system that requires so many plants of a prescribed size and habit, often spaced in a linear manner (with results not always appreciated by the public (see Figure 2.59)), this system allows considerable leeway in the use of a variety of elements as the designer sees fit to achieve the desired results. In addition, "point credits" can be achieved for preserving existing vegetation on site.

Landscape elements in this system and their point values are listed in Table 2.103.

The point system calculates the number of required trees for each site, based on the number of parking stalls, area of storage space and number of loading berths in the design. Total required canopy trees and total points devoted to a palette of landscape elements are figured in the following manner.

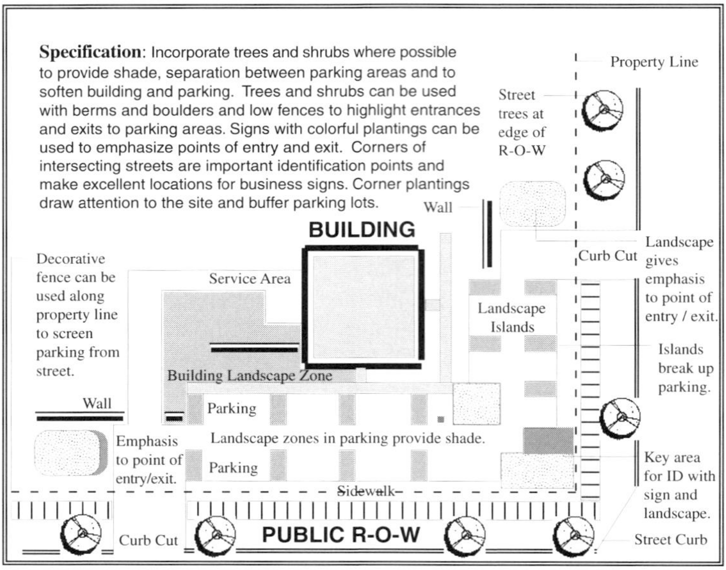

FIGURE 2.58. Building site landscape areas, Madison, Wisconsin.

February 3, 1995

Dear Town Officials,

It was brought to our attention at the February 2nd Plan Commission meeting that the Town Planner is proposing a "Subdivision Landscaping Requirement" ordinance. We have reviewed Section 21.0813 of the Land Divison Ordinance amendment for street trees and are opposed . . .

Should you still elect to proceed with this ordinance, even after public hearing, please consult with a landscape architect first, because row plantings of trees can make an area appear unattactive.

Sincerely yours,

Adele M. Broussard
Town of Richfield Property Owners
and Taxpayers

FIGURE 2.59. Facsimile of letter from those who oppose a landscape ordinance, West Bend, Wisconsin.

TABLE 2.103 Landscape Point System of Value, Madison, Wisconsin

Landscape Element	*Point Value*	*Credit Value*
Canopy Tree 2″–2½″ caliper	75	75
Evergreen Tree 3′ height minimum	30	30
Canopy Tree or Small Tree 1½″–2″ caliper	30	30
Deciduous Shrub	3	3
Evergreen Shrub	5	5
Decorative Wall/Fence	10 per linear foot	
Earth Berm 30″ height	10 per linear foot	
Earth Berm 15″ height	5 per linear foot	

First, one (1) canopy tree (75 points) is required for every twelve (12) parking spaces. To calculate the number of trees required, divide the number of parking stalls by twelve (12) and add one (1) tree.

Second, total points for landscape elements are also determined by the number of parking stalls. The city provides a table, "Point Schedule for Landscape Elements," in which the required number of points are shown.

Landscape requirements for storage areas are determined by dividing the total square footage of an on-site storage area by three hundred (300) square feet. This converts area to number of stalls. The number of stalls can then be used to determine the number of trees and number of required points. For example, a ten thousand (10,000) square foot storage area is equivalent to thirty-three (33) stalls or three (3) trees, and one hundred sixty (160) points.

For loading berths, add seventy-five (75) points for each berth.

In lots containing more than fifty (50) stalls with more than two (2) drive aisles or more than two (2) parking bays, at least one-half (½) of the required trees would be planted in interior islands. Vehicular use areas with fewer than four (4) stalls are not regulated under this ordinance.

To assist with the understanding and application of this ordinance, the city has prepared some useful documents. It has, for instance, developed a Landscape Worksheet with tables that makes it easy to calculate points and determine the required number of trees. In addition, it has put together a highly design-oriented graphic document titled "A New Approach to Parking Lot Landscaping." The document explains the ordinance and offers parking lot design tips and comments on the proper use of tree protection, plant material, earth berms, walls and fences. Examples are included, showing the proper way to calculate the point system from a parking lot site plan.

An accompanying pamphlet addresses parking lot site plan approval and provides handy information for the designer, landscape architect, architect, engineer

TABLE 2.104. Landscape Plan Application Requirements, Madison, Wisconsin

Scaled Drawings
Conditional Use or PUD/SIP Approval Letter
Driveway Opening Permit Application
Easement for Joint Driveway Use
Land Disturbing Activity Permit
Erosion Control Plan
Landscape Worksheet
Outdoor Lighting Plan

or permit applicant. Contained within are checklists, application forms, plan approval procedures and a Land Disturbing Permit Application. In addition, design standards for parking lots and outdoor lighting are included. Examples of plan drawings, showing parking lot layout, drainage, landscaping and erosion control, are also found in this graphically illustrated document.

Table 2.104 summarizes some of the information that must be prepared with the landscape plan and submitted to the city in order to receive parking lot construction approval.

Slinger

Zoning Ordinance, Chapter XXXI, "Performance Standards," draft, n.d.

In this community the landscape ordinance is included in the zoning ordinance, in the same chapter that regulates radioactivity, electrical disturbances, noise, odors, glare, heat, air pollution, water quality, fire and explosive hazards.

The village requires submission of a landscape plan illustrating "basic requirements" (design components) and "requirement specifications" (standards). The landscape plan must show plantings for green space, street trees, front yard plantings, parking islands, "building corners," yard (building) foundations, dumpsters and buffers. The basic requirements are formula based rather than design based. For instance, technical requirements are based on percentages, quantities, linear footage or area measure. Some of the requirements are simply indicated as "required" or "not applicable."

Basic requirements are zoning district specific. Requirement specifications cover plant materials, sizes, design recommendations and buffer types and composition.

This is a very general "first-generation" landscape ordinance, typical in areas of rapid growth, such as are found in Washington County, Wisconsin.

Other Landscape Ordinances

The following is a list of other landscape ordinances of the United States that are not annotated in this book but are in the author's Green Law Database.

Indian Well, California
Stockton, California
Sunnyvale, California
Douglas County/Castle Rock, Colorado
Windsor, Connecticut
West Palm Beach, Florida
Fulton County, Georgia
Elgin, Illinois
Rockford, Illinois
Winnetka, Illinois
Canton, Michigan
Egan, Minnesota
Borough of Garwood, New Jersey
Hackensack Meadowland District, New Jersey (14 municipalities)
Garner, North Carolina
Tulsa, Oklahoma
Peach Tree City, Pennsylvania
Beaumont, Texas
Fort Worth, Texas (draft ordinance)
Lubbock, Texas
Leesburg, Virginia
City of Port Angeles, Washington
Eau Claire, Wisconsin
City of Riverfalls, Wisconsin

APPENDIX A

Model and Specimen Green Laws

Nature in the city is becoming a scarce resource. Development and growth to house an increasing population is taking its toll on nature's fragile elements.

At one time in most American cities, expansive areas were devoted to meadow, pasture and forest or could be found within an easy walk from the town center. Many cities were founded or settled on nature's lakes, rivers and slow-moving streams that provided ample water for human consumption, industry and wildlife. Soils in these towns were loose, fertile and adaptable to many uses, at the same time performing air cleansing services and providing a medium for urban horticulture. Nature could be enjoyed in parks, on broad boulevards, along drainage channels, on steep slopes and within public reserves. Nature could be found in tiny green spaces of the humblest of neighborhoods. Even large, rambling private estates contributed to nature in the city.

Who is responsible for nature in the city? The answer, of course, is obvious. We are! But often the subtle importance of nature to livability in the city is overlooked for seemingly more important urban issues such as employment, public services, politics and economic growth. Nature deserves our constant attention and can make our modern cities and towns as livable as they were in the past.

Environment, we learn from recent research on the subject, is important to all critical urban issues. In fact, recent scientific study indicates that trees do much to make city life more enjoyable, thereby increasing employment opportunities, expanding economic growth potential and reducing the cost of energy consumption and city services. Managing nature in the city requires legislation. Legislation, in the form of landscape ordinances, tree ordinances and site design ordinances, is one of the newest methods of assisting nature in the city.

In fact, landscape ordinances are springing up around the nation in response to the public desire to assist nature in the city and keep its bountiful resources working toward city livability. Landscape ordinances are some of the most recent planning tools available to see that nature is preserved, protected or enhanced in the cities of America.

The landscape ordinances that follow are model and specimen ordinances that have been prepared to assist communities in establishing their own landscape ordinances. They may be used as legislative models, or as frameworks, to write an ordinance by any city, town, village, county, planning board or public agency wishing to establish a community green law. Consultants and citizens groups may also find them useful in lobbying for more effective legislation directed toward assisting nature in the city. The specimens provided here from the Louisiana towns and cities of Baton Rouge, Covington and Denham Springs are contemporary models that may be crafted as local landscape ordinances for large, medium or small towns.

Several standard forms have been identified as part of this study, and facsimiles of them have been included as models of administrative forms. These models may be used to write local forms that can be used in the administration of the ordinances. Figure A.1 is a good example of a form which must be filed by developers to certify that landscaping has been installed in conformance with plans and specifications. The form is signed by the landscape architect who prepared the plan.

Figure A.2 is a tree removal and land clearing permit. This type of form is submitted prior to site clearing as a way of identifying significant trees and preserving them from destruction. Few communities across the country presently do this now. This type of permit is generally part of a land alteration ordinance.

In the western states, water preservation is sometimes an issue defined in landscape ordinances. Figure A.3 is a facsimile of a form from a water conservation program as used in Napa, California.

Fees are a necessary part of administering landscape ordinances. Most communities charge a small fee, sometimes based upon a percentage of the cost of improvements, for reviewing landscape plans and inspecting the work following installation of landscaping. Figure A.4 is a facsimile form which is used in Ventura County, California, for the purpose of collecting and recording plan review and inspection fees. Fees are usually paid to the local building permit office.

Checklists are special kinds of forms that are created to record all important aspects of some engineering or design procedure. Checklists ensure that nothing is overlooked during the preparation of landscape plans and specifications or during the preparation of landscape permits. Some communities in this study have created checklists for plan review, thus ensuring that all important parts of the drawings and specifications are carefully checked for compliance with the landscape ordinance requirements. Figures A.5, A.6 and A.7 have been assembled from data contained within original ordinances used for this study. They have been compiled into these checklists from several sources to illustrate the important design requirements that city inspectors look for when reviewing landscape designs, irrigation designs and tree surveys.

CITY OF GLENDALE
PUBLIC WORKS/BUILDING SECTION
633 E. Broadway, Room #101
Glendale, CA 91206-4390
818-956-4835

LANDSCAPING CERTIFICATION
For
MULTIPLE DWELLING ZONED PROJECTS

This is to certify that all landscaping and irrigation improvements have been installed in substantial conformance with approved plans for the project located at:

612 N. Columbus
NUMBER STREET

Glendale, CA 91203
CITY

Landscape Architect
D. E. Deubler
(Name - Print)

1403 - B Kenneth Road
Glendale, CA 91201
(Address)

(504) 766-0922
(Telephone)

(Signature)

(California State License No.)

(Date of Certification)

FIGURE A.1. Facsimile landscape permit, Glendale, California.

City of Tampa Permit Section
Department of Housing and
Development Coordination
306 East Jackson Street
Tampa, Florida 33602

City Seal

APPLICATION FOR TREE REMOVAL AND SITE CLEARING PERMIT

PLEASE TYPE OR PRINT CLEARLY

1. Contractor / Qualifer Name	1 a. Qualifer's Social Security Number
2. Business Name	3. Applicant's Name (if other than contractor)
4. Property Owner's Name Street Address City State Zip Code Daytime Telephone Number (Number where owner can be contacted between 8am and 5 pm weekdays.)	5. Name of Person to be contacted regarding this project Street Address City State Zip Code Daytime Telephone Number (Number where project contact person can be contacted between 8am and 5 pm weekdays.)

6. PROJECT NUMBER	7. Job / Site Address
8. Legal Description Lot Block Subdivision	8. Lot Or Parcel Size _________sq. ft. _________acres
10. Project Type *Check one:* ☐ Tree Removal ☐ Site Clearing ☐ Both ☐ Pruning of Trees in Right-of-way	11. Site Clearing For ☐ Construction ☐ Underbrush Only ☐ Foundation Area Only ☐ Subdivision or PUD Common Areas

12. Description of Work to be performed under this permit

13. Number of trees to be Removed or Pruned ________________	13a. Check One ☐ Residential ☐ Commercial	14. Reason For Removal ☐ Construction ☐ Dead, Diseased or Damaged ☐ Hazardous Location ☐ Other ________________
15. Method of Removal ☐ Cutting Transplanting on Site ☐ Transplanting Off-Site	16. Does subject parcel directly abut jurisdictional wetland conservation areas? ☐ Yes ☐ No	17. If yes, will proposed development occur within 30 feet landward of the wetland? ☐ Yes ☐ No

18. Permit Fees are calculated by Permit Technician at time of submission.

19. I certify, together with plans and specifications, this application shows a true representation of the work to be accomplished under this permit. It is understood that any false information or deviation from the original documents will render this permit issued under this application null and void, unless approved by the Director of Parks Department. The permit issued under this application is invalid after 6 months if the project is not started for which this permit was issued, and there will be no refund. I agree to conform to all building department regulations and ordinances regulating building and zoning. I will replace trees as required by Article XII of Chapter 45, City of Tampa Code.
NOTE: IT IS THE RESPONSIBILITY OF THE PERMIT HOLDER TO CALL FOR ALL INSPECTIONS.
FAILURE TO COMPLY WITH THE MECHANIC'S LIEN LAW CAN RESULT IN THE PROPERTY OWNER PAYING TWICE FOR BUILDING IMPROVEMENTS.

20. Signature of Applicant Date

FIGURE A.2. Facsimile tree removal and site clearing permit, Tampa, Florida.

WATER CONSERVATION CONCEPT STATEMENT
(Please print or type in all applicable spaces)

PROJECT ADDRESS:______________________________________

PROJECT NUMBER:______________________________________

PROJECT SITE:____

LANDSCAPE ARCHITECT / IRRIGATION DESIGNER

Name:____
Address:____
____

Daytime Phone No.:_____________________________________

INCLUDED IN THIS PROJECT SUBMITTAL ARE:
____ Landscape Design Plan
____ Irrigation System Design Plan
____ Irrigation Schedules
1. Maximum allowable factor =
(22 gal / yr / sq ft) × (sq ft of landscaped area)
2. Estimated Annual Water Use________gals.
3. If #2 exceeds #1, please explain below.

____ Maintenance Schedule
____ Grading Design Plan
____ Soils Analysis

BRIEFLY DESCRIBE THE PLANNING AND DESIGN FEATURES THAT ARE INTENDED TO ACHIEVE CONSERVATION AND EFFICIENCY IN WATER USE.
____
____
____
____
____
____

Signature:___________________________________

Title:_______________________________________

FIGURE A.3. Facsimile of Water Conservation Statement, Napa, California.

VENTURA COUNTY
CALIFORNIA

RESOURCE MANAGEMENT AGENCY
PLANNING DIVISION

REIMBURSEMENT AGREEMENT FOR LANDSCAPE PLAN REVIEW

Permit / Entitlement No (s).:____

I, the undersigned Principal or Agency, hereby authorize the County of Ventura to review the submitted Landscape Plans for the above referenced permit / entitlement request (s) in accordance with the Ventura County Ordinance Code. I am herewith depositing $__________ to cover staff review, coordination and processing cost based on real time expended.

I understand that if the final cost is less than the deposit fee, the unused portion of the deposit will be refunded to me. I further understand that if the final cost is more than the deposit fee, I shall pay the balance due.

Name of Principal* (print or type):______________________________

Address of Principal (do not use PO Box): ______________________

____

Name of Agency (if different from Principal):______________________

Address of Agency (do not use PO Box):__________________________

Signature:________________________ Date__________________________

* If a corporation, list corporate offficer (s) authorized to act on behalf corporation.

FIGURE A.4. Facsimile, Reimbursement Agreement for Landscape Plan Review, Ventura County, California.

LANDSCAPE DESIGN CHECKLIST

	Required	Optional
GENERAL		
1. North Point		
Scale		
Designer's Name		
Landscape Architect's Registration Seal		
Certification of Compliance Statement		
Date		
Project Name		
Project Owner or Contractor		
LOCATION		
2. Street Address and Number		
Property Lines & Setback Lines		
Servitudes & Easements		
Utilities & Utility Connections		
Existing Public Features, Walks, Curbs, etc.		
Underground Structures		
SITE FEATURES		
3. Contours and Critical Elevations		
Natural Features, Wetlands, Conservation Areas etc.		
Existing And Proposed Site Structures		
(Buildings, Walks, Drives, Parking, Decks, Storage, Walls, Fences, etc.)		
EXISTING TREES		
4. Landmark, Ancient & Unique Trees		
Protected Trees		
Trees over 6" DBH		
Tree Groves		
Root Zone Elevations of All Trees to Be Preserved		
Special Habitats, Plants, Animals, Water Zones		
Diseased and Infested Trees		
DESIGN COMPONENTS		
5. Street Tree Plantings		
Street Yard Planting Zone		
Vehicular Use Areas (VUA)		
Interior Parking Plantings		
VUA Screens		
Street Wall Plantings		
Open Space Planting Zones		
Side Yard Buffers		
Rear Yard Buffers		
Storage, Loading & Refuse Screening		
Landscape Structures, Walls, Fences, Fountain, Artworks		
Storm Water Management Features		
Site Grading and Earth Berm Design		
Signage Planting Zones		
Special Design Components		
CALCULATIONS & LANDSCAPE PLAN SCHEDULES		
6. Landscape Zone Area Requirements		
Linear Footage Requirements		
Open Space Area Planting Calculations		
Landscape Point System Calculations		
Tree Credit Calculations		
Proposed Plant List & Nonliving Material Schedule		

SUBMITTAL NOTICE Designer is to submit three (3) complete sets of drawings along with all required calculations and schedules, applicable Permit and Plan Review Fees to the Inspection & Permits Office, Public Works Division, located in the City Hall Building.

FIGURE A.5. Specimen landscape design checklist, Louisiana State University.

IRRIGATION DESIGN CHECKLIST

	Required	Optional
GENERAL		
1. North Point		
Scale		
Designer Name		
Landscape Architect / Irrigation Designer Registration No.		
Certification of Compliance Statement		
Date		
Project Name		
Project Owner or Contractor		
LOCATION		
2. Street Address and Number		
Property Lines & Setback Lines		
Servitudes & Easements		
Utilities & Utility Connections		
Existing Public Features, Walks, Curbs, etc.		
Underground Structures		
SITE FEATURES		
3. Contours and Critical Elevations		
Soil Types and Infiltration Rate (USDA Standards)		
Existing And Proposed Site Structures (Buildings, Walks, Drives, Parking, Decks, Storage,Walls, Fences, etc.)		
WATER SYSTEM FEATURES		
4. Water Connection Meter, Pressure, Water Source		
Type of System		
Design Operating Pressure		
Flow Rate per Zone, Depths of Application		
Total Volume Required		
Yearly Water Budget Requirements per City Code		
Application Rates per Zone		
DESIGN COMPONENTS		
5. Main Connection Gate Valve		
Backflow Preventer		
Sprinkler Zones		
Pipe—Locations, Sizes, Pipe Pressure Rating		
Valves		
Sprinker Heads and Joint		
Drip Emitters or Drip Pipe		
Controllers—Location, Type, Schedule		
Rain Sensor Device		
Electrical Supply, Valve Wiring, Transformer		
Pipe Depth and Backfill		
Other System Components, (Nozzles, Check Valves, Nipples, Risers, Wires)		
Irrigation Specifications		
Irrigation Layout Plan & Details		
CALCULATIONS & IRRIGATION PLAN SCHEDULES		
6. Hydrozone Area Calculations		
Linear Footage Calculations		
Sprinker Zone Application Rates Calculations		
Yearly Water Use Budget Calculations		
Pressure / Pressure Loss Calculations		

SUBMITTAL NOTICE Designer is to submit three (3) complete sets of drawings along with all required calculations and schedules, applicable Permit and Plan Review Fees to the Inspection & Permits Office, Public Works Division, located in the City Hall Building.

FIGURE A.6. Specimen irrigation design checklist, Louisiana State University.

TREE SURVEY CHECKLIST

	Required	Optional
GENERAL		
1. North Point		
Scale		
Tree Consultant Name		
Landscape Architect's, Urban Forester's Registration No.		
Certification of Compliance Statement		
Date		
Project Name		
Project Owner or Contractor		
LOCATION		
2. Street Address and Number		
Property Lines		
Servitudes & Easements		
Existing Public Features, Walks, Curbs, etc.		
SITE FEATURES		
3. Contours and General Land Slope		
Vegetation Types		
Existing Ecological Zones		
Habitat Features (Geological, Zoological, Botanical)		
TREE FEATURES		
4. Water Connection Meter, Pressure, Water Source		
Type of System		
Design Operating Pressure		
Flow Rate per Zone, Depths of Application		
Total Volume Required		
Yearly Water Budget Requirements per City Code		
Application Rates per Zone		
SURVEY COMPONENTS		
5. Sensitive Habitat Zones		
Unique Trees, Species, Size, Health		
Landmark and Ancient Trees, Species, Size, Health		
Location of All Trees over 6" DBH		
Location of All Trees Classified as Protected Trees		
Prohibited Trees, Species, Size, Location		
Hazardous Trees		
Soils—Erosion Analysis		
Location of All Trees to Be Removed		
Tree Protection Devices and Installation Details		
Identification of Critical Root Zones		
Pruning Specifications		
Shadow Pattern Determination		
Microclimates		
Schedule of Replacement Trees		
Schedule of Trees & Shrubs to Be Relocated		
CALCULATIONS & TREE SURVEY SCHEDULES		
6. Clearing & Grubbing Standards		
Site Access, Clearing and Storage Areas Delineated		
Delineation of Tree Protection Zones, Area Measure		
Tree Removal Locations & Specifications		
Limits of Site Grading & Fill		
Basal Area Calculations		

SUBMITTAL NOTICE Designer is to submit three (3) complete sets of drawings along with all required calculations and schedules, applicable Permit and Plan Review Fees to the Inspection & Permits Office, Public Works Division, located in the City Hall Building.

FIGURE A.7. Specimen tree survey checklist, Louisiana State University.

Many of the ordinances in this nationwide study specify the exact procedure to be followed to submit landscape plans for public review. The city of Austin, Texas, has simplified the process into a general flow chart. Figure A.8 is a facsimile of the process used in this Texas community. As can be seen, the landscape plans are reviewed and approved as an essential part of the building permit approval process. When building plans are reviewed, the landscape plan is also reviewed. Both building and landscaping are tied to the Certificate of Occupancy, and this is how Austin enforces compliance with building codes and landscape ordinance requirements.

Figure A.9 is a facsimile of a certificate that is filed when irrigation plans are given to the City of Roseville, California. The certificate must be filled out by the landscape architect with information that will allow city engineers to determine the water requirements of new construction projects.

This appendix may be used to craft local landscape ordinances and standard forms. For instance, in the outline to the Model California Tree Ordinance, Figure A.10, one would expect to find standard forms as a part of Section 15. Figure A.11 shows the simple graphic conventions that are used to depict certain landscape elements.

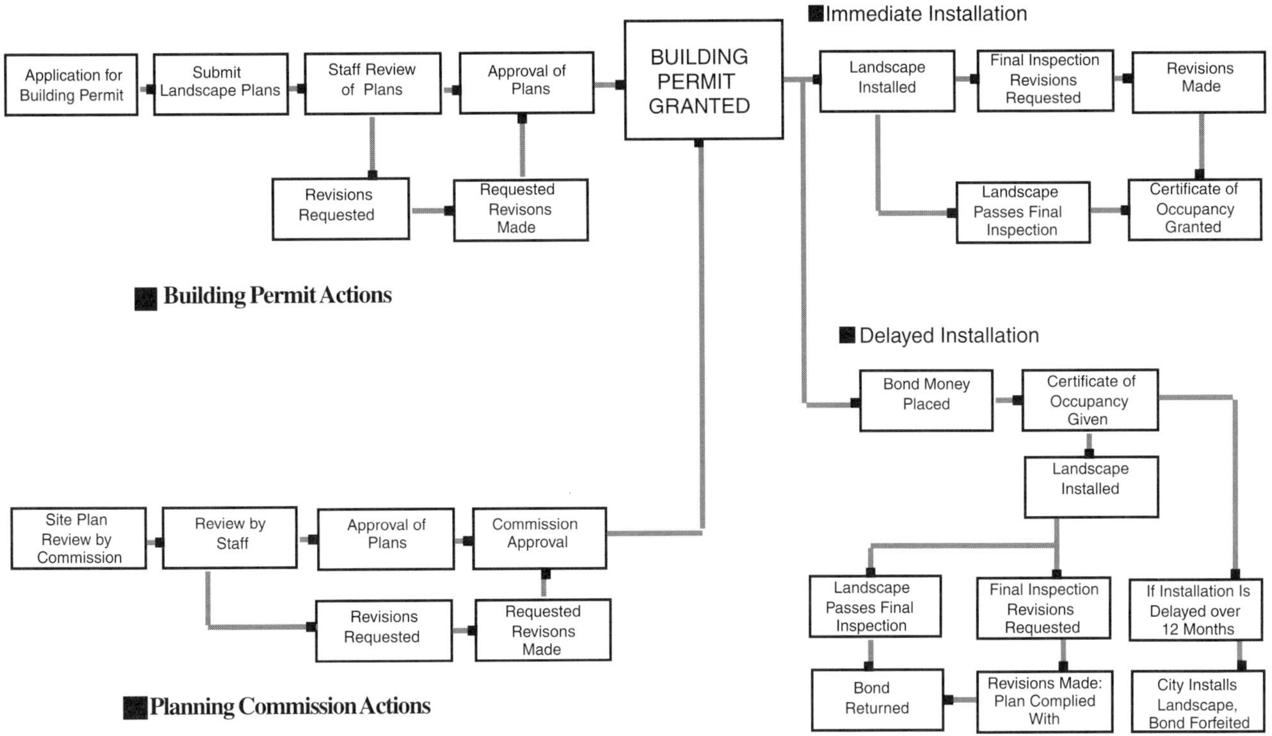

Notes 1. Upon Request Of Owner 2. Made Within 9-12 Months After Certificate of Occupancy Granted 3. Alternative Compliance Possible 4. Questions Should Be Directed to the City Building Inspection Department, Landscape Coordinator

FIGURE A.8. Facsimile of a typical landscape ordinance approval process flowchart, Austin, Texas.

CITY OF ROSEVILLE
Certificate of Compliance

Project Name:____

Project Location:____

PRELIMINARY PROJECT DOCUMENTATION SUBMITTAL
Check indicating submittal and fill in appropriate blanks.

_____1. Total Planting Area:_________________square feet
_____2. Planting Value (per planting criteria):________square feet
_____3. Estimated Total Water Use:____________(gallons per year)
_____4. Estimated Average Planted Area Precipitation: ____ (inches per year)
_____5. Landscape Design Plan
_____6. Irrigation Design Plan
_____7. Grading Design Plan

Comments:

I / We certify that the project has been designed in accordance with the Water Efficient Landscape Requirements.

____
Landscape Architect Signature   Date   State License Number

FIGURE A.9. Facsimile of a Certificate of Compliance, Roseville, California.

Section 1—Title
Section 2—Findings
Section 3—Purpose and Intent
Section 4—Definitions
Section 5—Determination of Definitions
Section 6—Jurisdiction
Section 7—Policies Regarding Trees
Section 8—Local Government Disclaims Liability
Section 9—Interference with Planting, Maintenance and Removal Unlawful
Section 10—Appeals
Section 11—Penalty for Violation
Section 12—Enforcement
Section 13—Performance Evaluation of Ordinance
Section 14—Severability
Section 15—Designate Administrative Responsibilities

Additional Optional Ordinance Provisions

Establish a Tree Board or Tree Commission
Specify cooperation between department and agencies
Develop a comprehensive management plan
Resolution of conflicts between trees and structures
Exemption from California Solar Shade Control Act
Responsibilities of property owners
Help for citizens performing tree maintenance
Topping prohibited
Permit required for planting trees in public rights-of-way
Planting requirements
Situations that are declared to be public nuisances
Licensing of private tree care firms
Harming public trees prohibited
Permit required to remove or prune city-owned trees
Permit required to remove or prune protected private trees
Conservation of forest and woodland resources during development
Procedure to be followed in resolving tree disputes
Standards for resolution of tree disputes
Apportionment of tree disputes resolution costs
Recording for notification of future owners
Enforcement of tree dispute resolutions

FIGURE A.10. Outline to the California Model Tree Ordinance, California Urban Forestry Program.

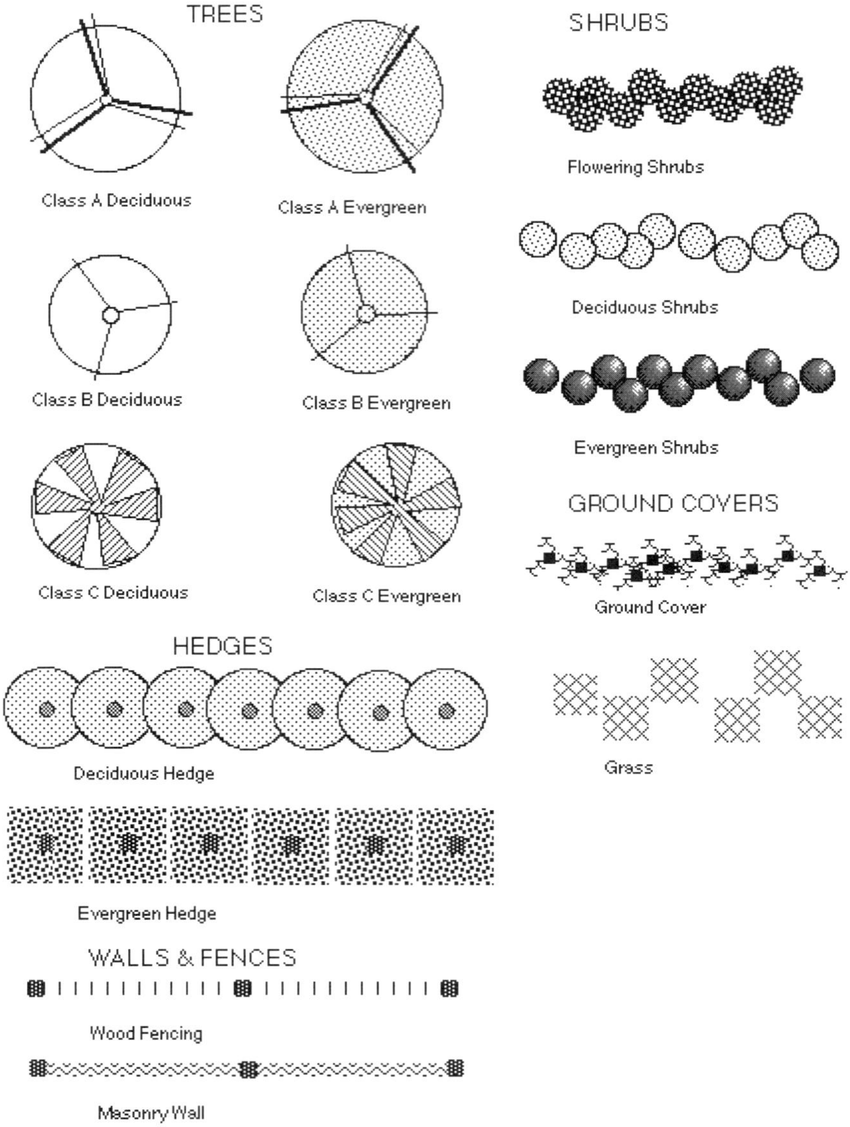

FIGURE A.11. Key to descriptive graphics, Abbey Associates Landscape Architects.

COVINGTON, LOUISIANA, LANDSCAPE ORDINANCE*

Section 4.4 Minimum Landscape Requirements

The following are the Minimum Landscape Requirements for the designated zoning districts. Each shall meet the criteria set forth below.

4.401 Purpose

The purpose of this Section is to promote the health, safety and general welfare of the public; to facilitate the creation of a convenient, attractive and harmonious community; to conserve natural resources including adequate air and water; to conserve properties and their values; to preserve the character of an area by preventing the harmful effects of prejudicial uses; and to encourage the appropriate use of the land. More specifically this Section is intended to make incompatible uses compatible by requiring a screen or buffer between uses in order to minimize the harmful impact of noise, dust, and other debris, motor vehicle headlight glare or other artificial light intrusion, and other objectionable activities or impacts conducted on or created by an adjoining or nearby use. Additionally, this Section is intended to require the landscaping of certain parking lots in order to reduce the harmful effects of wind and air turbulence, heat and noise, and the glare of motor vehicle lights; to preserve underground water reservoirs and to permit the return of precipitation to the groundwater strata; to act as a natural drainage system and ameliorate storm water drainage problems; to reduce the level of carbon dioxide and return pure oxygen to the atmosphere; to prevent storm erosion; to provide shade; and to enhance the blighted appearance of parking lots.

4.402 Applicability

The provisions of this Section shall apply to all Commercial, Industrial, Multi-family of three units or more, Religious, Educational and Industrial Uses; and Conditional Uses as deemed necessary and appropriate by the Zoning Commission in the Public Hearing for that Conditional Use. This Section shall not apply to those areas located in the Division of St. John (Downtown).

4.403 Standards

The following standards shall apply to the installation and maintenance of all landscaping, screening and barriers required by this Section.

The owner/developer is advised that licensed nurserymen and horticulturists are certified by the State of Louisiana and carry plant materials that are certified disease and insect free.

*Revised April 24, 1989, Covington Planning and Zoning Commission.

1. A minimum of twenty-five (25) square feet, with minimum side dimensions of five (5), is required for each tree planted.
2. All landscaping shall be installed in a sound workmanlike manner and according to accepted good planting procedures.
3. Trees shall be minimum of eight (8) feet in height immediately after planting and shrubs shall be three (3) feet in height immediately after planting within the front/side/rear yard planting area and vehicular use areas. Two six (6) foot trees may be substituted for one eight (8) foot tree.
4. Generally, planting required by this Section should be in an irregular line and spaced at random.
6. [sic] Existing vegetation which is suitable for use in compliance with the requirements of this Section shall be protected according to the provisions as set forth in Section 4.406

4.404 Landscape Plan and Planting Requirements

1. A landscape plan shall be submitted and approved as part of the building permit as required by the provisions of Section 4.402-Applicability above.
2. Such landscaping plans shall be drawn to scale, including dimensions and distances, clearly delineate all existing and proposed parking spaces or other vehicle areas, access aisles, driveways, and the location, size and description of all landscaping materials.
3. Street Planting Area Requirements

   Street Planting area is defined as the unpaved area of land located between the property line that abuts a public right-of-way and any building or vehicular use area, designated for the preservation and placement of plant materials. If a building site has two or more street planting areas, each street planting area is to be considered separately. If a building site is composed of two or more lots, the building site shall be viewed under the minimum landscape ordinance as one lot (building site).

   a. The street planting area shall be a minimum of 15 feet in depth for all Multi-family, C-1, C-2, C-3, C-4, C-5, Commercial Zoned property, Religious, Educational and Institutional Uses and Conditional Uses requiring review and approval by the Zoning Commission; Single Family Residences and Duplexes are excluded from this ordinance. Other requirements shall be as follows:

      i. The street planting area shall contain a minimum of one (1) Class A tree (see definition) for every twenty (20) linear feet of building site frontage or fraction thereof. The required number of trees may be located anywhere within the street planting area.

      ii. Where the street planting area as defined herein falls within or overlaps a utility company right-of-way or easement, the street planting requirements shall be as follows:

1. An additional fifteen (15) foot strip of land contiguous to and extending the full length of the street planting area to include the required number of trees as specified in Section 4.401 (3) a. i.; or,
2. Street planting area requirements as set forth in 4.404 (3) a. i. to be planted in landscaped islands adjacent to the street planting area for a depth not exceeding twenty (20) feet in addition to the planting of two (2) class "C" trees as defined herein for each twenty (20) linear feet of street frontage.

b. The street planting area shall be a minimum of 15 feet in depth for all M-1, M-2, and M-3 Industrial Zones Uses and Industrial Conditional Use Permits that require review and approval by the Zoning Commission. Other requirements shall be as follows:

   i. Each site shall contain a minimum of one (1) Class A tree and one (1) Class B tree in the street planting area for every twenty (20) linear feet of building frontage or fraction thereof. The required number of trees may be located anywhere within the street planting area.

c. Accessways

   Accessways through the periphery of an off-street parking or other vehicular use area shall be a minimum of twenty-four feet wide for two-way traffic and a minimum of twelve (12) feet to a maximum of fifteen (15) feet wide for one-way traffic. For street frontage up to one hundred (100) linear feet, no more than two (2) one-way accessways shall be permitted. For more than one hundred (100) feet of frontage, one additional two-way accessway may be permitted for each additional one hundred (100) feet of frontage or major fraction thereof (51 feet or greater) See Exhibit "A."

d. Site Triangle

   Site distance for landscaping adjacent to public rights-of-way and point of access.

   i. When an accessway intersects a public right of way, or when the subject property abuts the intersection of two (2) or more public rights-of-way, all material within the triangular areas described below shall provide unobstructed cross-visibility at a level between two and one-half ($2\frac{1}{2}$) feet and eight (8) feet, and further, shall be located so as not to create a traffic hazard.
   ii. Landscape material except grass or ground cover shall not be located closer than three (3) feet from the edge of any accessway pavement.

4. Buffer Planting Area Requirements (where applicable)

   Buffer Planting Area is defined as the unpaved area of land located between the side or rear property line abutting property zoned A-1, A-2, A-3 Residential and any building or vehicular use area, designated for the preservation and placement of plant materials.

The Buffer Planting Area requirements shall be as follows:

a. Buffer Planting Areas shall only be provided where property zoned A-5, C-1, C-2, C-3, C-4, C-5, and all Conditional Use Permits (except Industrial) requiring review and approval by the Zoning Commission abuts property zoned for single family residential, duplex use, or adjacent single family dwellings.

   The depth of the Side Buffer Planting Area for non-corner lots, if required shall be calculated using the front footage of the property as a guide. The depth of the Rear Buffer Planting Area for non-corner lots shall be calculated using the depth of the property as a guide. For corner lots, the width shall be calculated using the shortest side bordering a street and the depth shall be calculated using the longest side bordering a street. This calculated buffer planting area shall be a minimum requirement.

   i. Five (5) feet for the first one hundred fifty (150) feet of lot depth or width or fraction thereof; and five (5) additional feet for each additional one hundred fifty (150) feet of lot depth or width or fraction thereof. The Side Buffer Planting Area need not exceed ten (10) feet and the Rear Buffer Planting Area need not exceed fifteen (15) feet.
   ii. One (1) Class A tree for each ten (10) feet of lot depth and /or width and a 70% sight obscuring screen of living or 100% sight obscuring screen of non-living landscape material. (See definition for sight obscuring screen.)

b. M-1, M-2, M-3 Zoning Districts and Conditional Industrial Use Permits. Buffer Planting Areas shall only be provided where M-1, M-2, M-3 District or Conditional Industrial Use in any zoned area abuts any zoned area or use other than industrial (M-1, M-2, M-3).

   i. Twenty-five (25) foot deep Buffer Planting Area shall be provided, where applicable.
   ii. One (1) Class A tree for each ten (10) feet of lot depth and /or width and a 70% opaque sight obscuring screen of living or 100% opaque sight obscuring screen of non-living landscape material. (See definition for sight obscuring screen.)

5. Parking Requirements

   Two (2) Class B trees shall be provided for every eight (8) parking spaces or fraction thereof, excluding commercial parking garages and multi-level parking. The location of said trees shall be located anywhere in the parking area or adjacent to the parking area, exclusive of any other requirements.

6. Trash and Garbage Screening Requirements

   Storage areas containing three (3) or more refuse, garbage or rubbish containers or one (1) or more dumpsters shall be screened on all sides with a six (6) foot high 70% obscuring screen of living or 100% sight obscuring screen of non-living landscape material.

4.405 Maintenance

1. The owner, or his agent, shall be responsible for the maintenance, repair and replacement of all landscaping materials and barriers as may be required by the provisions of the Section.
2. All plant material shall be tended and maintained in a healthy growing condition, replaced when necessary and kept free of refuse and debris.

4.406 Preservation of Existing Plant Materials

In all Commercial, Industrial, Multi-Family of three units or more, Religious, Educational, and Institutional uses; and Conditional Uses as deemed necessary and appropriate by the Zoning Commission in the Public Hearing for that Conditional Use, excluding those areas located in the Division of St. John (Downtown), all Class "A" trees greater than twelve (12) inches in diameter measured four and one-half ($4\frac{1}{2}$) feet above the ground, and all Class "B" trees greater that six (6) inches in diameter measured four and one-half ($4\frac{1}{2}$) feet above the ground that are located in the Street Planting Area as defined in Section 4.404 (3), shall be preserved regardless of the number of said trees, but in no case shall this requirement create a traffic hazard as per Section 4.404 (3) d.

In all applicable zones, credit may be received toward the landscape planting requirements by preserving existing trees.

1. The owner/developer should try to preserve native trees and shrubs in the design and implementation of the landscape plan.
2. Exchange rate—For each existing tree preserved one tree shall be credited toward the satisfaction of the minimum planting requirements.
3. These credits shall only be given if the trees preserved are located in or within fifteen (15) feet of the specific area (Street/Buffer Planting Areas and Parking Areas).

   For example: The trees preserved in the Street Planting Area shall be given credit for the Street Planting Requirements only. Credit for trees preserved in the parking area shall apply only to the parking requirements, etc.
4. It shall be the responsibility of the land owner to use reasonable care in maintaining preserved trees. If a preserved tree dies, it is the responsibility of the owner to replace said tree with a tree of the appropriate Class within six (6) months. The owner or his agent shall be responsible for maintaining all plant materials required by the ordinance in good living condition.

5. For each tree to be credited, a planting area or open ground space of at least twenty-five (25) square feet shall be required for trees of up to 4 inches in diameter. For each additional 2 inches of tree diameter of the preserved tree an additional 25 square feet of planting area or open ground space shall be required. For example:

Tree Diameter	*Area*
4″	25 square feet
6″	50 square feet
8″	75 square feet
10″	100 square feet
24″	275 square feet

6. During construction, planting or open ground areas surrounding preserved trees shall be protected sufficiently to prevent earth compaction of the root zone. Planting or open ground areas shall be located so that the minimum distance from the trunk of the preserved tree to the perimeter of such designate area shall be at least two-thirds (⅔) of the maximum distance from the trunk of the preserved tree to the perimeter of such designated area.
7. Should any tree required by this ordinance to be preserved or planted die, it shall be the responsibility of the owner to replace the dead tree with the same number of total circumference inches of the dead tree.
8. All live oak trees in excess of twelve (12) inches in diameter at four and one-half (4½) feet above the ground (DBH) shall be preserved.

4.407 Permits and Inspections Required

1. Prior to clearing and grubbing operations, a building permit must be obtained from the building inspector.
2. See Section 4.404 above for the landscape plan requirements.
3. A certificate from the building inspector shall be required prior to occupancy. This certification shall indicate that the owner/developer is in compliance with minimum landscape requirements.
4. All minimum landscape requirements shall apply in all instances where there is a change in use that would increase the parking requirements as set forth herein above, or where the change of use requires the issuance of a building permit.
5. See Section 3.3 Permits and Certificates, for additional information regarding building permits.

4.408 Adjustments

Any adjustments, appeals or variances to this Section shall be heard by the Covington Board of Adjustments.

4.409 Definitions

1. Accessway: A way of approaching or entering a property.
2. Street Planting Area: An area of land between the property line and any vehicular use area or building that is intended for the placement or preservation of landscape materials.
3. Ground Cover: Plant material which reaches a maximum height of not more that twelve (12) inches.
4. Landscaping Material: Material such as, but not limited to, living trees, shrubs, vines, lawn grass, ground cover, landscape water features, and non-living durable materials commonly used in landscaping including, but not limited to, rocks, pebbles, sands, decorative walls and fences, brick pavers, earthen mounds, but excluding paving for vehicular use.
5. Planting Area: Any area designed for landscape material installation having a minimum area of twenty-five (25) square feet, with a minimum of five (5) feet on the side.
6. Buffer Planting Area/Side and Rear Yard Planting Areas: The unpaved area of land located between the side or rear property line abutting property zoned Residential, and any building or vehicular use area, designated for the preservation and placement of plant materials.
7. Sight Obscuring Screen: A 100% opaque visual screen with a minimum height of six (6) feet, if non-living material is used. If living material is used, it shall be at least 70% sight obscuring and be a minimum of four (4) feet in height immediately after planting and shall consist of plants that reach a minimum of six (6) feet in height at maturity.
8. Sight Triangle: The triangle at either side of an accessway or public right-of-way with sides of a specific length each along the public right-of-way/or accessway.
9. **Tree—Class A:** Any self-supporting woody plant of species which normally grows to an overall height of at least fifty (50) feet, usually with one main stem or trunk, and many branches. It may appear to have several stems or trunks, as in several varieties of oaks. (See Part P for examples).
10. **Tree—Class B:** Any self supporting woody plant of species which normally grows to an overall height of at least twenty-five (25) feet, usually with one main stem or trunk, and many branches. It may appear to have several stems or trunks, for example Crape Myrtle. (See Part P for examples).
11. **Tree—Class C:** Any self-supporting woody plant of species which normally grows to an overall height of at least fifteen (15) feet. It may appear to have several stems or trunks, for example Wax Myrtle. (See Part P for examples.)
12. Understory Plants: An underlying layer of low vegetation including all shrubs and trees 35 feet or smaller.

4.410 Examples of Class A, Class B, and Class C Trees and Evergreen Shrubs

Class A Trees

Acer rubrum "Drummondii"—Swamp Red Maple
Acer saccharinum—Silver Maple
Carya cordiformis—Bitternut Hickory
Carya illinoinensis—Pecan
Celtis laevigata—Sugar Hackberry
Cryptomeria japonica—Japanese Cedar
Cunninghamia lanceolata—Cunninghamia Fir
Fagus grandifolia—American Beech
Fraxinus pennsylvanica—Green Ash
Ginkgo biloba—Ginkgo
Gleditsia triancanathos—Honey Locust
Juglans nigra—Black Walnut
Juniperus virginiana—Eastern Red Cedar
Liriodendron tulipifera—Tuliptree, Yellow Poplar
Magnolia acuminata—Cucumber Magnolia
Magnolia grandiflora—Southern Magnolia
Morus rubra—Red Mulberry
Nyssa sylvatica—Black Gum
Pinus echinata—Shortleaf Pine
Pinus glabra—Spruce Pine
Pinus palustris—Longleaf Pine
Pinus taeda—Loblolly Pine
Platanus occidentalis—Sycamore
Populus deltoides—Cottonwood
Quercus acutissima—Sawtooth Oak
Quercus alba—White Oak
Quercus falcata—Southern Red Oak
Quercus falcata "pagodifolia"—Cherry Bark Oak
Quercus michauxii—Cow Oak
Quercus nigra—Water Oak
Quercus phellos—Willow Oak
Quercus shumardii—Shumard Oak
Quercus virginiana—Southern Live Oak
Salix nigra—Black Willow
Taxodium distichum—Common Bald Cypress
Tilia americana—American Linden
Ulmus americana—American Elm
Ulmus crassifolio—Cedar Elm

Class B Trees

Acer negundo—Boxelder
Albizia julibrissin—Mimosa
Betula nigra—River Birch
Broussonetia papyrifera—Paper Mulberry

Catalpa bignoniodes—Catalpa
Cedrus deodara—Deodar Cedar
Cercis canadensis—Redbud
Cinnamonum camphora—Camphor
Cornus florida—Flowering Dogwood
Diospyros virginiana—Common Persimmon
Firmiana simplex—Chinese Parasol Tree
Gordonia lasinanthus—Gordonia, Loblloly Bay
Ilex opaca—American Holly
Juniperus virginiana "canaertii"—Canaert Eastern Red Cedar
Koelreuteria bipennata—Golden Rain Tree
Lagerstroemia indica—Crape Myrtle
Magnolia heptapeta—White Saucer Magnolia
Magnolia virginiana—Sweet Bay Magnolia
Melia azedarach—Chinaberry
Ostrya virginiana—Hop Hornbeam
Parkinsonia aculeata—Jerusalem Thorn
Pistacia chinensis—Pistachio
Populus alba—White/Silver Popular
Quercus acuta—Japanese Evergreen Oak
Robinia pseudoacacia—Black Locust
Salix babylonica—Weeping Willow
Ulmus pumila—Siberian Elm
Zanthoxylum clava-herculis—Toothache Tree/Prickly Ash
Ziziphus jujuba-Jujube—Chinese Date

Class C Trees

Assimina triloba—Pawpaw
Carpinus caroliniana—Ironwood
Chionanthus virginicus—White Fringe Tree
Crataegus marshallii—Parsley Hawthorn
Crataegus opaca—Mayhaw
Crataegus viridus—Greenhaw
Eriobotrya japonica—Japanese Plum
Halesia diptera—Silver Bell
Hamamelis virginiana—Witch Hazel
Ilex decidua—Deciduous Holly
Malus angustifolia—Southern Crab Apple
Malus floribunda—Japanese Flowering Crab Apple
Magnolia soulangiana—Oriental Magnolia
Myrica cerifera—Wax Myrtle
Lagerstroemia indica—Crape Myrtle (selected varieties)
Oxydendrum arboreum—Sourwood
Prunus americana—Wild Plum/American plum
Prunus campanulata—Taiwan Flowering Cherry
Prunus cerasifera—Purple Leaf Plum

Prunus mexicana—Mexican Plum
Prunus serotina—Black Cherry
Prunus serrulata—Japanese Flowering Cherry
Pyrus Calleryana "Bradford"—Bradford Flowering Pear
Pyrus communis—Common Pear
Rhamnus Caroliniana—Carolina Buckthorn
Rhus copallina—Flameleaf Sumac
Sapium sebiferum—Chinese Tallow Tree
Sassafras albidum—Sassafras
Ulmus alata—Winged Elm

DENHAM SPRINGS, LOUISIANA, LANDSCAPE ORDINANCE*

Outline of the Landscape Ordinance Denham Springs, Louisiana

Section 13.0	Short Title
Section 13.1	Purpose
Section 13.2	Applicability of Landscape Ordinance
Section 13.3	Definitions
Section 13.4	Landscape Design Standards
Section 13.5	Landscape Design Submission Standards
Section 13.6	Alternative Compliance
Section 13.7	Permit and Inspection Requirements
Section 13.8	Enforcement Appeals and Penalties
Section 13.9	Administrative Guidelines
Section 13.10	Conflicts
Section 13.11	Severability
Section 13.12	Effective Date

Section 13.0 Short Title, Minimum Landscape Requirements

An ordinance amending Zoning Code of the City of Denham Springs so as to add a Landscape Ordinance of minimum landscape requirements. This ordinance shall be referred to as "Denham Springs Landscape Ordinance."

Section 13.1 Purpose

The purpose of this Part is to protect and enhance the community's environmental, economic and aesthetic resources consistent with the goals of the city's governing body thereby promoting the public health, safety and general welfare of the citizens and contributing to the quality of life by encouraging a high level of design in the development of the city.

---

*October 24, 1995

Section 13.2 Applicability of Landscape Ordinance

The provisions of this Part shall apply to all commercial, industrial, multi-family, religious, educational and institutional land uses that are developed after the effective date of this ordinance or that require the issuance of a building permit for alteration or an addition.

Section 13.3 Definitions

The following definitions shall apply to this ordinance.

1. Ground Cover—Material planted in such a way as to form a continuous cover over the ground that can be maintained at a height not more than twelve (12) inches.
2. Landscape Area—An unbuilt-upon area of land in which landscape materials are placed, planted or maintained, exclusive of servitudes.
3. Landscape Design shall mean the preparation of graphic and written criteria, specifications, and detailed landscape design plans to arrange and modify the effects of natural features such as plantings, ground and water forms, circulation, walks and other landscape features to comply with the provisions of this ordinance.
4. Shrub—A woody perennial plant differing from a perennial herb by its persistent and woody stems, and from a tree by its low stature (generally obtaining a height less than eight (8) feet) and its habit of branching from the base.
5. Trees—Class "A"—Any self-supporting woody plant of a species which normally grows to an overall height of at least fifty (50) feet, usually with one main stem or trunk and many branches, as in several varieties of oak trees.
6. Tree—Class "B"—Any self-supporting woody plant of a species which normally grows to an overall height of at least twenty-five (25) feet, with either one main stem or trunk with many branches, or several stems or trunks. Crape myrtles, for example.

Section 13.4 Landscape Design Standards

The Landscape Ordinance Review Committee shall develop design standards, subject to approval of the Mayor and Board of Aldermen, which shall apply to the design, installation and maintenance of all landscaping regulated by this ordinance. These design standards are to be consistent with standards published by the Louisiana Association of Nurserymen and the Louisiana Horticulture Commission.

A. The following Landscape Areas shall be planted and maintained according to the design standards referred to above.
   1. Street planting areas
   2. Sight triangle areas at street intersections

3. Buffer planting areas, along side and rear property lines
4. Vehicular use areas within parking lots and auto storage areas
5. Parking lot screening areas
5. Vehicular loading or storage areas
6. Trash and garbage storage areas
7. Storm water retention areas

B. Material used in the design must meet standards published by the American Society of Nurserymen in "American Standard for Nursery Stock," latest edition.

Section 13.5 Landscape Design Plan Requirements

1. All building permit applications covered by this ordinance shall be accompanied by a landscape design. This landscape design plan shall be drawn to scale by a Louisiana Horticulture Commission license holder authorized to design such plans and shall include such design criteria that may be required by the Landscape Ordinance Review Committee to interpret the extent of the permit application.
2. Landscape design plan technical standards as specified in standards published by the Louisiana Association of Nurserymen and the Louisiana Horticulture Commission, shall apply to the design, installation and maintenance of all landscaping required by this section.

Section 13.6 Alternative Compliance

1. The site design standards contained in this Part are intended to encourage development which is economically viable and environmentally sensitive. Project conditions associated with individual sites may justify approval of alternative methods of compliance with the landscape design standards. Conditions may arise where normal compliance is impractical or impossible, or where maximum achievement of the City's objectives can only be obtained through alternative compliance. Such conditions are to be approved by the Landscape Ordinance Review Committee on a case by case basis.
   A. Tree Credits. The Landscape Ordinance Review Committee may grant tree credits for preservation of existing trees and natural elements on a site by site basis.
   B. Exemptions. Exemptions from some of the requirements of this Part may be granted on a case by case basis for preservation of existing trees and natural elements.

Section 13.7 Permits and Inspection Requirements

1. The property owner must obtain from the City Building Inspector a Clearing Permit approved by the Landscape Ordinance Review Committee prior to any clearing of tracts of one (1) acre or more.

2. A Landscape Design shall be submitted along with the Building Plans when applying for a Building Permit. The landscape design shall be approved by the Landscape Ordinance Review Committee who must have a Landscape Architect registered in the State of Louisiana as a member.
3. No Building Permit shall be issued until the Landscape Design is approved by the Landscape Ordinance Review Committee.
4. A Landscape Certificate, indicating compliance with the requirements of this Part shall be obtained from the Landscape Ordinance Review Committee upon completion of landscaping and shall be presented to the City Building Official prior to the issuance of a Certificate of Occupancy.
5. The Landscape Certificate may be revoked for failure to maintain plant materials and planting areas if so determined through periodic inspection by the Landscape Ordinance Review Committee. If a Landscape Certificate is revoked, the Owner will need to reapply for and obtain a new Landscape Certificate in order to maintain the Certificate of Occupancy.

Section 13.8 Enforcement, Appeals and Penalties

1. The Landscape Ordinance Review Committee shall enforce the requirements set forth in this Part and also shall be responsible for performing necessary inspections to determine if the required landscaping has been installed according to the approved landscape design.
2. No Certificate of Occupancy shall be issued until the landscape requirements are met as shown on the approved landscape design and given final approval by the Landscape Ordinance Review Committee unless a performance bond in the amount of the estimated cost of the landscaping as determined by the Landscape Ordinance Review Committee is posted by the owner and/or developer of the property. If the owner and/or developer has not been issued a Landscape Certificate within sixty (60) days of the posting of the bond, the Landscape Ordinance Review Committee may place the owner and/or developer in default and utilize the bond proceeds to complete the required landscaping. The occupancy of any premises prior to the issuance of a Landscape Certificate shall be unlawful.
3. Any applicant denied a Landscape Certificate or who has had his Landscape Design rejected may appeal to the Mayor and Board of Aldermen within 15 days of notice of denial. The appeal must be in writing and fully state the reason or reasons for the appeal. The appeal must also be accompanied by a copy of the landscape design submitted to the Landscape Ordinance Review Committee.
4. The Landscape Ordinance Review Committee shall be composed of eight members appointed by the Mayor, subject to approval of the Board of Aldermen, who shall appoint such members as the following:

a) Denham Springs Tree Commission, member
b) Board of Alderman, member
c) A Landscape Architect, licensed in the State of Louisiana
d) A licensed landscape contractor
e) Livingston Parish Board of Realtors, member
f) A professional arborist
g) Two citizens, appointed at large

Any five members of said Committee shall constitute a quorum. Said committee shall meet at least once a month to review landscape designs and conduct the business of the Committee.

5. The Mayor and Board of Aldermen are hereby directed and authorized as a committee with full powers to act and review all appeals from the denial of a certificate or the rejection of a Landscape Design.
6. Upon the filing of an appeal, the Mayor and Board of Aldermen shall conduct a hearing on the appeal within 15 days of notice of filing. The City Clerk shall notify the appellant and the Landscape Ordinance Review Committee of the scheduled date of the hearing. The Mayor and Board of Aldermen shall establish rules and regulations for their own procedure at the hearings.
7. A decision of the Mayor and Board of Aldermen to modify or reverse a decision of the Landscape Ordinance Review Committee shall be in writing and shall set forth the reasons therefor. The decision shall also specify the conditions upon which the modification is made.
8. Any person or corporation who shall violate any of the provisions of this Ordinance or fail to comply therewith or with any of the requirements thereof, or who shall alter any planting or structure in violation of any detail statement or landscape design submitted and approved thereunder shall be guilty of a misdemeanor and shall be fined not less than twenty-five ($25.00) dollars, not more than one hundred ($100.00) dollars or be imprisoned for more than thirty (30) days for each day that the violation continues and each day such violation shall be permitted to exist shall constitute a separate offense.

Section 13.9 Administrative Guidelines

1. The Landscape Ordinance Review Committee shall adopt administrative guidelines to this ordinance in the form of Landscape Design Standards consisting of rules, regulations, procedures, approved plant material lists and landscape design requirements to be known as Landscape Ordinance, Design Guidelines for the administration and enforcement of this Ordinance.
2. Changes or modifications to the administrative guidelines shall be made by vote of the Landscape Ordinance Review Committee.
3. The City of Denham Springs through the Inspection Division of the Department of Public Works shall be authorized to collect a fifty ($50.00) dollar application fee to cover processing charges as required for the implementation of this ordinance. Such fees shall be set by resolution.

Section 13.10 Conflicts

If provisions of this ordinance conflict with other ordinances or regulations, the more stringent limitation or requirements shall govern or prevail to the extent of the conflict.

Section 13.11 Severability

If any section, subsection, sentence clause, provision or part of this Ordinance shall be held invalid for any reason, the remainder of this Ordinance shall not be affected thereby, but shall remain in full force and effect.

Section 13.12 Effective Date

1. This ordinance shall take effect ________,1995.
2. The terms of this Ordinance shall apply to all new permit applications for land alteration, vegetation removal or development filed on or after the effective date.

BATON ROUGE, LOUISIANA, LANDSCAPE ORDINANCE, CHAPTER 18: LANDSCAPE AND TREES*

Section 18.1 Purpose

The purpose of this Part is to protect and enhance the community's environmental, economic and aesthetic resources consistent with the goals of the City-Parish Comprehensive Land Use And Development Plan (Horizon Plan) thereby promoting the public health, safety and general welfare of the citizens and contributing to the quality of life by encouraging a high level of design in the development of the City and Parish.

Section 18.2 Applicability of Landscape Requirements

The provisions of this Part shall apply to:

A. All new commercial, industrial, multifamily, religious, educational, institutional, and public and semipublic land uses that are developed after January 19, 1994.

B. Development that requires the issuance of a building permit for a building addition amounting to more than fifty percent of existing street facade.

C. New development on lots with less than fifteen thousand (15,000) square feet within a multifamily, commercial or industrial-type subdivision that was approved prior to January 19, 1994, shall be exempted from the requirements of this Chapter. This exemption shall expire on January 19, 2004.

---

*East Baton Rouge Parish, Uniform Development Code, October 1997

Section 18.3 Landscape Standards

A. The following areas of a lot shall be developed and maintained in accordance with landscape standards set forth hereinafter:
   1. Street planting areas
   2. Sight triangle areas at street intersections
   3. Buffer planting areas, along side and rear property lines
   4. Vehicular use areas within parking lots and auto storage areas
   5. Trash and garbage storage areas (located less than one-hundred feet from a public street).

B. The following Standards shall be included in the Landscape Plan.
   1. All landscaping shall be installed in a sound manner and in accordance with accepted standards of the Louisiana Nurseryman's Manual for the Environmental Horticulture Industry.
   2. Plant material shall be true to name, variety and size and shall conform to all applicable provisions of the American Standards for Nursery Stock, latest edition.
   3. All single trunk trees shall have a minimum of two-and-one-half (2½) inch caliper immediately after planting. Two multitrunk trees with a minimum one (1) inch caliper per trunk may be substituted for each single trunk tree.
   4. Multitrunk trees shall have main stems with a minimum one (1) inch caliper per trunk immediately after planting. All multitrunk trees shall have a minimum of three (3) trunks.
   5. Ground covers (other than turfgrass) shall be minimum of four (4) inch container stock spaced twelve (12) inches on center. Two-and-one-half (2½) inch container stock may be substituted and spaced eight (8) inches on center.
   6. A minimum of one hundred (100) square feet for each Class "A" tree or fifty (50) square feet for each Class "B" tree of non-paved area is required for each tree where it is planted.
   7. No tree or shrub shall be planted in any servitude or easement without the written permission of the user agency or agencies.

C. Technical requirements for the installation of plant materials and landscape area site development shall be as follows.
   1. Street Planting Area Requirements + Vehicular Use Area Requirements + Bufferyards Requirements + Developed Site Area Requirements = Total Landscape Requirements.
   2. There shall be two (2) Class "A" trees or four (4) Class "B" trees for each ten thousand (10,000) square feet, or fraction thereof, of developed site area. On a site with buildings exceeding fifty thousand (50,000) square feet, fifty (50) percent of required trees shall be Class "A".

3. The street planting area shall contain a minimum of one (1) Class "A" tree or two (2) Class "B" trees for every sixty (60) linear feet of street frontage, or fraction thereof, measured at the property line. The required trees may be located anywhere within the street planting area. Corner lots with frontage on more than one street shall calculate the street planting requirement along the entire street frontage.
4. A standard bufferyard width is imposed, with a prescribed number of plants per one hundred (100) feet. (see Appendix D) Each optional bufferyard can fluctuate in width and in the amount of required plant materials based on the "plant unit multiplier". The plant unit multiplier, which can range from forty-five hundredths (.45) to one and five tenths (1.5), is multiplied by the required "plant units" (found in the legend). When a computation using the "plant unit multiplier" results in a fraction of five tenths (0.5) or greater, the planting requirement shall be rounded up to the next whole number.

   The number of plant materials, the structure required and the location of the structure are provided for in Bufferyard Alternatives (A, B, C and D). Height, material and opacity standards for designated fences, berms and masonry walls can be found on the Structure Required page.
5. Any wall shall be constructed in a durable fashion with a finished surface of brick, stone or other decorative masonry material approved by the Building Official.

   Fences shall be constructed in a durable fashion with weather resistant wood and be of a consistent pattern. All materials used in the construction of a fence shall be designed and intended for such use. Notwithstanding the forgoing, the Director of Landscape and Forestry may approve a buffer fence/wall constructed of other materials provided the materials and finish used will provide generally the same degree of opacity, durability, and aesthetic compatibility with adjoining residential areas as weather resistant wood. A finished side of all walls or fences shall face the common property line boundary. No wall or fence used for screening purposes shall be less than three (3) feet nor greater than eight (8) feet in height above grade.

   Prescribed fences or walls may be waived if a building, fence, or wall of at least equivalent height, opacity, and maintenance exists immediately abutting and on the opposite side of said property line.
6. All berms shall be planted with both shrubs and groundcovers to leave no bare earth. All shrubs shall be a species that can be expected to materially screen the development site within two (2) years of planting. The slope of a berm shall be of a grade that is suitable for maintenance and soil stability while taking into

consideration the type of plantings and groundcover that will be utilized but in no case shall a berm be less than three (3) feet in height. Nuisance vining plants that have a tendency to spread to other properties, are not permitted as berm groundcover. Designated berms (B1 & B2) may be curvilinear in design. Combined fence and berm height at any point must meet designated minimum height requirements.

7. Vehicular use areas shall be required to have a minimum of five (5) percent of the total vehicular use area landscaped. Such landscaping shall be distributed within the vehicular use area. Class "A" trees peripheral to the vehicular use area may be counted if a minimum of forty (40) percent of their canopies, at maturity, can be expected to shade or overlap the vehicular use area. Such trees will not, however, be counted to either the overall site tree requirements not the street planting area requirements. The landscaping shall be installed accordingly:
   a. For vehicular use areas of one to fifty (50) parking spaces, one (1) Class "A" tree or two (2) Class "B" trees for every twenty-five (25) parking spaces, or fraction thereof.
   b. For vehicular use areas of fifty (50) to one hundred (100) parking spaces, one (1) Class "A" tree or two (2) Class "B" trees for every eighteen (18) parking spaces, or fraction thereof.
   c. For vehicular use areas of over one hundred (100) parking spaces, one (1) Class "A" tree or two (2) Class "B" trees for every twelve (12) parking spaces, or fraction thereof.
   d. All such landscaped areas shall be protected from vehicular access to these areas.
8. For new vehicular use areas on sites zoned C-5, permanent landscaping shall be installed, as follows:
   a. Trees shall be planted at the rate of one (1) Class "A" tree or two (2) Class "B" trees per twelve (12) parking spaces, or fraction thereof.
   b. Required trees may be planted within the vehicular use area or along its perimeter. Where such a planting of trees may not be entirely accommodated within the property lines of the site, some or all of said trees may be planted within the public right-of-way in accordance with the Downtown Development District Street Tree Plan as reviewed by the Downtown Development District Commission.
   c. Residual areas not used for vehicular use or access shall be landscaped.
9. Technical requirements for the maintenance of plant materials and landscape areas shall be as follows.
   a. The owner, or his agent, shall be responsible for the maintenance, repair and replacement of all landscape

materials as may be required by the provisions of this Unified Development Code.

b. Landscape maintenance specifications require that all landscaping shall be maintained in a sound manner and in accordance with accepted maintenance procedures as established by the Louisiana Association of Nurserymen.

c. All plant materials and planted areas shall be tended and maintained in a healthy growing condition; replaced when necessary and kept free of refuse and debris.

10. Existing trees may be credited towards the landscape materials required by this part.

a. In all applicable zoning districts, credit may be applied toward the tree planting requirements of this Unified Development Code by the preservation of existing trees within Street Planting Areas, Buffer Areas and other areas of the site left undisturbed by construction.

b. The owner is encouraged to preserve as many existing trees and shrubs as possible in the design and implementation of the landscape plan.

c. Trees preserved in the street planting areas shall be credited toward street planting requirements, trees preserved in vehicular use areas be credited toward vehicular use area requirements and trees preserved in a buffer planting area shall be credited toward buffer area planting requirements.

d. It shall be the responsibility of the owner to use reasonable care to maintain preserved trees. If a preserved tree dies within five years, it is the responsibility of the owner to replace that tree with the number of trees credited on a Class matching basis within six months. The owner shall be responsible for maintaining all plant materials required by this Unified Development Code in good living condition.

e. Tree credit rate for each tree preserved shall be determined by the following schedule:

Existing Dripline Diameter of Preserved Tree(s)*	**OR**	**Existing Trunk Diameter of Preserved Tree(s)****	**Number of Tree Credits**
50 feet or greater in spread		26 inches or greater in diameter	5
40–49 feet in spread		20 inches in diameter	4
20–39 feet in spread		9–19 inches in diameter	3
6–10 feet in spread		3–8 inches in diameter	2

* Dripline Diameter measurement shall be rounded off to the nearest foot.

** Diameter of trunk of preserved tree shall be rounded off to the nearest inch, measured at a height four and one half ($4^1/_2$) feet above natural grade.

i. All other trees preserved will receive one credit with the exception of Chinese Tallow (Sapium sebiferum), Black Willow (Salix nigra), Cottonwood (Populus deltoides), Camphor Tree (Cinnamomum camphora) and other trees with life spans of twenty years or less.

ii. If any preserved tree dies within five years of construction on the preservation site, one tree shall be replaced for each tree credited against such preserved tree that dies.

f. In order to receive credit for preserved trees, the owner must include as part of the Landscape Plan submittal a Tree Preservation Plan which must be approved by the Director of Landscape and Forestry.

i. The Tree Preservation Plan shall include the location, size, and condition of each tree to be preserved, along with an indication of proposed development features which may impact such trees, and any other pertinent information as required by the Director of Landscape and Forestry to evaluate existing and proposed conditions.

ii. The Tree Preservation Plan shall include a detailed description of all methods to be used to ensure the survival of all trees scheduled for preservation credit, including information that may be required by the Director of Landscape and Forestry to interpret the intent and methodology proposed.

iii. All tree preservation methodology shall conform to the standards of the Louisiana Department of Agriculture and Forestry, the Louisiana Horticulture Commission, and the International Society of Arboriculture.

Section 18.4 Landscape Plan Requirements

A. All building permit applications covered by this Unified Development Code shall be accompanied by a landscape plan. This landscape plan shall be drawn in accordance with Louisiana Horticulture Law and shall include such criteria that may be required by the Director of Landscape and Forestry or City-Parish building Official to interpret the extent of the permit application. All landscape plans shall bear the official seal and signature of a Landscape Architect licensed in the State of Louisiana, an official Landscape Contractor's identification number, or a statement, bearing the signature of the preparer of the plan, certifying that the plan was prepared in accordance with Louisiana Horticulture Law.

B. Standards, as specified in Section 18.3 (Landscape Standards), shall apply to the design, installation and maintenance of all landscaping required.

Section 18.5 Alternative Compliance

A. The Landscape Standards contained in Section 18.3 are intended to encourage development which is economically viable and environmentally sensitive. The standards are not intended to be so specific as to inhibit creative development. Project conditions associated with individual sites may justify approval of alternative methods of compliance with the Landscape Standards. Conditions may arise where normal compliance is impractical or impossible, or where maximum achievement of the City-Parish's objectives can only be obtained through alternative compliance. Such conditions are contained within the Landscape Standards.

B. Requests for alternative compliance will be accepted for any permit application to which the requirements of this Chapter of the Unified Development Code apply, when one or more of the following conditions are met:

  1. Topography, soil, vegetation, drainage or other site conditions are such that full compliance is impractical.
  2. Improved environmental quality would result from the alternative compliance provisions of this Chapter of the Unified Development Code.
  3. Spatial limitations, unusually shaped pieces of land, unusual servitude requirements or prevailing practices in the surrounding neighborhood may justify alternative compliance for in-fill sites.
  4. Change on an existing site where requirements of this Chapter of the Unified Development Code are not spatially possible. Public safety considerations make alternative compliance necessary.
  5. Existing lots in approved multi-family, commercial and industrial subdivisions which exist on January 19, 1994.

C. A request for alternative compliance shall be submitted to the Director of Landscape and Forestry at the time the Landscape Plan is submitted. The Director of Landscape and Forestry shall not reduce requirements of Chapter 18 by more than fifty (50) percent. The decision of the Director of Landscape and Forestry will be final, unless the applicant appeals per Section 18.7.

D. Requests for alternative compliance shall be accompanied by sufficient written explanation and Landscape Plan drawings to allow appropriate evaluation and decision by the Director of Landscape and Forestry.

E. In a situation where compliance with this Chapter of the Unified Development Code is not possible, and there is no feasible alternative for compliance the applicant shall apply to the Planning Commission and the Metropolitan Council for a waiver of this Chapter of the Unified Development Code.

Section 18.6 Permits and Inspection Requirements

A. Prior to any clearing of tracts of five acres or more, the property owner shall obtain approval from the Department of Public Works who shall notify the Director of Landscape and Forestry. Property owners are encouraged to identify significant trees on sites and to seek the assistance of the Office of Landscape and Forestry in preserving them.

B. A Landscape Plan shall be submitted along with the building plans when applying for a building permit. The Landscape Plan shall be approved by the Director of Landscape and Forestry (who must be a Landscape Architect registered in the State of Louisiana) prior to issuance of the building permit.

C. If the owner or developer has not installed the approved landscaping within ninety (90) days of the completion of the building, the Director of Landscape and Forestry may place the owner in default which shall constitute a violation of this section of the Unified Development Code. Such violation shall subject the owner to a fine of fifty dollars per day for each day that the required landscaping is not completed.

D. Failure to maintain plant materials and planting areas as determined through periodic inspection by the Director of Landscape and Forestry shall constitute a violation of this Chapter of the Unified Development Code. Such violation shall subject the owner to a fine of fifty (50.00) dollars per day for each day that the required landscaping is not maintained.

Section 18.7 Enforcement, Appeals and Penalties

A. The Director of Landscape and Forestry shall enforce the requirements set forth in this Part and also shall be responsible for performing necessary inspections to determine if the required landscaping has been installed according to the approved Landscape Plan.

B. The Director of Landscape and Forestry shall review each Landscape Plan and within ten (10) days from receipt of such plan either approve or issue a written denial.

C. Any applicant whose Landscape Plan is rejected may appeal to the Tree and Landscape Commission within thirty (30) days of written notice of rejection. The appeal must be in writing and fully state the reason or reasons for the appeal. A copy of the Landscape Plan submitted to the building Official must also accompany the appeal.

D. Upon the receipt of an appeal, the Tree and Landscape Commission shall hear the appeal at their next scheduled meeting, provided that notification has occurred at least fifteen (15) days prior to any scheduled meeting. The Commission shall notify the applicant and the Director of Landscape and Forestry of the scheduled date of the hearing. The Commission shall establish rules and regulations for its own procedure at the hearings.

E. A decision of the Tree and Landscape Commission to modify or reverse a decision of the Director of Landscape and Forestry shall be in writing and shall set forth the reasons therefor. The decision shall also specify the conditions upon which the modification is made.
F. A decision of the Tree and Landscape Commission may be appealed to the Planning Commission and the Metropolitan Council.

Section 18.8 Administrative Guidelines

A. The Director of Landscape and Forestry shall prepare administrative guidelines to this Chapter of the Unified Development Code consisting of rules, regulations, procedures, and landscape drawing requirements for the administration and enforcement of this Chapter of the Unified Development Code. These guidelines shall be approved by the Landscape Review Committee.
B. Changes or modifications to the Landscape Standards shall be approved by majority vote of the Landscape Review Committee, the Planning Commission and the Metropolitan Council following public hearings.
C. The City-Parish of East Baton Rouge through the Inspection Division of the Department of Public Works shall be authorized to collect a fifty (50.00) dollar application fee to cover processing charges which shall be included in the total building permit fees as required for the implementation of this Unified Development Code.

Kay O. Ourso

APPENDIX B

Directory to Landscape Ordinances

ALABAMA

Fairhope
c/o Jubilee Landscape Incorporated
Landscape Design & Construction
P.O. Box 991
Fairhope, AL 36533

City of Huntsville
Planning Department
308 Fountain Circle
Huntsville, AL 35801
205-532-7353
fax 205-535-4236

City of Mobile
Land Use Administration
Land Use/Code Administration
Department
P.O. Box 1827
111 South Royal Street
Mobile, AL 36633-1827
205-434-5895

ALASKA

Anchorage
Department of Community Planning
P.O. Box 196650
Anchorage, AK 99519-6650
907-343-4222

ARIZONA

City of Glendale
Engineering Department
5850 W. Glendale Avenue
Glendale, AZ 85301
602-930-3630
fax 602-915-2689

City of Mesa
Planning and Community Development
55 North Center Street
P.O. Box 1466
Mesa, AZ 85211-1466
602-644-2185

City of Tempe
Community Development Department
115 East Fifth Street
Tempe, AZ 85281
602-350-8331
fax 602-350-8872

ARKANSAS

City of Fayetteville
Planning Department
113 West Mountain Street
Fayetteville, AR 72701
501-521-7700
fax 501-575-8257

Hot Springs
Hot Springs/Garland County
Beautification Commission
c/o Bob Byers, Landscape Architect
Twentieth Century Gardens
498 Arkridge Road
Hot Springs, AR 71913
501-262-2711

City of Little Rock
Department of Neighborhood
Revitalization and Planning
723 W. Markham, 2nd Floor
Little Rock, AR 72201-1334
501-371-4864
fax 501-371-6863

CALIFORNIA

City of Davis
Planning and Building Department
23 Russell Boulevard
Davis, CA 95616
916-757-5610
fax 916-758-0204

Glendale
Public Works/Building Section
633 E. Broadway, Room 101
Glendale, CA 91206-4390
818-956-4835

City of Hayward
Department of Community and
Economic Development
25151 Clawiter Road
Hayward, CA 94545-2731
510-293-5000
fax 510-293-1590

City of Irvine
Community Development
Department
One Civic Center Plaza
P.O. Box 19575
Irvine, CA 92713

City of Long Beach
City Attorney for Long Beach
333 West Ocean Boulevard
Long Beach, CA 90802
213-590-6061

City of Los Angeles
Department of Planning
Plan Approval Section
221 North Figueroa Street, Room 1500
Mail Stop 395
Los Angles, CA 90012-2601
212-580-5562
fax 213-2403005

Mariposa County
Planning Manager-Landscape Architect
P.O. Box 2039
Mariposa, CA 95338
209-966-5151
fax 209-742-5024

City of Napa
Planning Department
P.O. Box 660
Napa, CA 94559-0660
707-257-9530
fax 707-257-9522

City of National City
Planning Department
1243 National City Boulevard
National City, CA 91950
619-336-4310

Oakland
East Bay Municipal Utility District
375 Eleventh Street
Oakland, CA 94607-4240
415-287-0590

City of Ontario
Community Services Agency
Landscape Planner
303 East "B" Street
Ontario, CA 91764
714-986-1151

City of Palm Springs
Planning Division
Palm Springs, CA
619-323-8245

City of Riverside
Department of City Planning
City Hall, Room 655
Los Angeles, CA 90012

City of Roseville
c/o HLA Group
1990 Third Street
Sacramento, CA 95814
916-447-7400
fax 916-447-8270

City of San Diego
c/o Robin Shifflet & Associates
3749 Texas Street
San Diego, CA 92104
fax 619-543-9325

San Diego
City of San Diego
Planning Department
San Diego, CA 92101
619-236-6460

City of South San Francisco
Department of Economic and
Community Development
City Hall
400 Grand Avenue
P.O. Box 711
South San Francisco, CA 94083
415-877-3990
fax 415-872-3269

State of California, Model Water
Efficient Landscape Ordinance
Sacramento
State of California—The Resources
Agency
Department of Water Resources
P.O. Box 942836
Sacramento, CA 94236-0001

COLORADO

Aspen
130 South Galena Street
Aspen, CO 81611
970-920-5093
fax 970-920-5439

Town of Breckenridge
P.O. Box 168
Breckenridge, CO 80424
303-453-3183
fax 303-547-3104

City of Colorado Springs
Parks and Recreation Department
1401 Recreation Highway
Colorado Springs, CO 80905
715-578-6640

City and County of Denver
Department of Parks-Recreation
2300 15th Street
Denver, CO 80202-1139

City of Fort Collins
281 North College Avenue
Fort Collins, CO 80522-0580
303-221-6360

City of Lakewood
Planning, Permits and Public Works
445 South Allison Parkway
Lakewood, CO 80226-3105
303-987-7519
fax 303-987-7678

City of Pueblo
Department of Planning and
Development
211 East D Street
Pueblo, CO 81001
719-543-6006

City of Thornton
9500 Civic Center Drive
P.O. Box 291220
Thornton, CO 80229-1220

CONNECTICUT

Town of Wilton
Planning and Zoning Commission
Wilton Town Hall
Wilton, CT 06897
203-834-9250

FLORIDA

Central Florida Cities:
- Orange County
- St. Lucie County
- Dade County
- Gainesville
- Homestead
- Indian River
- Lake Mary

Maitland
Sanford
Oviedo
Orlando
Altamonet Springs

c/o Foster Conant & Associates
455 South Orange Avenue, Suite 501
Orlando, FL 32801-3355
407-648-2225
fax 407-648-0175

Cooper City
P.O. Box 290910
9090 Southwest 50th Place
Cooper City, FL 33329-0910
305-434-4300
fax 305-434-5099

Collier County Government
Office of Capital Projects Management
3301 Tamiami Trail East
Naples, FL 33962
941-774-8192
fax 941-774-9370

City of Coral Gables
Office of Planning Director
P.O. Box 141549
Coral Gables, FL 33141-1549

Coral Springs
9551 West Sample Road
P.O. Box 754502
Coral Springs, FL 33075-4501
305-344-1155

Dania
City Hall
100 West Dania Boulevard
Dania, FL 33004

Town of Davie
Development Services Department
Planning and Zoning Division
6591 Orange Drive
Davie, FL 33314-3399
945-797-1103
fax 954-979-1086

City of Daytona Beach
P.O. Box 2451
Daytona Beach, FL 32115-2451
904-258-3117
fax 904-947-3020

City of Delray Beach
Community Improvement Department
100 N.W. First Avenue
Delray Beach, FL 33444
407-243-7226

Hollywood
City of Hollywood
Community Planning Department
2600 Hollywood Boulevard, Room 315
P.O. Box 229045
Hollywood, FL 33022-9045

City of Jacksonville
Engineering Division
220 E. Bay Street, #901
Jacksonville, FL 32202
904-630-1363

Lee County Division of Planning and Construction
2100 Second Street
Fort Meyers, FL 33901

Lighthouse Point
City of Lighthouse Point
P.O. Box 5100
2200 N.E. 38th Street
Lighthouse Point, FL 33064
305-943-6500

Margate
City of Margate
Department of Environmental and Engineering Services
1001 W. River Drive
Margate, FL 33063
(305) 972-0828
fax 305-978-3498

City of Miami
Department of Community Planning and Revitalization
444 S.W. Second Avenue
Miami, FL 33130
305-416-1400
fax 305-416-2156

North Lauderdale
City of North Lauderdale
Community Development Department
701 S.W. 71st Avenue
North Lauderdale, FL 33068-2395
305-724-7069
fax 305-720-2064

City of North Miami
776 N.E. 125th Street
N. Miami, FL 33161
fax 305-899-0497

City of North Miami Beach
17011 N.E. 19th Avenue
North Miami, FL 33162-3194
305-948-2966

Oakland Park
City of Oakland Park
3650 N.E. 12th Avenue
Oakland Park, FL 33334

City of Orlando
Bureau of Parks and Special Facilities
1206 W. Columbia Street
Orlando, FL 32805
407-849-2287

City of Ormond Beach
Planning and Zoning
22 South Beach Street
P.O. Box 277
Ormond Beach, FL 32175-0277
904-676-3238
fax 904-676-3330

Parkland
City of Parkland
Planning Department
6500 Parkside Drive
Parkland, FL 33067
305-753-5040
fax 305-341-5161

Pembroke Pines
City of Pembroke Pines
Planning/Landscape Division
10100 Pines Boulevard
Pembroke Pines, FL 33026
305-435-6513

Plantation
City of Plantation
Landscape Department
400 N.W. 73rd Avenue
Plantation, FL 33317-1678
305-797-2200

Pompano Beach
City of Pompano Beach—Zoning
P.O. Drawer 1300
100 W. Atlantic Boulevard
Pompano Beach, FL 33061
954-786-4634

Sunrise
City of Sunrise
Planning and Engineering
10770 West Oakland Park Boulevard
Sunrise, FL 33351
305-746-3270
fax 305-746-3287

City of St. Petersburg
Planning Department
P.O. Box 2842
St. Petersburg, FL 33731
813-892-5182

Tampa-Hillsborough County
Natural Resources Planning
Planning and Development Management Department
Office of the County Administrator
P.O. Box 1110
Tampa, FL 33601
813-272-5710

City of Tampa, Parks Department
7525 North Boulevard
Tampa, FL 33604
813-931-2121
fax 813-931-2120

Volusia County
Growth Management and Environmental Services Division
123 West Indiana Avenue
DeLand, FL 32720-4253
904-736-5959

GEORGIA

Americus
c/o Ellis, Easterlin, Peagler, Gatewood, Harper & Skipper, Attorneys at Law
P.O. Box 488
Americus, GA 31709
912-924-9316
fax 912-924-6248

Gwinnett County
Planning Department, Land Development Section
75 Langley Drive
Lawrenceville, GA 30245
404-822-7510

Oconee County
Planning Department
P.O. Box 145
Watkinsville, GA 30677
706-769-3910

HAWAII

City and County of Honolulu
Facilities Development Division
650 South King Street
Honolulu, HI 96813

ILLINOIS

Bolingbrook
375 W. Briarcliff Road
Bolingbrook, IL 60439-0951
708-759-0400
fax 708-759-0545

Bartlett
Teska Associates, Inc.
627 Grove Street
Evanston, IL 60201
847-869-2015
fax 847-869-2059

Village of Cherry Valley
202 E. State Street
Cherry Valley, IL 61016
815-332-3441
fax 815-332-3414

Chicago
c/o Landscape Architects/Land Planners
417 S. Dearborn Street, Suite 510
Chicago, IL 60605
312-663-5494
fax 312-663-5497

City of Danville
Planning Department
17 West Main Street
Danville, IL 61832

DuPage County Development Department
Planning Division
421 North County Farm Road
Wheaton, IL 60187
708-682-7230
fax 708-682-7179

Village of Arlington Heights
Bensenville
Village of Bannockburn
Schaumburg

Village of Machesney Park
Director of Planning and Zoning
Chad Atkinson
300 Machesney Road
Machesney Park, IL 61115-2495
815-877-5432
fax 815-877-6958

City of Peoria
Planning and Growth Management
City Hall Building
419 Fulton Street, Room 404
Peoria, IL 61602
309-672-8556
fax 309-672-0925

City of Rockford
425 East State Street
Rockford, Illinois 61104
815-987-5585

South Holland
c/o Paul Handing, ASLA
4864 W. Augusta Boulevard
Monee, IL 60449
708-534-0887

City of Wheaton
Mr. James P. Kozik
303 West Wesley Street
Box 727
Wheaton, IL 60189-0727

INDIANA

City of West Lafayette
Clerk-Treasurer
City Hall
609 West Navajo Street
West Lafayette, IN 47906
317-463-3571

IOWA

City of Davenport
Construction and Engineering Department
226 West Fourth Street
Davenport, IA 52801
319-326-7766

KANSAS

Kansas City
Department of Development/Planning and Zoning Division
Municipal Office Building
701 North 7th Street
Kansas City, KS 66101

Lawrence-Douglas County Metropolitan Planning Office
P.O. Box 708
6th and Massachusetts Street
Lawrence, KS 66044-0708
913-832-3160
fax 913-832-3150

City of Leawood
4800 Town Center Drive
Leawood, KS 66211
913-339-6700
fax 913-339-6781

Lenexa, Kansas
City of Lenexa
12350 W. 87th Street Parkway
P.O. Box 14888
Lenexa, KS 66215

Overland Park
City of Overland Park
Department of Planning and Research
8500 Santa Fe Drive
Overland Park, KS 66212

Wichita-Sedgwick County
Metropolitan Area Planning Department
City Hall, Tenth Floor
455 North Main Street
Wichita, KS 67202-1688
316-286-4421

KENTUCKY

Louisville
Louisville and Jefferson County Planning Commission
531 Court Place, Suite 900
Louisville, KY 40202-3396

LOUISIANA

Caddo Parish
Caddo Parish Commission
Caddo Parish Courthouse
Shreveport, LA 71101
318-226-6900

City of Covington
Mayor's Office
Hon. Keith Villere, ASLA
P.O. Box 778
Covington, LA 70433
504-892-1811

City-Parish of East Baton Rouge
Office of Landscape and Forestry
P.O. Box 1471
Baton Rouge, LA 70821

Denham Springs
James Durbin, Alderman
112 Hummell Avenue
Denham Springs, LA 70727-0608
504-665-8117
fax 504-664-7973

Hammond
City of Hammond
Buildings and Streets Department
P.O. Box 2788
Hammond, LA 70404
504-542-3400

Jefferson Parish
Jefferson Parish Planning Department
P.O. Box 10242
Jefferson, LA 70181-0242
504-736-6320

Jennings
City of Jennings
Inspector's Office
P.O. Box 1249
Jennings, LA 70546
318-824-0432

Kenner
City of Kenner
Planning Department, Director of Planning
1801 Williams Boulevard
Kenner, LA 70062
504-468-7200

Lafayette
City of Lafayette
Planning and Development Management Department
P.O. Box 4017-C
Lafayette, LA 70502
318-261-8445

Lake Charles
City of Lake Charles
Planning and Development
P.O. Box 1178
Lake Charles, LA 70602
318-491-1200

Leesville
City of Leesville Planning Commission
P.O. Drawer 350
Leesville, LA 71446
318-239-2444

Mandeville
City of Mandeville
Planning Department, Director of Planning
3101 E. Causeway Approach
Mandeville, LA 70448
Hon. Paul Spitzfaden, Mayor
504-626-3144

Monroe
City of Monroe
Planning and Zoning
P.O. Box 123
Monroe, LA 71201-0123
318-329-2218

New Orleans
City of New Orleans
City Planning Commission
Room 9W, City Hall
1300 Perdido Street
New Orleans, LA 70112
504-565-7000

Ruston
City of Ruston
P.O. Box 280
Ruston, LA 71273
318-251-8640

Shreveport
Metropolitan Planning Commission
1234 Texas Avenue
P.O. Box 31109
Shreveport, LA 71101
318-226-5766

Slidell
City of Slidell Planning Department
P.O. Box 828
Slidell, LA 70459
Hon. Sam Caruso, Mayor
504-643-3434

St. Tammany Parish
Development and Permits Department
St. Tammany Parish Police Jury
P.O. Box 628
Covington, LA 70434
504-898-2529
504-646-4085

MAINE

City of Bangor
73 Harlow Street
Bangor, ME 04401
207-945-4400

MARYLAND

City of Annapolis
Department of Planning and Zoning
160 Duke of Gloucester Street
Annapolis, MD 21401
410-263-7961
fax 410-263-3322

Prince George's County
County Administration Building
14741 Governor Oden Bowie Drive
Upper Marlboro, MD 20772
301-952-3600

Queen Anne's County
Department of Planning and Zoning
County Office Building
208 N. Commerce Street
Centreville, MD 21617
410-758-1255
fax 410-758-0366

MASSACHUSETTS

City of Somerville
City Hall
93 Highland Avenue
Somerville, MA 02143
617-625-6600

MICHIGAN

City of Ann Arbor
Planning Director
100 N. Fifth Avenue
Ann Arbor, MI 48107

County of Emmet
Department of Planning and Zoning
200 Division Street
Petoskey, MI 49770

City of Southfield
Parks and Recreation
26000 Evergreen Road
P.O. Box 2055
Southfield, MI 48037-2055

Sumpter Township
23480 Sumpter Road
Belleville, MI 48111
313-461-6201

City of Warren
Planning Commission
29500 Van Dyke Avenue
Warren. MI 48093

MINNESOTA

City of St. Paul
Office of License, Inspection and Environmental Protection
350 St. Peter Street, Suite 310
St. Paul, MN 55102-1510
612-266-9086
fax 612-266-9099

MISSISSIPPI

Jackson
Division of Metropolitan Planning and Development
200 South President Street
P.O. Box 22568
Jackson, MS 39225-2568
601-960-2071

City of Vicksburg
P.O. Box 150
Vicksburg, MS 39181

MISSOURI

Blue Springs
City Planning
903 West Main Street
Blue Springs, MO 64015

Independence
City of Independence
Community Development Department
111 E. Maple
Independence, MO 64051-0519

Lee's Summit
207 W.W. Market
P.O. Box 1600
Lee's Summit, MO 64063

NEBRASKA

City of Kearney
Department of Public Works
18 East 22nd Street
P.O. Box 1180
Kearney, NE 68848-1180
308-233-3215
fax 308-234-6399

Lincoln
City Planning Department
555 South 10th Street
Lincoln, NE 68508

Omaha
City of Omaha
Planning Department
1819 Farnam Street, Suite 1111
Omaha, Nebraska 68183-0110
402-444-5200
fax 402-444-6140

NEVADA

City of Las Vegas
Comprehensive Planning
500 S. Grand Central Parkway
P.O. Box 551744
Las Vegas, NV 89155-1744
702-455-4314
fax 702-455-3271

City of Sparks
Planning & Community Development Department
P.O. Box 857
Sparks, NV 89432-0857
702-353-2340
fax 702-353-2489

NEW HAMPSHIRE

City of Concord
Planning Department
41 Green Street
Concord, NH 03301
603-225-8515

NEW JERSEY

East Windsor
c/o Melillo & Bauer Associates
Landscape Architecture
P.O. Box 1005
302 Hawthorne Avenue
Point Pleasant Beach, NJ 08742
908-295-9630
908-295-8406

Mendham
c/o Anna Cheng Young & Associates
Landscape Architects
246 Talmage Road
Mendham, NJ 07945

Borough of Paramus
Jockish Square
Paramus, NJ 07652

City of Piscataway
Municipal Complex
455 Hoes Lane
Piscataway, NJ 08854
908-562-6570
fax 908-562-1337

Randolf
Township of Randolph
Municipal Building
502 Millbrook Avenue
Randolph, NJ 07869
201-989-7100
201-989-7076

NEW MEXICO

City of Albuquerque
Parks and General Services Department
One Civic Plaza
P.O. Box 1293
Albuquerque, NM 87103

NEW YORK

Town of Clifton Park
One Town Hall Plaza
Clifton Park, NY 12065
518-371-6054
fax 518-371-1136

Town of Hempstead
Parks Department
200 North Franklin Street
Hempstead, NY 11550
516-292-9000
fax 516-292-6024

City of Watertown
Planning Department
245 Washington Street
Municipal Building, Suite 302
Watertown, NY 13601-3380
315-785-7730
fax 315-782-9014

NORTH CAROLINA

Cary
Town of Cary
316 North Academy Street
P.O. Box 1147
Cary, NC 27512-1147

Town of Chapel Hill
306 North Columbia Street
Chapel Hill, NC 27516
919-968-2700

Charlotte-Mecklenburg Government
Charlotte Engineering Department
600 E. Fourth Street
Charlotte, NC 28202

City of Greensboro
General Services Department
P.O. Box 3136
Greensboro, NC 27402-3136

City of Hickory
Department of Planning and Development
P.O. Box 398
Hickory, NC 28603-0398
704-323-7422
fax 704-323-7550

City of Kinston
Department of Planning and Development
P.O. Drawer 339
Kinston, NC 28502
919-939-3253
fax 919-939-3127

Orange County
Planning Department
306F Revere Road
Hillsborough, NC 27278
919-732-8181

City of Raleigh
Planning Department
222 West Hargett Street
P.O. Box 590
Raleigh, NC 27602
919-890-3658
fax 919-890-3690

City-County Planning Board of Forsyth County and Winston-Salem
P.O. Box 2511
Winston-Salem, NC 27102
910-727-2087
fax 910-748-3163

OHIO

City of Cleveland
Research, Planning and Development
1501 North Marginal Road
Cleveland, OH 44114
216-664-3284

Hilliard
c/o Edsall & Associates
Land Planners-Landscape Architects
754 Neil Avenue
Columbus, OH 43215
614-221-0580

Dublin
City of Dublin
Planning and Zoning
5131 Post Road, Suite 105
Dublin, OH 43017
614-761-6553

City of Kettering
Planning and Development
3600 Shroyer Road
Kettering, OH 45429

Vandalia
c/o Edsall & Associates
Landscape Architects-Land Planners
754 Neil Avenue
Columbus, OH 43215
614-221-0580

OKLAHOMA

City of Oklahoma City
Oklahoma Planning Department
420 West Main Street, 9th Floor
Oklahoma City, OK 73102
405-297-3908
fax 405-297-1631

City of Stillwater
Community Development Department
Planning Division
P.O. Box 1449
Stillwater, OK 74076

OREGON

City of Ashland
Department of Community Development
City Hall
20 East Main Street
Ashland, OR 97520
503-482-3211

City of Medford
c/o Galbraith & Smith PC
Landscape Architects-Site Planners
815 East Jackson Street
Medford, OR 97504
503-770-7964
fax 503-770-5164

City of Phoenix
P.O. Box 666
Phoenix, OR 97535

City of Portland
Bureau of Planning
1120 SW Fifth, Room 1002
Portland, OR 97204-1966
503-823-7700
fax 503-823-7800

PENNSYLVANIA

Findlay Township
P.O. Box W, Route 30
Clinton, PA 15026

Upper Macungie Township
Urban Research and Development Corporation
28 Bethlehem Plaza
Bethlehem, PA 18018
610-865-0701
fax 610-868-7613

SOUTH CAROLINA

Anderson County
Anderson County Planning
P.O. 8002
101 South Main Street
Anderson, SC 29622
803-260-4043
fax 803-260-4613

City of Beaufort
Department of Planning
P.O. Drawer 1167
Beaufort, SC 29901
803-525-7011
fax 803-525-7013

City of Hilton Head Island
Natural Resources Administrator
One Town Center Court
Hilton Head Island, SC 29928
803-686-0904
fax 803-842-7728

Town of Mount Pleasant
Department of Planning and Engineering
P.O. Box 745
Mount Pleasant, SC 29465
803-884-1229

City of Myrtle Beach
Drawer 2468
Myrtle Beach, SC 29576
803-626-7645
fax 803-448-3627

SOUTH DAKOTA

Rapid City
Planning Department
300 Sixth Street
Rapid City, SD 57701
605-394-4120
fax 605-394-6636

City of Sioux Falls
Planning and Building Services
City Hall
224 West Ninth Street
Sioux Falls, SD 57104-6407
605-367-7130
fax 605-367-7801

TENNESSEE

Town of Collierville
Department of Planning
151 Walnut Street
Collierville, TN 38017
901-853-3279
fax 901-853-3233

Bartlett
c/o Fisher, Phillips, Arnold, Inc.
Engineers-Planners-Landscape Architects
475 Jack Kramer Drive
Memphis, TN 38117
901-761-1811

Nashville
Metropolitan Planning Commission
730 Second Avenue South
Nashville, TN 37201

Metropolitan Government of Nashville and Davidson County
Department of Codes Administration
Metro Howard Building
700 Second Avenue
Nashville, TN 37201
615-862-6500
fax 615-862-6514

TEXAS

Austin
City of Austin
Planning Department
P.O. Box 1088
Austin, TX 78767
512-499-6438

City of College Station, Texas
P.O. Box 9960
College Station, TX 77842
409-764-3412

City of Denton
City Hall West
221 Elm
Denton, TX 76201
817-566-8350

Farmers Branch
Planning Director
P.O. Box 819010
Farmers Branch, TX 75381-9010

City of Galveston
823 Rosenburg Avenue
Galveston, TX 77553
409-766-2106

Garland
City of Garland
P.O. Box 469002
Garland, TX 75046

Grand Prairie
Department of Planning
P.O. Box 530011
Grand Prairie, TX 75053-0011
214-660-8255
fax 214-262-4642

Houston
City of Houston
Parks and Recreation Department
P.O. Box 1562
Houston, TX 77251
713-845-1128

Irving
City of Irving Community Development
825 W. Irving Boulevard
Irving, TX 75060
214-721-2427

Plano
City of Plano
Planning and Transportation Department
P.O. Box 860358
Plano, TX 75086-0358
214-424-6531

City of Round Rock
State Preservation Board
Stephen F. Austin State Office Building, Suite 1029
P.O. Box 13286
Austin, TX 78711
512-463-5495

City of San Marcos
Assistant to the City Manager
630 East Hopkins Street
San Marcos, TX 78666
512-353-4444
fax 512-396-4656

Southlake
Planning and Zoning
667 N. Carroll Avenue
Southlake, TX 76092
(817) 481-5581
fax 817-481-0036

VIRGINIA

Hampton Roads
Planning District Commission
723 Woodlake Drive
Chesapeake, VA 23320
804-420-8300

City of Chesapeake
City of Norfolk
City of Suffolk
City of Virginia Beach
City of Williamsburg

City of Norfolk
Department of City Planning and Codes Administration
508 City Hall Building
Norfolk, VA 23501

County of Spotsylvania
Planning Department
P.O. Box 876
Spotsylvania, VA 22563
540-582-7146
fax 540-582-1032

Yorktown
County of York
Department of Community Development
P.O. Box 532
Yorktown, VA 23690-0532

WASHINGTON

City of Auburn
Planning Department
25 West Main
Auburn, WA 98001
206-804-5031

City of Bellevue
Planning and Development Division
P.O. Box 90012
11511 Main Street
Bellevue, WA 98009-9012
206-451-4109
fax 206-451-7259

City of Federal Way
33530 First Way South
Federal Way, WA 98003
206-661-4109
fax 206-661-4129

Medina
c/o The Berger Partnership, P.S.
Landscape Architecture-Site Planning
2021 Minor East
Seattle, WA 98102
(206) 325-6877
fax 206-323-6867

Pullman
Washington State University
Facilities Development, Commons Office
P.O. Box 643611
Pullman, WA 99164-3611
509-335-2192
fax 509-335-6875

City of Spokane
Parks Department
North 809 Washington
Spokane, WA 99201
509-625-6670
fax 509-625-6958

WISCONSIN

Brookfield
Planning Director
2000 N. Calhoun Road
Brookfield, WI 53005
414-782-9650

Kenosha County
Office of Planning and Development
19600 75th Street
P.O. Box 520
Bristol, WI 53104-0520

City of Madison
Department of Planning and Development
Madison Municipal Building
215 Martin Luther King Jr. Boulevard
P.O. Box 2985
Madison, WI 53701-2985
608-267-8741
fax 608-267-8739

Washington County
Land Use and Park Department
432 East Washington Street, Room 150
West Bend, WI 53095-7986
414-335-4445

APPENDIX C

Additional Help

Additional help and information on landscape ordinances and tree ordinances can be found at the School of Landscape Architecture, Louisiana State University, Baton Rouge, LA 70803. Locate the Green Law Web Page on the Internet to find further information concerning landscape ordinances and green laws. The Green Law Web Page has been created as a research web site to provide a forum of information concerning landscape ordinances and other related green laws.

You will find this web page at **http://www.design.lsu/edu/greenlaws**

The author is indebted to the East Baton Rouge Parish Tree Commission, the Louisiana Arborists Association, the International Society of Arboriculture and many individuals who have contributed to this creation. Several published documents have assisted with this endeavor. They include outline ordinances published by the Louisiana Association of Nurserymen, the National Arbor Day Foundation and the International Society of Arboriculture. These are listed in the bibliography and are required background reading for anyone wishing to establish a tree ordinance.

An excellent companion reference to this book is the *Municipal Tree Manual*, 1990, published by the International Society of Arboriculture and compiled by Philip J. Hoefer, E. B. Himelick and David F. DeVoto. Their contribution to this effort is greatly appreciated.

This study was funded by an America the Beautiful Grant from the Louisiana Department of Agriculture and Forestry through the Louisiana Association of Nurserymen. Walter Imahara, Warren Meadows and the entire Board of Directors of the Louisiana Association of Nurserymen are to be thanked for their concern for the environment of Louisiana.

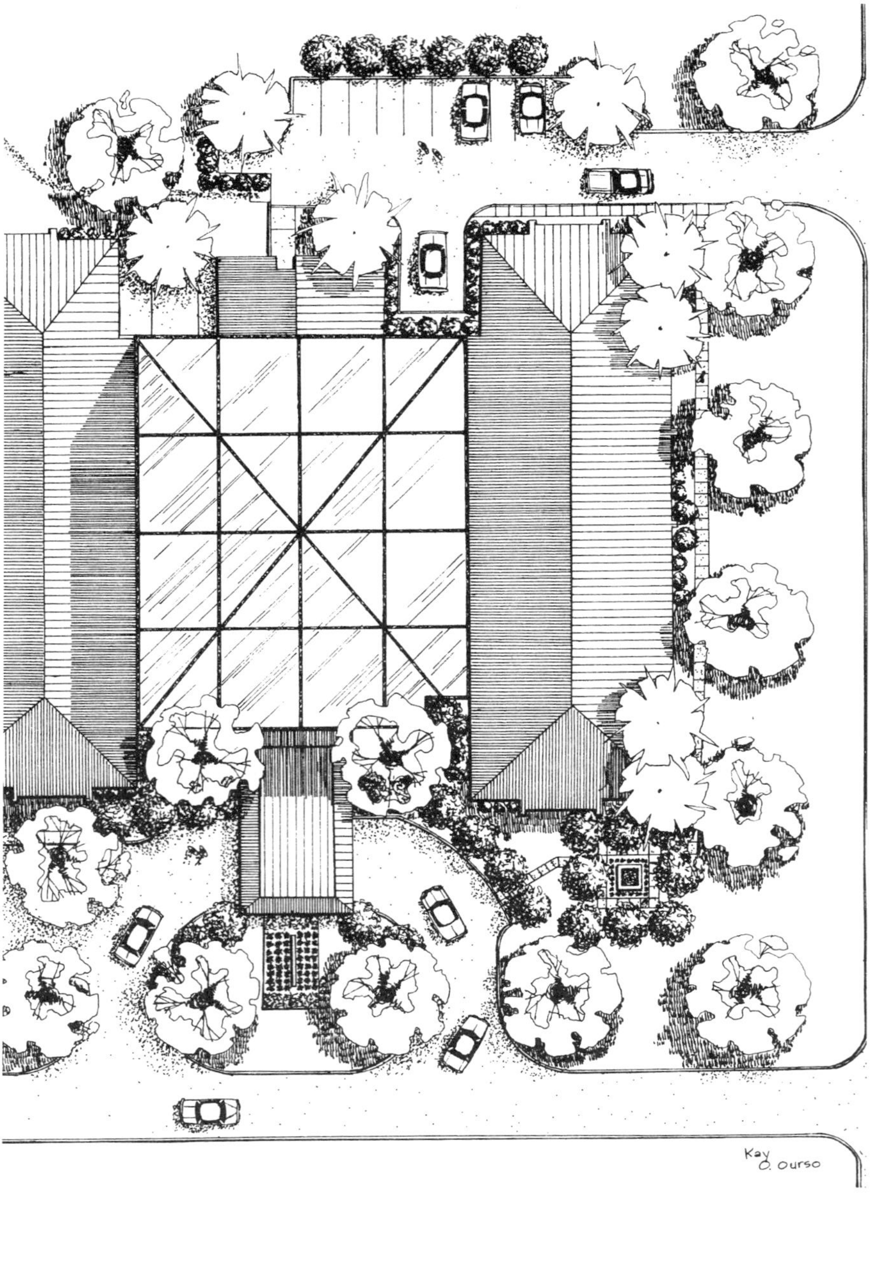
Kay
O. Ourso

Standard Landscape Ordinance Definitions

One of the critical subsections of a well written landscape ordinance is a section that describes the technical terms used to describe the design components, technical standards and administrative requirements.

Because landscape ordinances are based on language as well as design, many of the technical terms are unknown to developers, builders and community officials. An understanding of these definitions will allow readers of ordinances to better grasp the meaning of the section that pertains to each definition.

Careful readers will note that many of these definitions have spatial connotations. A number of them pertain to the geography of a development site. Words like *street yard, hydrozone, street wall* and *detention basin* have specific site reference, so this list can be considered a primer of site plan lexicon appropriate for the education of young planners, landscape architects, engineers, architects and builders.

The definitions that follow are derived from two sources. Most have been extracted from ordinances in this study, and credit for these ordinance definitions are stated along with the definition itself. Definitions credited to Louisiana State University have been developed as part of this study by the author. These definitions explain relatively rare but important situations found in more than five (5) ordinances but for which no effective or inclusive definition was ever written. This is the first attempt so define them.

Definitions have been carefully chosen to be as self-explanatory as possible. In several instances, multiple definitions are given. This is done with the hope of better defining the term or, more usually, highlighting regional differences in vocabulary or simply changes over time caused by changing practices. Some regional differences can be noted in the annotations that follow.

The definitions may be utilized by any community that cares to use them in code revisions. They have been written here with the hope of standardizing landscape ordinance vocabulary, thereby leading to a wider understanding of green laws and more universal application in design.

AAN Standards. The American Standard for Nursery Stock, published by the American Association of Nurserymen (AAN), 1980 or current edition. Memphis, Tennessee.

Access Way. A paved area intended to provide ingress and egress of vehicular traffic from a public right-of-way to an off-street parking area. Pompano Beach, Florida.

Administrative Standards. The set of rules, procedures and requirements set forth in a landscape ordinance associated with making permit application, assembling materials for pubic review, meeting the requirements of the landscape ordinance, seeking approvals, enforcement, conducting site inspections and filing reports. Louisiana State University.

Alley. A public thoroughfare, other than a street or highway, providing a means of vehicular access to abutting property. May be considered a street in those cases where a subdivision has been recorded containing lots that abut only on an alley. Los Angeles, California.

Arborist or Urban Forester. A person trained in arboriculture, forestry, landscape architecture, horticulture, or related fields and experienced in the conservation and preservation of native and ornamental trees. Williamsburg, Virginia.

Architectural Screen. A durable wood fence or masonry wall that screens the view from the street to off-street parking and related vehicular use areas. Corpus Christi, Texas.

Attached Sidewalk. A sidewalk attached directly to the back of the roadway curb. Denver, Colorado.

Berm. A mound of soil, either natural or man-made, used to screen and visually separate, in part or entirely, one area, site or property from the view of another area. East Windsor, New Jersey.

Buffering. The use of landscaping (other than mere grass on flat terrain), or the use of landscaping along with berms, walls or decorative fences, that at least partially and periodically obstruct the view from the street, in a continuous manner, of vehicular use areas, parking lots and their parked cars, and detention ponds. Austin, Texas.

Buffer Yard. A landscaped area provided to separate and partially obstruct the view of two (2) adjacent land uses or properties from one another. Omaha, Nebraska.

Buildable Lot Area. That portion of a lot or parcel excluding the required yards, easements and areas within future right-of-way width lines in accordance with Chapter 13. Mesa, Arizona.

Building Site. That portion of a lot that is occupied by a building or that portion of a site that is proposed to be occupied by a building and for which a building permit has been issued. Aiken, South Carolina.

Certificate of Completion. An official document issued by the county evidencing that facilities constructed in support of a subdivision have been completed in a form and manner acceptable to the county. Orange County, Florida.

Champion Trees. Those trees that have been identified by the state division of forestry as being the largest of their species within the state. Gainesville, Florida.

Clearing. Includes, but is not limited to, the removal of trees, understory, shrubbery, brush, ground cover and/or topsoil from any part of the land but does not include maintenance mowing. Brevard County, Florida.

Comprehensive Landscape Ordinance. A very sophisticated ordinance that regulates not only landscaping but land alteration, tree protection, tree removal, storm water management, erosion control, ground water recharge and land clearing. Louisiana State University.

Compatible Use. Any activity carried on in a building, structure or tract of land that is able to exist harmoniously with any activity carried on in a building, structure or tract of land adjacent to the primary use. Independence, Missouri.

Conservancy Area. An area designated on a recorded plat, deed or covenant to protect the natural features of the area. Bannockburn, Illinois.

Critical Root Zone (CRZ). The minimum area beneath a tree that must be left undisturbed in order to preserve a sufficient root mass to give a tree a reasonable chance of survival. The critical root zone is typically represented by a concentric circle centering on the tree trunk with a radius equal in feet to one (1) times the number of inches of the trunk diameter:

$$(\text{CRZ in ft} = 1 \times \text{D in.})$$

Alpharetta, Georgia.

Critical Root Zone. Generally a circular area surrounding a tree, the center of which is the center of the tree trunk and the radius is the distance from the outside of the trunk to any point twelve (12) times the diameter, as measured at four and one-half ($4\frac{1}{2}$) feet from the ground on the low side of the trunk, which points constitute the circumference of the critical root zone. Raleigh, North Carolina.

Curb Cut. Any break in the curb for a vehicle entry or driveway apron. Denver, Colorado.

DBH—Diameter At Breast Height. The diameter of a tree measured at a point four and one-half ($4\frac{1}{2}$) feet above the ground. Fayetteville, Arkansas.

Designated Official. The landscape architect, arborist, building official or other person designated by the city, from time to time, to review surveys, plans and programs as required. Medina, Washington.

Density Factor. A unit of measure used to prescribe the calculated tree coverage on a site. Alpharetta, Georgia.

Design Manual. A companion document prepared to summarize the technical language of a landscape ordinance and the administrative procedures involved with preparing landscape design plans to seek building permits, tree removal permits and land alteration permits. A well-written design manual describes the contextual, administrative and technical aspects of the ordinance.

Design manuals generally contain information that is helpful to designers, such as formulas, tables, diagrams, typical construction details, materials lists, standard specifications and helpful appendix material. Design manuals are written in easy-to-understand language and are illustrated with graphics so that city officials, permit applicants and property owners can understand the technical terms of landscape architecture, construction, horticulture and forestry contained within the landscape ordinance. Louisiana State University.

Detached Sidewalk. A sidewalk that is not attached to the street curb. Detached sidewalks generally occur in residential areas and are normally separated from the curb by a tree lawn. Denver, Colorado.

Detention. A temporary storage of a determined quantity of water with a release rate that is either fixed or variable. Shreveport, Louisiana.

Developed Area. That portion of a plot or parcel on which a building, structure, pavement or other improvements have been placed. Rapid City, South Dakota.

Development Permit. A permit issued by the city that authorizes development activity and includes, but is not limited to, a soil erosion permit, clearing and grubbing permit, land disturbance permit and/or building permit. Alpharetta, Georgia.

Diameter at Breast Height (DBH). The diameter in inches of a tree measured at four and one-half ($4\frac{1}{2}$) feet above the existing grade. (DBH shall be used to measure existing trees to remain). Barlett, Tennessee.

Drainage Plan. A detailed plan prepared in graphical format with or on a detailed grading plan addressing on-site and off-site drainage control, flood control and erosion control issues. Shreveport, Louisiana.

Drip Line. A vertical line extending from the outermost portion of the tree canopy to the ground. Hilton Head Island, South Carolina.

Easement. A grant by a property owner of the use of land for a specific purpose. Fairfax County, Virginia.

Entry Walk. The narrow walkway in residential areas that leads from and is perpendicular to the curb and to the detached sidewalk, crossing the tree lawn. Denver, Colorado.

Equivalent Replacement. A tree that is of the same species and matches or exceeds the size, height and spread of a removed tree. Pompano Beach, Florida.

Equivalent Value. An amount of money that reflects the estimated cost of replacing a tree. Pompano Beach, Florida.

Exceptional Specimen Tree. Any tree that is determined by the city council to be of unique and intrinsic value to the general public because of its size, age, historic association or ecological value, or any tree designated a Florida State Champion, United States Champion or World Champion by the American Forestry Association. Jacksonville, Florida

Existing Vegetation to Be Preserved. Any viable grouping of or single existing evergreen or deciduous trees and associated understory for which tree or buffer preservation credit is being requested. Houston, Texas.

Foundation Area. The ground area immediately adjacent to a building on all sides thereof. Foundation areas extend a minimum of four (4) feet in all directions from the foundation of the building. Bartlett, Illinois.

Foundation Planting. Plant material placed in near proximity to building foundations, located in planting beds arranged to complement the building elevations and connect the building to the site. Parkland, Florida.

Gray Wood. The portion of a palm trunk that is mature hardwood, measured from the top of the root ball to the base of the new, green, soft, terminal growth or fronds. Coral Springs, Florida.

Green Area. An area of living landscape material. Ocean Springs, Mississippi.

Green Law. A sobriquet for the term *landscape ordinance* or any site-specific law that preserves, protects or enhances natural systems on a defined parcel of land or zoned development site. Common green laws include postconstruction landscape ordinances, tree preservation ordinances and land alteration ordinances whose prime purpose is the protection of native habitat, including vegetation, soils, natural drainage and wildlife. Louisiana State University.

Greenspace Percentage. For the purposes of this community's ordinance, the greenspace percentage includes all planted areas interior to the property lines. The percentage is calculated as follows: 100% – impervious surface percentage = greenspace percentage. Greenspace is to be planted with trees, shrubs, ground cover or grass, consistent with good landscape design. West Lafayette, Indiana.

Grey Water. Untreated household waste water from clothes and dish washing, bath water, etc. Grey water does not include water flushed down toilets. National City, California.

Ground Cover. Plant material that normally reaches a maximum height of not more than eighteen (18) inches. North Lauderdale, Florida.

Ground Cover. Living landscape materials or low-growing plants, other than turf grasses, installed in such a manner as to provide a continuous cover of the ground surface. Wichita, Kansas.

Hardscape. Any permanent, nonliving site improvements, including, but not limited to, pavement, curbing, wheel stops, steps, walls, fences, fountains, sculpture, railings, lighting, irrigation fixtures and other similar fixtures. Daytona Beach, Florida.

Hatracking. To flat-cut the top of a tree, severing the leader or leaders, or pruning a tree by stubbing off mature wood larger than three (3) inches in diameter. Plantation, Florida.

Heavy Vehicle Loading Area. A paved area designed to accommodate the maneuvering, loading and unloading and parking of commercial vehicles having a length of twenty-seven (27) feet or greater. Garland, Texas.

Heat Island. An unnaturally high temperature microclimate resulting from (solar) radiation from impervious surfaces. Dade County, Florida.

Hedge. An evenly spaced planting of shrubs that forms a compact, dense, visually opaque living barrier. Dania, Florida.

Hedge. A growth of vegetation, cultivated in such a manner as to produce a barrier to inhibit passage or to obscure view, that is more than twelve (12) inches in height. Where there are interruptions of growth by vertical space having a horizontal distance of more than twenty-four (24) inches in every four (4) feet, such growth shall not be considered a hedge. This definition is not intended to regulate individual shrubs, plants or trees. Beverly Hills, California.

Hedgerow. A row of shrubs and/or trees that occurs along the borders of fields. Sometimes purposely planted for wind and erosion control in agricultural areas. More commonly, an area along a road or field boundary that has grown up with various plants seeded by wind, water, birds, etc. DuPage, Illinois.

Historic Tree. Any live oak that has a caliper of twenty-four (24) inches or greater; any red cedar that has a caliper of twelve (12) inches or greater; any longleaf pine or magnolia tree that has a caliper of twenty (20) inches or greater. Lake Mary, Florida.

Historic Tree. A tree that has been designated by the Metropolitan Beautification and Environmental Commission, with advice from the Tree Advisory Committee and with consent of the property owner, as of notable historical interest and value to Metropolitan Nashville and Davidson County because of its location or historical association with the community. Nashville, Tennessee.

Hollywood Driveway. Two paved wheel tracks, each between two and one-half ($2\frac{1}{2}$) and three and one-half ($3\frac{1}{2}$) feet wide, separated by a planted strip at least three (3) feet wide. Los Angeles, California.

Hydrozone. A portion of a landscaped area having plants with similar water needs that are served by one irrigation valve, or a set of valves with the same schedule. National City, California.

Impervious Surface. Land area covered by a surface treatment that hinders the ability of the underlying soils to percolate water. Lake Mary, Florida.

Impervious Surface Percentage. For the purpose of this community's ordinance, "impervious surface percentage" (ISP) is an intensity measurement of the impervious surfaces, which include building footprint, parking lots, loading areas and sidewalks interior to the property line and all other impervious surfaces. The ISP is calculated by expressing the following fraction as a percentage: Total area of impervious surface on site × 100/total area of the site. West Lafayette, Indiana.

Interior Landscaped Area. That area inside the perimeter of a site that is permeable and capable of being planted with live landscape materials. Jackson, Mississippi.

Interior Landscaping. The use of landscape materials within the boundaries of a parcel, including parking areas. Hilliard, Ohio.

Island. In road and parking area design, a raised planting area, usually curbed, placed to guide traffic, separate lanes, limit paving (impervious surface), preserve existing vegetation and increase aesthetic quality. East Windsor, New Jersey.

Islands, Center. Center islands are located between bays of head-in parking and run the length of the parking bays. DuPage County, Illinois.

Islands, Corner. Corner islands are located between two (2) bays of parking that are at an angle relative to each other and at the edge of the parking lot. DuPage County, Illinois.

Islands, Drive. Drive islands are located between a bay of parking and an access drive. DuPage County, Illinois.

Islands, End. End islands are located at the ends of a double bay of parking. DuPage County, Illinois.

Islands, Half End. Half end islands are located at the ends of a single bay of parking. DuPage, Illinois.

Islands, Intermediate. Intermediate islands are located within a parking bay row. Dupage County, Illinois.

Land-Altering Activity. Any change to existing land, including, but not limited to, clearing, grading, excavating, filling or other construction activities, such as for parking lots, residential and commercial buildings, retaining walls, storm drainage systems and utility main installations, or repairs thereof, any of which would physically alter the existing conditions and/or vegetative cover on the land. Shreveport, Louisiana.

Land Clearing. Those operations whereby trees and vegetation are removed and that occur previous to construction of buildings, road right-of-way excavation, utility excavation, grubbing and any other necessary clearing operation. Southfield, Michigan.

Landing Walk. A twelve (12) to twenty-four (24) inch wide paved strip along the back of a curb to facilitate stepping in and out of vehicles. Denver, Colorado.

Landmark Tree. A tree that has special significance because one or more of the following criteria apply: rare species, old age, size, location, association with a historical event or person, scenic enhancement or unique characteristics. Dalton, Georgia.

Landscape Architectural Plans. All plans, specifications, or reports prepared or issued by a registered landscape architect and filed for public record, which are to be signed by the registered landscape architect, dated and stamped with his or her seal. Plantation, Florida.

Landscape Design Components. Sections of a landscape ordinance making reference to specific parts of a site, building lot or development property that must be designed using standards, specifications or technical requirements specified in that ordinance. For example, "This Chapter shall regulate landscaping of five (5) distinct areas of the building lot as follows: (1) street yards, (2) landscape buffers, (3) storage area screening, (4) parking lots, (5) storm water detention areas." Louisiana State University.

Landscaping. Any combination of living plants, such as trees, shrubs, vines, ground covers, flowers or grass; natural features such as rock, stone, bark chips or shavings; and structural features, including, but not limited to, fountains, reflecting pools, outdoor artwork, screen walls, fences, or benches. Colorado Springs, Colorado.

Landscaping Bank Clause. Language that sets up a procedure, a "landscape bank," allowing mitigated plantings on public lands or an equivalent replacement value payment to a city landscaping account for trees or landscaping that must be removed or installed but cannot be accomplished on the development site as a result of various circumstances. In true bank fashion, landscape credits may be borrowed, loaned, bought, sold or traded. Interest payments and administrative fees may be collected. Louisiana State University.

Landscape Irrigation Audit. A process to perform site inspections, evaluate irrigation systems and develop efficient irrigation schedules. Napa, California.

Landscape Ordinance. A public law, requiring public review and approval of a permit, often contained within a zoning ordinance or land development code, that regulates landscape design, landscaping and landscape installation and maintenance. Louisiana State University.

Landscape Ordinance Standards. Specifications, requirements, quality determinations or performance guidelines for judging acceptable compliance with the provisions of a landscape ordinance. For example, "ground cover shall be container stock meeting the standards specified in the 'American Standard for Nursery Stock,' latest edition, published by the American Association of Nurserymen." Louisiana State University.

Landscape Plan. The preparation of graphic and written criteria, specifications and detailed plans to arrange and modify the effects of natural features such as plantings, ground and water forms, circulation, walks and other features to comply with the provisions of an ordinance. Baton Rouge, Louisiana.

Landscape Plan. A scaled plan that clearly delineates vehicular use areas and displays and describes all landscaping, to include methods of irrigation and maintenance of landscaped areas. Orange County, Florida.

Landscaped Street Yard. The area of a lot that lies between the street right-of-way line and the actual front wall of a building, parallel to the street, until an imaginary extension of such front building wall line intersects the side property lines. In determining the actual building wall of a building for the purposes of this community's ordinance, steps and unenclosed porches are to be excluded, but such building wall line will follow and include the irregular indentations of the building. Durham, New Hampshire.

Legacy Oak. A private or public oak identified through research as having historical significance or occurring on a site with historical significance. The tree must be of seventeen (17) feet circumference or a minimum of one hundred (100) years old or have unique form or character, or have good public visibility or special qualification as a result of tree descendancy, being a memorial tree, being designated a Bicentennial Oak or being listed as a member of the Live Oak Society. Baton Rouge, Louisiana.

Light Vehicle Loading Area. A paved area designed to accommodate the maneuvering, loading and unloading and parking of commercial vehicles having a length of less than twenty-seven (27) feet. Garland, Texas.

Loading Areas. Trash collection areas of dumpster-type refuse containers, outdoor loading and unloading spaces, docks, outdoor shipping and receiving areas, outdoor bulk storage of materials or parts thereof, and outdoor repair areas of any service stations, safety equipment, inspection stations or dealers. Lafayette, Louisiana.

Lot, Area. The remaining site area after deleting all portions for existing and proposed perimeter rights-of-way and alleys. Mesa, Arizona.

Low Water Use Plants. Plants that are able to survive without supplemental water after they have become established. Albuquerque, New Mexico.

Mulch. Any material such as leaves, bark, straw, or other materials left loose and applied to the soil surface to reduce evaporation. Albuquerque, New Mexico.

Native Grasses. Species of perennial grass other than those designated as noxious weeds by the State of Kansas. Lawrence, Kansas.

Native Plant Community. A natural association of plants dominated by one or more prominent native plant species or by characteristic physical attributes. Dade County, Florida.

Natural Area. An area identified on an approved site plan containing natural vegetation that will remain undisturbed when the property is fully developed. Coral Springs, Florida.

Net Lot Area. The area within lot boundaries of all lands comprising a site. Net lot area will not include any portion of the abutting dedicated streets, alleys, waterways, canals, lakes or any other such dedications. Dade County, Florida.

Off-Street Parking and Other Vehicular Use Area. Any area, excluding public rights-of-way, used for the purpose of driving, maneuvering, parking, storing or display of motor vehicles, boats, trailers, mobile homes and recreational vehicles, including new and used automobile lots, and other parking lot uses, excluding minimum parking requirements for single-family residences. Maitland, Florida.

Opacity. An imaginary vertical plane extending from the established grade to a required height, of which a required percentage of the vertical plane will be visually screened from adjacent property use. Dublin, Ohio.

Open Space. The unoccupied portion of a lot or building site that is open to the sky and that may or may not contain landscaping, landscaping structures or outdoor recreational facilities. Pullman, Washington.

Open Space Ratio. The proportion of a site consisting of open space, being natural areas, gardens, recreational areas, greenways and lawns, which shall be calculated using the base site area. Davenport, Iowa.

Outdoor Storage Area. An area for storage of equipment, materials, goods and supplies, including the keeping of automobiles, trucks, boats, trailers, buses and lawn and garden equipment, that are not entirely enclosed within a building and that are not on temporary display for the purpose of being immediately for sale to the public at large (where permitted by the zoning ordinance). Garland, Texas.

Parking Area Landscape Zones. *Terminal islands* are placed at the ends of a row of parking spaces. *Interior islands* are placed within individual rows of contiguous parking spaces. *Divider medians* are placed where any row of contiguous parking spaces is located so as to abut an interior driveway rather than another row of contiguous parking spaces. North Miami Beach, Florida.

Parking Lot Island. An area of ground within the boundary of any parking lot, which has curbing adjacent to all paved areas. Planting islands are used for traffic control and to provide space for landscaping that helps screen and shade parking lots. DuPage, Illinois.

Perimeter Landscape Strip. A landscaped area that separates the vehicular use area from adjoining property and/or a public right-of-way. Its purpose is to enhance the visual appearance of the site and to provide screening of the vehicular use area and certain other activities from the public right-of-way and abutting property. Little Rock, Arkansas.

Perimeter Landscaping. The use of landscape materials within and adjacent to the outer boundary of a parcel. Hilliard, Ohio.

Permeable Pavement. A paving material that permits water penetration to a soil depth of eighteen (18) inches or more. Permeable pavement may consist of nonporous surface materials, poured or laid in sections not exceeding one square foot in area and collectively comprising less than two-thirds (⅔) of the total surface area. Dallas, Texas.

Permit. An official document authorizing performance of a specific activity regulated by the community's ordinance. Tampa, Florida.

Pervious Area. The area of a plot remaining after the impervious areas are subtracted. The impervious areas include the areas covered by structure, vehicular use areas, storage areas or display areas, access ways, pedestrian pavement and wet retention areas. Pompano Beach, Florida.

Plantable Area. The pervious surface area expressed in square footage available for the preservation or planting of trees. The plantable area does not include that portion of the lot that is covered by buildings and structures permitted pursuant to the maximum lot coverage standards of the city. Alpharetta, Georgia.

Postconstruction Certification Statement. A statement that is filed with municipal officials by the landscape architect certifying that all landscape construction has been implemented according to the requirements of the landscape ordinance or any public law that may apply. Louisiana State University.

Property. The real property included within the boundaries of any lot approved and recorded in the plat records of the county, or an unplatted tract or parcel of land as described and recorded in the real property records of the county. Denton, Texas.

Protected Tree. A tree of five (5) inches or greater DBH, unless otherwise exempted in this community's ordinance. All mangrove trees and cypress trees, regardless of diameter, shall be defined as protected trees. Tampa, Florida.

PVA. Off-street parking and vehicular use areas, an area other than on a public right-of-way designated for the parking and movement of vehicles. Huntsville, Alabama

Reclaimed Water. Water that as a result of treatment of waste water, is suitable for a direct beneficial use or controlled use other than human consumption. Davis, California.

Registered Landscape Architect. A person who holds a license to practice landscape architecture as defined in and in accordance with state law. Tampa, Florida.

Retention Area. An area designed and used for the temporary or permanent storage of storm water runoff, which may be either dry or wet. Wet retention areas must be at least one-half (½) acre in size, with an average width of not less than one hundred (100) feet, a minimum depth of eight (8) feet below groundwater level and maximum side slopes of four to one (4:1) to a point five (5) feet below water level. North Miami Beach, Florida.

Screening. Decorative, solid-faced fencing, walls, earthen berms or dense vegetation used undividually or in combination for the purpose of concealing from view the area behind such fencing, walls or vegetation. The installed height of such screening is to be no less than 6 (six) feet and no more than 8 (eight) feet. Bolingbrook, Illinois.

Sign Monument Zone. An area of a site dedicated or permitted to the erection of a sign or sign cluster usually less than six (6) feet in height, often lighted and planted with low, brightly colored seasonal flowers. Louisiana State University.

Single-Issue Landscape Ordinance. Sometimes referred to as a "first-generation landscape ordinance," this type of ordinance pertains to a single landscape issue such as parking lots, buffers, screen or trees. Louisiana State University.

Sight Triangle. The area on either side of an access way at its junction with a street forming a triangle within which clear visibility of approaching vehicular or pedestrian traffic is to be maintained. New Orleans, Louisiana.

Specimen Tree. A tree with any individual trunk that has a DBH of eighteen (18) inches or greater. Dade County, Florida.

Specimen Tree. A particularly special example of a species because of its size, age, habit or any trait that either epitomizes the character of species or makes the tree an unusual example of its species. Prince George's County, Virginia.

Storage Area. Any exterior area used for the keeping of garbage or trash cans, dumpsters, newspaper containers, oil and bottled gas tanks, swimming pool equipment, air conditioners and mechanical appurtenances. North Lauderdale, Florida.

Street Frontage. The length of a property abutting one side of a street, measured along the dividing line between the property and the street. Wichita, Kansas.

Street Trees. Trees, shrubs, bushes and all other woody vegetation on land lying between the property lines on either side of all streets, avenues or ways within a city/village. State of Nebraska.

Street Tree Planting Area. The area of a development site that lies between the street right-of-way line and the edge of the street curb parallel to the street. This land is publicly owned but is often used for street tree planting and maintenance. Louisiana State University.

Street Wall. Any building wall fronting on a street. Corpus Christi, Texas.

Street Yard. The area of a lot that lies between the street right-of-way line and the actual front wall line of a building, as such building wall line extends from the outward corners of the building, parallel to the street, until such imaginary extensions of such front building wall line intersect the side property lines. Austin, Texas.

Technical Requirements. Criteria of a technical nature, usually specified in quantities, dimensions and sizes and spelled out in a landscape ordinance to guide designers in the proper design of various parts of the site, building lot or development property. For example, "Plantings for all interior parking lots islands or peninsulas shall be four (4)-inch, container-grown ground cover plants twelve (12) inches tall, stagger spaced twelve (12) inches on center and planted in eight (8) inches of specified bed preparation materials to the same depth as nursery grown. Louisiana State University.

Tree Bank. A fund established by a city to provide an opportunity to make a cash payment to the city in lieu of providing required landscape stock on a site. Altamonte Springs, Florida.

Tree Conservation. Providing for optimum overall tree coverage and specific tree placement by a combination of retaining certain existing trees and planting new ones, as appropriate. Beaufort, South Carolina.

Tree—Class A. Any self-supporting woody plant of a species that normally grows to an overall height of at least fifty (50) feet, usually with one (1) main stem or trunk, and many branches. It may appear to have several stems or trunks, as in several varieties of oaks. Covington, Louisiana.

Tree—Class B. Any self-supporting woody plant of a species that normally grows to an overall height of at least twenty-five (25) feet, usually with one main stem or trunk, and many branches. It may appear to have several stems or trunks; for example, crape myrtle. Covington, Louisiana.

Tree—Class C. Any self-supporting woody plant of a species that normally grows to an overall height of at least fifteen (15) feet. It may appear to have several stems or trunks; for example, wax myrtle. Covington, Louisiana.

Tree Density Standard (TDS). The minimum number of Tree Density Units per acre that must be achieved on a property after development. Gwinnett County, Georgia.

Tree Density Unit (TDU). A credit assigned to a tree based on the diameter of the tree, in accordance with tables defined in the ordinance of this community. Gwinnett County, Georgia.

Tree Ordinance. A public law developed to organize a municipal urban forestry program, formulate a tree commission and control the planting, removal and care of public and/or private trees. Louisiana State University.

Tree Preservation. Retaining an existing tree on site, or an orientation toward providing for maximum tree coverage on a site by retaining existing trees, especially those of high value, rather than by replanting. Beaufort South Carolina.

Tree Protection Area (TPA). Any portion of a site wherein are located existing trees that are proposed to be preserved in order to comply with the requirements of the ordinance of this community. Gwinnett County, Georgia.

Tree Protection Zone. The area around a tree corresponding to the drip line or ten (10) feet in all directions from the trunk. Hilton Head Island, South Carolina.

Tree Replacement Schedule. A plan showing the location, species and sizes of all replacement trees. A replacement tree is any tree that is planted in order to replace an existing tree. Mount Pleasant, South Carolina.

Utility Service Area. An area that contains any surface-mounted HVAC equipment or freestanding above-ground devices, such as utility boxes, booster stations, switch boxes and transformers, that are part of an underground utility system. Americus, Georgia.

Vehicular Encroachment. Any portion of a motor vehicle, outside the boundaries of a vehicular use area, that protrudes into a landscape area. Dania, Florida.

Vehicular Use Area. Any area of a lot not located within any enclosed or partially enclosed structure and that is devoted to a use by or for motor vehicles, including parking (accessory or nonaccessory) or storage of automobiles, trucks or other vehicles; loading areas; service areas and drives; and access drives and driveways. Chicago, Illinois.

Vehicular Use Areas. All areas subject to vehicular traffic, including access ways, driveways, loading areas, service areas, and parking stalls for all types of vehicles. This definition does not include covered parking structures or underground parking lots. San Diego, California.

Visual Screen. A physical obstruction used to separate two areas or uses, which is at least seventy-five (75) percent opaque. Visual screens are to consist of living plant material, natural or man-made construction material or a combination thereof. North Lauderdale, Florida.

Visual Enhancement Landscaping. Consists of landscaping or the retention of natural vegetation that provides definition of land uses or softens the impact of one land use on another. Anchorage, Alaska.

Water Harvesting. Any combination of techniques that results in storm or flood waters captured on-site, for later plant use or return to the water table. Sparks, Nevada.

Water Waste. The nonbeneficial use of water supplied by the municipal water supply system. An example is landscape water applied in such a manner, rate and/or quantity that it regularly overflows the landscaped area being irrigated and runs onto adjacent property or a public right-of-way. Albuquerque, New Mexico.

Wetland Mitigation. (1) Methods for eliminating potential damage or destruction to wetlands and/or (2) creation of wetlands from uplands to offset the loss of protected wetlands. Southfield, Michigan.

Wetland Vegetation. Plants, including, but not limited to, trees, shrubs, and herbaceous plants, that exhibit adaptations to allow, under normal conditions, germination or propagation and to allow growth with at least their root systems in water or saturated soil. Southfield, Michigan.

Woodland. A tract of land dominated by trees but usually also containing woody shrubs, grasses and other vegetation. For purposes of this community's ordinance, the term *woodland* will incorporate *woods, woodland areas, wooded areas, forest, forested areas* and any other terminology commonly recognized to have the same meaning. Yorktown, Virginia.

Yard Area. That portion of any site covered by the front, side and rear yard areas as established by the minimum setback requirements in the zoning ordinance of the city for the respective zoning district. Aiken, South Carolina.

Yard Setback Area. The front, side and rear yard setbacks as required by the applicable zoning regulations of the city Margate, Florida.

Yard, Waterfront. The yard adjacent to a waterway fifty (50) feet or more in average width adjoining the yard, with width measured from the mean high-water line. As used in the code of this community, waterfront property is hereby defined as property abutting open water, bays, bayous, wetlands, lakes, canals, aquatic conservation areas, aquatic preservation areas and similar waterways. Tampa, Florida.

Xeriscape®. A set of garden design and landscape maintenance principles that promote good horticultural practices and efficient use of water. The term *Xeriscape* is a registered trademark of the National Xeriscape Council and means water-conserving drought-tolerant landscaping. Oviedo, Florida.

Selected Bibliography

I. Books and Technical Manuals

Abbey, D. G. *Guide to Writing a Landscape Ordinance*. Louisiana Association of Nurserymen, Baton Rouge, LA, 1988.

Abbey, D. G. *Guide to Writing a City Tree Ordinance*. Louisiana Association of Nurserymen, Baton Rouge, LA, 1993.

Bernhardt, E. A., and T. J. Swiecki. *Guidelines for Developing and Evaluating Tree Ordinances*. California Department of Forestry and Fire Protection Urban Forestry Program, Sacramento, CA, 1991.

Fazio, James. *How to Write a Municipal Tree Ordinance*, Bulletin No. 9. National Arbor Day Foundation, Nebraska City, NE, 1991.

Deneke, G. *Urban Forestry*, 2d ed. John Wiley & Sons, New York, NY, 1986.

Duerksen, Christopher J., and Suzanne Richman. *Tree Conservation Ordinances*, PAS Report Number 446. American Planning Association, Chicago, IL, 1993.

Goodman, G. *Ordinance Analysis No. 10, Trees*. Michigan Municipal League, Ann Arbor, MI 1984.

Haar, Charles. *Land Use Planning, A Casebook on the Use, Misuse, and Re-use of Urban Land*. Little Brown and Company, Boston, 1971.

Hoefer, P., E. Himelick, and D. DeVoto. *Municipal Tree Manual*. International Society of Arboriculture, Urbana, IL, 1990.

Miller, R. W. *Urban Forestry*. Prentice-Hall, Englewood Cliffs, NJ, 1988.

Moll, Gary, and Sara Ebenreck. *Shading Our Cities*. Island Press, Washington DC, 1989.

Moll, Gary, and Stanley Young. *Growing Greener Cities*. Living Planet Press, Los Angeles, CA, 1992.

Robinette, Gary O. *Local Landscape Ordinances*. Agora Communicatons, Plano, TX, 1992.

Weber, C. C. 1989. "Developing a Successful Tree Ordinance." In G. Moll and S. Ebenreck. *Shading Our Cities*. Island Press, Washington DC, 1989.

Wenger, Karl. *Forestry Handbook*, 2d ed. John Wiley & Sons, New York, NY, 1984.

II. Periodicals

Beatty, R.A., and C. T. Heckman. "Survey of Urban Tree Programs in the United States." *Urban Ecology* 5 (1980/1981): 81–102.

Corwin, M. A. "Parking Lot Landscaping." *Planning Advisory Service*: No. 335. American Society of Planning Officials.

Dorney, R. S., B. Evered, and C. M. Kitchen. "Effects of Tree Conservation in the Urbanizing Fringe of Southern Ontario Cities: 1970–1984." *Urban Ecology* 9 (1986): 289–308.

Duerksen, Christopher J. "Beyond Ecology and Economics." *Urban Land* (January 1986): 34–35.

Floyd, Charles F. "Requiem for the Highway Beautification Act." *American Planning Association Journal* 48:4 (1982) 441–53.

Tiller, Kay. "Los Angeles Landscape Ordinance Sets National Precedent." *Landscape Architect and Specifer News* 12, no. 9 (September 1996).

Moll, Gary. "The State of Our City Forests." *American Forests* (May/June 1987): 61–64.

Robson, H. 1983. "Municipal Ordinances, Relation to Trees," *Journal of Arboriculture* 9:128–136.

Tereshkovich, G. 1990. "Texas Municipal Tree and Landscape Ordinances," *Journal of Arboriculture* 16 (3): 62–65.

Urban Forests Magazine, American Forestry Association, P.O. Box 2000, Washington DC 20013.

Walsh, Susan. "City Legislation Lags." *Landscape Architecture* 77, no. 5 (September/October 1987): 16–17.

Weinberg, Scott. "Environmental Quality Points." *Landscape Architecture* 75, no. 2 (March/April): 97–98.

Yost, Owen G. "Regulations at Center Stage." *Landscape Architecture* 77, no. 2 (March/April 1987): 93–94.

III. Papers

Chadwick, L. C. "Some Important Aspects of a Municipal Street Tree Ordinance." Columbus, OH. *Proceedings of the International Shade Tree Conference* 48: 53–58.

Fazio, J. K. 1993. " How to Write a Municipal Tree Ordinance." Nebraska City, NE, National Arbor Day Foundation. *Tree City USA Bulletin No. 9.*

Grey, Gene. "Tree Ordinances and Related Policy." Department of Forestry, Kansas State University. *Proceedings of the National Urban Forestry Conference*, November 13–16, 1978. Washington DC, 627–631.

Hoefer, P. 1990. "Developing a Tree Ordinance." *Proceedings of the Fourth Urban Forestry Conference*, St. Louis, October 1989. Washington DC, American Forestry Association.

Jennings, N. E. "Tree Ordinances for Small Towns." University of Nebraska, Lincoln. *Proceedings of the National Urban Forestry Conference*. November 13–16, 1978. Washington DC, 743–748.

Laguaite, Timothy P. "A Documentation of and Recommended Solutions for Site Planning and Design Problems." unpublished thesis, Louisiana State University, Baton Rouge, 1985.

Macie, E., 1990. *Proceedings of the Fourth Urban Forestry Conference*, St. Louis, October 1989. Washington DC, American Forestry Association.

Mooter, D. P. 1985. "Shade Tree Ordinances," Conference Papers. *Eighth Annual Trees for Nebraska Conference*, Lincoln, NE, February 1985.

Satterthwaite, H. E. 1984. "Shade Tree Ordinances," *Shade Tree* 57:73–77.

Siems, C. 1990. "Tree Protection Ordinances." *Proceedings of the 11th Minnesota Society of Arboriculture*, Duluth, MN, Minnesota Society of Arboriculture.

Spitzer, H. A. 1987. "Oak Tree Ordinances," *Proceedings, Multiple Use Management of California Hardwood Resources*, San Luis Obisbo, November 1986. U.S. Forest Service, General Technology Report PSW-100.

Waltersheidt, M. J. "Planning an Urban Forestry Program for a Small Community." Texas A&M University, College Station. *Proceedings of the National Urban Forestry Conference*, November 13–16, 1978. Washington DC 708–713.

Weber, C. C. 1989. "Developing a Successful Urban Tree Ordinance," *Proceedings of the Second National Urban Forestry Conference*, Cincinnati, October 1982. American Forestry Association, Washington DC.

Wray, P. "Sample Tree Ordinances for Iowa Communities," Iowa State University, Cooperative Extension Services, P.M.-1429c.

IV. Miscellaneous Publications

Abbey, D. G. "Landscape Ordinances in North Louisiana," *Louisiana's Nurserymen Magazine* 13, no. 1 (Spring 1990).

Abbey, D. G. "Covington's Green Law." *Louisiana's Nurserymen Magazine* 12, no. 3 (Fall 1989).

Abbey, D. G. "Green Laws In The City of New Orleans." *Louisiana's Nurserymen Magazine* 12, no. 2 (Summer 1989).

Abbey, D. G. "Green Laws For Louisiana." *Louisiana's Nurserymen Magazine* 10, no. 3 (Winter 1987).

Abbey, D. G. "Green Laws for Louisiana." *The Louisiana Landscape Architect* 3, issue 4. Louisiana Chapter, ASLA, Baton Rouge, 1987.

V. Relevant Web Sites on the Internet

http://www.design.lsu.edu/greenlaws (LSU Green Law Web Page)
http://www.amfor.org (American Forests)
http://www.arborday.org (Arbor Day Foundation)
http://www.ag.uiuc.edu/~isa/(International Society of Arboriculture)
http://salem10nt.odf.state.or.us/pubaff/goals/gir12.htm (State of Oregon Urban Forestry)
http://www.uga.edu/~soforext (Southern Regional Urban Forestry)
http://envhort.ucdavis.edu (UC Davis Environmental Horticulture)
http://st120.cesuga.edu/forestry/forestry (University of Georgia Community Forestry)
gopher://minerva.forestry.umn.edu:70/11urb (Minnesota Urban Forestry Bibliography)

INDEX

For an alphabetical listing of states, counties, and cities, see the Contents on page v.